THE PACIFIC WAR REMEMBERED

THE
PACIFIC WAR
REMEMBERED

AN ORAL HISTORY COLLECTION

Edited by John T. Mason, Jr.

NAVAL INSTITUTE PRESS
Annapolis, Maryland

Library of Congress Cataloging-in-Publication Data

The Pacific war remembered.

  Bibliography: p.
  1. World War, 1939–1945—Pacific Ocean—Sources.
2. World War, 1939–1945—Personal narratives, American.
I. Mason, John T., 1909–
D767.P33   1986   940.54′26   86-5438
ISBN 0-87021-522-1

Printed in the United States of America

To Betty

CONTENTS

CONTENTS

ABBREVIATIONS

ABDA	American-British-Dutch-Australian
ACI	air combat intelligence
AK	cargo ship
AKA	attack cargo ship
AP	armor piercing
APA	attack transport
APD	high-speed transport
ARS	salvage ship
ASDIC	echo sounding gear
BAR	Browning automatic rifle
BOQ	bachelor officers quarters
BuShips	Bureau of Ships
CEC	Civil Engineering Corps
CO	commanding officer
ComAirSol	Commander, Air, Solomons
CVE	aircraft carrier
DesRon	destroyer squadron
DUKW	amphibious truck
FRUPac	fleet radio unit, Pacific
JICPOA	Joint Intelligence Committee, Pacific Ocean Area
LCC	landing craft, central
LCM	landing craft, mechanized
LCPR	landing craft, personnel, ramped
LCT	landing craft, tank
LCVP	landing craft, vehicle and personnel
LSD	landing ship, dock
LSM	landing ship, medium
LST	landing ship, tank
LSV	landing ship, vehicle
LVT	landing vehicle, tracked
PT	motor torpedo boat
SubPac	Submarines, Pacific

TBS	talk between ships
UDT	underwater demolition team
USAFFE	U.S. Armed Forces, Far East

MAPS

PREFACE

This is not an account of the war in the Pacific. Many good histories have been written about that war and many more will be written. The excerpts that follow come from the large collection of oral interviews I and others have conducted over the past twenty-four years with naval personnel, men and women, who participated in the Second World War and whose remembrances contribute color and something in the way of historical fact to the permanent record. In all instances they offer a unique point of view because they are personal. Their accounts do not necessarily reflect the overriding strategy of the situations in which they found themselves. In many cases where there was a master plan, they did not even know it.

Oral history is indeed the presentation of personal perspectives. It is colored by a man's predilections and by the great collection of events and experiences that have shaped his life. While he relives a particular event, these stand behind him as a stage setting stands behind actors speaking strong, vibrant words. For this reason oral history has sometimes been accused of being self-serving.

In the course of conducting interviews oral historians try to guard against this possibility as well as errors of fact. The interviewer serves, consciously, as a surrogate for the historical record. He has a role to play, a role that makes the interview a joint creation. It is not, as many assume, a soliloquy. The interviewer must be pleasant, unobtrusive, rarely appearing as devil's advocate. At the same time he must ask the right questions, know when a man's story is incomplete, and prod gently for more detail. He best performs his role when he does not reveal too much knowledge of an event. He is the willing student who sits at the feet of his mentor. All this takes preparation and detailed research of the period or event under scrutiny. Only out of such a chrysalis can significant questions emerge.

It is not only the interviewer who strives for historical accuracy. The men recorded in this collection went to great lengths to examine their own records, documents, photographs, and diaries to be certain of their facts. I tried always to encourage them in their endeavors. Admiral Sullivan spent many hours searching and sifting through his source materials before scheduling an interview. Only then did he relate his story to me, chapter by chapter. I had the feeling that he was a kind of specialized historian at work. The intriguing thing about his narrative is that no one else has told or could tell it. His has the imprint of authenticity and character on every page and could not be duplicated by the most profound, conscientious historian. In this sense Sully's story, like most of the other accounts here, is a verbal portrait of the man as well as a record of action. Of course the human mind is fallible, but when that mind has studied all the available records, what it tells from personal experience must be given a large amount of credence.

In recent years oral history has been used increasingly as source material. But it is a new kind of source material. It offers itself for testing, for correction, for amplification. The freedom given the interviewer to ask questions makes all this possible. Further room for clarification is provided by the methodology of the oral historian. He and the interviewee go over the transcripts of their conversation. This does more than catch the obvious errors of spelling and misunderstanding. It gives the participants a chance to see if in their exchange a wrong emphasis has been conveyed, for it is easy to be carried away in conversation and lose perspective. In the process of review gaps can be discovered and filled, repetition eliminated, inconsistencies spotted and resolved.

One of the great benefits of oral history is that it gives men and women who are not masters of the written word a chance to communicate in a medium in which they are comfortable. Admiral Kinkaid is a good example of one who was happy to have me tape his recollections because he found that his thoughts came forth more freely when spoken. The result is a picture of the Battle for Leyte Gulf as he understood it. He was the commander of the Seventh Fleet; he was in possession of a vast amount of information; he was a highly principled, conscientious man; and this is his version of what happened. Historians have given some of the incidents he talks about a different twist, but the fact remains that this is Tom Kinkaid's story and as such it has its own validity.

Although the overall impact of this collection might be termed impressionistic, the selections have been made with some thought and purpose. They are not intended to give exhaustive coverage of the war in the Pacific. Neither every major battle nor every geographical area is represented. A full account is, of course, beyond the capacity of a series of excerpts from interviews. There was, however, an attempt to choose segments of the war story that add something of importance to the historical record. There was also an effort to draw on accounts that are vivid, or eloquent, or meticulous in their appraisal of events. Many of the excerpts are interlarded with humor, for even the grimmest battles have their lighter moments.

No one part of the war is given more attention than another. Inevitably, this reflects my own ideas for the oral history collection I began at the U.S. Naval Institute in the late sixties and worked on for thirteen years. It was my thought that the collection should touch on every aspect of naval activity in the Second World War without bias or overemphasis. My colleagues and I interviewed men and women from a variety of backgrounds: surface ships, carriers, submarines, gunnery, aircraft, intelligence, logistics.* I hoped to achieve a well-balanced picture of the war by reaching out to people who had served in many different capacities and who were not always in the topmost ranks at the time of the actions they described.

Getting back to the volume at hand, I think one thing the oral history vignettes here share is an emphasis on innovation and pragmatism, a certain freedom to act that bore much fruit. During the Pacific war, when carrier battles and amphibious landings were undertaken for the first time on a large scale and across huge distances, self-reliance and inventiveness came to the fore. Draper Kauffman's account of his work with the newly formed UDTs is a good example. He and his men developed techniques as they prepared for the landing on Saipan. They did not wait to apply for a patent. Red Ramage, skipper of the submarine *Parche,* implemented a new method for reloading torpedoes in the midst of battle, when lives were at stake and victory was elusive. Harry Hill's story of the conquest of Tinian demonstrates again how men can learn while an operation is under way, even men like Hill who were masters at coordinating services for amphibious warfare. Then there is Jimmy Thach's account of how he devised the Thach Weave, playing with kitchen matches on his dining room table. It was something that did much to guarantee victory at the Battle of Midway. Indeed, great ideas often come disguised in humble jackets.

Some of the excerpts in this book underscore the value of the intelligence community's services. Through the eyes of Art McCollum and through his careful calculations one can glimpse something of the contribution these men made to the war. Without them it might have ended very differently.

Many of the excerpts here also bespeak the compassion that is part of man's birthright, something that will out in spite of the rigors and inhumanity of war. The oral account from Paul Moore, who took part in one of the bloodiest and most protracted chapters in marine corps history, the struggle for Guadalcanal, is a perfect illustration. His was the contribution not of the professional marine but of the volunteer. He was a fledgling catapulted from the ivory tower of Yale University into the blood and stink of jungle warfare. That he was able to make this sudden transition without breaking, indeed,

*The reader interested in further pursuit of naval oral history can easily consult the U.S. Naval Institute and the Nimitz Library of the Naval Academy in Annapolis, the Naval Historical Center in Washington, D.C., or the Oral History Research Office at Columbia University in New York.

with a growing sympathy for his fellow man, compatriot and enemy alike, says something about war that is lacking in many written histories.

I have the greatest respect for men like Paul Moore, both commissioned and noncommissioned, who participated in the Pacific war. Their courage and their sacrifices were products of the human spirit. Even as they waged a terrible war, they often demonstrated what is best in man. This volume, above all, is a tribute to them.

These excerpts have been edited slightly in the interest of accuracy, brevity, and, in rare instances, for consistency of style. It was thought wise to break with the original interview format, the question and answer procedure, and use a first-person narrative. This does no disservice to the man whose oral history is excerpted, and it surely makes for greater facility in reading. Neither does it do disservice to the interviewer, for the ideas posed in questions are carried on in the narrative of the respondent.

Various people mentioned in the oral histories are listed at the back of the book. It should be noted, however, that in some instances the persons referred to cannot be identified at this late date and therefore do not appear in the list. Every attempt has been made in the case of military personnel to carry the ultimate rank reached in the service; where possible, rank at the time of an action described is also given. The pictures have been selected for their value as good likenesses. No attempt has been made to represent the men as they appeared when the incidents they describe took place. Yet a photograph of each narrator, no matter how far removed from the time of events, is a complement to the verbal portrait he paints.

Now for the most difficult part of my preface—expressing gratitude to all the good people who have contributed to this book. They are numerous.

First, of course, I am deeply indebted to the men who have given me permission to quote them, or to their heirs when they are no longer alive or available for comment. They were generous in their responses. In fact, talking by telephone with them after many years was the happiest experience of the entire process of producing this book. It was like going back to one's family after a long absence—warming, reassuring, and welcoming.

Next I acknowledge my indebtedness to those who gave me unremitting support and encouragement in my efforts to promote oral history: the late Professor Allan Nevins, eminent American historian and founder of the oral history movement of today; his distinguished successor, Louis Starr, head of the Columbia University Oral History Office; Judge Eller (Admiral Ernest Eller), who was director of the Navy Department's division of naval history when I first discovered the subject in 1960; his successor, Vice Admiral Edward Hooper, who saved my program at the Naval Institute when monies were running short; and Rear Admiral Jack Kane, who took over the office after Ed Hooper and continued the same enthusiastic support. Thanks in this area would not be complete if I did not pay tribute to Dean Allard, the tireless, indispensable head of the Naval Historical Center's operational archives.

There are thanks due also to my former colleagues at the Naval Institute: the late Commander R. T. E. Bowler, Jr., the secretary-treasurer who staunchly encouraged this enterprise; Tom Epley, director of the book department, not only a former colleague but also a friend; Paul Stillwell, my most worthy successor as director of oral history, and his obliging assistant, Susan Sweeney; Patty Maddocks, the resourceful librarian and ever-willing friend; Beverly Baum, who possesses a sixth sense in the design and layout of books; and Constance Buchanan, my editor, whose patience and wisdom guided me through the editing process. Alice Creighton of the Nimitz Library was of great assistance in finding photographs and maps, as was Agnes Hoover of the Naval Historical Center. And of course I owe much to Ronald Grele, the present director of the Columbia Oral History Office. Without a moment's hesitation he gave me permission to use excerpts from a number of memoirs for which the copyright is held by the trustees of Columbia University. I owe a word of thanks also to Commander Etta Belle Kitchen, for many years the recipient of SOS calls from me when I needed interviews conducted on the West Coast. Some of these are represented in this collection. And finally, with immense gratitude, I acknowledge the willing cooperation of Deborah Reid, my one-time transcriber at the Institute and more recently a very trusted helper with this volume.

THE PACIFIC WAR REMEMBERED

Inevitable is the word to describe the Japanese attacks on Pearl Harbor and Manila in December 1941. By that time the war party had gained ascendancy in Japan. Throughout the 1930s it had preached its philosophy of power, and gradually it had engulfed the more rational forces within the imperial government by wielding its growing military strength, assassinating government officials, trumpeting the need for a new order in East Asia, and instilling in the Japanese people a desire for what the Germans called *Lebensraum.*

Japan lacked the oil, tin, and other essentials required for modern industrial growth. Many of these raw materials abounded in accessible areas such as the Netherlands East Indies, Malaya, Indochina, and the Philippines. The temptation to invade was great, and there were historical precedents that seemingly justified acting on it. Was it not the "wealth of the Indies" that had appealed to the English, the Spanish, the Dutch, and the Portuguese in earlier centuries? This same appeal motivated the Japanese in the twentieth century. Another prod was Japan's experience after World War I. On the victorious Allied side, she had received valuable mandates for the Marianas, the Marshalls, the Carolines, and the Pelaus. This had given the aspiring industrial nation an appetite for power.

Power was what she sought in continental Asia early on. In 1915 Japan tried to force China to accept the Twenty-one Demands, which would have made that weak, disintegrating giant into a virtual protectorate. Growing tension in an inconclusive relationship reached a climax in the so-called China Incident of 7 July 1937. The Japanese army was ready to show its muscle after a concerted buildup. There was a cooked-up clash between Japanese troops on maneuvers and a Chinese outpost on the Marco Polo Bridge near Peking. The United States took the lead in diplomatic efforts to settle things peaceably, calling a conference of nineteen nations in Brussels to consider ways of ending the conflict. Japan, however, refused to participate. She insisted that the China Incident was her own affair.

The political life of Japan from the twenties on can be described as a

1

seesaw. The extreme militarists and the more temperate factions battled for control. The only hope of preserving peace in the far Pacific was for Western powers to encourage the less xenophobic elements in Japan. This opportunity was thrown away when the U.S. Congress passed the Immigration Act of 1924, which, in part, barred Japanese immigration to the United States. The insult to Japan was magnified by the Washington Naval Treaty of 1922 and a further restating of its provisions in London in 1930. The treaties established a 5:5:3 ratio of naval power between Great Britain, the United States, and Japan—equal strength for the two former and lesser strength for the latter. This only goaded the militant Japanese on. Jingoists made the ratio into a slogan to whip up hatred against the United States. They told their countrymen that Americans wanted to keep the Japanese down for ever.

An incident that might have pushed the Japanese further toward war involved the USS *Panay*, a river gunboat that patrolled the Yangtze River to protect American commerce and nationals. In November 1937 Chiang Kai-shek's government was forced to evacuate Nanking because the Japanese army was rapidly approaching. The American ambassador and part of his staff followed Chiang to Chungking. The rest of the staff remained for another week and then departed in the *Panay*. Although the Japanese government was duly informed of this move, the gunboat was dive-bombed and sunk and the survivors were strafed as they sought the shore. Several were killed and others wounded. The Japanese government promptly apologized for the incident and said it was a case of mistaken identity. Subsequent evidence disproved this, but the United States was so anxious to avoid conflict that she readily accepted Japan's assertion. America was relieved. War was avoided.

In 1938 encouragement of a more subtle nature was proffered the militarists in Japan. The U.S. Congress had directed the secretary of the navy to appoint a board that would report on the need for additional naval and air bases in the United States and her possessions. The results of this board, the Hepburn Report, were made available on 1 December. Not all of the recommendations were implemented by Congress. A call to improve the military base on Guam, an American possession in the Mariana Islands, was rejected. Guam, a strategic outpost of U.S. power, was too near the Japanese homeland to go unnoticed. Some of the members of the House who voted against the provision stated the reason for its defeat: fear of appearing to challenge Japan. This was the attitude of many Americans at that time. The United States had emerged from World War I saying, "No more wars."

A rational solution to head-on conflict was once more a possibility, albeit not a promising one, when Admiral Mitsumasa Yonai, minister of the navy, formed a new cabinet early in 1940. His was a conciliatory group that wished to make overtures to the United States. But all efforts were doomed to failure. The Japanese asked for the impossible. They asked for acceptance of their position in China, which was in violation of existing treaties. The United States refused, the Yonai ministry resigned. From that point on the voice of reason was largely submerged in Japan.

There was another development that paralleled the rise of the Japanese militarists. The United States was applying a growing list of sanctions against Japan. They began with the "moral embargo" of 1938, when the exportation of planes and equipment from the United States to countries bombing civilians was stopped. This was a direct reaction to the more and more frequent Japanese attacks on targets in China, including American churches and hospitals. It was said that the most dangerous spot during an air raid in China was an American mission. That embargo was followed in July 1940 by an act of Congress strengthening the U.S. national defense and authorizing the president to "prohibit or curtail" the export of any military equipment, munitions, or machine tools "whenever he determined that would be in the interest of national defense." As a result of that act the president put an embargo on the export to Japan of strategic minerals, chemicals, aircraft engines, iron, and steel scrap.

The president's total embargo of iron and steel scrap came on the heels of a significant Japanese move. On 27 September Japan signed the Tripartite Pact with Nazi Germany and Fascist Italy. Now Japan formally recognized the Hitlerian "New Order in Europe," and the other two powers recognized the leadership of Japan in the establishment of a "New Order in Greater East Asia." Each of the three powers agreed to assist the others if "attacked by a power at present not involved in the European war or in the Sino-Japanese conflict"—notably, the United States.

There was no turning back now. The United States had no intention of totally reversing her foreign policy toward Japan, restoring trade relations with that country, or acquiescing in further Japanese conquests. The consequence was Pearl Harbor and the attack on the Philippines.

*   *   *

As dawn broke over Pearl Harbor on 7 December 1941, the ninety-four units of the U.S. Pacific Fleet were at anchor, preparing to assume their duties of the day. The scene was a peaceful one, unhurried, normal. Suddenly, at 0755, the scenario changed. A veritable hail of death and destruction was launched from the sky by Japanese bombers and fighters. Three hundred and fifty-three aircraft, in two major waves, assaulted units of the Pacific Fleet. In less than two hours catastrophe was complete. The victors departed.

The newly designated enemy fleet, under the command of Vice Admiral Chuichi Nagumo, had achieved the total surprise that was planned. The attack was designed to cripple the Pacific Fleet and so prevent it from interfering with the pending Japanese plan to capture the Malayan Peninsula, the Philippines, and the Dutch East Indies. In the harbor eighteen American ships, including eight battleships, capsized or were sunk or heavily damaged. Navy and army aviation forces on the island were devastated. But the greatest loss of all was counted in personnel: 2,403 people—officers and men of the navy, marines, and civilians—were killed, missing, or fatally wounded; 1,178 others sustained wounds but survived. Those the chain of command held ultimately responsible for these losses, Admiral Husband E. Kimmel, in command of the fleet, and Lieutenant General Walter C. Short, in command of the army force, were relieved in the days that followed.

The Japanese, by a circuitous route from Japan, had come out of the north in a part of the ocean between the Aleutian Islands and Midway. It was a difficult route, but one that gave greater guarantee of safety from detection by American reconnaissance planes and merchant ships. When the striking force of six carriers, two battleships, three cruisers, and nine destroyers was within 250 miles of Oahu, the planes were launched. Because of their slower speed, a contingent of twenty-seven submarines had been sent in advance. Five of them carried midget subs, which were to penetrate the harbor itself.

Few losses were sustained by the Japanese fleet—only twenty-nine planes, and one large and five midget submarines. The other units returned to their homeland with an amazing victory to their credit. But they had at the same time inaugurated a fierce, bloody contest that was to endure for 1,364 days and would only end in disaster for the Japanese Empire.

The following excerpts are taken from interviews with two men who commemorated the attack by returning to the scene of the disaster forty years later. They came for a reunion with surviving colleagues; it was a time of strong emotions, of thanksgiving, of great joy and unmitigated sadness. The memories relived during this experience resulted in graphic accounts of the attack by these two men—James Leamon Forbis, a coxswain in the battleship *Arizona*, the most heavily damaged of all the battleships, and James Anderson, a corpsman in the USS *Solace*, the only hospital ship in the harbor at the time. Both provide vivid pictures of what the Japanese attack meant to the men of the U.S. Pacific Fleet.

NO MORE WAR GAMES

JAMES LEAMON FORBIS

JAMES LEAMON FORBIS enlisted in the navy in 1939. When war came on 7 December 1941 he was serving as a coxswain in the USS *Arizona*. Three days after this event he was assigned duty in the USS *Craven* (DD 382). He saw additional duty in World War II in the USS *Kalk* (DD 611) and the USS *De-Haven* (DD 727).

Forbis retired from the navy on 31 July 1961 in the rank of chief boatswain's mate. Later he served for some time as a personnel clerk for the U.S. Army. He lives in Louisville, Kentucky.

On the morning of December 7, 1941, I was aboard the battleship *Arizona*. I was a coxswain. That morning I was in the duty section on the bow of the ship doing the morning chores. I had breakfast, and after cleaning up one of my jobs was to go back and rig the stern of the ship on the port side so the chaplain could have church services. I had a detail of six or eight seamen. There was an awning over the stern. This was the officers' country. We rigged great flags around, the international alphabet flags which were used for visual

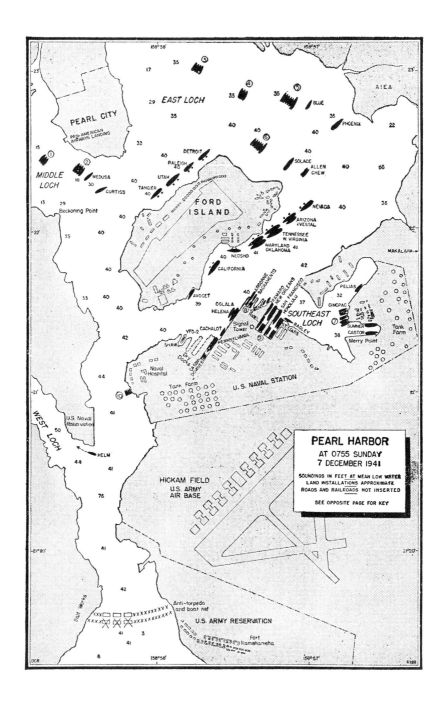

PEARL HARBOR
AT 0755 SUNDAY
7 DECEMBER 1941

SOUNDINGS IN FEET AT MEAN LOW WATER
LAND INSTALLATIONS APPROXIMATE
ROADS AND RAILROADS NOT INSERTED

SEE OPPOSITE PAGE FOR KEY

communication and which we also used for the services. We set up the portable organ, the pulpit and chairs. About the time we finished the bugler went on the fantail for morning colors. On normal Sundays they didn't use the band. The bugler took care of this function himself.

He had already sounded first call, which was scheduled for five minutes to eight. He was standing there awaiting eight o'clock when some planes came out of the east from Aiea. They were coming right out of the early morning sun and it was real bright. One of the seamen in my detail looked up into that sun. He couldn't see anything but he said, "Boy, I wish I was up there in one of them planes flying around this morning." I glanced up but couldn't see anything because of the blinding sun, and I said, "Yeah, I guess it's pretty nice up there." Then other planes started coming in over Hickam Field and the naval shipyard. They were dropping bombs as they came. Then they veered very sharply to the left.

Now, we were expecting the big carrier *Enterprise* to come in the day before and she hadn't come, so we thought, Maybe those are *Enterprise* planes. They were always playing war games out there, the army against the navy, in surprise attacks. So we thought, Maybe it's the crazy army air forces. They don't know when to quit. They even have to get after us on a Sunday morning.

When we had been out to sea previous to this, these army air corps pilots would come around and make runs on us and then drop little smoke bombs off the bow or the stern or the port so many yards out. They probably had sandbags with flares that'd make smoke. So this day we thought, That is what they are going to do.

But then the bombs were dropping and you could hear them exploding and *bang!*—one of them hit the bow of the ship. I told somebody with me, "Boy, somebody's going to catch hell now. They hit the ship." I still thought it was practice, but it was awful heavy for practice because it jarred that battleship.

Now we had been trained to close all the watertight doors and hatches in our part of the ship when air attacks started, so right away we did that. Then we were supposed to fill in on the antiaircraft battery. We ran up on the boat deck where the antiaircraft battery was, but it was already fully manned and firing.

Very shortly we knew they were Japanese planes. There was nothing for us to do but stand around, and that wasn't very safe because we were getting some shrapnel and strafing. Now our battle stations were in number-four gun turret, which was on the after part of the ship. So we went down to the third deck and aft to the powder-handling room and then started climbing up the ladder to the gun turret, for our station was up in the turret. I was on the ladder when a bomb hit on top of the turret. It ricocheted off and knocked me down to the lower handling room. There was a kind of flash and we got smoked out. You couldn't breathe that old stink in there, that smell. I got burned, but not bad. We all got scorched. Then we went over into number-three lower handling room. The compressed air lines had broken there and the compressed air was blowing the smoke out so you could breathe and live.

The last word that came over the public-address system was, "Fire on the quarterdeck." Well, number-three turret barbette sat on the quarterdeck area, and part of the gun-turret crew was there in the turret. One of the turret officers was in the turret and he was keeping us informed. He says, "There's nothing that we can do." We couldn't fire the main battery at the planes, for the guns were fourteen-inch, not lightweight antiaircraft weapons.

Another man and myself tried to get down to the after steering room of the ship, for we knew there were some gas masks stored there. We got down there in the dark—I don't know how we did, except that we knew that part of the ship pretty well. Well, we got down there, but the masks were locked up and we couldn't get to them, so we came back to number-three turret. There the officer was holding all of the number-three and number-four turret crew, at least half of the full crew. We stayed up in the pits.* The bloomers were off the guns so the smoke was coming in around them.† Evidently oil was burning. The uniform of the day at that time was white shorts and skivvy shirts. The only way we could think about keeping that smoke out was to take our undershirts off and our white shorts and cram them around the guns.

We stayed there until the officer told us to come out. We went down the ladder to the main deck, which was burning just a short distance above the break where the boat deck starts. From there the wind and the tide were coming out of the east and keeping the oil and the fire back from number-three and number-four turrets. I had my shoes off. I don't know why. They were shined shoes and I didn't want to wade in that water and oil in clean shined shoes. I don't know what I was thinking. I wasn't thinking.

When I came down that ladder with those shoes in my left hand I stepped in oil and water up to my knees. The stern part of the ship was sticking up dry. The ship was down by the bow and sitting on the bottom. I walked around number-four turret. It was dry. I set my shoes down under the overhang with the heels against the barbette, just like I was going to come back and get them.

---

*A pit was a depressed section in a gun-battery area where men could find some protection from strafing.

†A bloomer was a flexible cover attached to a turret's front armor plate. The bloomer protected the gunport from water and at the same time left the gun free to train on target. In the situation described here, the bloomers were off and the guns were without protection. As a result, the smoke from the oil fire on the quarterdeck was coming into the area from around the gun barrel. If the bloomers had been in place over the guns, perhaps there would have been enough protection to have momentarily kept smoke from seeping into the area where the men were.

Everything was really in a sad shape. It was torn up. There was bombing, burning, and people were in the water. Some boats were retrieving them. Lieutenant Commander Samuel Fuqua was on the stern. He was directing some operations—boats to pick up men and things of that sort. Everyone was leaving the ship. There were about a half-dozen of us getting some life rafts over the side to the men in the water. Some of them had been blown into the water and some of them had jumped.

About the time we came out of the pits the USS *Vestal* was tied alongside trying to get under way. Her mooring lines were over our heads. Turkey Graham, one of the *Arizona* men, had a fire axe and he was chopping the lines. I can recall somebody hollering and saying, "Hey, don't cut our mooring lines, we might need them." But Turkey went ahead and swung that axe and told them, "Get the hell out of here while you can." I understand that later he got the Navy Cross for that. We got some rafts into the water but the wind and the current were so strong they would carry the rafts right up to the fire. Meanwhile the boats were picking men off the rafts, and this at least gave them a temporary refuge and a little relief from the oil. It was really thick.

A few of us remained on board ship. We had briefly discussed the powder magazines. The fourteen-inch powder was directly below us. Once in a while somebody would say something about it. We knew the magazines were overdue. They were going to go. And we knew that if they did go, that deck would blow us awful high. So we got all the rafts over, and because there was nothing left for us to do we jumped into the water.

The old boat boom on the starboard side had been blown or knocked loose from its anchoring. It was still attached but it was in the water under the oil and you couldn't see it. I jumped in and hit it. I was almost knocked out, just about unconscious. One of the guys helped me recover and encouraged me until I finally could swim on my own. I started out half cuckoo from hitting that boat boom. He stayed with me. We swam over to the boat landing through the oil. I don't know how I made it. The good Lord was looking out for us.

I was really pooped when I got over there, swimming against the wind and the current and in that oil. I tried to climb up over the side of the launch when both I and it were covered with grease. It was quite a chore. I hollered up, and it so happened a friend of mine saw and heard me. I just can't imagine how he recognized me because I was greasy from one end to the other. He reached down and tried to hold on to me, but his hands slipped right off. So finally he turned around and hollered for help. "Some of you guys help me, here's Forbis down in the water." They pulled me up. I was more dead than alive. But it was only a temporary thing. I wasn't burned and had no serious injury.

When I got in that boat and looked back I got the full impact of what had happened in the harbor. I'll tell you, I couldn't believe I was alive.

There was a kind of air-raid shelter at this landing. The pilots from Ford Island lived there. Now the wives of the men and officers who lived on Ford Island were around that morning. They found some clean clothing and outfitted me. They wiped me down a little bit and put me in some sports clothes. In five minutes the oil soaked through those clothes. I was just like a soaped greasy rag. Then one of the wives said, "I know. There are more clothes back here. The oil won't come through them." So they put me in a navy captain's uniform with wings. Now mind you, I was barefooted, with no hat, in formal dress, tails and all. So I was Captain for a Day. I got a lot of respect around there. I was in my captain's uniform.

From there we went to the block arena and I slept in the arena that night. Then I went up to the marine barracks and they gave me a toothbrush and a razor. Three days later I was assigned to a destroyer, so I had another happy home. But every time somebody hollered boo or beat on the bulkhead I was about ready to jump over the side.

I might add that while I was waiting for the ship I had been assigned to there were a few small boats around. They were being taken here and there on chores of various kinds, so I, being a coxswain, was occasionally on one of these boats. A few men would go along with me. Three or four of us were making a trip and we stopped by the *Arizona*. They had put the fire out and things had cooled down enough for us to go aboard. It was pitiful. The decks were warped and there were bomb holes around. I went back into the turret I had been in. I retrieved the pair of shorts I had been wearing and the undershirt that I had crammed around the guns to keep the smoke out of the turret. I also found my cigarette lighter and knife and cigarette case, a few little things like that. But I didn't even look for the shoes; I never thought of it.

I can't believe there were any survivors below decks, because from midships forward the magazines had exploded internally. I later heard that the reason the magazines did not explode in the after part of the ship—the part I had been in—was because a fire-control man who was standing watch in the magazines had flooded them with water. If he hadn't done that there would have been very, very few survivors. I certainly wouldn't have survived if those magazines had gone up, and I don't think the others around me would have.

VIEW FROM THE USS *SOLACE*

JAMES ANDERSON

JAMES F. ANDERSON, born in Fort Worth, Texas, on 22 July 1923, has made a career as a navy enlisted man. At the time of the Japanese attack on Pearl Harbor he was serving as a hospital corpsman, first class, in the USS *Solace*, the only hospital ship at anchor in Pearl Harbor.

Anderson continued in the service until his retirement in 1960. His last duty was in the assault helicopter aircraft carrier *Thetis Bay* (CVHA). He lives in retirement in Austin, Texas.

On that particular morning we [the hospital ship *Solace*] were off the end of Ford Island with a clear view of Battleship Row. We were tied up between the old *Olympus*, Admiral George Dewey's ship, the repair ship *Dobbin*, and several destroyers. It had been my intention to go over to the cathedral that morning. I had cleaned up and was standing in line waiting for eight o'clock to roll around, when our liberty boats would come. We were standing at a large cargo hatch looking out across the bay and could clearly see the old battleship *Utah,* which was used as a target ship. I could see the men milling around on her deck as they waited to catch their liberty boats. About this time some planes came down through the mist of the early morning. I said to a friend beside me, "Well, it looks like we're going to have another one of those damn sham battles this morning."

But as these planes came in—there were five of them, I remember—they dropped torpedoes, and I said, "That's too much. They don't drop torpedoes." As the torpedoes were going through the water and before they hit the *Utah,* the planes flew up over the top of our ship. I could see the red balls on their wings. "My God, those are Japanese. Let's get this damn hatch shut."

At that moment the torpedoes hit the *Utah* and the ship appeared to jump—oh, ten, maybe twenty feet in the air. This giant ship. The decks of the *Utah* were loaded with lumber, for protection, I suppose, from the bombs that fell on them in target practice. Then the *Utah* seemed to go over, way over to one side. As it went, the lumber was flying across the deck knocking the men down. She looked as though she was going to capsize, but suddenly she stopped and reversed. All the lumber that had slid to one side now slid in the opposite direction. The men were scrambling to get away but it was knocking them over the side. Others were jumping into the water and I could see them swimming to Ford Island.

Three of us that were standing at this big iron cargo hatch reached out and pulled it shut. Normally it took an electric winch to pull it shut. How three of us did it I'll never know. Then I ran out on our quarterdeck to see what was happening there.

Our old chief pharmacist's mate came running out. He was pulling his suspenders up over his shoulders and was in his sock feet. The officer of the deck, a young ensign, was in absolute panic. He didn't know what to do. The chief sent him to the bridge and told him to make the ship ready for getting under way, then picked up the phone and told the engine room to fire up the boilers and make ready for getting under way.

All the men from my ward, following what we had learned from our drills in the past, began to put metal covers over the windows. (The *Solace* had been a passenger ship with windows up high.) While we were doing this, I kept turning around to see what was going on, and I saw more planes coming in, passing over Battleship Row dropping bombs. I remember very clearly what looked like a dive-bomber coming in over the *Arizona* and dropping a bomb. I saw that bomb go down through what looked like a stack, and almost instantly it cracked the bottom of the *Arizona,* blowing the whole bow loose. It rose out of the water and settled. I could see flames, fire, and smoke coming out of that ship, and I saw two men flying through the air and the fire, screaming as they went. Where they ended up I'll never know.

Meanwhile, we continued with our job and got the windows covered. Then we went into the ward and checked everything and made ready for patients to arrive. Four of us set to with plaster of Paris and all the kinds of bandage material that it mixes with. We were told to make plaster of Paris bandages as fast as we could, rolling them different lengths.

All this happened in maybe ten minutes—no more than that had elapsed.

At this point the Jap planes were coming in alongside us to bomb Ford Island. We could look straight into the cockpits and see the pilots as they went by us. They came that close because they knew they would not be harmed by us, a hospital ship. I knew that our ship was not out of danger— anything was a target.

Almost immediately we started getting casualties, and from that point on I was very busy in our surgical ward. I remember only one of the men we got was able to tell us his name. The others were all in such critical condition they couldn't talk at all. They were all very badly burned from the oil and flash burns. The one who gave us his name did not have a single stitch of clothing on. The only thing left was a web belt with his chief's buckle, his chief-master-at-arms' badge, and the letters USS *Nevada*. He survived but he had a very long cut down the top of his head and every time he breathed his scalp would open up and I could see his skull.

We were using tannic acid for the burns. Every sheet we had in the ward was immediately brown. Many of the men who came in had their ears burned completely off, their noses badly burned, and their fingers bent like candles from the intense heat they had been in. Their bodies were just like hot dogs that had fallen in the fire and burned. All we could do for those poor fellows was give them morphine and pour the tannic acid over them. We were making that from tea, boiling it up as strong as we could get it and bringing it straight to the ward from the galley.

I think we must have gone through forty-eight hours without any sleep— all spent tending to our patients. There was so much adrenalin pumped into the body a person couldn't sleep. But after forty-eight hours I got to the point where I was staggering around. One of the bunks became empty—a man died and we put him on a stretcher to take him down to our morgue. A nurse came along and said, "You get on that bunk and grab some sleep." I don't know how long I slept, but after a while somebody woke me up because another patient had to go in the bunk. I got up and went back to work again. Nobody ever thought of asking for relief.

In the days after the attack, boats from our hospital ship had the awful job of going out alongside the battleships and picking up the remains of the bodies that had floated to the surface. Our corpsmen tried very hard to salvage any part of a human body that could be identified. We brought these parts back and tried to identify fingerprints or teeth or anything of this kind. It was a gruesome job but we had to do it—the detail was assigned to us. The parts were brought to the morgue, where we would clean them of oil and try to identify them.

The United States had a longstanding plan, several times amended, that would go into effect if war against Japan broke out. Both the army and the navy agreed that the Philippine Islands were indefensible against a sustained Japanese attack. But if U.S. forces held Manila Bay and its environs, the American fleet could fight its way through the Japanese mandated islands on a rescue mission. This was the U.S. plan. It was shattered by Japanese actions in the Far East, which in the Philippines began with the 8 December (7 December U.S. time) attack on Manila.

The following excerpts all deal with the situation in the Far East, particularly in Manila. Each sheds a different light on conditions in the Asiatic Fleet at the time the Japanese invaded the Philippines, and yet in all there is an emphasis on preparations for the attack, the complexities of command relationships, and the need for more equipment and ships.

The first piece is from Admiral Thomas C. Hart, who at the outbreak of war was commander in chief of the Asiatic Fleet, headquartered at Manila. His account shows that, unlike leaders in Pearl Harbor, he expected an attack and was able to take steps in anticipation of it, even though he knew his minuscule forces would not be able to withstand a full-scale enemy onslaught. He also suggests that President Roosevelt may have been anxious to lure the Japanese into war. In the course of his talk Hart creates a sense of the inexorable descent of fate on an outpost of Western civilization.

The second excerpt is from then–Ensign Kemp Tolley, at the time a junior on the staff of Admiral Hart. Tolley, a gifted intelligence officer who had seen duty on the Yangtze River patrol, was well aware of the situation in Manila in December 1941. He saw the lack of communication between General Douglas MacArthur and Admiral Hart, and he deals with its ramifications in his remarks. MacArthur had retired from the army in 1937 and been commissioned field marshal of the Philippine army, in which capacity he had set about organizing the armed forces. But after the Japanese seizure of French Indochina in July 1941, he was recalled to active duty in the U.S. Army. His Philippine army was absorbed into the U.S. Army Forces, Far East.

The third excerpt is from Admiral Robert L. Dennison, once a captain on the staff of Admiral Hart and skipper of the destroyer *John D. Ford*. As one-time liaison between Admiral Hart and General MacArthur, his observations on the relationship between the army and the navy are pertinent. More important, his comments evoke the picture of an inadequate military force fleeing before an enemy war machine hell-bent on victory. Both Dennison and Hart show the dismal and necessary disintegration of the tiny Asiatic Fleet once it had to abandon its base in Manila Bay and seek shelter in the Dutch islands to the south.

WAR ON THE HORIZON

ADMIRAL THOMAS C. HART

THOMAS CHARLES HART was born in Davison, Michigan, on 12 June 1877. He graduated from the U.S. Naval Academy in 1897 and later attended both the Naval War College and the Army War College.

Hart served in Cuban waters during the Spanish-American War (1898), and after a series of early assignments he was commander of submarine divisions operating in the Pacific and the Atlantic during World War I. In 1918 he became director of submarines in the Office of the Chief of Naval Operations. During the 1920s he commanded the battleship *Mississippi* and later Submarine Divisions, Battle Fleet, and Submarine Force, U.S. Fleet. From 1931 to 1934 he was superintendent of the U.S. Naval Academy. In 1934 he was named Commander, Cruiser Division 6, Scouting Force, and later Commander, Cruisers, Scouting Force. He became commander in chief of the Asiatic Fleet in 1939 and was in Manila when the Japanese struck. He held the Allied ABDA command until 1942, when he returned to the United States and became a member of the navy's General Board.

In February 1945 he was appointed to the U.S. Senate to fill a vacancy from Connecticut. At that point he retired from the navy in the rank of admiral. Although invited to do so, he did not run for a full term in the Senate. Rather, he chose to return to his home in Sharon, Connecticut, where he lived until his death on 4 July 1971.

The Yonai cabinet resigned in Japan the summer of 1940. They had been fairly reasonable. I was concerned when those men left. Everyone in Washington was concerned; it was the first indication that the militarists were taking over in Tokyo. About that time our government embargoed the shipments of scrap iron and so forth to Japan. It marked the beginning of the economic squeeze.

The feeling kept growing that war was coming closer. I became disquieted enough to send one submarine unit south to Manila two months earlier than it would have gone otherwise.* It was slow and the rest of my ships were fast, so the move was intended to reduce our vulnerability while we were on the China coast.

We—or perhaps it was only I—became concerned about the number of wives and children in the Far East. They were members of the families of fleet personnel. A count disclosed that we had about two thousand women and children. So I began suggesting to the Navy Department that they all be sent home.

The Japanese entry into Indochina began in late August of 1940. That decidedly increased all of our apprehensions, for it disclosed what the Japanese were about. Fairly soon the Navy Department agreed that the Asiatic Fleet's women and children were to be sent home. I was taking the rap for it; news of it was not given out in Washington. I was told to make it public when I saw fit, but to proceed with plans. In the Far East everyone agreed that Old Man Hart had his wind up and was scared to death about something or other. I became as unpopular with the wives as I could possibly be. My wife and oldest daughter, who was with her in the Far East, didn't lead the procession back home but saw to it that they were not the last ones to go either. I was right about the matter, as things turned out. The army followed the same plan in a few months. But I was the one the women cursed. Some of them still speak to me about it. They tell me they would have scratched my eyes out if they could have gotten to me. But they bless me now.

By mid-October 1940 I became convinced that the place for me was with the fleet, and the place for the fleet was in the Philippines, not on the China coast. Our main job, as I saw it then, was to get ready for war. Protecting American interests on the China coast had not been reduced in importance, but it was no longer the main issue. On the fifteenth of October I sent the Navy Department a dispatch setting forth my views and saying that on such and such a date I was sailing for the Philippines with all the fleet except the river gunboats. The department's reply was queer. It said, "The State De-

*In those days it was the custom for the commander in chief of the Asiatic Fleet to station most of his units along the Chinese coast during the summer and in the fall to return most of them to Manila. On this occasion Admiral Hart sent some of his submarines back two months early because war threatened.

partment desires that you remain on the China coast." Expressing its con-currence, the Navy Department said I should send the fleet down but should myself stay on the China coast in the *Isabel,* my flag yacht. That was exactly the same policy they had followed in my predecessor's day.*

I didn't discuss the matter with my staff at all but immediately wrote a reply in which I again set forth the situation as I saw it. I ended my message, "Unless otherwise definitely ordered I am sailing for Manila within twenty-four hours." The reply to my first dispatch had said that it was the "desire" of the Navy Department, but I read between the lines and guessed it was not the desire of the Navy Department at all. The staff came running in with my draft for a dispatch and said, "You can't send this, you'll lose your job." I said I would accept the risk.

Soon after we sailed we got something that indicated department ap-proval. And in the next mail came a letter from Admiral Harold Stark, the chief of naval operations. "Of course you are right. . . . When I sent the dispatch I knew you'd do that." We had always believed in each other. He gave me absolute trust always. He took my part when there was anything wrong, and we corresponded very frankly.

Down in Manila we were working the fleet right along. The menace seemed to be growing all the time and with it the probability of a surprise attack. It was like walking around among crowds of people in the street and knowing that you had an enemy there who would hit you from behind without warning. So my problem was for the fleet to be sufficiently alert and not to be surprised, but at the same time I had to be careful not to wear my people out by keeping them under a constant alert. That would have had serious effects. You may have heard the expression, "Yes, that prizefighter was a good man but he left his fight in the dressing room. He went stale and was overtrained." I had to be the one who did the watching; I had to be certain there was no overtraining. That was one of the reasons there was pretty much strain on the commander.

That spring (1941) the fleet went down into the Sulu Chain for the first time to stay for a period of time. That gave us a chance to look around for a more secure harbor in case one was needed that far away. It was about nine hundred miles south of Manila.

As I look back now, President Roosevelt's freezing of Japanese financial credits by executive order in July 1941 looms even larger than it did then. It had worldwide repercussions and it created in the fleet an even stronger belief that the Japanese threat was bound to end in war. We in the fleet were

---

*The commander in chief of the Asiatic Fleet was a diplomatic representative in the Far East as well as commander of a fleet. In peacetime the commander in chief sent his ships south but remained himself off the Chinese coast, mainly around Shanghai. The State and Navy departments were advising Hart to follow peacetime procedure by staying behind.

given no official information about that action of the president. The State Department failed to inform the high commissioner to the Philippines and the War Department failed to inform General MacArthur. We first heard the news through a Hong Kong paper that some passenger brought to our command post in Manila. We in turn passed it out to the local papers, advising them to feature it as something of very great importance. We saw it as a serious threat to the Japanese in all respects. Japan was an Oriental nation that had become, in a relatively short period of time, one of the great nations of the earth. Its people still had something of an inferiority complex and they were very sensitive.

I can give you an apt illustration of my point. The port of Tarakan in northeast Borneo served one of the best Dutch oilfields. The oil had a paraffin instead of the usual asphalt base. Consequently it was in great demand. The Japanese had been importing it steadily. Shortly after President Roosevelt's executive order a large Japanese tanker arrived there for a load. It had been running back and forth in a routine way between Japan and Tarakan. The officials ashore and the officers of the tanker knew each other, and so the Japanese supposed this trip would be like the others. They were badly set back on their heels when the manager of the local oil company said, "No, I can't load you until I have the money."

Of course there was no cash available, and the ship lay there for weeks until the Japanese government was able to supply the funds for her cargo. The manager of the oil company was a good fellow. He was sorry for the Japanese captain, who had thrown up his hands at the news and said, "My tanks are empty. I haven't oil enough to run our dynamo or to cook our food." So the oil company sent out a boat daily with a small tank of oil. It was enough to run the tanker's auxiliary boiler for twenty-four hours at a time. The humiliation to the Japanese officers and all who knew about it was of course a matter of great moment.

At the very end of November 1941 I got an order from the Navy Department to dispatch some picket ships off the Indochina coast. The order came from the department, but we could see that it did not originate there, and for this reason: about the twenty-sixth of November we heard rumors of a Japanese expedition in Camranh Bay, which is a large harbor about 150 miles northeast of Saigon.*

The rumor was so definite that I felt, even before getting the dispatch, that we needed to do something about it. That involved considerable personal responsibility. I handled it this way. I directed a scouting flight, one

*Hart is suggesting that the dispatch originated with President Roosevelt. Ever since the dispatch was sent, there has been speculation about why the president wanted such a dangerous mission undertaken. Sending picket ships to the west China Sea and the Gulf of Siam (the areas specified in the dispatch) to report on Japanese movements could have provoked the Japanese and in turn justified an American declaration of war.

plane at a time, to be made every day the weather would permit, to look at Camranh Bay and the other one or two harbors of less importance in that vicinity. I asked for the best, wisest, and most careful pilots, and said that I wished to brief them myself before they flew. I briefed those airmen because I, and only I, was responsible in case anything went wrong. In the briefings I gave them what information there was and said, "Try to get confirmation and even full information, but try to do it without being seen, and don't bring on a war." Well, cloud conditions were such along the Indochina coast that it was not a very difficult thing to do, and they succeeded on most days. They found a large expedition of something like twenty good-sized ships in Camranh Bay, obviously military because there was air cover flying over them all the time. Our Catalinas had found and continued to watch the main part of the Japanese expedition, which was about to invade Malaya and capture Singapore.

I did not inform the Navy Department that those risky flights were being made. I decided they had to be something that only I could be blamed for. But we did send the information resulting from those flights to the department without saying how we got it. So when that order came to send three picket ships to the Indochina coast, it was after the Navy Department had learned about what there was in Camranh Bay. I of course speculated on the source of the order.

The Navy Department gave us a chance to drag our feet in the matter, because it said if we did not have suitable craft available we could commandeer small craft and fit them out for the purpose. That meant communicating by radio, which took a little time, and we did drag our feet. Actually, only one of the craft ever started—she was on the way to the Indochina coast when Pearl Harbor happened.

That was a queer situation. Although we and Washington had the information about the expedition along the coast, the department ordered these picket ships sent over there. Of course they would be sitting ducks for the Japanese navy, which was going up and down that coast. Now, anyone can draw an inference on that from what I've already said, but I'll go on a little farther.

During the congressional investigation of the Pearl Harbor incident by the Joint House and Senate Committee, I was called. I was a senator from Connecticut at the time; I spent most of one day on the witness stand. I knew that the call was coming, and I also knew the attitude of some of the members of the committee. I wondered if I would be called on to disclose this incident, and knew that if I did, it would be partisan ammunition which I would be supplying to Senator Ralph Brewster and some others. There was a decided partisan effort to find fault with President Roosevelt. This came to the surface during that inquiry. I was afraid that I might be called upon to tell it, and was delighted when I finished my testimony without any disclosure.

Since nothing untoward resulted, it was quite a minor incident which, I thought, should not cumber important things at that particular time. It does not matter now. Some time afterwards I found that Mr. Seth Richardson, who was the head of the committee's staff and a very able lawyer, did know all about it, but he did not question me concerning it. I was greatly relieved that I didn't get into the mess.

A picket ship of the sort the order referred to was a small ship designed merely to gather information. Compared with a plane, it was quite ineffective. The plane can see inside the harbor, while a small ship lying off the harbor is able to see very little. There was nothing to be gained whatever by sending pickets; indeed, there was a decided risk in it. It would have been risking personnel for no reason, and I am glad I dragged my feet. I never needed to make any inquiries later as to the source of this dispatch, for that I felt I knew.

ARMY SNUBS NAVY IN THE PHILIPPINES

REAR ADMIRAL KEMP TOLLEY

KEMP TOLLEY was born in Manila on 29 April 1908, the son of an army officer stationed there. He graduated from the U.S. Naval Academy in 1929. After some years of sea duty, Tolley was assigned independent intelligence duty in Europe from May 1934 to June 1936, where he received instruction in the Russian language.

He became aide to the commander of the South China Patrol in 1937, then executive officer of a gunboat on the upper Yangtze River. During this period he was also assigned to intelligence duty in Shanghai. After service at the Naval Academy as an instructor, he returned to the Yangtze River Patrol and later to Manila. There, in December 1941, he commissioned and took command of the yacht USS *Lanikai* and sailed her through the Japanese blockade, arriving in Australia three months later, after a trip of some four thousand miles. From May 1942 to May 1944 he served as assistant naval attaché in Moscow. The last year of World War II he spent with the Third Fleet in the Pacific, seeing action at Leyte, Iwo Jima, Okinawa, and Japan. His postwar assignments included a tour as director of the intelligence division at the Armed Forces Staff College in Norfolk, Virginia (1949–52); commander of Amphibious Squadron 5 (1954–56); and commander of fleet activities in Yokosuka (1958–59).

Tolley, who retired as a rear admiral in June 1959, lives in Moncton, Maryland, near the area his forebears settled two and a half centuries ago. He is the author of a number of books, including *Yangtze Patrol* and *The Cruise of the Lanikai,* and numerous articles for *Proceedings, Shipmate,* and other publications.

Then came the time to go north in the spring.* I had gotten pretty well acclimated to the leisurely atmosphere by then. The daily routine was to go ashore at four and have a swim in the Army-Navy Club pool. There was free lunch in the bar. Ladies weren't allowed, but the gentlemen would go in and eat what amounted to practically a dinner. It would be fried chicken one day, baked beans and hot dogs the next—quite an ample meal, washed down with innumerable mugs of San Miguel beer. Then you might take another swim or toddle on back to the ship to watch the movies. And that was the day. On the weekends, you might play some golf with a guy, or go about twenty or thirty miles in the country on a picnic, or borrow a banca from someone and go out boating on the bay. It was a very leisurely life. We all drank far too much. The older officers were more likely to be found at the Polo Club, where there was a heavy sprinkling of rich Filipinos—real blue-blooded Manila.

As for army personnel, we saw very little of them. There were a few around Manila, but they might as well have not existed. The army had a small headquarters in the walled city in Manila, but the big establishment was on Corregidor or at Fort McKinley—the infantry post, which was about an hour by streetcar or maybe thirty minutes by automobile. Up to the start of World War II, there was no contact of any substantial or serious nature between the army and the navy. Even at the outbreak of the war, relations were very tenuous and unsatisfactory, I think. It was well established that Admiral Hart and General Douglas MacArthur were at dagger points. There was no cooperative enterprise between them at all. I think this was true of the joint services everywhere.

It was in some respects a matter of personalities, because Admiral Hart had got on very well with the two previous commanders in the Philippine Department,† Major General George Grunert and Major General Walter Grant. They went home, and the army organization completely changed when USAFFE was established and Douglas MacArthur was recalled from inactive duty. He had retired as chief of staff of the army in, I guess, 1935 or 1936, and had been invited by the Philippine government in the rank of field

---

*The time is April 1940. The Asiatic Fleet customarily spent the winter months in Manila and went to the northern China coast for the summer.

†That is, the part of the Department of the U.S. Army assigned to the Phillipines.

marshal to train and head their military forces. He was wholly aloof then from the U.S. Army in the Philippines. He stuck to his work and got very high marks from Hart. Hart felt that MacArthur was doing an excellent job, and he actually wrote in a note that he thought MacArthur was one of the best investments the Philippine government had ever made.

Shortly before the outbreak of World War II USAFFE was set up. MacArthur was recalled to head it and was made a lieutenant general. He was a major general on the retired list. He had been a four-star general as chief of staff of the army, but as a lieutenant general he was still one grade junior to Hart. The field marshal title had disappeared.

Now this irked old Mac to no end, because he had been a brigadier general in France in World War I, commanding a division when Hart was in short pants, relatively speaking. And he had commanded submarines in England and later on the East Coast of the United States. But here was Hart in the Philippines. I think MacArthur was about two years younger. Hart was almost retirement age, and he passed retirement age before he got out of there. So they were very slow reaching amicable terms. MacArthur, very reluctantly, and after a long delay—something like a month—called on Hart, and Hart returned the call the next day just to show him what good manners we all have in the navy.

Sometime after that Hart managed to get MacArthur over for a conference, and he couldn't shut him up. The only thing MacArthur wanted to talk about was his problems and what he planned to do. He said he had wanted to build a navy in the Philippines while he had been field marshal. That's what they needed, more of the motor torpedo boats to protect the coastline. And furthermore, he had no interest whatever in the American navy situation and its plans. He said sort of offhandedly, "I know the navy has its plans, we have our plans, but I see no point of conflict, so let's just carry on as before."

About that time, Hart, in all innocence, sent out a message to the shore navy in Shanghai, to navy purchasing, and to the South China patrol in Hong Kong saying that when army troops came through, they would be under the control of the navy shore patrol. This was because the shore patrol was more cognizant of local conditions and had all the angles and had connections with the right people. Of course Hart's directive was illegal. To make things worse, he sent a mimeographed copy of the dispatch to MacArthur's headquarters, which MacArthur read after it had been sent out. Well, MacArthur was furious. He said, "This is absolutely an incredible faux pas on the part of the navy, one that will arouse the ire of every army man in the Far East." He didn't even bother to tell Hart this. He went over everybody's head and wrote directly to Harold Stark, the chief of naval operations, not even his own boss, and said, "This is insufferable. I won't put up with it." Of course, that was not an ideal way to start a bosom friendship.

25

Then Hart proposed in a letter to MacArthur the idea that if army airplanes—there were then something like thirty-five or forty B-17 bombers and about eighty or ninety observation and fighter planes—were operating over navy ships, the reasonable precaution would be to let the navy ships control the airplanes so that they wouldn't get bombed by mistake. In other words, Hart told him to do it like the navy did: when airplanes came within the air control of ships afloat in the area, the ships should take control. They should tell the aircraft which way to fly so they wouldn't drop their eggs on the wrong basket.

MacArthur didn't answer this for two weeks, and when he did his was the most blistering reply you can imagine one officer writing to another. In effect it said, "If we can dignify the piddling excuse you have for a fleet under that name, it is even more ridiculous that it should be allowed to control the powerful striking force which my air arm comprises. If you feel that it is necessary for me to get permission to act under your control while my aircraft are over your ships, I say the whole idea is totally unacceptable." Hart gave up after that. He didn't even want to speak to the guy.

On one occasion, some time after that, MacArthur got a message saying he was being promised a heavy augmentation of air power, which would arrive pretty soon. He was living in the Manila Hotel, in the penthouse suite which had originally been built for Manuel Quezon, then president of the Philippines. It was a gorgeous place—simply a palace—on top of the old Manila Hotel. Hart was living all by himself in a modest bedroom three or four decks below. (When he was at home and available to callers, he would put his hat in the window; anybody walking by who saw the admiral's cap there knew he was allowed to come in and have a drink. That was his "in" card, so to speak.) So when MacArthur got that message he had Mrs. MacArthur phone down to Hart to be sure he was home. MacArthur wouldn't waste his energy. He put on his bathrobe and his house slippers and trotted down to Hart's place to read him the message he had just received. And then he said, "Now look at this, Tom. When you get something like this you can really call yourself something. You can pretend you have got power." And out he went. It was that sort of relationship at the top which made any conceivable type of cooperation impossible down below.

Captain Dennison, a real diplomat and a wise man, did the very best he could as liaison officer. Every morning he would turn up at MacArthur's headquarters to listen to the briefing of the general. He and MacArthur were on pretty good terms. MacArthur respected him, apparently trusted him, and confided in him as much as he felt was necessary. (Dennison said later in an oral history interview that he thought MacArthur, who regarded the seagoing service as a separate world, treated him as a kind of ambassador from the navy.)

I think there is no doubt that if there had been closer cooperation between Hart and MacArthur, the situation at the outbreak of the war would have been different. It was absolutely a lead pipe cinch that the only Japanese landing in force could have been in Lingayen Gulf. Under those circumstances, naval effort could have been and should have been directed at that area, certainly by submarines if nothing else. The fact that our torpedoes were defective undoubtedly would have had a strong bearing on any real action, but the fact that none of the submarines were there—they all came later, and only in ones and twos—can only have helped Japanese invasion forces at the beach.

There is yet another aspect of this. Hart offered the Fourth Marine Regiment to MacArthur with several suggestions. One was that they be broken up and put in small units of ones and twos in the Philippine reserve divisions to stiffen their morale. Another was that they act as military advisors, because most of the Philippine reserve divisions were absolutely green. Some of them had no uniforms, some of them had never fired a shot out of the artillery. The officers were totally incompetent, in most cases singularly devoid of military knowledge. About all they did was knock each other out saluting.

But the answer from MacArthur was no. The Fourth Regiment would be held in reserve. There are, of course, all sorts of ideas about what should have been done and what wasn't done, but MacArthur's idea was to use his green forces on the beach and have the seasoned forces used as reserves. As a result, of course, the Fourth Marines did not see action, except in the final defense of Corregidor, when it was far too late. If MacArthur had used his good troops, which were the marines, and one or two of his own regiments plus the Philippine scouts at the Lingayen Beach line, where the Japanese were in total disarray, the result might have been different. The Japanese had a very bad time getting ashore. The weather was lousy. They had miscalculated on the beaches in spite of high-level reconnaissance the week before and espionage for years. In general, it was more by luck than good management that they got ashore without opposition. The opposition that MacArthur expected to put up with those reserve divisions simply disintegrated. They had no cohesion, no know-how. With the first burst of machine-gun fire, off they went, leaving their equipment behind. If the good troops had been on hand, things undoubtedly would have been different.

As far as I know, there was not even a close enough meeting of minds for MacArthur to have disclosed to Hart what his troop disposition plan was. There was no exchange of plans.

Of course, Hart was very badly let down in two respects. First of all, at a presentation he had heard MacArthur talking with the British commander in chief from Singapore, who was in Manila. This was way back in October 1941. MacArthur was convincing, and absolutely sure of himself and his ability to hang on not only to Luzon but to all of the Philippine Islands,

27

JAPANESE INVASIONS
OF THE
PHILIPPINE ISLANDS
DECEMBER 1941

■ US Airfields

Nautical Miles

including the big island down south, Mindanao. He had recommended to the War Department that he be allowed to spread his troops out instead of concentrating all of them on Luzon. He had three divisions on Mindanao and quite a few scattered around other places. If all of those had been on Luzon and properly handled, things might have been different. However, Mac gave Hart an impression of such utter satisfaction and assuredness that Hart was won over. The admiral figured, This guy is so sure of being able to hold Luzon, why should I retreat to Singapore or the Dutch East Indies, which my basic plans call for? Why shouldn't I try to fight it from Manila Bay? This guy has got airplanes. He says he can stop anything on the beaches. He can knock the Japs out of the air. They can't fly this far, for their planes aren't very long range. He didn't say a word about aircraft carriers. Why don't I try to fight it from Manila?

So Hart sent Admiral Stark a message about it. This was the second letdown. It took exactly one month for the Navy Department to answer, and the answer was no. Hart fully expected that they would let him do what he wanted. After all, by that time he had exchanged dozens and dozens of letters with Stark. They started out calling each other Stark and Hart and wound up calling each other Betty and Tommy. They were on the best of terms in their correspondence. So I suspect Hart felt that anything he proposed that was remotely within reason would get a cheery "Aye, aye!" from Stark. Anyway, by the time the reply came it was too late for Hart to ship lots of his stuff down south—torpedoes, spare parts, fuel, torpedo warheads, that sort of thing.

On the other hand, you can hardly say it was a letdown for Hart when all the navy ships were deployed, with the exception of two crippled destroyers under repair in Cavite and the submarines, which were normally in Manila Bay anyway, the logical place to operate from. All of the ships were safely out, and all of the big seaplanes were safely dispersed in three or four different places. On the morning of the outbreak, when MacArthur's air forces were destroyed largely on the ground, the navy didn't lose a stick. Nothing was harmed at all, because no ships or navy aircraft were there. They had been deployed and dispersed just exactly as Hart wanted them to be.

There are some people who wonder why in the world the submarines weren't deployed where Japanese ships were likely to concentrate—why a half-dozen of them weren't down trailing the Japanese force, which was obviously on its way to Malaya. I have never heard that point discussed, and I have never heard Admiral Hart give any explanation one way or another. All except two of the submarines were concentrated in Manila Bay. They were on patrol in the vicinity of the Philippines. None of them were out on the trade routes or the invasion routes. And, of course, nobody knew about the defective torpedo. Moreover, at the beginning of the war, people were not as much on their toes as they were six or eight months later. They simply didn't have the attack technique. They were a little spooky. They were green. They had done many a practice run, but there is a big difference between practicing a run on your friend and having a swarm of antisubmarine craft over the top of you.

There is absolutely nothing the navy could have done without air cover. There was no navy air at all except the PBYs, which were, even for their day and age, large, slow, vulnerable, and only fit for long-range scouting. In no sense were they combat aircraft. They could carry bombs, but they couldn't rise to high altitude and their maneuvering capabilities were poor. So as an offensive force they were out of the picture completely. Actually, the only point in having them out there was that, before the war started, they were on neutrality patrol and were good for checking on merchant ships of the various belligerent powers who might or might not have been trying to take advantage of Philippine neutrality. They became expert at identification as a result. When they saw a destroyer they didn't call it a battleship like the army aircraft were always doing. But without air cover, and with the destruction of MacArthur's air force, the utter lack of any cohesion in the control of these aircraft made it wholly impossible for the little forces the navy had to do any good or keep the sea near Japanese forces.

The United States had thirteen destroyers out there. Those four-pipers had one three-inch gun with iron sights. In other words, it was about as close to useless as anything you could imagine, even against close-in aircraft. That was all we had—all the destroyers had—one three-inch iron-sight antiaircraft gun which tended to jam after about the third shot. The only really up-to-date ship out there with any decent antiaircraft armament was the cruiser *Houston,* and as it turned out, she was resupplied by ammunition from the cruiser USS *Boise,* which had to retire from the field due to damage to her bottom. So what could the navy have done? That is all there was. Because of those circumstances, it is useless to condemn the navy. It was not a war fleet. It was strictly a fleet for showing the flag. It wasn't a fighting fleet, with the exception of the subs.

THE PHILIPPINES: PRELUDE TO DEPARTURE

ADMIRAL ROBERT LEE DENNISON

ROBERT LEE DENNISON was born in Warren, Pennsylvania, on 13 April 1901 and graduated from the U.S. Naval Academy in 1923. He completed the Academy's postgraduate course and received a master of science degree from Pennsylvania State College in 1930. He earned the degree of doctor of engineering from Johns Hopkins University in 1935.

Dennison qualified as a submariner at New London in 1925 and joined the submarine *S-8*. From 1930 to 1941 he had sea duty alternating with two shore assignments. He was on the staff of Commander in Chief, Asiatic Fleet, at the outbreak of war and with Allied Naval Forces, East Australia, early in 1942. Later that year he became chief of staff to Commander, Amphibious Force, Pacific Fleet, and participated in the Aleutian Islands campaign. In 1943, as a captain, he was assigned to the Joint War Plans Committee of the Joint Chiefs of Staff. In 1946–47 he was assistant chief of naval operations for politico-military affairs. He commanded the battleship *Missouri* in 1947–48 and then became naval aide to President Harry Truman. He was promoted to the rank of rear admiral in 1953 and became commander of Cruiser Division 4. Two more tours in the Navy Department followed. Dennison commanded the First Fleet from June 1956 to July 1958. In March 1959 he became a four-star admiral and took command of Naval Forces, Eastern Atlantic and Mediterranean.

In February 1960 he became Commander in Chief, Atlantic, and Supreme Allied Commander, Atlantic. He served in this capacity during the Cuban Missile Crisis and retired on 1 May 1963. Admiral Dennison died on 14 March 1980.

My title on the admiral's staff was assistant war plans officer. Hart made me his contact with General MacArthur also, for there was no personal interaction between Hart's staff and MacArthur's staff. Actually, this duty of mine didn't serve much purpose until the war did break out.

There was a big difference in age and rank between MacArthur and me, but MacArthur proved to be completely open with me. When I first reported to him he called his staff in and instructed them in my presence to show me all the dispatches exchanged between themselves and Washington. He said he intended to do the same.

I was amazed. I didn't then know as much about army customs as I do now. I was appalled to find Major General Charles Willoughby, MacArthur's G-2, telling the G-2 in the War Department things that were completely different from what MacArthur was telling the chief of staff of the army. There were no interstaff communications worth a damn.

I had several very interesting experiences with MacArthur which threw a little light on him. Before Cavite was destroyed on December 10, he had moved to headquarters in a wooden building on the top of a wall—it's a walled city. In the wall there were tunnels and bomb shelters. I was in his office one day in this ramshackle building when the air-raid alarm went off. We didn't have any guns, the ammunition was all gone, so we couldn't reach the bombers anyway at the altitude they were flying; they could just bomb at will. Their practice was to make dummy runs to test out the wind and all that, then they'd make a firing run and let go. Well, in this particular raid we were the target. When the alarm went off, MacArthur's staff beat it to a tunnel with their files and their gas masks. I eased forward to the edge of my chair to leave, thinking, of course, that MacArthur would be going to the bomb shelter. When he saw what I was doing he said, "I'm enjoying our conversation and I'd like to continue it, if you would care to stay here with me." So I thought, If he can take it, I can. How ridiculous. He's the one that ought to be in a bomb shelter. So we sat and continued our conversation with all these bombs going off around us. Thank God the building wasn't hit. But that was MacArthur. He was fatalistic.

I went over to MacArthur's headquarters one morning around nine o'clock. The general said to me, "Before I talk with you I want you to hear what I'm going to tell my staff." So he called his staff in and said, "Gentlemen, I'm going to declare Manila an open city as of midnight tonight (December 25)." This was really an ancient concept of war, the idea being that the city would not support any military activities and therefore the enemy would spare it, not pillage it, not knock it down or capture it. This was the first that anybody had heard of the matter, so after he got through I said, "May I go back and talk to Admiral Hart?" which I did. I told Admiral Hart that I'd just heard General MacArthur tell his staff that he intended to declare Manila an open city as of midnight that night.

Well, Hart didn't usually show much emotion, but this time he said, "What!" Then he got up out of his chair and said, "Come around here and sit down and write that down." So I wrote down a simple sentence: "At 9:10 this morning General MacArthur told me" and so on. He sat down again and read it and he still couldn't believe it. He'd been making plans to operate some units out of Manila, and we had moved the submarine tender *Canopus* alongside the seawall in the port district. We'd taken off warheads and torpedo exploders and distributed them all over that general area so they wouldn't be concentrated any place, and we had put some camouflage over the *Canopus*. She was in shoal water so that, were she hit, she wouldn't submerge. We were planning on continuing submarine operations. We had barges of fuel oil all around the Manila area and all kinds of supplies which we couldn't possibly get out. We needed time, certainly more than a few hours, which meant that we couldn't back up this concept of an open city. We had to have those supplies. MacArthur didn't comprehend what this would mean to us.

Before Admiral Hart left Manila he polled his staff—the few of them that were left, for he had sent most of them, including his chief of staff, down to Java. He polled his staff to ask us whether we felt he should stay. Of course we all knew damned well that what we said didn't make any difference anyhow. We told him he wasn't serving any useful purpose there in Manila. He had sent his flagship down to Java and he was now based ashore. We didn't have any more ships around the bay except some destroyers (I think there were three), a few submarines, and the *Canopus*, the submarine tender. We were going to try and operate the submarines out of Subic Bay.

"You ought to go," was the advice of the remaining members of his staff. So he left on the USS *Shark* early on December 26. Before he left he ordered me to go to Corregidor, where Admiral Francis Rockwell was. Rockwell was commandant of the Sixteenth Naval District and was given the job of operating the Asiatic Fleet naval forces left in the area.

Finally the submarines had to go because the *Canopus* was hit. We were under aerial surveillance all the time. The submarines had to sit on the bottom during daylight when they came off patrol and then surface at night for replenishment, after which they submerged again. (This was in tropical waters and the heat was very uncomfortable.) We didn't have the ships or supplies to operate with. So finally we just had to get out. The destroyers were sent out too and they all got down to Java.

When I reported to Admiral Rockwell I had to pick up the threads with MacArthur, who had insisted on setting up headquarters for himself and his chief of staff, Lieutenant General Richard Sutherland, in an old wooden building on top of a rock. The rest of his staff and Admiral Rockwell and his people were down in the tunnels of Corregidor. Later they almost had to carry MacArthur off the top of that rock.

I went to talk with MacArthur at his headquarters and to ask him what his plans were. He and Sutherland broke out some gasoline company's road maps. They didn't have any army maps; those had all been lost, burned or bombed. MacArthur very painstakingly went over exactly what his troop movements were going to be. By that time the Japanese had landed south of Manila and were moving north. They were being opposed by Philippine forces with some U.S. officers. The general told me exactly when the Japanese were going to come through Manila.

I said, "Well, can't you just hold them till we get these supplies out of there?"

"No," he said, "I can't afford to let these troops engage them because I could never get them disengaged. They're not well enough trained. They'd just get in there and be absorbed and lost, but they can slow the Japanese down." Then he told me about the movement of troops through Manila and also the forces that had gone down to Bataan. At that time, which was, I guess, maybe January, he predicted almost to a day how long Bataan could hold out. This was not speculation on his part. This was seasoned military judgment.

Finally Admiral Hart sent for me to come down to Java. At that time I was acting chief of staff to Admiral Rockwell. I went down in the submarine *Permit*. We did a war patrol on the way down. It lasted for something like forty days, and by the time I got to Java Hart had just left and turned over that command to Vice Admiral William Glassford, commander of the Yangtze Patrol. He had not been on Hart's staff. Hart, at that time, was also the ABDA Float, the American-British-Dutch-Australian forces. Hart was relieved of his ABDA command by Vice Admiral Helfrich of the Dutch navy on the grounds that the Dutch really ought to be in command in their home territory. Of course, Helfrich didn't have any concept of how to handle task forces, not that he had all that much power. The Dutch navy was of a different kind and mostly submarines. It wasn't equipped for operations like that.

Glassford went up to Badung, in the mountains above Djakarta, and he called me there along with some other officers. The remainder of the staff was to get aboard some tender and go to Australia. We stayed in Badung almost until the day the Japanese invaded in the north. Then I went out again by submarine and Glassford went by plane, a KLM airliner. We met in the Freemantle area. The commands had all dissipated, and we were the last to leave. But before we left Helfrich had called a conference of all the senior commanders there. I learned that he had stationed a tanker about halfway between Java and Ceylon. He hadn't told anybody about this except the Dutch. Obviously he planned to pull out and have his own ships refueled before going on to Ceylon. I told Glassford that Helfrich didn't know we were leaving, but at this meeting the British and Australian admirals said they were through, that they'd used up everything they had and were getting out.

Glassford played a hell of a good game of poker. He told Helfrich that we would stay with him to the end. Later Glassford said to me, "I was the last to leave the meeting and Helfrich called me back and said, 'Glassford, there is one thing I want you to understand. I appreciate your offer and I'll never forget it. But I don't intend to stay here and become a prisoner of war.'"

The Asiatic Fleet as a whole wasn't designed so much for fighting purposes as it was for politico-military purposes. It had very little power. The submarines were by far its most powerful component. The ships were, by and large, pretty old. The *Houston* was a fairly modern ship. The *Marblehead* was not one of our newest by any means. The destroyers were old. So there was not much we could have done to stop any real invasion. The army didn't have very much real air power out there either. They had bombers at Clark Field, but MacArthur simply could not believe that we would be attacked by a force that came out of Formosa, and so he held those planes on the field until they were lost completely in a Japanese raid. About one-third of the fighter planes and over half the bombers were destroyed on December 8. This dismayed the army air forces people no end. There just wasn't anything like the power out there that would be required for air cover or opposition to an invasion operation or air-to-air combat.

I was in Cavite just after it was hit on December 10. MacArthur had sent me over there. It was completely devastated. Manila wasn't seriously damaged until much later. MacArthur's declaring it an open city wasn't helpful at all. Nothing happened. The Japanese weren't interested in destroying Manila in those days. They wanted the city, not a bunch of rubble. Of course, towards the end of the war it was a different story.

The lack of communication and cooperation between the army and navy commands in the Philippines was similar to the situation at Pearl Harbor. You must realize that this was long before there was any real liaison between the army and the navy. The navy, with its marine corps, had a built-in amphibious-landing capability, though the marines were not intended for operations much beyond the beach line. We didn't have any plans in those days for the use of army forces in amphibious operations. There just wasn't any understanding of the complementary roles of the army and the navy.

MacArthur had a very elementary understanding of the use of a navy. He, like a good many army officers of his time, looked on a navy as a seaward extension of the army's flank and that's all. This attitude became very plain later on when we moved from Australia through the islands up to the Philippines. Of course, this concept horrified naval officers, although we brought some of it on ourselves. We never really supported MacArthur with the Seventh Fleet. We were fighting our own war.

MacArthur's plan of approaching Japan from the south did not include naval forces or naval air. His original plan was to move in four- to six-hundred-mile jumps, which he considered to be the range of land-based air, objective after objective, marching all the way up to the southern tip of Mindanao and moving further up. After learning of his strategy of jumping into Leyte Gulf, many of us thought it would make a lot more sense to bypass the Philippines entirely. But we would have to do that almost over MacArthur's dead body.

There wasn't any naval officer I know, Halsey or anybody else, who didn't think bypassing the Philippines was the way to do it. This step-by-step idea I use as an illustration of the difference in the thinking of the army and the navy in those days. We had not moved in the same kind of environment.

I think it wasn't until Admiral Nimitz and Admiral King came along that an understanding between the two services began to develop. Admiral Nimitz was very, very keen on this particular subject. He believed with all his heart, and quite properly so, that our security depended on some kind of a linkage, or at least some understanding, between the army and the navy. Of course, this was before the days of the air force. I am sure that with an air force he would have felt the same. Anyway, we did in effect have an air force in World War II.

General MacArthur's treatment of me was quite different from his treatment of his own staff. He was very autocratic with his own people. It seemed to me that he didn't really confide in or trust anybody, with the possible exception of General Sutherland. But even then I don't think there was any real understanding between them. His treatment of me I think underlines the fact that he looked upon the navy as something entirely apart from the army. He dealt with me courteously, as the representative of another service. It was his gentlemanly way of acting. He made it clear that I wasn't under his orders. He was a thorough gentleman. There was no question about that.

We didn't get any help out in Manila from the good old Navy Department either. I remember in the very early days of the war, when we were getting the hell kicked out of us, the Bureau of Engineering sent out a dispatch ordering us to send in samples of fuel oil from the Japanese ships that we'd sunk. Well, we hadn't sunk any ships. There was an air of unreality about that dispatch.

With the Javanese there was also a sense of unreality. When I got to Soerabaja in February or March 1942, the people there didn't even know a war was on. It was a long way away and they only came in contact with a few of us, who went to clubs and dances there. There was no real concern on their part. They weren't going to be invaded. Ridiculous.

The same atmosphere prevailed in Australia when I arrived there. Actually, it was even worse. We ran into some very serious labor difficulties that interfered with the operation of our own ships. The workers still wanted to go to the races, work only eight hours a day, and go on strike if they didn't like things.

The SeaBees have a unique record. They have reason to be proud of it. The official story deals with statistics, which in the aggregrate are impressive: 247 battalions were formed in the course of the war; 22,000 miles of roads were built; men were stationed at 375 areas around the globe; 700 Purple Hearts were awarded. The list goes on and on. But it is the men, not the statistics, that tell the story best, about the bridges, the camps, the airfields and ports they built in the heat of the jungle, in the drenching rains of a tropical island, under the deadly sniping of the defending Japanese.

Rear Admiral Ben Moreell, chief of the Bureau of Yard and Docks from 1937 to 1945, was responsible for this service. He served as a young officer in the navy's Civil Engineering Corps during World War I, an assignment that gave him experience with construction workers. As World War II approached he thought of the need for construction battalions in the navy, and his suggestion gave rise to an official organization. Officers in the Construction Corps, drawn largely from the Civil Engineering Corps and the engineering professions, were given full autonomy over their men. This was a major departure from the navy's peacetime practice of allowing only line officers to command. Into the ranks came carpenters, mechanics, steelworkers, electricians, truck drivers, bull dozer operators, and "patriotic artisans," men whose energy and willingness to contribute to the war effort were represented in the graphic insignia of their organization: a flying bee wearing a sailor's cap and carrying a tommygun, a wrench, and a hammer.

The fact that the SeaBees were an integral part of the navy, that they were men under full military discipline, made for relative harmony when they worked alongside the marines, the navy, and the army in hot spots such as Guadalcanal, Tulagi, Espíritu Santo, Bougainville, Iwo Jima, and Okinawa. Apparently it was during their baptism under fire on Guadalcanal, where they worked in tandem with the marines after September 1942, that the popular name SeaBees was bestowed upon the construction battalions. They had become a part of the total war effort and had no loyalties other than those due their commanding officers, their flag, and their country. In this respect their service differed from that of the merchant marine, where conditions of service, working hours, and overtime were still matters to be negotiated with individual employers.

Their record on Tulagi is an illustration of their service and cooperation. There they built a tank farm and fueling station at the navy's temporary naval base. They erected a PT boat base, a hospital, fuel oil tanks, and connecting pipelines. On their own, and without any prodding, they elected to help the commander of the naval base. In one year they performed ship repairs of one kind or another on about 450 vessels. This included the installation of new propellers on 120 of them. There were no dry docks, so the propellers had to be changed under water. The men converted ordinary gas masks into diving masks; they ran oxygen from compressors into hose lines through filters; they made filters from bales of cotton; they built their own underwater cutting torches; they set up a complete machine shop on shore and did work that the ships themselves could not perform. All of these tasks were performed under conditions less than ideal. Tulagi was jungle country, where rainfall averaged 320 inches per year.

Such efforts were partly morale building. They were partly an escape from boredom, we are told, but they were also the efforts of men anxious to get the war over, men who discovered how innovative and versatile they could be in the face of necessity. Captain Willard G. Triest, whose oral history follows, once remarked to me, "We found that more square pegs could be put into round holes than you could imagine." A man could be a carpenter in the daytime, the operator of a film projector at night, he could sing in the choir on a Sunday, man an antiaircraft gun during the week, or join the crew of a PT boat at night. It was a constant source of discovery, this use of latent talents in the war effort.

The selection from Captain Triest, at the time of events a lieutenant commander in the naval reserve, reveals the groundwork performed for the very first project of the construction battalions, organized only weeks after the Japanese attack on Pearl Harbor. We see the almost frenetic development of Operation Bobcat, the plan that resulted in the building of a complete military base and fueling station on Bora Bora in the central Pacific. The base facilitated the effort to send urgent supplies to Australia and was to become a vital link in American cooperation with allies in the South Pacific. Triest's story is an admixture of humor, earnestness, and dogged determination—all characteristics that surface time and again as the bloody war unfolded.

GEARING UP FOR OPERATION BOBCAT

CAPTAIN WILLARD G. TRIEST

Willard Gustav Triest, born in 1905 in New York City, attended the Hill School in Pennsylvania and the Rensselaer Poly-technic Institute in Rensselaer, New York. He was born into an engineering family: both his father and his maternal grandfather were involved with the construction of the Brook-lyn Bridge. When that project ended Triest's father continued in the heavy construction business in New York City. In the 1920s, after he completed his education, young Triest joined his father's firm.

Triest was commissioned in the U.S. Navy's Civil Engineering Corps in December 1941. He was first detailed to Quonset Point, Rhode Island, where he served as domestic project manager for the civilian lend-lease construction work in Iceland, Ireland, Scotland, the Azores, and finally Bora Bora in the Society Islands. In 1943 he had duty as a lieutenant commander with the Fifty-seventh SeaBees on Espíritu Santo in the Pacific and as a commander of the Twenty-seventh SeaBees on Tulagi, Guadalcanal, Emirau, and Okinawa. A month after leaving the SeaBees, in March 1946, he was back in uniform for a short time to administer a five-state area. At that time President Truman took over the coal mines.

From 1950 on Triest was occupied with engineering projects in the area of Annapolis, Maryland, including the building of the Severn River Bridge. As head of

the Triest Manufacturing Works in Annapolis, he was one of the developers of the
navy's modern lightweight refueling-at-sea system.

Mr. Triest makes his home in Annapolis, Maryland.

On New Year's Eve, 1941, I got a call from my counterpart in the Bureau of
Yards and Docks in Washington, Lieutenant Commander Wayne van Leer,
who was a deputy to Captain Everett Huntington, the man in charge of the
base section of the bureau. He asked for Captain Raymond Miller, and
unfortunately the captain was out on some inspection trip, so he said, "Well,
I'll have to talk to you. Get some pencils and a sheaf of paper because we're
going to be talking for some time." For four hours he dictated the requirements for a supersecret base, to be known as Bobcat, which was to be built in
the Society Islands one thousand miles south of Honolulu—the first fueling
station on the way to Australia. We were to design all the construction
facilities, including the tank farm, pipelines, submarine-loading facilities (by
submarine I mean submarine hoses led out to buoys in the harbor for
refueling ships), and the equipment necessary to build an airfield, hospital,
and living facilities for five thousand army personnel. This all had to be done
and the equipment accumulated—about twenty thousand tons of it—and
loaded on two ships in Quonset Point in two weeks—I repeat in two weeks!

The captain came back, and I told him that I had this long conversation
with Commander van Leer and showed him my sheaf of notes. When I
explained at some length he of course became very much interested in the
project, as I had become, and said, "Well, go ahead. Do anything that's
necessary."

This plan was probably born in Washington just about the twenty-fifth of
December 1941, and the word to go ahead was given to me on the thirty-first.

The captain asked me what my plans were, and I said, "Well, the only
thing I think we can do is to go right to Standard Oil or one of the majors and
have them undertake it." Of course, we would use the same procedure that
had been used for bases in Iceland, Scotland, and Northern Ireland. We
would design in New York, turn the construction requirements over to the
procurement staff of George A. Fuller and Merritt, Chapman and Scott, and
they would then accumulate the material, load it aboard ships, and ship it
out.

I went to New York next afternoon, New Year's Day, and met Charlie
Adoue, leading designer with Standard Oil of New Jersey, about four
o'clock. I laid the whole program out to him and said that this was a 3A
priority program as far as we were concerned (with only an A rating), we had
to stop what we were doing in order to get this job out, and we had just two
weeks in which to do it. Further, one of the specifications was that we were to

recruit an engineer whom we could commission to build it because in searching through their files the navy people found they didn't have a single construction man who was in any way familiar with pipelines and tank farms. None. Also, they could find no welders, who were to be an essential part of this job. You couldn't pry a welder loose from a shipyard to save your soul. There were precious few qualified construction men loose and the navy had none other than those in shipyards. So the second most important part of our job was to conscript the first construction detachment to be sent out in uniform. The contractors were not going to build.

They were called a construction detachment at this time, not yet Sea-Bees, because it had been envisioned that construction battalions would be formed which would consist of five companies each. I don't know whether we called this a detachment or a company at that time, but these were construction people, actual mechanics under CEC officers, not under CEC officers who were supervisory personnel in the shipyards and public works offices. Admiral Moreell actually started using naval construction personnel at the end of World War I.

We worked, all of us, most of that night to get the basic layout and essential plans committed to paper. We'd been told by the bureau that the only map or drawing of the island was an old German geographical study that had been made some twenty or thirty years before, and there were no pictures available except in a motion picture called "Tabu." It was a Hollywood film made on the island five or six years before. We viewed the movie and it gave us an idea of the terrain. This was a great help. We had to guess the height of the hills on the island to determine how we could sink the fuel tanks into the side of the hills for camouflage purposes—a specific requirement—and the distance from the hills to the waterfront. Then we had to estimate the distance out to the ships to judge the lengths of hose lines for fueling purposes. This was all conjecture. We had nothing to go on.

In any event, we set about getting the design force working on this thing as soon as we'd viewed the motion picture. Then Charlie and I turned our attention to recruiting personnel, including the principal officers necessary to build this base. We had to have what is called a pipeline superintendent. We planned to send out a detachment or company of about 250 men with the requisite number of officers, but the principal officer had to be a tank farm man. We talked this over with Cap Finney of Standard Oil, in charge of pipelines and tank farms, and he said, "Well, there's one man we have named Shorty Duddleston, who is our superintendent on the Portland-Montreal pipeline, and he's about finished up there." (That was a twenty-inch pipeline they were just completing between Portland, Maine, and Montreal.) "I suggest you call him and see what you can do."

So I got on the telephone and told him what was happening—that the navy had a very special job I was assigned to, and one of our assignments was

43

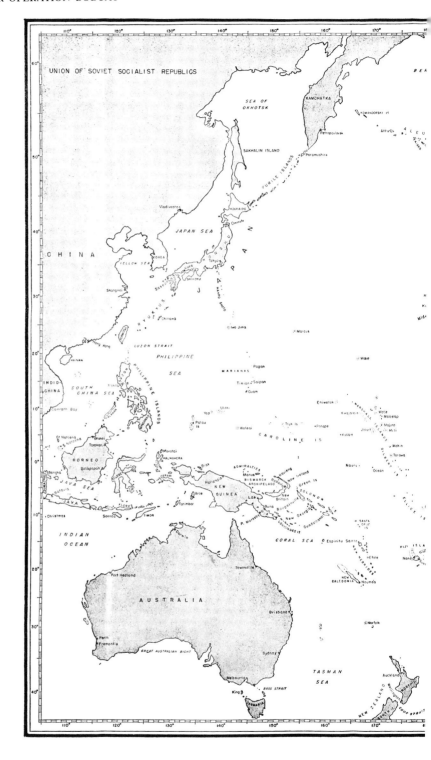

44

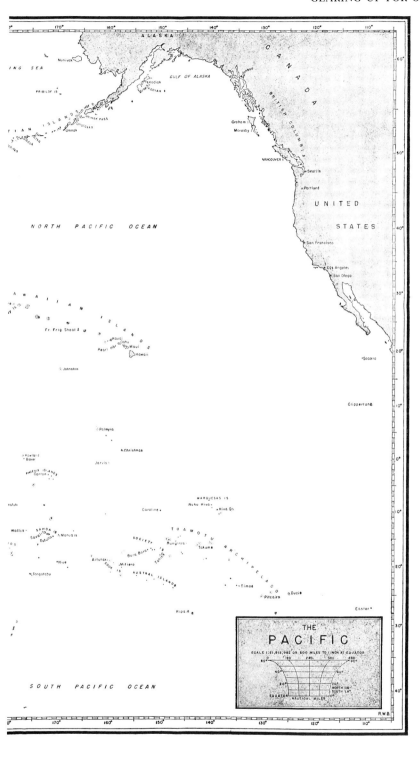

45

to recruit an officer with pipeline and tank farm experience who would go out with a uniformed force to build these facilities.

He said, "You couldn't pay me enough to do that. I'm getting twenty-five thousand dollars a year. What would you pay me?"

I said, "I really don't know—six thousand or seven thousand. But you have to consider the urgency of the mission and the needs of your country. I'll talk to Standard Oil about it and they'll do something for you, but I can't offer you any more than your rank would command."

He said, "What kind of a rank are you offering me?"

I thought quickly and, tongue in cheek, said, "Two and a half stripes," knowing full well that the navy wasn't giving any more than two stripes to officers being recruited at that time.

Anyway, he said, "I'll think it over. Call me back."

So I arranged to call him back in the morning and we had another twenty minutes' conversation, and by the time I'd finished he had agreed to take on the job. "All right," he said, "I'll be in New York Sunday morning," which was the next day. On Sunday he came into the office about eight o'clock and we worked all day and laid the whole thing out for him, even though he was a civilian and this was a top-secret job. We hadn't time to get him a clearance. He told me that he wasn't physically fit and so he would probably need a lot of medical waivers and so on. I found out that he had no more than a high-school education, and this was another roadblock because no officer was given a commission unless he had a college degree or the equivalent thereof. The long and short of it is that we worked all day and he was thoroughly indoctrinated in what had to be done and how fast. Then he asked the sixty-four-dollar question: "Where are you going to get the men?"

And I said, "We're going to get the men out of the receiving barracks in Charleston and we're going to recruit welders. We know we've got to get a welding chief for you and as many other welders as we can, and I propose to go to the oil fields in Louisiana and Texas and get them that way."

We took a sleeper to Washington. We were to meet Admiral Moreell and Captain Huntington on Monday morning at eight o'clock. We arrived about five minutes of eight and van Leer was jumping up and down in the Bureau of Yards and Docks and so was Captain Huntington. They said "For God's sake, the admiral and Admiral King are waiting for you upstairs. The chief's room number is 4645."

I had brought my secretary, "Admiral" French, down because every spare moment I was dictating memorandums to her, and the idea was that she could transcribe them when we were there and be available to take more dictation. In the meantime, I was covering all this with orders to the contractors. So I said, "If you'll give 'Admiral' French a desk and a typewriter she can go to work while we're busy."

I went up with Duddleston to see the admiral. Duddleston was still in civilian clothes, of course. We went into Admiral Moreell's office, and his chief of staff jumped up and said, "Oh my goodness, yes, the admiral's waiting for you." He knocked on the door and Admiral Moreell opened it. Right behind him was another very distinguished admiral whom I learned was Admiral King. We walked in and I introduced them to Duddleston.

Admiral King said, "Come in, son, come in, just the man we're waiting for." And as I stood there, Admiral King put his arm around one of Duddleston's shoulders and Admiral Moreell put his around the other shoulder, and the three of them walked to the window to the admiral's desk, where they all sat down. I stood there, first on one foot and then the other, while they talked to him, and they began describing the job immediately.

As he sat there with his hat in his hand, Duddleston said, "Well, gentlemen, I'm still a civilian. I'm not cleared for this sort of thing."

The admiral said, "Pay no attention to that. We'll take care of it. Triest, you can be excused now. We'll talk."

So I went back down to the bureau, and for about three hours talked and dictated some more and discussed the job with van Leer and Captain Huntington. Then they called me back upstairs about twelve or one o'clock, and Admiral Moreell said, "Triest, Duddleston is going to join us, and I want you to get him in uniform by five o'clock this afternoon."

"Yes, sir." So I took him down to see Commander Perry, who was our liaison between the bureau and the Bureau of Personnel.

Commander Perry said, "What's this all about?"

"I have a man here that I've got to get in uniform. He is going out to Bobcat and it's extremely urgent, as you may have heard. I have to have him in uniform by five o'clock."

"What? That's impossible. You know the procedure around here."

I said, "I'm sorry, sir, but if you'll just call Admiral Moreell he'll tell you himself."

So he dialed. "Chief, Lieutenant Triest is down here with a man he wants—yes, sir. Yes, sir." And that was that.

He started filling out the necessary forms, and when he found out about Duddleston's education, he said, "High school. You know this is impossible. I can't get a commission for a man who hasn't had a college education."

I said again, "I'm sorry, but you heard the admiral."

"Yes, I heard him." He filled out the form a little further and then said, "Now how about the letters of recommendation?"

I replied, "Admiral King will give him one, Admiral Moreell another, Captain Huntington and Commander van Leer, and I'll give him one."

More disgusted grunts and then, "Okay, okay. How about a physical?"

"Well, sir, he hasn't had a physical, obviously."

"Well, take him down to see Captain So and So in charge of the infirmary."

I went to the infirmary and spoke to the chief, who said he would take care of the matter. But I said I had better speak to the captain because of the need to have this man in uniform in about two and a half hours. I was ushered in to the captain. I told him my problem and he said, "This is highly unusual."

"I appreciate that, sir, but it has to be done."

"What about his physical qualifications?"

Duddleston broke in, "Captain, let me interrupt. I'm color-blind, I'm flat-footed, I'm knock-kneed, I have less than half my teeth, and whatever else may be wrong, I don't know, but I'm in fine shape."

The captain remarked, "This is impossible. You know that."

I said again, "Yes, sir, I know. Would you mind calling Admiral Moreell? He will straighten it out."

So he called the admiral and started, "Chief, Lieutenant Triest—yes, sir. Yes, sir, right away." So he called his staff in and gave them instructions to give Duddleston a physical and make it as complete as they could within an hour's time. He successfully passed with eight waivers.

At four o'clock I went back to New York to get on with my work. Duddleston was to call me at seven-thirty. In the meantime I had called my tailor in New York and he had promised to keep three men overtime to fit the uniforms. Duddleston was to call me with his measurements by five o'clock and was due back in New York by ten that night. He called on schedule. He had two secretaries in the Bureau of Yards and Docks taking his measurements over the telephone, and I relayed them to the tailor.

Duddleston arrived in New York at ten-thirty that night. I went with him to the tailor's and he was fitted into his clothes and ready to go. On the sidewalk he said, "Say, you know, I don't even know how to salute."

"You just follow me," I said. "Here's a man coming right now." It was a gob across the street with his hands in his pea jacket. "You start across the street when he does and you just watch him. When he salutes you, you answer. Don't salute first. Wait till he salutes, then you answer."

We stood there with great amusement watching Duddleston waiting for the light on Fifty-second and Madison. As the light changed the gob started to cross. You could see Duddleston's right hand getting ready to salute. In the meantime the gob had his hands still in his jacket and his white hat cocked at an angle and a big plug of tobacco in his mouth. His eye caught Duddleston, he turned his head the other way and let out a big plop of tobacco juice and didn't bother to salute, but Duddleston was so anxious that he saluted anyway. We just stood there and roared. It was a terribly funny incident. He boarded a special plane we had chartered and went to Fort Worth to say good-bye to his family. The plane waited and the next morning took him to Charleston.

Within a few days we had developed the specifications for the various pieces of equipment required, starting with the longest leadtime items, such as National Transit pumps for pumping the fuel oil through the submarine loading hose to the tanks on shore. It was Charlie Adoue's business and I took his lead completely. He knew exactly what had to be done. In a matter of hours he had the whole procedure laid out in his mind. He issued the basic orders I gave to the contractors. They had to find sources of supply. In many cases we supplied the sources, because they were not familiar with either the tank farm business or the pipeline business. National Transit pumps to them were Greek words.

The contractors had fifty men busy expediting my orders to the various manufacturers and suppliers throughout the country, including, for example, the purchase and transportation of steel tanks which we had to buy in Texas and have trucked to Quonset. The submarine loading hose we got from Hewitt-Robbins in Buffalo and they had to have special priorities. We only had a 1A priority. That was all we could get. They were making hoses for the air force with a 3A priority, so I had to spend literally hundreds of dollars telephoning the resident naval inspectors of various plants to persuade them that ours was really a much more urgent program than any they were working on. I simply said that I was working on the highest priority job that the CEC had, under direct orders from Admiral Moreell and Admiral King, and they just had to get it out, in one week including the time it took to truck hoses to Quonset.

The Bureau of Yards and Docks could not get a higher priority for the project. The highest priorities were going to naval aviation supplies and army aviation supplies. The 3A priority was tantamount to the most urgent requirements the country had. It was just laid at my door to persuade the naval inspectors that ours was equally important and somehow had to be worked in. I called the resident inspector at the National Transit Company about pumps, and he said, "Well, we have to have bearings. We have no bearings for these pumps."

"Where do the bearings come from?"

"From the Hyatt Roller Bearing Company."

So I called Hyatt and spoke to the resident inspector there. He said, "We're backed up with 3A priority bearings for the next four months. We couldn't think of giving them to you."

"Come on, now, get down to earth. We have to have them and I don't want to have to go to the White House to get orders directly to you to get those bearings. We must have the pumps, and if necessary I'll go through Admiral King to the White House. This is my job and it's going to be done. We have to have those bearings and they must be delivered to National Transit in three days."

And so it went with everything we asked for. The long and short of it is that within ten days something around eighteen thousand tons of equipment had been accumulated either by direct purchase from the outside or by taking it from stock at Quonset Point. And the ships were there, two freighters. We loaded about nine thousand tons on each freighter.

In the meantime, after Duddleston was recruited, it became necessary to find a welder, a chief welder that we could also get into uniform. I think I spent some fifteen hundred dollars in seven days on the telephone calling up every construction company and every oil company that I could find in the registers. I'd get a lead on a man and they'd say, "Well, he's out in the field. I can't reach him but he lives in such and such a place and generally has dinner at such and such a tavern, usually around six o'clock." I would call that tavern at six o'clock and get him on the phone. But I couldn't persuade any of them. Finally I found a man I did persuade to join up. He asked what he should do and I said, "Say good-bye to your family. Of course, we'll pay your fare to Charleston, and you report there in two days and start your school." This was a real breakthrough, and with his help I finally got half a dozen more with the inevitable hassle about medical waivers. In the meantime we had conscripted 250 men from various receiving stations in New York and Charleston and other places, and they were sent to Charleston. Then three or four other officers were assigned to Duddleston from the CEC. In Charleston they started getting these forces into shape, seeing to their equipment and so on. Then we loaded all kinds of steel plate and angles on board so additional men could be taught welding. They figured that they had to have about seventeen welders, and the chief's responsibility was to train these men (draftees) en route. So we had welding equipment, including generators, on deck, and they set up schools on one of the two ships to train the boys in the art of welding as they sailed from Charleston to Bora Bora.

As I said, we had accumulated about eighteen thousand tons of equipment and stowed it aboard these two vessels at Quonset Point, but there were still two thousand tons that couldn't make it. It was being trucked in from various places around the country. There was no doubt that we had to get this equipment aboard the vessels, and so we accumulated a convoy of four hundred trucks with two drivers each, drums of gasoline, water, box lunches, etc. We started them off in convoy, and they went directly from Quonset Point, right through New York City, and on down to Charleston in two and a half days, stopping twice for more fuel. They took turns sleeping and they were met at every state line by state troopers. They went through New York City as one solid convoy, four hundred trucks, across the George Washington Bridge. They got there on time, they put the cargo on board in time, the men were there, and we got back only one telegram saying that one valve, or some small part, was missing. That was the only feedback we had.

That's what the contractors did, and they did a magnificent job. They knew that business—getting materials, handling them, transporting them, and so on. It was their particular forte.

50

Ready cash for financing was made available in their basic contract, which at that time had grown from seven hundred million to some astronomical sum.

The conclusion to this project was building the base. Duddleston did an excellent job. He went from there to build eight or ten other fueling stations across the Pacific. I didn't see him again. I heard from him from time to time. I think he finished up Bora Bora about August of that year and was assigned to another base. And in November of 1942 I was myself assigned to a construction battalion—at that time they were called SeaBees—so I got out of the design business and into the actual construction myself.

When the Japanese juggernaut struck at Manila on 8 December 1941 (7 December at Pearl Harbor), all the components of the small Asiatic Fleet were scattered quickly. As a base Manila was soon denied to Admiral Hart, the commander in chief of the fleet. General MacArthur declared the city open on 25 December. The admiral then left for Surabaya, in Java, where he established headquarters. That became the base for Admiral William Glassford's Task Force 5, the striking force of the fleet. Other elements of the fleet were sent to Darwin, on the northern coast of Australia, where a service base was established for the submarines and the patrol aircraft (PBYs) that remained of Patrol Wing 10.

Admiral Hart had twenty-eight PBYs when the war broke out. They were the eyes of his fleet and their patrolling abilities were invaluable, but they were slow and vulnerable. On 12 December, at Olongapo in Subic Bay, a quarter of them were destroyed at their moorings by Japanese Zeros. From that point on the enemy had complete mastery of the air around Luzon. Almost immediately thereafter Hart ordered the commanding officer of his PBYs to take the tender *Childs* to safety in the lower Philippines and eventually to Darwin.

The Japanese moved rapidly to take over the Philippines and the Dutch East Indies. Only pockets of resistance remained in the early days of 1942. Bataan and Corregidor, at the entrance to Manila Bay, held out until 6 May 1942. Java, in the Netherlands East Indies, remained an outpost, but it too fell by 9 March. Japanese plans for their attack on this stronghold included the severance of that island's communications with Australia, particularly the new Allied base at Darwin.

To that end they assembled the most powerful striking force they had sent on a single mission since the attack on Pearl Harbor. Four carriers, two battleships, and numerous other units made up the flotilla. The Allies had nothing capable of stopping such an armada, even for a moment. A total of 242 planes, from fleet units and land bases, sortied against Darwin on 19 February. They came in waves, heavy high-level bombers and dive-bombers. They attacked the ships in the anchorage and they hit the airport before Allied planes could take off. They strafed the town and dealt Darwin an altogether devastating blow. Eight ships were lost in the harbor, nine others were damaged; the airport was demolished, military stores were destroyed, and the town was abandoned for fear of a return visit by the marauders. Admiral Glassford made a hasty decision to retire what remained of his tenders and auxiliaries to Exmouth Gulf in western Australia.

It was on the very date of this deadly attack on Darwin that Lieutenant Thomas H. Moorer and his crew in their PBY, one of the few remaining Catalinas from Patrol Wing 10, had an encounter with destiny. This gripping story of human endurance has been included because it paints an indelible picture of the hardships American flyers and sailors endured in the early days of the war in the Pacific. At that time optimism had vanished and disaster had overtaken the inadequate American forces. But at that time also men demonstrated real tenacity, an ability to be innovative with what tools were available. Several other excerpts in this book illustrate the skillful use of those tools in the early dark days. The scattered elements of the old Asiatic Fleet, struggling in the face of terrible odds, gave us some of the finest chapters in naval history.

A PBY MEETS WITH DESTINY

ADMIRAL THOMAS H. MOORER

Thomas Hinman Moorer, who was born in Mount Willing, Alabama, on 9 February 1912, graduated from the U.S. Naval Academy in 1933. Named naval aviator in 1936 after completing the course at the naval air station in Pensacola, he was with a fighter squadron until 1939, when he joined Patrol Squadron 22.

Moorer was stationed at Pearl Harbor when the war began. His squadron was sent against the Japanese in the Philippines and Java. From July 1942 to 1945 he was an observer in the United Kingdom; commander of Bombing Squadron 132 out of Key West; and gunnery and tactical officer on the staff of Commander, Air Force, Atlantic. With the end of hostilities Moorer had tours with the Strategic Bombing Survey in Japan; with the Naval Aviation Ordnance Test Station in Virginia; as operations officer on carriers in the Atlantic; as experimental officer at the Naval Ordnance Test Station in California; with the Naval War College; as aide to the assistant secretary of the navy for air; and as commander of the USS *Salisbury Sound*. In 1957 Moorer was promoted to rear admiral, and there followed a series of major advancements: two tours in the Navy Department; command of Carrier Division 6; command of the Seventh Fleet in the Far East; commander in chief of the Pacific Fleet; command of NATO'S Allied Command, Atlantic; and commander in chief of the U.S. Atlantic Fleet. Moorer was named chief of naval operations in 1967 and reappointed to this office in 1969. On 14 April 1970 he became chairman of the Joint Chiefs of Staff, in which capacity he served until his retirement on 1 July 1974.

Admiral Moorer has remained almost as active in retirement as he was during the years of his notable career. Recently he began work on a biography.

We were operating out of Darwin, Australia, at the time. It happened on the nineteenth of February, 1942. We had some information about four Japanese carriers being down in the vicinity of Ambon, an island of the Moluccas in the Malay Archipelago. My mission was to locate them. There was a low ceiling that day. I had just cleared Bathurst Island, northwest of the Australian coast, and observed a ship, so I went down to take a look. It was a Philippine ship. I satisfied myself that it was a peaceful ship, and I was in the act of climbing to go off and continue my patrol when I saw nine Japanese fighters. They had peeled off from a whole formation that was headed for Darwin. We were at about a thousand feet when they attacked the plane and set it afire. We didn't have any leak-proof tanks, and they were shooting little low-muzzle-velocity twenty-millimeter guns. You could actually see the bullets. They had practically no velocity and they were explosive. When the plane caught fire it burned all the fabric. The rear part of the wing was all fabric, as well as the rudder and elevators. There were two great big gas tanks up forward. I was surprised to see us still flying when all the fabric burned off. The tail was also of fabric and it burned off on one side. It was very hard to fly at that point. I didn't have much control. I recognized that I had to land right away. I released the bombs because I was afraid they were going to explode, and of course there was danger that the gasoline would explode. However, I managed to land downwind in the water.

The Japs attacked until they were satisfied that the plane was going down. They could see it going down because the fire was extending well past the tail. It was my good fortune that they had other things to do. They couldn't let their bombers run off and get to Darwin before they did, so they didn't fool around with me very much. They made about two passes each and then charged off to overtake the bombers.

We had a crew of eight and we had two rubber boats. Three of us had been hit by Japanese fire. The radioman had a bad ankle and I was hit in the leg. We got out as quickly as we could because the plane was burning furiously. It had swung into the wind, and everybody was up in the bow to get clear of the flames. The gasoline was coming out of the tanks in several streams about the size of your thumb. I had a full load of fuel, because I had only been in the air about an hour and a half and had taken on about three thousand gallons before taking off.

One of our rubber boats had been shot up and was full of holes, so we all had to get into the other one. The master of a Philippine ship, who had seen us go down, came over to pick up the survivors. It happened to be one of five ships that had been chartered by the U.S. government to take ammunition over to Corregidor. All five were ordered to take different routes in the hope that one of them would slip through. When we got aboard and I found out that he was loaded with ammo, I told my crew to go back to the stern and be prepared to abandon ship, because I felt fairly certain that the Japanese were going to attack sooner or later.

While we were aboard, Japanese seaplanes came over from a cruiser (they had seaplanes on their cruisers as we did in those days). They carried one-hundred-pound bombs and two of them tried to bomb the ship. They missed but they did drop four bombs. The captain's tactic was to stop the ship any time he got attacked. This was, of course, the worst thing he could do.

After we had been aboard about two hours, I was back on the fantail and looked up to see nine dive-bombers stacked up and coming right down on us. I told my crew to jump over the side. I knew what was going to happen. Only one boy failed to do so. I don't know whether he had gone up forward at that time or what. But I know we never saw him again.

We had life jackets. As we jumped over the side the ship was hit in the bow. The first bomb hit and blew all the ammo out, and then blew the bow off the ship. As I recall, the water was about two hundred feet deep in that area. When the bow was blown off, the ship went right down and stuck in the mud. About half of it was exposed at forty-five degrees. It happened in just seconds. The two screws were still turning. Most of the Filipinos who were lost were in the engineering spaces.

The Japs bombed the hell out of the ship. They even bombed it after the bow end was in the mud and the stern was sticking up. There were two lifeboats aft on the stern, so we finally swam back to the ship and climbed aboard after the Japs had left.

We cut those two boats loose. I put my copilot, Ensign Moseley, in one. (He was killed in the Battle of Midway later.) I manned the other boat and we paddled around and collected our own people—the seven of us remaining. Then we rescued about forty Filipinos.

We were well north of Bathurst Island, about 150 miles from Darwin. So I planned to sail southeast and go back to Australia.

The young Filipinos were panic-stricken and some were horribly burned. But we picked them up and started to get organized. Then again the Japs came over and strafed the boats and we all jumped out. This was a separate group of Japs who came out from their carrier.

We had a hell of a time getting the Filipinos back in the boats again, but we finally did, as many as we could find. The two boats were still together so we started sailing southeast. We sailed and sailed until the following night. About midnight, I believe it was, I heard breakers. We grounded and beached in the surf. It turned out to be Bathurst Island. Some of those young Filipinos jumped out of the boats. They were so frightened that they just jumped out and made for the jungle. I don't know where they went. They may still be down there for all I know. They wouldn't wait until we got organized ashore. I wouldn't let anybody leave the beach once we got ashore.

We had people that were seriously burned. My radioman couldn't walk because of his ankle. I knew there was a small church on the opposite side of the island, for I had seen it from the air. I didn't know whether there were any people there, but I thought we'd try to walk around the island. We tried but we just couldn't do it.

I had made one major mistake. I had taken my shoes off while I was swimming. That was one thing that was later put into the survival manual, because it's the worst thing you can do. The shoes are the most important thing you've got if you do get ashore. Otherwise your feet get sunburned and cut. So I was barefooted. We didn't get very far along the beach. We went back to where we came ashore.

It got very cold at night. I remember we all slept in the sand. You'd dig a big trench with your hands and cover yourself with the sand. There was warmth in that because it got hot during the day.

Of course we had no water. The reflection of the heat from the beach would split the rain squalls. They would come right up to the beach and you'd get all set to have some good water. Then the squall would split, and half of it would go around one side and half around the other. Then the two halves would join up again and just disappear. It never did rain on the island.

All we had to drink was condensed milk, for that is what they carried in those Philippine boats. It was the worst-tasting milk—I guess it was caribou. Anyway, if you can think of anything worse than Philippine condensed milk I'd like to see it.

Finally we wrote in the sand. I had everybody write WATER MEDICINE in big letters. They were letters as long as that lamp over there. We didn't have anything else to do. Sure enough, in a couple of days or so a Lockheed Hudson came out on reconnaissance and saw the writing. He waved his wings to indicate he understood, went back to Darwin, and then came back out.

They dropped water to us but we got only some of it. It was in glass bottles, and when it hit the beach some of the bottles broke. We also got medicine. They had a note which said, "A corvette will come back and pick you up early in the morning." Well, sure enough, at daylight we looked out and there was this little Australian corvette.

The skipper was a hell of a guy. He was an Australian reserve officer and had been in all of the action around Crete when the Germans made their air assault. He thought this mission in the corvette was nothing. He was on vacation. "Old chap, this is nothing," he said.

So we got everybody aboard and started back to Darwin when an Emily flying boat came over. The corvette had one three-inch antiaircraft gun. The Japanese Emily had twelve one-hundred-pound bombs. It made twelve passes at us and dropped the bombs one at a time. The captain had a tar barrel on the stern of the ship and he set that off. Every time the Jap aircraft arrived at the release point the captain would back down into the smoke—downwind right into the smoke made by this tar barrel—so the Emily couldn't see him. It never did touch us, even though it dropped bombs in succession. The Emily did that all morning, but finally the pilot ran out of fuel, I guess, and shoved off. We were three or four miles out from Bathurst Island when this happened. Then we sailed on to Darwin. When we arrived we found the town was absolutely deserted. We went back to the hotel I was familiar with, for I had been there before.

There was food in the cupboards, but there wasn't a human soul in that hotel. We, the seven-man crew, set up shop. We moved in. It wasn't long before the military police came along. They patrolled around the town when no one was there. The only way I could identify myself was with my Annapolis ring. I was barefooted and in shorts, with no shirt, nothing else. I finally convinced them I was an American. So they sent messages for us, and finally Lieutenant Tommy Christopher came up to get us and took us down to Perth. We had set up headquarters in Perth. Practically all the ships from the Dutch East Indies had gone to Perth.

We were in the deserted hotel at Darwin for about three days. We didn't have much else, but we did have ten thousand cases of beer—San Miguel beer. And we helped ourselves. It seems that the *Gold Star* was a transport that once a year took San Miguel beer from the Philippines to Guam. When the war broke out Guam was captured and the *Gold Star* was diverted and ordered to Darwin, where she unloaded her cargo of beer on the dock.

In January 1942 Admiral Ernest J. King gave an extraordinary assignment to his air operations officer, Captain Donald B. ("Wu") Duncan. It was to study the possibility of staging a raid on Tokyo from one of the navy's aircraft carriers, using army air forces planes and their pilots in the effort. General Henry H. Arnold of the army air forces responded with enthusiasm when the project was mentioned to him, proposing the services of Lieutenant Colonel Jimmy Doolittle and some of the air forces' medium bombers, the B-25s. They had adequate range and power for such a venture.

Admiral King felt that such a raid would boost the morale of the American people, who had been badly shaken by the success of the Japanese in their surprise attack on Pearl Harbor. Impatient and uninformed people were complaining. "Where is the navy?" they asked. "Why don't we do something?"

Duncan, a careful, meticulous man, gave immediate thought to all the ramifications of the proposal. In a few days he was able to come back to Admiral King and assure him that the project was not only possible but feasible. Things were set in motion with great speed. General Arnold was cooperative, and Colonel Doolittle's help was soon enlisted.

Doolittle would assemble the necessary men at Eglin Field in Florida, where they would train for a few weeks. Their planes would be given special equipment for carrier launching. Since army air forces pilots were unfamiliar with carriers, Lieutenant (later Rear Admiral) Henry L. Miller of the navy, a skilled pilot, was delegated to coach them.

In the following excerpt, Captain Duncan goes into detail about the plans that were formulated and then implemented by the navy and army air forces. His report on the subject was so highly classified that no copies of it were made. There existed only his handwritten original. It was eventually given to Captain Miles Browning, Admiral William Halsey's operations officer. Duncan made a trip to Hawaii to acquaint Admirals Nimitz and Halsey with the details of the plan and to convey to the former directly from Admiral King the necessary orders to carry out the project.

A second excerpt follows from Rear Admiral Miller. He was brought into the plan as a pilot-teacher without any knowledge of the project or the objective. Only by deduction was he able to learn about the raid. Miller's skill and his engaging personality aided him in persuading Colonel Doolittle to take him along from Florida to the California coast, where he continued for a short time longer the training of the army air forces pilots. Then his persuasive powers got him a still greater favor—permission to accompany the army fliers on the carrier *Hornet* to the launching spot in the Pacific. Later he was called to Washington to make a detailed report on the launchings to the navy and army secretaries and to Admiral King.

SECRET PLANNING FOR THE TOKYO RAID

ADMIRAL DONALD B. DUNCAN

DONALD BRADLEY DUNCAN, born in Michigan on 1 September 1896, graduated from the U.S. Naval Academy in 1917. He received flight training at Pensacola in 1920–21 and was designated naval aviator. He did postgraduate study at Annapolis and in 1926 earned a master of science degree from Harvard University.

Duncan's early duty at sea was primarily in carriers. On shore he served in several capacities in the Bureau of Aeronautics. He was executive officer at the naval air station in Pensacola, and in 1941 he took command of the USS *Long Island,* the first merchant ship converted to an aircraft carrier escort. He commissioned and became commanding officer of the USS *Essex* in 1942 and participated in the attacks on Wake and Marcus islands. He served on the staff of the Commander in Chief, Pacific Fleet, and later was Deputy Commander in Chief, Pacific Fleet, with the rank of vice admiral. He had a tour of duty as deputy chief of naval operations for air and later was named Commander, Second Task Fleet.

Admiral Duncan retired in 1957 in the rank of admiral. After retirement he became governor of the Naval Home in Philadelphia. He died in Pensacola, Florida, where he had his residence, on 8 September 1975.

In the early spring of 1942 came what many people remember well and very few people had anything to do with putting together—the Tokyo Raid, in which army aircraft under Jimmy Doolittle operated from the *Hornet* in company with the *Enterprise* and some cruisers and destroyers that made up the task force that performed the famous Tokyo Raid under the direct command of Bill Halsey.

I was involved in that operation, at least in the planning and preparation stage. I've always wished that I might have gone along, at least on part of it, but that was not my lot. My work on it was finished when they sailed from San Francisco. Up until then I was very much in the center of the operation.

I can tell you the whole story. I brought along a letter which I wrote to Admiral King to refresh his memory a little later on. And I think it might be well for me to quote from this letter, which outlines the operation, as I tell the story. I won't say what is coming from the letter and what is coming from my recollections—it's all the same source. I might say at the outset that this letter I wrote in 1949 was a result of a request from him for me to refresh his memory, so that he could reply to a letter from Judge Samuel Rosenman, who was very close to the administration and who wanted to gather some material about the raid, which he had discussed with the president in the early days of the war.

My story begins with a Sunday in January of 1942. I got a call from Captain Francis Low, my immediate superior in Admiral King's office, to come down to the Navy Department. He had something to talk to me about. So I got down there as soon as I could, and he told me that he had had a discussion the night before with Admiral King. He lived on the *Dauntless* with Admiral King, on the little flagship that the admiral had tied up in the navy yard. They used to spend many evenings talking over various problems that came up, so they had gotten on this particular subject the night before Low called me. They had a discussion on the possibility of using some army bombers from an aircraft carrier to bomb Japan. That, of course, had been thought of by a lot of people. I say that it was thought about, but I just mean the *idea* of bombing Japan. You'll recall the cries: "Where is the navy?" and "Why don't we do something?" These were the genesis of the idea to bomb Japan.

Low said to me, when I got down to headquarters, that the admiral wanted me to look into it and see whether it would be feasible—the idea being, of course, to find an airplane that could be launched from well outside the three-hundred-mile range from the Japanese coast, at which distance we were informed the Japanese were patrolling with aircraft.

I started in right away and made a preliminary survey of the situation, considering such factors as the availability of a carrier, the practicability of some takeoff trials, the performance data of the various army aircraft which might be used, the weather, things the pilots might strike in Japan with the force that could be provided. And within a very few days, maybe two or three, I had enough information to tell Admiral King that I considered the project feasible, and that I thought two carriers should be used. The first proposal made to me was for one carrier. I told the admiral I thought two should be used—one to carry the bombers, and one to carry naval aircraft, probably fighters, for the protection of the task force. The B-25 appeared to be the best airplane, and I recommended that we proceed with the preparation of plans which could then await implementation as circumstances permitted.

I believe this was the time Admiral King went to General Arnold, the head of the army air forces, with the proposal which Admiral King later told me was immediately and enthusiastically concurred in by General Arnold. As a matter of fact, at that time Arnold had quite a number of B-25s being modified to carry additional gasoline, as they were thinking about raiding Japan from Chinese airfields at the time, which they later did. So he had some airplanes which could be utilized for a carrier raid, and he was enthusiastic about going along with us in our plan for the raid. That was in January 1942.

I then proceeded to make a detailed study and prepare an outline operation plan, of which there was only one copy ever made. I wrote it in longhand, and that was so nobody except those who had to know about it would ever have a chance of seeing it. In the meantime, General Arnold had at once organized the army air forces' contingent under Lieutenant Colonel Doolittle, later a general. The first step was the conversion of the airplanes, and that was already under way.

I had a good deal of assistance from a good many people in the collection of data. Many agencies contributed material without knowing the real purpose. In no case was the reason for the collection of data revealed to anyone in its entirety at that time. The arrangements for the takeoff trials I had completed myself. I found that there were some B-25s in Norfolk making passage from one airfield to another. I was able to commandeer them through General Arnold's office. And the aircraft carrier *Hornet* was in Norfolk, in the process of shaking down and getting ready to join the fleet, so she looked like a natural for the job.

The arrangements for the takeoff trials were completed, and the trials were conducted from the *Hornet* off Norfolk during early February. So that got done at quite an early stage.

I did all this by legwork. I had to talk to people, and I went out on the *Hornet* when she conducted the trials and saw the two airplanes take off from her. They took off easily in the space that it was calculated they would need, and it was a very fine performance. They were just the common B-25s that the air force used. We extrapolated for the extra weight and we knew just how much more distance they would need, if any, on the takeoff. All I wanted to make sure of was that our calculations were correct on the wing-tip clearance, the positioning on deck, and the ability to pick up speed, and that the tests were successfully run. So we knew the B-25 was the airplane, having actually sent it off from the ship that was going to do the launching.

I had already had the *Hornet* in mind to do this operation, if it were conducted, because she was due to finish her shakedown and go around to the Pacific coast at just about the time everything else would be in order and the operation was ready to start. So, although nobody on the *Hornet* knew it, they were destined for the operation some time before they actually performed it. That made my friend Pete Mitscher, commanding officer of the *Hornet,* unhappy; he was not let in on the full plan until quite late in the business.

The trials, as I said, confirmed the estimates made and indicated that we would have no trouble launching about sixteen aircraft. The conversion of the aircraft progressed—that is, additional fuel was provided for—and they were moved to Eglin Field in Florida for installation of special equipment and the training of pilots in carrier takeoff procedure. They had to be trained to take off in a way that was quite unfamiliar to people who had nothing to do with carriers; they had to take off with a heavy load at low speed. That was a little difficult for them, but they responded nobly and really did a marvelous job of it.

We had an officer who was very familiar with aircraft operating from carriers and takeoff and landing techniques, Henry L. ("Hank") Miller. Hank was then a lieutenant or junior lieutenant commander. He went to Eglin Field and trained Doolittle's people in takeoff technique. They also used their time down there in some additional fitting out of the aircraft, getting them ready for this operation. But of course at that time none of them knew what this was all about.

General Arnold had decided—I asked him this question myself, and he told me what the answer was—that the airplanes, after leaving the carrier and bombing Japan, should proceed to bases in China. I had talked to him about the possibility of either doing that or flying back to the vicinity of the carriers and ditching alongside, where the personnel could be picked up, because of course they couldn't land aboard. The general told me that he would make arrangements for them to land in fields being prepared secretly in parts of China where the Japanese were not.

At that particular time, that is, in mid-February, as far as I know, Low and myself and Admiral King and General Arnold were the only people who knew about the whole plan. As I said, the president had discussed with some people how we were to get at Japan with aircraft, but nothing on this particular plan had been told to him at that time. Now, those four people in mid-February were the only ones who really knew what was cooking.

After the flying-off trials at Norfolk, the *Hornet,* with a couple of tankers and destroyers, departed for the West Coast. She arrived at San Diego about the middle of March and prepared to join up with the Pacific Fleet and take up duties as an active carrier.

About the fifteenth of March Admiral King called me in and said that he had been talking to General Arnold, that General Arnold felt his people were ready to go or nearly so, and that he wanted me to tell him when we would be ready to set this thing up. I told him I felt we could set it up right away, the *Hornet* having gotten out to the West Coast and Doolittle's people having been pretty well trained. And I told the admiral that with his approval I would arrange to discuss the whole thing with Doolittle, show him the plan, and proceed myself at once to Pearl Harbor to present the plan to Admiral Nimitz and Admiral Halsey. This the admiral approved, and I went over to talk to General Arnold, I think on the fifteenth of March. I told him I was leaving for Pearl Harbor as soon as possible and would like to go over the plan with Doolittle. I can remember exactly how General Arnold reacted to that. He opened the door of his inner office, where we were together, and called out to one of the people in his outer office and said, "Get Doolittle up here right away, tonight!"

So the next morning I met Doolittle. He had been in Florida and had got aboard an airplane and come up that night. I wasn't sure whether he'd get there because the weather was pretty stinking, to use an old expression, but he was there on the morning of the sixteenth and we got together. I took out my copy of the plan I had written. Fortunately he could read my writing, and so he sat down and read the whole plan. I called it an outline plan. It had a weather annex and a proposed route, and it covered the process of getting the airplanes embarked and mentioned the ships we expected to use—everything I could think of that was needed to present to the commander in chief of the Pacific and to General Arnold and to Doolittle. He read it once, and with no questions to ask said, "That's fine."

I told him I was leaving the next morning to go to Pearl to present the plan. He said his people were ready to leave Florida and they would go to Sacramento to wait for last-minute instructions on joining the ship.

Colonel Doolittle had been informed of some of the aspects of this thing before I conferred with him on the sixteenth of March, but he, like others involved, had not been told of the whole plan or seen how we proposed to carry it out. (Of course, it didn't take much thinking on his part to realize that he was going to do something from an aircraft carrier.) That was the first time he became acquainted with the whole plan, and it was the first time he was told what we proposed with reference to embarking the aircraft and other naval aspects of the plan.

I proceeded to Pearl Harbor on the seventeenth of March and arrived on the nineteenth. I went right to Admiral Nimitz, told him briefly what was going on, and arranged for him to get Admiral Halsey and a few selected members of his staff, whom he had to have acquainted with it. We set up a meeting for me to present the plan, which I did. I had been told by Admiral King to tell Admiral Nimitz that this was not a proposal made for him to consider but a plan to be carried out by him. So that cleared up any matter of whether we should do it or not; it was on the books by then.

I presented the plan to Admiral Nimitz and Admiral Halsey and the selected members of their staffs, who had to know a good part of it. Admiral Halsey said he considered the plan to be feasible and he would make immediate preparations to go to the West Coast and confer with Doolittle.

I might say that I had a rather interesting experience, which taught me something on my way to Pearl Harbor. I had gotten orders from the Bureau of Navigation to proceed to Pearl Harbor by air, but I hadn't taken the precaution to tell them to give me top priority. So I got started from Washington all right and got a commercial airliner. I believe in Albuquerque or some place, in the middle of the night, I was awakened by the stewardess, who told me that I would have to disembark from the airplane when we landed at the next stop because the army air forces had a number of pilots traveling under top priority. They had delivered airplanes there and were going back to San Francisco; they had to have my spot on the plane. I told her that I couldn't get off, that I was under orders which required me to make a connection at San Francisco and go to Hawaii the next day. She said that their instructions were to have me get off. I said, "I'm not getting off." So a few minutes later the pilot came back and said that their instructions were to go along with the priority established and that I would have to get off the airplane. I said I wouldn't get off. I showed him my orders, which were so worded as to be completely secure; they simply said that I was to go to Pearl Harbor for a conference. I showed him those and he was moved and sympathetic but said that somebody would have to tell him to let me stay on the plane. So I suggested that he might, when we landed, call up General Arnold in Washington and tell him that he was about to throw Captain Duncan off the airplane and put on Second Lieutenant Humptydump, and what should he do about it. So he said he would talk it over with the people getting on the plane when we got in, and if that didn't work he would call up Washington for instructions. I said, "That's fine, but if I leave the airplane you will have to carry me off. I'm not going to get out of this bunk and off the airplane." The next thing I knew it was morning and I was still on the plane and heading for San Francisco. One of the pilots who was scheduled to get aboard said that he wanted to stay over another day and that would suit him fine, so he dropped out of the picture and let me fly instead.

After the conference on the nineteenth of March I left Admiral Nimitz's office and went over and boarded the *Enterprise* and talked to Admiral Halsey some more and to Captain Miles Browning, his operations officer. Browning, of course, had to know about the plan; he had been in the conference we had with Admiral Nimitz. I gave him this copy of the plan, which I thought I would not need anymore. I've regretted it ever since, or I regretted that I didn't make an arrangement with him to get it back, because I realized afterwards—that is, sometime afterwards—that it would have been quite an historic document. Whatever happened to it I don't know. I simply cautioned Browning to lock it up securely, and as far as I was concerned it was Admiral Halsey's. That's the last I ever heard of it.

As soon as Admiral Halsey and Admiral Nimitz had concurred and had gotten everything out of me that they could or needed, I sent a dispatch, which I had prearranged, to Captain Low in Admiral King's headquarters in Washington. The purpose of this was to get Doolittle and his "troops" moved from Eglin Field to Sacramento. The wording of that dispatch was very simple and I think quite secret. It was a personal from me to Low which said, "Tell Jimmy to get on his horse." That was all that was needed to get Doolittle and Company moved from Florida to Sacramento right away.

I then proceeded to San Diego and went aboard the *Hornet*. By that time it was tied up at the dock at the air station there. I went into a huddle with Captain Mitscher, at which time I acquainted him with all the details of the operation. He thought it was wonderful, and he appreciated being told in person by a man who had been in this business from the start. He was a little miffed because he hadn't been told sooner, but in my opinion he didn't have to be told sooner. That was the criterion I used—that is, people wouldn't know anything until they had to know, and then only what they had to know and nothing else. I would be the judge of that.

That was the situation when I went back to Washington and told Admiral King that the thing was all laid on and would proceed according to plan.

In 1949 Admiral King said in his letter to me that President Roosevelt and even Secretary Knox were not told about the plan until the planes had taken off from the *Hornet*.

TRAINING THE DOOLITTLE FLIERS

REAR ADMIRAL HENRY L. MILLER

HENRY LOUIS MILLER was born in Fairbanks, Alaska, on 18 July 1912. He graduated from the U.S. Naval Academy in 1934 and was designated naval aviator in 1938 after training at Pensacola. He later completed the bombardier's course and the all-weather flight course. In 1942, as flight instructor at the naval air station in Ellyson Field, Florida, he trained the "Tokyo Raiders" in carrier takeoffs.

During World War II Miller commanded air groups on the USS *Princeton* and the USS *Hancock*. Among his later commands was a triple-duty assignment in 1955 as Commander, U.S. Naval Station, Sangley Point; Commander, Fleet Air, Philippines; and Commander, Naval Air Bases, Philippines. He was selected for rear admiral on 22 July 1959, and by 1960 he was chief of staff to Commander, Naval Air Force, Pacific. Later he commanded Carrier Division 15 (1961–62) and, in September 1964, Carrier Division 3 and Task Force 77, the carrier striking force of the Seventh Fleet. In February 1965, as commander of Task Force 77, he launched the first of a succession of aircraft carrier strikes on North Vietnam from the decks of the USS *Ranger, Coral Sea,* and *Hancock*. In October of that year he took the nuclear-powered task group, the USS *Enterprise* and the USS *Bainbridge,* from Norfolk to Subic Bay, and in December 1965 he engaged the first nuclear-powered task force in combat with the enemy in Vietnam. Miller's concluding duty was as commander of the Naval Air Test Center at Patuxent River, Maryland.

Miller, who retired on 1 September 1971, lives in Lexington, Maryland.

When the war broke out I was stationed at Pensacola for duty as a flight training officer. So in February 1942, when I received a set of orders to go to Eglin Field for some special duty, I was delighted.

The navy gave me an old SBU plane that they pulled out of the boondocks at Ellyson Field. It had been in the sand down there. I was told to fly to Eglin Field, about a thirty-minute ride from Pensacola. I went down on a Sunday and reported to the colonel in charge of the base. I read him my orders and said, "Do you know what I'm down here for?" And he said no. I explained to him that I was an instructor at Pensacola. I was a carrier pilot before I came back to Pensacola as an instructor. Now I was supposed to teach some army air forces pilots how to take off from a carrier. He still said he didn't have any idea of why I came down there, so I was just getting up to say it must have been a mistake, when I asked him if he knew anything about Lieutenant Colonel Doolittle's detachment. With that he closed the doors and practically asked me to talk in a whisper.

I mentioned Doolittle's name because I had talked to the assistant training officer at Pensacola and he had told me my orders had something to do with Lieutenant Colonel Doolittle—and Doolittle was then identified as the famous flier, Jimmy Doolittle.

The colonel at Eglin Field then drove me over to the place where I was to stay. After I got my gear squared away he took me down to a building set aside for Lieutenant Colonel Doolittle's B-25 detachment. Doolittle wasn't there, nor was his executive officer, Major Jack Hilger. So I talked with Captain Edward York and Lieutenant David Jones. I told them who I was and what I was supposed to do—teach them carrier takeoffs. They said, "Have you ever flown a B-25?" I'd never even seen one. So with that we went down the line.

We climbed into a B-25 and we went over to the field that was assigned to us exclusively. I then gave them some simple instruction on the steps necessary in a carrier takeoff. I hadn't had time to examine the plane, but I did have a feel for it. They told me about the speed they'd been using for takeoffs—110 miles an hour. On our first takeoff they observed the airspeed and it showed sixty-five to sixty-seven miles an hour. They said, "That is impossible. You can't do that." Well, the B-25 we flew that day had a light load, so I said, "Okay, come on back and we'll land and try it again." The second takeoff indicated an airspeed of seventy miles an hour when we got in the air, and they were convinced that a B-25 could take off at that slow speed.

Just before we finished our work that first day, I went over to the room that had been assigned to me to get my flight jacket because it was chilly. As I looked around I thought, Gee whiz, here I am a lieutenant in the navy and this army air forces gives me a dirty, junky room like this! No carpet on the deck, just cold concrete . . . And look at that crummy bed! So with that I put on my jacket and wondered who else was staying in this little cell block. I went out to look for the name of the place and read VIP Quarters. I said to myself, "They must be kidding." So I went on to the next room and looked at the nameplate and it read Lieutenant Colonel Doolittle. I went on to the next one and it said Charles F. Kettering (he was vice president of General Motors). So again I said, "My gosh, this is pretty fast company I'm in. I'd better not complain about this horrible room because evidently those guys have the same kind of horrible room." That's the way the army lived at that time. That's the way they lived all over the United States.

Of course, I soon found out where this special group of army fliers was going. But my only navy contact was Captain Donald B. ("Wu") Duncan, who was a special assistant to Admiral Ernie King, the chief of naval operations. I took my orders from Lieutenant Colonel Doolittle and Captain Duncan.

This training period at Eglin Field was supposed to take about fifteen days, after which I was to go back to Pensacola. However, we did have some foggy days and so it was going to take longer. That didn't create any problem, because Jimmy Doolittle, on his trips to Washington, would keep Captain Duncan informed, and Duncan in turn would give me permission to stay at the field as long as I wanted on this set of orders.

For the purpose of this particular mission, the B-25s were going to be at thirty-one-thousand pounds, and that was two-thousand pounds over the maximum designed load. So for the training period I checked out all the pilots for light loads, then intermediate loads, and then finally for the maximum load they would take on this raid. Everybody did pretty well. We had extra crews. I took data on each one of the pilots and marked off the field. We had observers. I borrowed pilots to act as observers. We got a portable anemometer to find out how much wind they had. We measured the distance for each plane that got off. I recorded all that data. Also, in the cockpit I observed techniques, because there you get a feel for who's a good pilot and who isn't, no matter what his takeoff distance is.

Everything appeared to be going on schedule, and we came to the last day of training. A day or two later the planes were scheduled to shove off for the West Coast. On that last day I checked out all the men, except the last one, a pilot by the name of Lieutenant Bates. He finished his trials, but I wasn't satisfied because he was letting the plane fly him, so I said, "Okay, all observers get out. Bates, you have to try it again. You fly this plane smoothly. You fly the plane. Don't let it fly you. Once more around."

Well, we took off. He took off in a skid. He pushed into a harder skid but he didn't push the throttle to the floorboard and the plane settled right back down on the runway on its belly. We came to an abrupt stop. It didn't catch fire. We were lucky, because we had gasoline all over that plane. All the pilots were there watching it. Fortunately I had a firetruck there for the first time in days, and everything turned out okay.

The next day Jimmy Doolittle came back from Washington and said, "I hear you had an accident."

I said, "Yes, sir, but there's nothing wrong with the technique or with the plane. What was wrong was Bates. He just wasn't flying the airplane. The airplane was flying him."

So Jimmy Doolittle said, "Okay. You know I'm going to the West Coast today and we're going to pick up another instructor out there to give us some more of this."

And I said, "You know, Colonel, it's a matter of professional pride with me. I don't want anybody on the West Coast telling you, 'No, let's start all over with this technique.' I'd like to go with you if we're going to have time to do more of this practice out there."

And with that he said, "Okay, if it's all right with Washington, you can fly out with me this afternoon."

So I called up Pensacola and had some laundry flown down, and they picked up my airplane and anemometer and junk and took it back. I flew out to the West Coast to Sacramento with Jimmy Doolittle.

We put the planes in the depot at Sacramento to get a recheck and to get them all set to go aboard the carrier. As each plane would come out of that interim overhaul period, I'd take it up with the crew to Willows, California, and give them takeoff lessons at Willows.

Then on the last day Jimmy Doolittle said, "We'll finish up at Willows, then we're going to fly down to Alameda and go aboard the *Hornet*. How do you think everybody's doing?"

"Oh," I said, "I think there is no strain at all. I think everybody's doing great."

We were taking extra crews, and so he said, "Would you list the crews in order of takeoff expertise—1, 2, 3, 4, 5, 6, 7?"

They were going to take fifteen airplanes and we had eighteen or nineteen crews. So I listed the people in order of what I thought was their ability. General Doolittle and Major Hilger and a couple of others were looking over the list. Hilger said he thought Bates should join one of the crews that went and wondered why I objected. I explained the accident to him and said, "After we crashed, the crew were going to jump out of the windows right into those whirling props. I grabbed both of them and said, 'Sit down and wait until those props stop. Turn off all your switches.' The switches were still on. I reached back to get my pencil and notebook and when I came on back the props had stopped and they had jumped out. I looked—they had turned off all the switches and then turned them all on again." So I said to Hilger, "You know, when you get over enemy territory, when you have some of those Japs chasing you, you've got to be really sharp and you've got to be thinking all the time. If you panic, you're lost. I wouldn't take Bates." And they didn't take Bates.

Just before going aboard, Jimmy Doolittle asked me what I thought of the crews. I said I didn't think there'd be any trouble at all. I said, "You know, Colonel, if you want proof, I've had less time in the B-25 than anybody. You can take one extra along—a sixteenth airplane—and when we get one hundred miles out of San Francisco I'll take it off. I'll deliver it back to Columbia, South Carolina, to the army, and then go back to Pensacola."

He didn't say yea or nay. So I finished that day up at Willows checking out everybody I could and got in the last plane going to Alameda. When I landed there, Jimmy Doolittle came over to me and said he'd just been aboard ship. He saw some old navy friends there: Captain Pete Mitscher, the skipper of the *Hornet,* Commander George Henderson, who was the executive officer, Commander Apollo Soucek, who was the air officer, and Marcel Gwinn, who was the assistant air officer.

Doolittle said, "You know, I talked to them about your idea of taking an extra plane along and they agree, so we'll take sixteen and launch you one hundred miles out."

So the big day arrived. We sailed, and just before lunch I was up on the flight deck and there was Jimmy Doolittle. We had parked the airplanes. We had about 495 feet for takeoff. He said, "Well, Hank, how does it look to you?"

I said, "Oh, gee, this is a breeze."

"Well, let's get up in that airplane and look," said he. So he got in the cockpit and I was in the copilot's seat. "This looks like a short distance."

And I said, "You see where that tool kit is way up the deck by that island structure?"

"Yes."

"That's where I used to take off in fighters on the *Saratoga* and the *Lexington.*"

And he said, "Henry, what name do they use in the navy for bullshit?"

With that we went down to chow, and just before I finished my dessert, I was told to report to the bridge.

I got up on the bridge and Pete Mitscher said, "Well, Miller, I don't think I'll be able to give you forty knots of wind over the deck."

"Captain," I said, "we don't need that anyway because we have 495 feet.

I taught these guys how to take off from an aircraft carrier with forty knots of wind and 250 feet. We have lots of room." And I told him the story about talking with Jimmy Doolittle just before lunch.

With that, Captain Mitscher said to me, "Well, Miller, do you have an extra pair of pants with you?"

"Oh, yes sir. I brought all my baggage with me because I'm going to fly nonstop to Columbia, South Carolina."

And he said, "We'll take that extra plane."

I replied, "Captain, will you drop me off at the next mail buoy, please? By the time I finish this trip I will have traveled halfway around the world on a telephone call, and I'll be an ensign when I get back." I told Pete Mitscher that I was tickled to death, because from the very beginning when I heard there was going to be a raid on Tokyo, I wanted to go to the takeoff spot. I was delighted with that.

Every day the pilots were aboard the *Hornet* en route to the far Pacific, they would get an intelligence briefing, go over all the equipment in the airplanes, and get in a sizable amount of poker as well. They roomed with navy fliers and navy ships' officers. They were a great bunch of people. They were all volunteers for this, of course, and they knew that it was going to be pretty difficult. After they got through bombing Japan they were supposed to fly down the coast, then cut in. I think they were supposed to go in at the thirty-eighth parallel and fly to one field that was going to be held by Chinese guerrillas. There they were to land, take on enough gasoline from hand pumps out of drums to fly on to Chungking, turn the planes over to Chiang Kai-shek and his people, then come out of China and back to the States. They were going to take off just before dark.

Jimmy Doolittle was to be the first off. He was going to carry firebombs and drop them on his targets in the Tokyo area just at dusk. The other planes would be coming in, say, a half an hour to an hour afterwards, and they would be bombing targets in the Tokyo area from the light of the fires that were caused by Doolittle's bombs.

Well, the day arrived and everybody was supposed to stay in the ready rooms all day long. The task force was going to be at general quarters; they had to be on the alert. All the planes that were spotted for takeoff were tied down. It was a wet, windy, rough, miserable morning. Just at daylight the task force picked up a couple of Jap fishing boats. The cruisers started firing at the boats. They did a horrible job of hitting them. There were also some *Enterprise* planes in the air. They were dive-bombing and strafing the boats but had just as hard a time trying to hit them. Admiral Halsey, who was in charge, was afraid that the boats would get off a radio message to Tokyo, so he sent a message over to the *Hornet:* "Launch army pilots." And when I got up on deck and told Colonel Doolittle, he said, "Would you help get the pilots in the airplanes?'' So this I did. We launched the first one, Jimmy Doolittle, at eight-twenty that morning. He did a fine job. He's a great aviator. He did it just like the book says.

We were over six hundred miles from the Japanese coast, so we knew the pilots didn't have a Chinaman's chance of getting to China with those airplanes. It was just too far a trip. Additionally, going into Tokyo they were hitting much stronger head winds than were anticipated. The planned distance for the takeoff had been about two hundred miles from the coast.

The planes went in. We estimated they would be over the Tokyo area about five or ten minutes after one o'clock that day. So at ten minutes after one we were listening on board the *Hornet,* and the Tokyo radio came on the air and said that enemy bombers had dropped bombs in the area. They were all excited and then *bang*—they went off the air. We knew that the planes had got there and that the raid was successful; for the real purpose of the raid was to do some damage and to show the Japanese people that we could reach them.* Additionally, it was a tremendous shot in the arm for the American people.

---

*Thirteen of the B-25s dropped bombs on Tokyo. Three others concentrated with incendiaries on Nagoya and Kobe. Defending forces were caught unprepared, even though the Japanese pilot ships had forewarned them. The damage inflicted was not great, but the message came through to the Japanese people that their cities were not immune to air attack. The Japanese government released very little information about the raid, and damaged areas of the cities were declared off bounds to the populace.

Not one of the attacking planes was lost over Japan. Seventy-one of the eighty pilots and crewmen who had participated in the raid survived. One man was killed in a parachute drop over China and four others were drowned. Eight men were captured by the Japanese in China. Three of them were executed and one other died in prison.

"The fruits of victory are tumbling into our mouths too quickly," observed Emperor Hirohito on 9 March 1942, the occasion of his forty-second birthday. It was a prescient remark. By this date the Japanese military had completed the first operational phase of its overall Pacific plan, and in double-quick time. Rangoon fell on 9 March, just hours before the last Allied troops on Java had surrendered.

Now the Japanese high command deemed it necessary to move at an even faster pace if the empire were to gain its ultimate objective. Admiral Isoroku Yamamoto, commander in chief of the Imperial Navy, was discerning enough to fear the strength of the United States. He had served in Washington and knew something of the potential of U.S. industry. He also figured that when the U.S. Navy was ready to launch a counterattack it would do so from Australia, where bases and airfields were available. To forestall such a development Japan had to capture Port Moresby, a seaport on the south coast of New Guinea, only 350 miles from the coast of Australia. Japan also had to take Tulagi in the Solomon Islands and move down to New Caledonia, the Fijis, and Samoa. It was imperative to isolate Australia before the U.S. giant got on his feet.

Implementation of this grand strategy had begun in January 1942 with the capture of Rabaul, a town on New Britain in the Bismarck Archipelago. It was being rapidly turned into a major naval and air base. This move was followed in February by the capture of Lae, on New Guinea's northeast coast, and in March by the capture of Salamaua (nineteen miles south of Lae). Both Lae and Salamaua became supply bases, important to the Japanese because they were only two hundred miles due north of Port Moresby.

In March 1942 the gist of Japanese strategy became known to Washington and to Admiral Nimitz at Pearl Harbor. They asked Captain Joseph Rochefort, the navy's brilliant code breaker, to give them an estimate of Japanese intentions, and in a remarkable analysis he predicted that with the East Indies secured by the enemy and the Indian Ocean swept clear of Allied forces, the next Japanese campaign would be in the area of New Guinea. Rochefort's perspicacity was based in some measure on America's growing ability to read the Japanese naval code. The intelligence staff in Pearl Harbor had begun to suspect that the Japanese were about to make a play around the southern end of the U.S. defense line. If that should result in the loss of Port Moresby it would be a first-class disaster for America.

All this led inevitably to the Battle of the Coral Sea (3–8 May 1942), the first carrier battle of the Pacific war. In this action both sides made mistakes—so many, in fact, that Samuel Eliot Morison dubbed it the Battle of Naval Errors. In the following selection from the oral history of Lieutenant Paul D. Stroop, at the time flag secretary to Rear Admiral Aubrey W. Fitch in the *Lexington,* we can see the errors of each side being played out, including those that led to the sinking of the "Lady Lex."

The loss of the *Lexington* came to be seen as the factor that tipped the scales in favor of Japan. But if, in a tactical sense, Japan won the encounter, in a strategic sense victory belonged to the United States. Captain Liddell Hart, military historian, has written that the Japanese effort at Coral Sea was an example of "strategic overreach."* This is an apt description. After the battle the Japanese invasion force had to withdraw without reaching its goal, and the effort to capture Port Moresby was never made again.

*Quoted in Morison, *The Two-Ocean War*, p. 140.

LOSS OF THE "LADY LEX"

VICE ADMIRAL PAUL D. STROOP

PAUL DAVID STROOP was born in Zanesville, Ohio, on 30 October 1904. In 1926 he graduated from the U.S. Naval Academy. After duty in the USS *Arkansas,* at the Washington Navy Yard, and at the naval air station in Hampton Roads, Virginia, he competed in the Olympic games (1928). In 1929 he took a course in flight training at Pensacola, upon completion of which he was designated naval aviator.

He served for three years in torpedo and patrol squadrons based on the tender USS *Wright.* Next he studied at the postgraduate school in Annapolis, had duty with a bombing squadron based on the *Ranger* and the *Lexington,* and served with scouting squadrons on the *Portland.* After a tour in the Bureau of Aeronautics, he became aide and flag secretary to the commander of Carrier Division 1. Various other duties followed in the central and South Pacific, and in February 1944 he became responsible for aviation plans on the staff of Commander in Chief, U.S. Fleet. In this period he attended Allied Military Staff conferences at Quebec, Malta, Yalta, and Potsdam.

In 1945–46 Stroop had duty on the staff of Commander, Fifth Fleet, in the western Pacific and then as fleet aviation officer on the staff of Commander in Chief, Pacific Fleet. Next came three years at the general line school in Monterey, California, and the National War College in Washington. After this last duty he commanded two carriers successively, then became commander of the Naval Ordnance Test Station, Inyokern, California; the senior naval member of the Weapons Systems Evaluation Group; and deputy chief of the Bureau of Ordnance. On 14 March 1958 he became chief of the Bureau of Ordnance, then chief of the newly created Bureau of Naval Weapons. Detached in 1962, he assumed the position of Commander, Naval Air Force, Pacific Fleet.

Stroop retired in the rank of vice admiral on 1 November 1965. He lives in San Diego, California.

Early in April 1942 we were still in Pearl Harbor and Admiral Fitch, commanding Task Group 17.5, was designated to go to sea in the *Lexington*. Our orders were to carry us down into the South Pacific. In preparation, the *Lexington* was put in the navy yard at Pearl Harbor. I remember a considerable number of twenty-millimeter guns were mounted on her gallery decks, around the perimeter of the flight deck. We sailed about the fifteenth of April and were in company with some cruisers and destroyers. In the South Pacific we were to rendezvous with Rear Admiral Frank Jack Fletcher, who was flying his flag in the *Yorktown*. At the same time we were to be joined by a force of Australian ships under Rear Admiral J. G. Crece, RN. We didn't realize we were going into a carrier action with the Japanese, but intelligence we received on the way down indicated that there was a great deal of Japanese activity, particularly along the coast of New Guinea. Our mission had been merely to go down and strengthen the U.S. force in the South Pacific and probably make some raids on Japanese installations ashore.

We entered the Coral Sea around the first of May 1942. I remember quite distinctly that the first communication we had from our Royal Navy friend, Admiral Crece, evaluated the importance of the Coral Sea area. He said that our combined forces should do all they could to keep the Japanese from coming into the area. By this time the Japanese had landed on the north coast of New Guinea. There was strong evidence they were going to come around the eastern tip of that island and make a landing at Port Moresby. This was an important outpost of the British empire.

The *Yorktown,* of course, had preceded us into the Coral Sea, and about the first of May raided the new Japanese installations at Tulagi Island. After that raid she and her accompanying cruisers and destroyers were to link up with our force and with the Australian ships. That took place on the fifth or sixth of May. The night of the sixth was spent refueling, topping off destroyers, and refueling the carriers. We were getting ready for what was to be the Coral Sea battle.

I was serving as staff navigator and was concerned that our refueling course—it was probably going to take all night to refuel—wasn't the best one to get us into the position we wanted to be in the morning of 7 May. So we made a very deliberate slow change during the night. We changed just a few degrees at a time to a new course that would take us in a northerly direction and get us closer to the area where we thought we might find Japanese carriers.

On the morning of the seventh we sent out our scouting planes from the *Lexington* and the *Yorktown*. Not only were we searching for the two Japanese carriers *Zuikaku* and *Shokaku,* but we were also quite interested in the invasion force. Our intelligence had told us this was coming around the eastern tip of New Guinea. The objective was to use our scouting planes and cover the outer limits of our search sector completely. I think that in this particular case they went out about 250 miles. Unfortunately, on the seventh the Japanese carriers had the advantage of weather cover and were not discovered by our forces. We also had the advantage of weather cover and were not discovered by the Japanese until very late in the evening. It was too late for them to launch an attack. We assumed at that point that the *Zuikaku* and *Shokaku* were out of range. We hadn't seen them so we didn't really know where they were.

We did get a contact report, as I recall, from an army air corps B-17 on the Japanese invasion force that was coming around the coast of New Guinea. So we sent our attack forces in that direction—torpedo planes and dive-bombers. They found a certain number of ships plus a converted carrier, the *Shoho,* and one cruiser. Our forces made a very successful attack, but it amounted to an overkill on the carrier. Probably fourteen torpedoes were put in her and many bombs were dropped. She sank immediately. As I look back on it, it was too bad that the attack hadn't been better coordinated, with some of our force spread around on other ships. It was of course our first battle of this kind, so everybody went after the big prize and sank her very quickly. We really didn't know what we were going to find in the invasion force. The initial contact report from the army air corps aviator was not very complete. It read something like this: "A large number of boats headed in several directions."

I remember my friend Lieutenant Commander Bob Dixon was leading one segment of the attack force. We were out of voice communication with him during the time of the attack and on part of the return trip. But as soon as Bob could get a message through, he called the ship and sent the message that became rather famous: "Scratch one flattop."

On the evening of May 7 we had recovered all of our search planes, and we ran a cruising formation at dusk when we sighted some lights coming over the horizon. On the *Lexington* we thought that these were probably some of our own planes from the *Yorktown,* for we were not sure that she had got them all back yet. I remember noticing the port running lights of the formation. One of the things that struck me as odd was their red color. They had a sort of a bluish tint, red-blue tint, and that was different from what we had on our own planes. Just about that time a ship in our destroyer screen began firing. A voice message went out on the TBS to the skipper of the destroyer, Commander Charles Chillingworth, a friend of mine. It told him to stop firing, for these were undoubtedly friendly planes coming in. And Chillingworth came right back on the TBS and said, "I know Japanese planes when I see them." Well, these were Japanese planes; they had mistaken the *Yorktown* and the *Lexington* formation for their own ships. They were coming in with their lights on and were ready to get into the landing formation.

There was a lot of confusion, but after Chillingworth identified them as enemy planes everybody began shooting. There were lots of fireworks. The Japanese planes broke up their formation, turned out their lights, and disappeared. We followed them on radar and lost them at about forty miles.

I have always figured that the Japanese carriers and our carriers after dark that night had got quite close to each other. Radar was not very well developed in those days, and the enemy ships could still have been close even though they were over the radar horizon. It was true also that our intelligence unit had tuned in on their airplane landing frequency and could hear the Japanese carriers talking to the pilots in the air. This was another indication that the Japanese carriers were not too far away. I even discussed with Admiral Fitch the possibility of having a destroyer attack that night, but he felt that the distance was probably too great and it would be too difficult to locate them.

I remember one conversation of a Japanese pilot that was reported to me. He couldn't get his wheels down, so the carrier told him that he would have to land in the water. They wouldn't take him aboard. They didn't want to clutter up their flight deck with a crash when they had other planes coming aboard. After he got this order he requested that the carrier shine a light on the water so he'd have a spot to land on.

Late that afternoon, after our planes had got back from their attack on the invasion force off the New Guinea coast, we began getting indications on the radar screen of unidentified aircraft in the vicinity. With that we put fighters in the air and vectored them out. The fighters from the *Lexington* were led by Lieutenant Commander Paul Ramsey. According to his story, he came out of a cloud deck and under the clouds he found a formation of Japanese attack planes. Apparently they had been sent in our direction and had not found our carriers. He came out behind them and was in perfect position. Immediately he was able to shoot down the last two planes in the Jap formation. I remember when Ramsey got back to the *Lexington*. During our trip south from Pearl Harbor he'd grown a luxuriant mustache. He said that as soon as he shot down his first Japanese plane he would shave this mustache off. When he approached the *Lexington* he made a quick circle around the ship with his canopy open. He was stroking his mustache, indicating that he wasn't going to have it much longer. And he landed aboard and shaved it off that night.

All of this made it obvious to us and to the Japanese that we were quite close to each other that night and would probably have an engagement the next day. I think the record shows that the Japanese carriers went north during the night and the *Yorktown* and *Lexington* went south, getting prepared for the next day's operations.

I went to sleep that night but I wakened early. I remember I had to get up in a hurry when a bundle of intelligence dispatches were made available to me. It was probably three-thirty in the morning. I didn't have time to shave, so I put my electric razor in my pocket thinking I would have some time on the bridge the next day. I never had that opportunity. I still had the razor when I abandoned ship.

I began analyzing the dispatches with the chief of staff. I had a young ensign as assistant intelligence officer and he proved quite helpful. Admiral Fitch, of course, read all the dispatches, and we discussed them together.

We started our search groups out right at daylight. The senior officer of the search squadron was Lieutenant Commander Bob Dixon. He took what he thought was the most likely sector. It turned out that he was practically right. The first sighting was made probably around eight o'clock or nine o'clock in the morning by one of Dixon's squadron pilots. He found the *Zuikaku* and the *Shokaku* and sent the message back. Dixon himself then moved into that sector and sent the young pilot back. Dixon stayed as long as he could in the vicinity of the carriers, giving us the locations, speeds, and directions of their movements. He did a perfectly classic job of shadowing them, taking advantage of cloud cover when he could. I might add that Bob Dixon, in my opinion, was one of the great heroes of this two-day operation. He had led the attack on the *Shoho* and then did a tremendously fine job of shadowing the *Zuikaku* and *Shokaku* and surviving. This was considered a very dangerous task—to remain in the vicinity of enemy carriers where you could be the target of higher-performance fighter planes. Dixon did it and got away with it. He had been a test pilot and learned early in the game how to economize on fuel and get the most out of an engine. This certainly stood him in good stead that day. When all the search planes came back and Bob Dixon hadn't arrived, we figured that something had happened to him. About an hour after everybody thought he would be out of fuel he showed up over the horizon and landed aboard. He had floated in the vicinity of the Japanese carriers and conserved his fuel.

Well, after the initial report came the obvious decision was made to send off the attack planes from the *Yorktown* and the *Lexington* and order them to make a coordinated attack on the *Zuikaku* and the *Shokaku*. The distance was a little greater than we would have liked for all our air group, particularly the TBMs, the torpedo planes. They were carrying the heavy torpedo loads and would not have too much range. I have forgotten how great the distance was to the Japanese carriers—it may have been something over two hundred

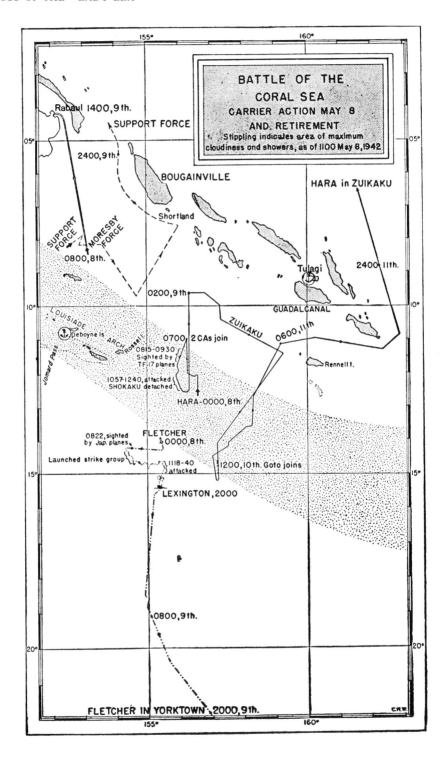

BATTLE OF THE
CORAL SEA
CARRIER ACTION MAY 8
AND RETIREMENT
Stippling indicates area of maximum
cloudiness and showers, as of 1100 May 8,1942

miles. At any rate, we sent them out at about maximum range. An attack was scheduled to take place at about eleven o'clock or eleven-fifteen in the morning.

Our carriers remained in the vicinity of the launchings at various courses and speeds, waiting for the return of the scout planes. These they took aboard, and then they waited for the attack planes to come back. They were due back about one-thirty in the afternoon. About eleven o'clock we began getting indications on the radar of a large group of planes approaching us. We figured that the Japanese were doing the same thing we were. They had their attack planes coming down. The *Lexington* and the *Yorktown* were in an area of good visibility, whereas the *Zuikaku* and the *Shokaku* still had the advantage of cloud cover. This to a considerable degree affected the action, because a good many of our attack planes could not make contact with them. Our planes that did were quite effective. They damaged the *Shokaku* considerably and the other carrier slightly. However, the Japanese managed to control the damage and get away.

Our attack was not a coordinated attack. Each squadron was led separately by the squadron commander. The air group commander was not in contact with them or lost contact. But he, Lieutenant Commander Bill Ault, arrived over the enemy carriers with only four aircraft in his particular section. He went on in, attacked, and himself claimed a thousand-pound hit.

A combination of the weather and lack of coordination, I feel, made us less than successful in attacking the Japanese carriers. We should have been more effective than we were.

As the enemy aircraft were approaching, around eleven o'clock, I remember making an entry in the war diary because I thought maybe later on I wouldn't be able to make entries in the log. I was keeping the war diary in longhand in a ledger on the bridge. I made an entry at eleven-twenty: "Under attack by enemy aircraft." That turned out to be exactly right. We began seeing enemy planes overhead and they came down in a very well coordinated attack with torpedo planes and dive-bombers.

I can remember standing on the bridge and watching the dive-bombers come down. These had fixed landing gear. You were convinced that the pilot in the plane had the bridge of your ship right in his sight. You knew it and it didn't look good. Fortunately they were not strafing, because if they had been I'm sure they would have made the topside untenable. The minute the pilot released his bomb you could see it taking a different trajectory from the aircraft itself. Generally it fell short, because their dive wasn't quite as steep as it should have been, and you knew that particular bomb wasn't going to hit you. It might hit the side of the ship. I was fascinated watching the bomb leave the airplane and realizing it was probably going to fall short.

The torpedo planes came in about the same time in a fine, nicely coordinated attack and launched their torpedoes at about a thousand yards. They were down to flight-deck level when they dropped the torpedoes. And of course they were successful. I believe we got four torpedo hits. In the official account that was finally sent out, only two torpedo hits were recorded. I personally believe that this is wrong. The *Lexington* probably took four. I believe all the torpedo hits were on the port side and pretty well distributed along the length of the ship, because immediately after the attack we took a port list and I watched some of the torpedo planes passing from port to starboard. They'd launch their torpedoes, and then some of them would fly very close to the ship to get a look at us. They were curious and sort of thumbed their noses at us. We were shooting at them with our new 20mms and not hitting them at all. The tracers were falling astern of the planes. It was very discouraging to see enemy planes pass within range of your guns and not be able to knock them down. You had some personal interest in what they were doing and you were scared, all at the same time. As far as the senior people were concerned, we were completely helpless. We were depending on the training that had been given the fighter pilots in the air and on the training and practice the gunners had. The commanding officer of the ship, Captain Frederick C. Sherman, was very busy twisting his ship, trying to avoid torpedoes. I think he was successful in some cases.

I think the *Lexington* took three bomb hits. One of the most spectacular was on the port gun gallery. A bomb exploded and immediately burned and killed gun crews in that area. I remember walking down there when the attack was over and there were the marine gunners, burned right at their stations on the guns. That particular bomb started a fire down in the officers' country, the next deck below. The living quarters were set on fire and a couple of the stewards who were down in the pantry were killed. I remember that particularly, because I considered going down later and getting into the stateroom and taking out some gear from the safe. It couldn't be done. We had another bomb in the after part of the island or stack and another one aft in the boat pocket where the captain's gig was stored. All these bombs started fires which we figured we could control and put out.

We learned a lot from this action. We learned that our ships were tinder. They had too much inflammable stuff aboard. The furniture in the admiral's cabin, for example, was wood and fabric. That burned. Paint all over the ship had an oil base, and wherever we got a fire the paint on the bulkhead burned. That had to be corrected. We learned that our fire-fighting equipment was not adequate, that we needed to redesign our hoses and hose nozzles for fog instead of solid water.

Even though we took three bombs and four torpedoes, we were still able to make, I believe, twenty-seven knots. We had the ship under control. An hour after the attack she was back on an even keel by counterflooding. Pop Healy, the damage-control officer, came up on the bridge and discussed things with the captain. He was down in central station where he took charge of the damage-control parties and counterflooding. After the attack we were able to steam into the wind. We landed some aircraft aboard. Bob Dixon was the last one. He came aboard in the afternoon.

The *Yorktown* was suffering the same kind of attack. She took one bomb that went down about four decks and exploded, but she was in much better shape than the *Lexington*. The *Yorktown* was able to have her damage repaired and go on to the Battle of Midway, where she was lost.

We kept under way, making about twenty-seven knots. After we got our planes back aboard the decision was made to head for Australia. I laid out a course for Brisbane, where we could get our battle damage repaired. The other ships formed up—the cruisers, the destroyers, and the *Yorktown*—and we were headed for Brisbane.

Along about two or two-thirty in the afternoon we heard a rather loud submerged explosion. My first reaction was that a Japanese submarine had sighted us and fired a torpedo which probably had an influence fuze and had gone off under the hull. It seemed like that kind of an explosion, deep down and probably under the ship. We found out later that it was not an enemy torpedo at all. It was gasoline fuel. The bomb hits had caused the fuel to leak. It had collected in the elevator well and some spark had set off the fumes. The immediate effects were disastrous. As soon as the explosion occurred communication between the bridge and central station was lost. (Later testimony showed that Pop Healy and his crew in central station were wiped out at that time.) Fires throughout the ship were accelerated by the explosion. Another fire developed underneath the number-two elevator. The elevator was flush with the flight deck and you could see the flames coming out. Word came almost immediately that the engineering spaces were untenable and had to be abandoned, so the engineering crews on the afternoon watch shut down the main engines. Here was the ship dead in the water and, worst of all, she had no fire-fighting capability. All power was lost. From then on the case was hopeless. We actually had a destroyer alongside to try and get hoses over, but this was completely impracticable. The fires kept increasing in size, and by three o'clock the decision was made to get the wounded off the ship and the air group personnel as well. These people were not needed in the fighting of fires and they could be useful if the ship was lost. Destroyers came alongside and got them off about three-thirty.

We continued trying to fight the fires, but it became increasingly evident that the ship couldn't be saved. It was also evident that staying aboard much longer was very dangerous.

Apparently on the hangar deck torpedo warheads were going off from the storage aft. Flames were erupting with increasing frequency around the perimeter of the elevator. They would shoot up two or three feet. They sounded like a freight train rumbling up the hangar deck.

Finally Admiral Fitch, in order, I think, to ease the captain into making the proper decision, said, "Well, Fred, it's about time to get the men off." This was around five o'clock in the afternoon. So the order was given to abandon ship. Everybody sensed this was the proper thing to do and that they ought to do it in a hurry. We had lines over the side. The sea was calm, the water was warm, it was still daylight—all in all it was a pretty good situation. There were destroyers and cruisers in the vicinity of the ship so we had places to go. The men started going down over the side on these lines and they were being picked up by boats from the other ships. We didn't have any of our own in the water, but we did have a destroyer alongside, almost continuously taking people off from the air group, the wounded first, and when the order was given, other people. We had a total of around 2,500 to 3,000 personnel on board. Only about 150 were killed in the whole action, and many of them were victims of the initial attacks on the ship and the internal explosion down deep in the ship, where all the crew of the central station were wiped out.

I remained on the bridge with Admiral Fitch, his orderly, the chief of staff, the communications officer, and the flag lieutenant. We were probably the last to abandon ship except for the captain. Captain Sherman went down on the flight deck and, according to his story, made a trip aft and inspected the ship to see that everybody was off, for he intended to carry out the tradition of the captain being the last man off the ship. The admiral and the few of us on the staff left the bridge and selected port side forward as the place where we would go over the side. I remember going across the flight deck and realizing it was pretty hot. Very soon the whole thing was going to be in flames. On port side forward we had what little breeze there was. That made it the coolest part of the ship. There were large mooring line hawsers laid over the side. They made it very easy to haul yourself down into the water where boats were ready to pick up survivors. I was prepared to jump because I didn't realize that these lines were still available. If the ship erupted in flames I knew we were going to want to get into the water in a hurry. But actually we had plenty of time.

I remember as we crossed the flight deck an interesting thing happened. The admiral's marine orderly was still with him. As the admiral walked across the deck the orderly was in an absolutely correct position, one step to the left and one to the rear. He was carrying the admiral's coat over his arm, and it turned out that the admiral was the only officer who arrived on the rescue ship with a jacket because his orderly had seen to that. The orderly also had kept all of the dispatches that were handed to the admiral during the action. When the admiral read a dispatch he'd give it to his orderly, who'd put it in his pocket. This was to be important later on.

One of my jobs as flag secretary had been to keep the war diary, so before I left the bridge I tore all the pertinent pages out of the diary and folded them up in a square and stuffed them in my pocket. This also proved useful in writing a battle report later.

When we arrived at the forward port side of the flight deck the sun was just going down. The boats that had been in the water picking up survivors were all heavily loaded and were heading back to their ships. There was no boat immediately available for the admiral and the rest of us, so I silhouetted myself at the edge of the flight deck and began trying to attract the attention of the nearest cruiser. Pretty soon I got an acknowledgment by searchlight. They saw that I was trying to semaphore to them. At the Naval Academy we had to learn to semaphore on cruises, and now, fifteen years later, the knowledge came back. I sent a message: "Send a boat for admiral." The message got through and right away a motor launch came round from the bow of the cruiser and headed for our spot. When the boat was quite close we started to go down the lines over the side. I remember the admiral's orderly trying to insist that the admiral go first. The marine was still very proper. Finally the admiral got a little annoyed and ordered the man to go down. Of course the admiral wanted to be the last one to leave the flight deck.

The communications officer, Lieutenant Bowen, and I had selected the same line to go down, and we didn't argue over protocol. I got on first and started lowering away. I'd been a rope climber at the Naval Academy. Now I never felt stronger in my life. So I started down and got to the water. I didn't want to get my feet wet and the boat wasn't there yet. I'd timed my descent so that I'd get down about the same time the boat arrived, so I stopped with my feet just short of the water. Then I felt Lieutenant Bowen's feet on my shoulder. He was much heavier and longer, and I guess didn't have the strength to hang on any longer. He said, "Pardon me, sir, while I pass you." And then he dropped off the line and went into the water. The waves wet the lower part of my body and I remember worrying about my electric razor. It was still in my pocket. I didn't want that to get wet. Before I left the bridge I'd taken some cellulose tape and wound it around my watch, for I figured it was going to get wet and I wanted to protect it. The boat then got under the line the admiral and the orderly were hanging on to and picked them up dry-shod. When they got on the cruiser the orderly still had the admiral's coat and still had the dispatches. I hung on my line until the boat came over and picked me up.

Then we cruised alongside the *Lexington* to pick up a few others who had come down and were still in the water. I had an inflatable aircraft life preserver on, but I hadn't inflated it. I didn't need to.

The rescue craft did a fine job of picking everybody up. Of course this was because they had a lot of time, the weather was good, the water was warm, and it was still daylight.

Captain Sherman left the ship aft and was rescued by another boat and put aboard another ship. We were taken to Admiral Kinkaid's flagship and went right up to the bridge. It was getting quite dark, and just about the time we got to the bridge there was a tremendous explosion on the *Lexington* and a whole elevator, number two, right abeam of the island, was lifted out of the ship and followed by a solid mass of flame which went as high as the mast of the ship. Then the whole bridge area broke out in flames. It was quite spectacular, silhouetted against the night sky.

We probably had fifty aircraft parked, tied down in the launching area of the flight deck. Many of these planes had ammunition in their fixed guns and fuel in their tanks. They made a most spectacular fire. As they burned the ammunition cooked off and the night sky was filled with tracers coming off the after deck.

The task force then was ordered to steam away and one destroyer, the *Phelps,* was left behind with orders to sink the *Lexington.* Four torpedoes exploded in her and she sank. Afterwards there was a tremendous underwater explosion. The captain of the *Phelps* later reported that he thought he had been torpedoed, but of course it was the effect of this underwater explosion on the *Lexington.*

The task force then steamed down toward Noumea, where some survivors were gathering. All were taken in various ships to Tonga Tabu, where we found the *Yorktown.* At that time Admiral Fitch's whole staff reassembled in her. It was there that I organized the battle report for the carrier part of the Coral Sea action. It was signed by Admiral Fitch, who had been given tactical command of the two carriers by Admiral Fletcher on the date of the battle.

Admiral Nimitz characterized the Battle of Midway as "a victory of intelligence, bravely and wisely applied." It was certainly that. It was also the second of five great naval battles of the Pacific war in which aircraft played the dominant role.

The American high command, having perceived that air power would be the key to the coming battle, had placed all its emphasis on the destruction of the Japanese carriers. Yet when the battle came the Americans had only three carriers, while the Japanese fleet comprised eight carriers, eleven battleships, and an immense number of supporting vessels.

Admiral Nimitz laid on his naval commanders, Admirals Fletcher and Spruance, an order which paraphrased said, "You are to fight cautiously and are to meet a superior enemy force without unduly exposing your own." Now that seemed like a difficult task, but they were able to comply by skillfully using the intelligence that was theirs.

The U.S. command had two great advantages. The first was knowledge of Admiral Isoroku Yamamoto's operational order covering the forthcoming engagement. On May 20 he had detailed the complete order of battle for the Japanese assault on the Aleutians and Midway, identified in his dispatch only as AF. The dispatch was intercepted in its entirety and identified by the fleet radio unit in the Pacific. Five days after its receipt Captain Joseph J. Rochefort, officer in charge of the combat intelligence unit at Pearl Harbor, was able to deliver personally to Admiral Nimitz a decrypted form of the Yamamoto order that was nearly ninety percent complete. Only the Japanese internal time-date cipher had not been broken, but by working frantically on this problem two members of FRUPac were able to come forth with the actual dates: 3 June for a Japanese diversionary air strike on Dutch Harbor, Alaska, and 4 June for the assault on Midway itself.

Admiral Nimitz and his intelligence officer accepted the data as authentic and formed their plans accordingly. Certain quarters in Washington were not so convinced and continued to think of a forthcoming assault by the Japanese as possibly aimed at the West Coast of the United States.

The second great advantage for the Americans, which went hand in glove with the intelligence data at their disposal, was the ability to use surprise as a factor. As for the Japanese, the most obvious reason for the miscarriage of their plans was a failure to achieve the surprise on which they had counted. Enemy submarines assigned the task did not take station between Pearl Harbor and Midway until 1 June, because the Japanese command had assumed that, in ignorance of the pending attack, the Americans were not likely to sortie from Pearl Harbor before the actual Japanese assault on Midway. In fact, three U.S. carriers and their escorts had already crossed the Japanese patrol line before the submarines were on station. If Japanese submarines had been there, the outcome of the Battle of Midway would have been vastly different.

Many of the heroic efforts of American personnel in the Battle of Midway are well known—the great exploits of Torpedo Squadron 8 from the carrier *Hornet*, for example, and of the thirty pilots and crewmen who did not return. Perhaps not as well known were the efforts prior to the battle of Lieutenant Commander John ("Jimmy") Thach, who as early as 1941 wrestled with the problem of the Japanese Zero, the fighter plane whose reputation had preceded it to American shores. Thach, at the time of events narrated a squadron commander on the *Yorktown*, wanted in particular to find some technique that would enable U.S. fighters to cope with this formidable enemy. He developed the theory that a two-plane fighter section would be superior to the accepted three-plane formation, a highly inventive solution eventually known as the Thach Weave. The account of its creation is part of his oral history. Included as well is an account of Thach's exploits and those of his men when they served on the carrier *Yorktown* in the Battle of Midway. It was there that the Weave, which Thach taught not only to his own pilots but also to the army air forces and the navy's Operational Training Command, proved its worth.

After Midway a Japanese Zero was discovered downed in the Aleutians. Admiral James Russell talks about retrieving it from a bog on Akutan in July 1942, when he was a lieutenant commander with a patrol squadron in the Aleutians. This was a fortunate discovery for the Americans; the plane was repaired and they saw demonstrations of its maneuvering capabilities at airfields around the country. Jimmy Thach was one of the navy pilots who had the opportunity to fly against it and test his own theories of an adequate defense.

92

THE THACH WEAVE IS BORN

ADMIRAL JOHN S. THACH

JOHN SMITH THACH was born on 19 April 1905 in Pine Bluff, Arkansas, and graduated in 1927 from the U.S. Naval Academy. He was designated naval aviator after completing the course in Pensacola in 1930. Recognized early in his career as one of the navy's aerial gunnery experts, he became a test pilot for naval experimental aircraft.

At the time of Pearl Harbor Lieutenant Commander Thach was in command of Fighter Squadron 3. As air operations officer of the Fast Carrier Task Force, Thach developed the system of blanketing enemy airfields with a continuous patrol of carrier-based fighters that prevented land planes from taking off and systematically destroyed them on the ground. Under Admiral John Sydney McCain, he planned and directed the navy's final offensive blows against the Japanese homeland.

Postwar assignments included duty in naval air training and command of the USS *Sicily* during the Korean hostilities. In the rank of vice admiral he served as deputy chief of naval operations (air) from 1963 to 1965. On 25 March 1965 he was promoted to admiral and served as Commander in Chief, U.S. Naval Forces, Europe. He remained in this assignment until he retired on 1 May 1967. After that he resided in San Diego, California. Thach died on 15 April 1981.

It was in the spring of 1941 that we received an intelligence report of great significance. It had come out of China, where the Japanese and Chinese were at war and where there was aerial combat. The report described a new Japanese aircraft, a fighter, that performed far better than anything we had. It was reported to have a climb of more than five thousand feet per minute. It had very high speed and it could turn inside of any other aircraft. Well, those are the three advantages that a fighter pilot needs to have if he is going to be successful in combat. At least, he would like to have two out of the three—high speed and a high rate of climb with the ability to turn rapidly. Now you can turn altitude into speed just by putting your nose down, but you can't change the rate of climb or how tight an airplane will turn. That is built into it.

When I realized that this Japanese airplane—if the intelligence report out of China was correct—had us beat in all three categories, it was pretty discouraging. Some of our pilots just didn't believe it and said, "This can't be. It is a gross exaggeration."

We discussed the intelligence report in our squadron thoroughly. I remember noting the language in which the report was written. It was fighter pilot's language. Now whether it had been interpreted during translation, I don't know. I felt we should give it some credence because it sounded like a fighter pilot who knew what he was talking about. So I told my squadron, "All right, let's assume that it is exaggerated. Let's say the plane is only half as good as this report says it is. Let's put down these figures. Let's say it has only twenty-five-hundred feet per minute of climb. We have eleven hundred. Suppose it doesn't have such a high rate of turn. Cut that in half and it still looks like it can turn inside of us. Do the same thing with the speed. If you allow only half the speed reported, this plane would still do about the same as we do."

As it turned out, this Japanese plane did have a climb of about three thousand feet per minute. It could turn inside of anything and it did have a lot more speed than we did, even carrying more gasoline. This was the Zero.

I decided that we had better do something about this airplane. And I drew on my days on the football field and the basketball court. I know there that if you come up against somebody who is faster than you are, you have to trap him somehow so that he can't use his superiority, whatever that may be. You've got to bait him or do something of the kind.

I believed we had one advantage over the Japanese, if we could ever get into a position to use it. We had good guns and could shoot and hit even if we had only a fleeting second or two to take aim. So we must do something to entice the opponent flying in a Zero to give us that one all-important opportunity. I figured it was the only chance we had.

So every night when I came home I would work on this problem. We lived in a little rented house in Coronado, California. I used a box of kitchen matches and put them on the dining room table and let each one of them represent an airplane. In this way I could get as many airplanes in the air as I wanted in various formations and then try to decide what they ought to do. Usually I worked on this every night until about midnight. Madalyn, my wife, was worried that I was not getting enough sleep. So about eleven-fifty-five she would come to the table and say, "Jimmy, you know you are going to fly tomorrow. Don't you think it's time you got some sleep?" She was right. She knew I lost track of time when fiddling with those matches, and so I would put them away until the next night.

For years when I was flying in a fighter squadron one thing that sort of irked me and made me a little unhappy was the kind of formation we flew. It was with three-plane sections—a leader and two wingmen. If you're going to fight and do radical turns, this is an unwieldy formation. If the leader made a turn, say, to the left, and it was as quick and tight as he could turn, the inside man would slide over and probably right into the other wingman. This was true especially if the inside man was trying to get his sights on something at the same time the leader was. In order to fight in three-plane sections in that formation, I decided that each plane had to have three eyeballs: one to look at the leader, one to look through the gunsights, and one to keep an eye on the other wingman so that you didn't run into him.

Now, it was obvious that if we wanted to do something sudden to fool an enemy, we ought to eliminate one of those planes and just have a two-plane section. This is what I was doing in my experiment. Of course, at that time everybody was flying around in three-plane sections, both in the United States and in Europe.

I asked myself what would happen if you just had two-plane sections as part of a four-plane division or combat unit. In that case, you are in the air as a part of the combat unit and you see an enemy aircraft. You know that either you want to get him or you want to avoid getting shot down yourself. Now you don't run away from him unless you're sure you've got a headstart. Assuming that he has greater speed, you have to turn towards him. You turn towards him and hope that he won't get a good shot and that you will. Enemy aircraft in the area are coming in to attack you. They are off to the side and so you turn towards them. Well, they have got to pick some target. If we split a little wider apart at that point into a sort of wide formation, the enemy will have to take on one of the two-plane sections. If he goes after the one on the right, the one on the left, presumably, might have a chance to shoot him in a cross fire. "Let's try that," I thought. (I'd work on these problems every night and then next morning we'd try them in the air.)

Soon I realized that it wasn't any use flying these four planes very close together. You might as well start them out split. In that way you could separate them far enough so that if any enemy came after one, from above, ahead or astern, you might be able to confuse him by doing something he didn't expect. Then I decided we should have a standard distance between the two pairs of planes equal to the tactical diameter of the aircraft. That is the diameter of the tightest circle or half circle an aircraft can make. With the sections of aircraft split like this, if the enemy came from directly ahead, one section would have a head-on shot and the other section could turn in to get a crossing shot.

Now, if the enemy came from astern, we had a lookout doctrine that applied. The two-plane section on the right of the combat unit watched over the tails of the two-plane section on the left and vice versa. If you were on the right side you never needed to look to the right. You always kept an eye open over to the left. This was so that somebody would know if an enemy plane was coming up on the combat unit's tail.

Often I talked to myself while working on a problem of this kind. It seemed to help. So I said, "If we are really going to fool him we won't use any signals. We'll have to wait until he's almost within lethal firing range, and then the one who's watching him will make a sharp turn towards the plane being attacked. This is the signal that somebody is right within firing range on its tail. The pilot of the plane being attacked won't be able to see him because he can't see straight astern. So if you are in the left section and you see an enemy attacking the section on the right from astern, you turn hard right. What does this do? The attacking aircraft has to take a lead. If it's diving in, it has to take a lead, an extension of his target's flight line as he sees it. But his target suddenly turns after the enemy has committed himself. That throws off his lead and he's not going to hit. And if he tries to follow on around to get back his aim, he's got to do at least two maneuvers: he has got to put his wing down and then pull his nose back up again. That takes time. It brings him right into the gunsights of the other section of aircraft, which should have a good shot at him, either head on, if he continues to follow his target, or from a good side approach if he pulls out. Although he has superior performance, we have a shot at him, but he hasn't got a shot at us, at least not an accurate one."

This looked as though it was the only thing to do. I was very excited about this discovery with matches on the dining room table. I went into the bedroom. I thought maybe my wife was asleep. She wasn't. She was just waiting to tell me when it was midnight. So I cried, "Madalyn, I've got it. I've got it! Now you can get enough sleep for a change."

I wrote up my experiment and presented it to the squadron. We discussed it and I said, "We've got to practice this, but who's going to be the Zeros? How are we going to find airplanes of that sort, that fast and with that high a performance? I'll tell you what we'll do." I told Lieutenant Commander Edward ("Butch") O'Hare to take four aircraft and use full power. I would take four and put a little mark on the throttle quadrant and never advance it more than halfway. That gave him at least a superior performance, maybe double, maybe not, but somewhat better.

Well, we went up in the air and began the experiment. I had told Butch, "You attack from any direction you want and keep a good eye out and see what my maneuvering looks like. Does it look like it's any good? Is it giving you any trouble?" So he made all sorts of attacks, quite a few of them from overhead, coming down this way and that. It looked like a pretty good thing to me. Every time he came in to shoot—you can tell when an airplane is in position to shoot—we just kept weaving back and forth.

After we landed Butch came over to me and said, "Skipper, it really worked. It really worked. I couldn't make any attack without seeing the nose of one of your half-throttle airplanes pointed at me. So at least you were getting a shot even though I might also be getting a shot. At least it wasn't one-sided. Most of the time that sudden turn caught me a little bit by surprise because it seemed to be timed just right. I knew, of course, what you were going to do, but I couldn't tell exactly *when* and I didn't want to anticipate it. When I was committed and about to squeeze the trigger, he turned. I didn't think he saw me."

Of course he didn't. That is the beauty of it. You needed no communication. You were flying along watching the other two planes of your combat unit. They suddenly made a turn. You knew there was somebody on your tail and you had to turn in a hurry. That's all there was to it. You didn't need any radio.

So we felt a little better about the situation revealed in that intelligence report on the Zero. We had been proving all of our fighter lives that an airplane with superior performance could knock you out of the air. That was it. There was no question about it. If you met him he was going to get you, assuming he wasn't a stupid pilot. You can never assume the enemy is not going to be experienced and able to shoot. But now we had something to work on, to keep us from being demoralized. It also gave us something of a plan. I've always felt that in athletics, football or basketball or any competitive sport—and the same applies to combat—you've got to have a plan. Even though it proves to be a lousy plan, at least that is better than having no plan. If you start working at yours you might keep the enemy off balance.

I've read that I was supposed to have studied the combat reports of the Battle of the Coral Sea and then figured out this new technique in time for the Battle of Midway. This is not true. We had been practicing this maneuver for a long time, since the summer of 1941. Jimmy Flatley gave it the name Thach Weave. I didn't. But without that intelligence report that was said to have come out of China, I think we would have gone right along, fat, dumb, and happy, and eventually run into the Zero and not had nearly the success we did have. We would have been far worse off. In fact, we would have been in far worse shape in the early battles of the war.

THE THACH WEAVE PUT TO THE TEST, AND THE *YORKTOWN*'S DEMISE

ADMIRAL JOHN S. THACH

Our air group landed aboard the *Yorktown* about fifty miles at sea on May 30, the day she departed from Pearl Harbor. She had undergone a patch-up job there for damage received in the South Pacific. We were to join the *Enterprise* and the *Hornet*. Together these carriers formed two task groups: Task Force 17 with the *Yorktown* under Admiral Frank Jack Fletcher and Task Force 16 with the *Enterprise* and the *Hornet* under Admiral Raymond Spruance.

Before I left Pearl Harbor I was given very brief indications that we expected an attack, and obviously there was a big battle coming up in the middle of the Pacific. That night, after we got aboard and everything was buttoned up and we were headed toward Midway, all of the squadron pilots and the air group were brought into the wardroom. There the air officer of the *Yorktown* gave us a complete briefing on everything they knew about the opposition Japanese forces and their probable intentions.

They didn't tell us at the time of the briefing that the Japanese code had been broken and that most of the information was being obtained in that way. But very soon the navy patrol planes did pick up a large Japanese force and what we had heard was all verified then. Their obvious objective was Midway Island and they had more than enough to take that island. If they did, they probably would consider charging on down the Hawaiian Island chain.

We were all mightily impressed by what we heard at the briefing. A serious and crucial engagement was coming up. If we could win this one, we might be able to stop the Japanese advance. So we spent the time at hand

98

getting our ammunition ready, carefully checking and rechecking each airplane.

Then I got word that the commanding officer of the dive-bomber squadron and the commanding officer of Torpedo Squadron 3 wanted to have a conference, and I agreed. Lem Massey, commanding officer of the torpedo squadron, said he thought I ought to get up with the dive-bombers, "because that's where the Zeros are going to be. That's where they were in the Coral Sea battle." That became the subject of our conference, whether the fighter escort should go with the dive-bombers or the torpedo planes. We knew we didn't have enough escort planes to split them and send a few with each. My plan was for two divisions of eight each. That was the basic tactical breakdown we had developed. If you are going to send any number of airplanes that number has to be divisible by four, otherwise you are left with two planes that don't have wingmen. So we planned to send eight.

The other two squadrons began playing Alphonse and Gaston, each trying to give the fighters to the other, so I said, "How about letting me decide it?" I reasoned that since the torpedo planes in the Coral Sea battle had gotten in pretty much unopposed and had done their work in sinking ships, the Japanese would be more concerned about the torpedo planes here. The way to sink ships was to put a hole in the side of the ship below the waterline. That's what a torpedo was designed for. The Japanese knew this and they were going to be very concerned about any torpedo attack. They were going to try and knock it out before it got under way. So they finally agreed that I should go with the VT-3, the torpedo planes.

It may surprise people these days that I should be able to make such a decision. The truth is that in World War II, as a lieutenant, I made more decisions than some very high-ranking officers made in the Vietnam War. In that war the secretary of defense was telling us how many planes to send, what formation to fly, and at what altitude.

In my time we operated under a doctrine called good common sense. If you had enough of that, you would stack your fighters above the dive-bombers. You would have at least one division with them and at least one or more with the torpedo planes; for the torpedo planes were the old firetraps, slow and awkward and with no self-sealing tanks. They needed more protection. That governed our decision in this case. Our doctrine was flexible and depended on where we anticipated the enemy fighters might be. The TBDs of that time were called Devastators but were more devastating to the crews in them than to the enemy.

I was very concerned about whether the torpedo planes could get in to make their attack. I knew that if the Japanese were together in one formation and had a combat air patrol of defending fighters we would very likely be outnumbered. We were also concerned about the fact that the Zero fighter could outperform us in every way. We felt we had one advantage in that we could shoot better and we had better guns. But if you don't get a chance to shoot, better guns matter little.

I was thinking about all of this and also which pilots I would take with me. I didn't sleep much that night, but we were all pretty optimistic because we felt that we were going to get tactical surprise. We didn't think the Japanese knew we were anywhere near them. This was a great morale builder, thinking we were going to have one of the basic advantages of warfare on our side—surprise.

But then the next morning Captain Buckmaster of the *Yorktown* decided that only six fighters were to go. He wanted to keep as many as possible back to defend the *Yorktown*. If you send a strike against an enemy carrier force, why, usually you can expect an attack on yourself as well, unless enemy search planes fail to find you or you get all of the enemy right away and they have no aircraft in the air with suitable weapons to attack. So I had quickly to revise the formation that we were going to fly over the torpedo planes.

There were twelve torpedo planes for the attack and our six fighters. I put two fighter planes just astern of the torpedo planes, which were flying formation in the shape of a triangle. The two fighters were down at a lower altitude than the other four. We flew between one thousand and fifteen hundred feet above the torpedo planes. They were so slow, however, that we had to do S-turns in order to slow down and not run away from them.

We took off from the *Yorktown* by 0900. Those on the *Hornet* and *Enterprise* started taking off a little after 0700. Before leaving, I had a last-minute briefing in which I told the people going with me and those standing by for combat air patrol that I wanted the formation to stick together. Nobody was going to be a lone wolf because lone wolves don't live very long in the circumstances we were about to experience. We just had to stick together no matter what happened. I was convinced—and I thought they were, too—that was the best way to survive and protect the torpedo planes. Then I reminded them of the tricks we had heard about. Sometimes a Japanese fighter would fly up and pose himself in a position where it looked like you could easily go out and shoot him, for he was a little below you. He was giving you this advantage, but his friends were waiting topside to come down and pick you off if you pulled out alone. Our primary job was, I said, to protect the torpedo planes and keep the enemy fighters engaged as much as we could all the way in and all the way out. It was a pretty serious situation. We had got the information on how big a formation the Japanese had.

So we boarded our planes. All of us were highly excited and admittedly nervous. I think most other people did pretty much what I did. I kept going over my check-off list. As soon as we got in the air, I had each section test their guns so they'd be ready and see that all the switches were on and not on safety. This seemed to work all right, so in we went.

100

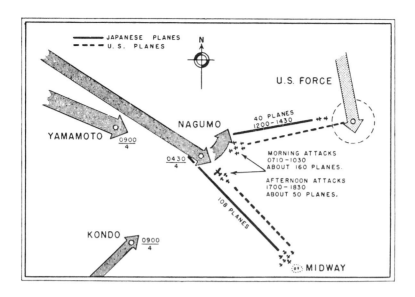

Lem Massey made a small change and we took off on a heading of about southwest. I wondered why he did that. Had he gotten some more information? About that time, looking ahead, I could see ships through the breaks in the little puffy clouds, and I figured that was the reason. We had just begun to approach about ten miles from the outer screen of this large force.* It looked like it was spread over the ocean. Several colored antiaircraft bursts were seen in our direction, one red and another one orange—and then no more. I wondered why they would be shooting at us, because we weren't quite within range. We weren't even nearly within range. The bursts came from the nearest ship, which was quite a distance from the main body of carriers and battleships. We soon had our answer. We'd been sighted from the surface screen and it was alerting the combat air patrol. A very short time after, Zero fighters came down on us—even before we got anywhere near antiaircraft range. I tried to count them. We had been trained to count things at a glance. I figured there were twenty.

Then one of our planes was burning. He pulled out and I didn't see him anymore. He was shot down right away. I didn't see the Zero that got him either. It didn't take me long, however, to realize that they were coming in a stream on us from astern. I was surprised they put so many Zeros on my six fighters. I had expected they would go for the torpedo planes first. They must have known we didn't have the quick acceleration to catch them, the way

*Vice Admiral Chuichi Nagumo's Carrier Striking Force, which consisted of four carriers, two battleships, three cruisers, and eleven destroyers.

101

they were coming in at high speed in rapid succession and zipping away. But then I saw they had a second large group that was streaming right past us and into the poor torpedo planes.

Macomber, leading the second duo of fighters, was too close to me to permit an effective weave, and I was not getting very good shots at the Zeros. I called him on the radio and said, "Open out more. About double your present distance and weave." No acknowledgment. His radio must have been bad. He has since stated it was.

How ironical this situation had become! I had spent almost a year developing what I was convinced was the only way to survive against the Zero and now we couldn't seem to do it. I kept wondering why Macomber was so close instead of being out in a position to weave. Of course, he had never practiced the weave. He was one of the VP-42 pilots based aboard the *Yorktown* during the Coral Sea battle and he had tangled with some Zeros then. Like the other former VP-42 pilots, he had reported to VF-3 just before we flew out to land aboard the *Yorktown* en route to Midway. I had assumed my exec, Don Lovelace, had briefed them or had them read the squadron tactical doctrine. Suddenly I realized that Don didn't have much time to brief anyone before falling victim to a grisly accident that claimed his life.* I had tried so hard to wipe that horrible event from my mind that I forgot Don was no longer with us.

Then I remembered telling my flight during the last-minute briefing to stick together. Macomber must have thought I meant for him to fly a closed-up formation. What I actually meant was I wanted no lone-wolf tactics. It was too late to correct that misunderstanding now. I couldn't see the two pilots who flew slightly below us with the torpedo planes, so I turned to my wingman, Ram Dibb, and said, "Pretend you are a section leader and move out far enough to weave." His voice sounded elated to get this "promotion" right in the middle of a battle.

Several Zeros came in on a head-on attack on the torpedo planes and burned Lem Massey's plane right away. It just exploded in flames. And beautifully timed, another group came in on the side against the torpedo planes. In the meantime, a number of Zeros were coming down in a string on our fighters. The air was just like a beehive, and I wasn't sure at that moment that anything would work. And then my weave began to work! I got a good shot at two Zeros and burned them. One of them had made a pass at my wingman, pulled out to the right, and then come back. We were weaving continuously. I got a head-on shot at him and just then Ram, the wingman, radioed, "There's a Zero on my tail." He didn't have to look back because the Zero wasn't directly astern. He was at about a forty-five-degree angle and

*Lieutenant Commander Donald A. Lovelace died in an accident on 2 June 1942 while on duty in the *Yorktown.*

beginning to follow Ram around, which gave me the head-on approach. I was really angry then. I was mad because my poor little wingman had never been in combat before. In fact, he had very little gunnery training. It was his first time flying from a carrier and this Zero was about to chew him to pieces. I probably should have ducked under the Zero, but I lost my temper and decided to keep my fire going into him so he'd pull out. He did, and I just missed him by a few feet. I saw flames coming out of the bottom of his airplane. This was like playing chicken on the highway with two automobiles headed for each other, except we were shooting at each other as well. It was a little foolhardy, but I think when I hit him it pulled his stick back and his nose went up. The first reaction on being hit is to jerk back. I wanted him to pull out. I was going to force him to pull out. That is a foolish thing to do. I didn't try that anymore. You really don't need to, because if you haven't hit by the time you get there you can certainly afford to duck under, and then you'll get away.

The Japs kept coming in. By this time we were over the screen and more of our torpedo planes were falling, but so were some Zeros. And we thought, At least we are keeping a lot of them engaged.

We could see the carriers now. They were steaming at very high speed and launching airplanes. And those planes looked like more fighters. I couldn't tell. I just got a glimpse. They were beginning to maneuver.

Now the torpedo planes had to split in order to make an effective attack. We used to call it the Anvil Attack. They would break up formation and spread out in a kind of a line on each side of the target, the carrier. The reason a formation of torpedo planes has to split is so they can come in against a carrier from various points around at least 180 degrees of the compass. If the target ship turns to the right, he has left a broadside shot for several torpedoes. If he turns to the left, then the ones on the other side get the same advantage. The ship can comb only one of the oncoming torpedoes. By combing I mean just heading right for the torpedo and barely avoiding it so that its extended track is parallel to the ship but clear of its side.

We fighters thought we were doing pretty well until our torpedo planes split. Then they were extremely vulnerable, just all alone with no protection. And the Zeros were coming in on us, the fighters, one after the other. Sometimes they came simultaneously from above and to the side. We couldn't stay with the torpedo planes except for the one or two that happened to be under us.

I kept counting the number of airplanes I knew I'd gotten in flames going down. I couldn't bother to wait for them to splash. But I could tell if they were flaming real good and there was something besides smoke. If you saw real red flames, why, you knew a plane had had it.

I had a little kneepad and I would mark on it every time I knew one was gone. Then I realized this was sort of foolish. Why was I making marks on my kneepad when the kneepad wasn't coming back? I was utterly convinced then that we weren't any of us coming back because there were still so many Zeros. They had already got one of our six, and two more of them I couldn't see anymore. There seemed to be only Macomber, Ram Dibb, and myself. Pure logic cried out that the enemy's superior performance and the number of Zeros he was throwing into the fight meant that we could not possibly survive. So I said to myself, "This counting is a foolish thing. It takes a second or two to look down to your kneepad and make the mark. It's a waste of time." And then I said, still talking to myself, "We're going to take a lot of them with us if they're going to get us all."

But we kept working on this weave and it seemed to work better and better. The reason I tell about stopping my act of counting is because ever since then I haven't had the slightest idea how many Zeros I shot down. I can't remember and I don't suppose it makes too much difference. It only shows that I was absolutely convinced that nobody could get out of there, that we weren't coming back and neither were any of the torpedo planes.

Then it seemed that the attacks began to slacken. I didn't know whether they were spreading out and working more on the unprotected torpedo planes. But the torpedo planes continued on in. I saw three or four of them get in and make an attack. I believe that at least one torpedo hit was made. Now all the records, including those of the Japanese, say that no torpedoes hit. I'm not sure that the people aboard a ship that is hit by dive-bombers really know whether they were hit by bombs or by torpedoes. I was aboard the *Saratoga* when she was torpedoed and the *Yorktown* when she was bombed and I couldn't tell the difference.

And then I saw a glint in the sun that looked like a beautiful silver waterfall. It was the dive-bombers coming in. I could see them very well because they came from the same direction as the Zeros. I'd never seen such superb dive-bombing. It looked to me like almost every bomb hit. Of course there were some near misses, but there weren't any wild ones. Explosions were occurring in the carriers. About that time the Zeros slacked off more. We stayed around. We escorted two torpedo planes out, one after the other, and tried to get them clear. Then we went back and picked up another one that we saw. We stayed right with him and over him, hoping that the Zeros wouldn't have him all to themselves.

After the dive-bomber attack was over, I stayed there between the screen and the carriers. A single Zero appeared, flying slowly below and to one side of us. I looked up toward the sun and, sure enough, there were his teammates poised like hawks waiting for one of us to take the bait. We didn't.

I could only see three carriers. I never did see a fourth one. And one of them, probably either the *Soryu* or the *Kaga*, was burning with bright pink flames and sometimes blue flames. I remember gauging the height of those flames by the length of the ship. The distance was about the same. It was just solid flame going skyward and there was a lot of smoke on top of that. Before I left the scene I saw three carriers burning pretty furiously. Then I came and picked up one torpedo plane and flew on back toward the *Yorktown* while providing protection for it.

In all I was over the Japanese fleet a full twenty minutes. I had enough gas because we took off later than the other people. The fighters were the last ones to take off.

In reflecting on this battle after the event, I realize that this classic coordinated attack, with the torpedo planes going in low and the dive-bombers coming in high and almost simultaneously, was effective. I think it is usually better if the dive-bombers do hit first, for then the torpedo planes can get in better among the confusion of the bombs bursting. Here was a sort of reverse of the Coral Sea battle. I also realized that the people who died hadn't given their lives in vain. They'd done a magnificent job of attracting all the enemy combat air patrol; all the protection that the Japanese carriers had was engaged and held down, so we did do something, and maybe far more than we thought at the time. We engaged enemy planes that might have gotten into the dive-bombers and prevented them from getting many hits.

On the way back to the *Yorktown,* while escorting the torpedo plane, I felt my shoes were a little squashy. I reached down and felt this slippery liquid all over my leg. I thought it was blood. It felt like blood. I didn't want to look at it, so I just didn't for a while. I wiggled my legs and they felt all right, except I remember a little place on my shin that didn't feel too good. I thought, I must have bumped it getting in the airplane. Then I picked up my glove and looked at it and it was oil. I was never so glad to see oil on my hands in all my life.

When we landed on board, the mechanic saw a hole in the gas tank and removed the tank to fix it. He opened it and found an incendiary bullet that was half burned. It had penetrated pretty near the bottom of the tank and had immediately been smothered by gasoline, so didn't do any damage, didn't set the tank on fire. The engine oil was all gone, but the good old engine had still ticked over and I had been able to get aboard ship. I had known while landing that I was low on oil because both my feet were wet with it and the oil pressure had dropped to zero. Apparently another Japanese bullet had shot an oil line away.

After we'd landed aboard, we were getting ready to go on a combat air patrol. In order to do so we were having the planes rearmed, refueled, and checked over and were taking stock of what we'd lost and what we had left. I was in the ready room while a combat air patrol of eight fighters was in the air over the ship. The rest of the fighter pilots were in the ready room when suddenly they picked up on radar an attack of about forty aircraft about thirty miles out. Actually I think it proved to be eighteen dive-bombers supported by six fighters.

They came on in. The combat air patrol did a terrific job and shot down most of them, but I think I'm correct in saying that four dive-bombers got through. I made my count this way. You could hear the antiaircraft fire in the ready room, which was at the flight-deck level in the *Yorktown*. The heavy five-inch gun goes off at a slower tempo than the smaller-caliber guns—then the forty-millimeter, the twenty-millimeter, and the little machine guns. When you hear the small-caliber guns, you know the enemy aircraft are pretty close. I counted this sequence four times, and we felt a couple of *thud*s, but it all seemed rather remote from the fighter pilot's ready room. If four got through they were very accurate, because they did get three hits on the *Yorktown*. One of them exploded down a smokestack and created quite a problem, setting the soot on fire and spreading it around. This stopped the ship. It blasted out all but one boiler, I think. Then—I am not sure of the time but it didn't seem very long—we heard that the engineers had run auxiliary flexible steam lines.

We got under way and we received word in the ready room that they thought we could make sixteen knots. And they asked could we take off. And I said, "Yes, we can take off, even though you are making less speed than that. We can start way back at the stern of the ship." There weren't many planes left aboard. They had not let the dive-bombers come aboard until we fighters were received. And then very, very soon after we landed the attack of the Jap dive-bombers came, so our dive-bombers didn't have time to get aboard and were still in the air.

We took stock of all the planes we had. When the initial Jap attack came, our men had to stop refueling our planes and purge the lines with carbon-dioxide gas. They were still fighting fires in some places when the ship got under way. And there was a fire caused by one of the bombs down near the main gasoline tank in a storeroom, so we couldn't get more gasoline. I said, "Let's take off all the airplanes that have as much as twenty gallons of gas and any ammunition we can get." So we did. We got together six or eight planes, and the ship got under way slowly and finally built up speed. I don't think it was making sixteen knots when I took off, because I just got over the bow and dipped a little bit. And just as we were rolling down the deck another attack came in. These were heavy torpedo planes, a squadron of torpedo planes from the one Japanese carrier that had not been found. They were escorted by six or eight fighters. Now we didn't have too many combat air patrol planes in the air at the time, only about four.

Even as we were rolling down the deck the antiaircraft fire had to open up, for the Jap planes were that close. I got my wheels up, with about thirty-six hard turns of a crank. There was nothing automatic about it. You just had to breathe through your mouth. I was looking out to see the firing on the starboard side and saw the plane with Milton Tootle, Ensign Tootle III. He didn't even get his wheels up but turned right toward the torpedo planes and into our own antiaircraft fire. He shot down a Japanese torpedo plane and it looked as if a Zero promptly shot him down. He was in the air less than sixty seconds. This is probably the shortest combat flight on record where a fighter shot down anything. Tootle said a Zero was shooting at him, but he was also, like the rest of us, in the middle of our own antiaircraft fire, so who knows who brought him down. I think the Zero probably did. Anyway, Tootle was picked out of the water and saved.

Now I saw a torpedo plane coming. They had split just like we did in our formations and they were coming in from different points of the compass at the *Yorktown*. The one I saw was real low on the water. I could see a bright red-colored insignia shaped like feathers on his tail, something no other Japanese aircraft had. I made a good side approach on him and got him on fire. The whole left wing was burning and I could see the ribs showing through the flames. But that devil stayed in the air until he got close enough and dropped his torpedo. That one hit the *Yorktown*. He was a dedicated torpedo plane pilot, for even though his plane was on fire and he was falling, he went ahead and dropped his torpedo. He fell into the water immediately after, very close to the ship.

These Japanese pilots were excellent in their tactics and in their determination. In fact, as far as determination was concerned, you could hardly tell any difference between the Japanese carrier-based pilots and the American carrier-based pilots. Nothing would stop them if they had anything to say about it.

So that stopped the ship. And then I had a little tangle with a Zero. Since we had never been able to join up in formation we just turned individually off the bow of the ship into the torpedo planes. I didn't have a wingman. In fact, I didn't see anybody else, but I did see the Zero and I went at him. He apparently had been fighting with some of our combat air patrol and was going to catch up with what he thought was left of his torpedo planes. I was hoping he wouldn't see me, but he did soon after I started for him; he just pulled up very neatly and came right over the top of my head and right on my tail. Fortunately there was a little cloud I was headed for. I went right into that cloud, did a split S, pulled out, and didn't see him any more. He almost had me. I had thought that before he saw me I could get a shot at him and then decide what to do.

The *Yorktown* never took airplanes aboard again. It was a very sad thing to see her listing more and more. I thought she was going to roll over and capsize. Apparently the skipper did also because it wasn't long before he ordered abandon ship. We in the air were directed to land aboard the *Enterprise*. She and the *Hornet* were sitting about fifty miles away, with plenty of combat air patrol over them, too far away to help the *Yorktown*.

A ZERO IS FOUND BOTTOM UP IN A BOG

ADMIRAL JAMES S. RUSSELL

JAMES SARGENT RUSSELL was born on 22 March 1903 in Tacoma, Washington. In 1926 he graduated from the U.S. Naval Academy, and following flight training at Pensacola he was designated naval aviator. His postgraduate studies included a tour at the Naval Academy (1932–34), and in 1935 he received a masters degree in aeronautical engineering from the California Institute of Technology.

The outbreak of World War II found Lieutenant Commander Russell in command of Patrol Squadron 42, which he led against Japanese forces in the Aleutian Islands campaign. He was decorated for leading his squadron in the face of enemy opposition and extremely hazardous weather conditions, and for establishing advanced bases in the area from which his squadron operated. In later significant assignments he served as director of Military Requirements, Bureau of Aeronautics (1943–44); a member of Air Technical Intelligence, Supreme Commander, Allied Powers, Japan (1945–46); a member of the U.S. Strategic Bombing Survey in Tokyo (1945–46); and commanding officer of the USS *Coral Sea* (1951–52). In 1955 he became chief of the Bureau of Aeronautics. He was awarded the Collier Trophy in 1956 for his development of the supersonic navy fighter, the *Crusader*. On 21 July 1958 he was promoted to admiral. He served as vice chief of naval operations from 1958 to 1961 and as Commander in Chief, Allied Forces, Southern Europe, from 1962 until his retirement on 1 April 1965.

Admiral Russell has been active in naval affairs since his retirement. He lives in Tacoma, Washington.

On the fourth of June 1942 Ensign Mitchell was shot down. I was sad about this, for he had had a very tough time. He had been patrolling overnight as usual on a southern sector of the Aleutian Islands, out of Cold Bay. He had received some bad gasoline from a tender—there was rust and salt water mixed up with his gasoline—and his engines were running rough. But he kept airborne and managed to get back to the base. We looked him over at Cold Bay and we cleaned out the side of his tankage that wasn't self-sealed, but the other side, where we had our bulletproof fuel cells, we just couldn't clean out. So we closed those off and filled his good side full of clean gasoline and sent him up to Kodiak, Alaska. I told him not to show up again until he had an airplane that he was satisfied he could fly.

He got to Kodiak and there was a lot of excitement up there. The wing commander had an operation order that he wanted to send down to his squadrons. Instead of getting Mitchell's plane back in shape, cleaning out the tanks on the bulletproof side, etc., the wing commander sent him back, still flying on the one good side, to deliver operational orders to me at Cold Bay and to Foley at Dutch Harbor. He landed at my place. I was very much annoyed to think that he didn't have his airplane back in shape.

Then he took off from there to make his delivery at Dutch Harbor. We always radioed in to any base before we landed to find out if the place was under attack and whether it was fit to land there. He followed this procedure. He radioed in to Dutch Harbor as he approached and they said, "No, we're under attack." Instead of going out into the Bering Sea and staying close until Dutch Harbor was open, or coming back to us at Cold Bay—and these two bases were fairly close together—he elected to go into Beaver Inlet. It's a very deep fjord on the eastern side of Unalaska Island, where Dutch Harbor is located.

Ensign Mitchell was very familiar with the country because he had flown the Dutch Harbor detachment; he'd had the four weeks of duty down there and he remembered that this particular fjord led into a rather open bay. It was completely surrounded by mountains but had open water. He decided to slide in there and wait until the attack was over. What he didn't know was that the *Ryujo*'s air group was coming around that side of the island.* They stopped him in there and a section of fighters peeled off and shot him down. There is every evidence that his waist gunner, whose name was Rawls, got in a lucky shot on a Zero, because one was found on Akutan Island, in the Aleutians, on its back in a marsh.

The reason I believe that it was Mitchell's waist gunner who winged the

---

*The *Ryujo* was one of two light cruisers in Japan's Second Mobile Force, which made attacks on Dutch Harbor on 3 and 4 June, inflicting some damage. The Japanese hoped their thrust at Alaska would deflect some of America's naval power from the Midway campaign. The only result of Japanese action in Alaska was the occupation of two relatively insignificant islands in the Aleutians, Attu and Kiska.

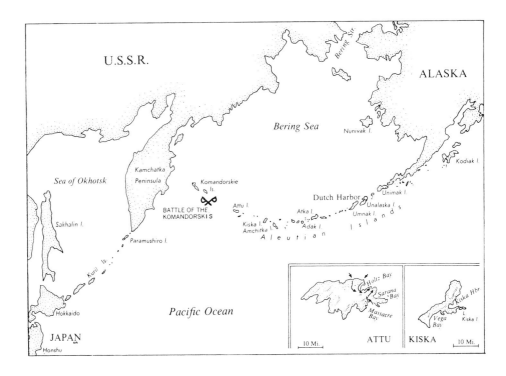

Zero is this: The bullet that brought the pilot down went in from the top and severed the oil return line leading from the oil cooler to the engine of the Zero. This caused a loss of oil. The flight petty officer flying the airplane saw his oil pressure drop and radioed to the *Ryujo*, saying, "I expect my engine to freeze up momentarily. I am losing oil pressure and I will make a forced landing on Akutan Island. Please send a submarine to pick me up." His plan was to land on the island, destroy his airplane by burning it, and walk down to the beach on Akutan Island to be picked up by a submarine which was cruising in the vicinity of Dutch Harbor. What he didn't realize was that this lovely meadow he picked out to make his landing on was a bog, as most level places in the Aleutians are. He lowered his wheels. If he'd left his wheels retracted, I think he would have gotten away with it very handily, but he didn't do this. He lowered his wheels. These immediately caught in the bog and flipped him over on his back. He broke his neck and was killed.

We found this airplane thirty days later.* Our planes were out looking for a missing Catalina and, flying over Akutan Island, they were amazed to find an airplane, with red apples on its wings, bottom up in the marsh on Akutan

*Presumably 4 July 1942.

110

Island. A salvage party was put together at Dutch Harbor. They went over to the scene of the wrecked Zero and disassembled it enough so they could get it down to the waterfront and on a lighter. Towed back over to Dutch Harbor, it was put on a freighter and brought down to the naval air overhaul facility at the naval air station at North Island, San Diego. It was repaired and flown by early October 1942.

The plane was a Zero Mark 2, one of the early Zeros, a beautifully put-together machine. I saw it in Dutch Harbor. Repaired, it was used to develop tactics against the Zero. Now the pilot who was assigned to it was Captain Melville ("Boogie") Hoffman, who was a former enlisted pilot, fighter pilot, and his sole duty was to become completely familiar with that airplane and its maneuvering capabilities and to dogfight against our pilots. This took place mainly around San Diego, but the plane was also flown at Wright Field and other places across the country. Jimmy Thach, who developed the Thach Weave against the Zeros in the early days of World War II, flew against it.

I have talked with Boogie Hoffman. He said they discovered the built-in incidence of the vertical surfaces of the Zero. These were designed to help meet the tremendous torque on takeoff, which you get normally with a big propeller like that on the Zero. You must carry a lot of right rudder as you make your take-off run because of the torque of the prop, and some of this torque load was relieved in the design of the Zero. But if the Zero got going at very high speed (the force against an airfoil varies with the square of its velocity), it would roll very fast toward the right and more slowly toward the left. So the tactic was, if you got in a brush with a Zero, to get him at high speed and roll to the left, for this was his slow roll direction. Now I think I'm correct—right and left—but at least I know you'd roll very fast in one direction and slow in the other, at high speed. And this tactic was, of course, used by us.

Masatake Okumiya, who wrote the book *Zero!,** the best history written on naval aviation in Japan, attaches a great deal of importance to the fact that the United States got a Zero early on in the war and could try it out and find out what its foibles in the air were.

*Masatake Okumiya and Jiro Horikoshi, with Martin Caidin (E.P. Dutton, 1956).

The death struggle of the *Yorktown* was a sad denouement to the great victory of Midway. After being torpedoed by the enemy on 4 June, she was abandoned by skipper and crew. All seemed lost. Overnight the picture improved and the skipper of her escort, the destroyer *Hughes*, radioed his opinion that she could be saved.

Admiral Nimitz in Pearl Harbor dispatched help at once. The minesweeper *Vireo* took the *Yorktown* in tow on 5 June but made little progress against the tradewinds. Early on the sixth the destroyer *Hammann* arrived, secured herself to the side of the giant carrier, and immediately landed a salvage party, which included the skipper of the *Yorktown*, Captain Elliott Buckmaster. They went to work and made considerable progress. A bevy of destroyers circled the stricken ship and her salvage party with sounding gear to help provide an antisubmarine screen.

The enemy was vigilant. A Japanese floatplane sighted the *Yorktown* early on the fifth and reported her as abandoned and drifting. Admiral Yamamoto dispatched the submarine *I-168* to find her and administer the coup de grâce. The carrier was sighted the next afternoon. The submarine penetrated the escort screen without difficulty and fired four torpedoes. Two of them found their mark in the *Yorktown* and still another hit the *Hammann*, breaking her in two and sinking her in four minutes. Captain Buckmaster still hoped for further salvage efforts on the morning of the seventh, but it was not to be. The *Yorktown* sank soon after dawn, an irreparable loss to the then limited forces of the navy.

Lieutenant Commander Joseph M. Worthington was skipper of the destroyer *Benham* during the Battle of Midway. The *Benham* escorted the *Hammann* to the listing carrier and remained to rescue hundreds of survivors when all was over.

BENHAM TO THE RESCUE

REAR ADMIRAL JOSEPH M. WORTHINGTON

JOSEPH MUSE WORTHINGTON, born in Annapolis, Maryland, on 11 March 1902, graduated from the U.S. Naval Academy in 1924. He attended the Army Industrial College in 1933 and the Naval War College in 1943.

After early sea duty and service as an instructor at the Naval Academy, Worthington had duty in 1940 as gunnery officer of the USS *Northampton*, where he did experimental work in the practical use of radar in gunfire control. In 1941 he assumed command of the destroyer *Benham* and took part in operations at Guadalcanal and Midway. In 1944 he joined the staff of Admiral Royal E. Ingersoll, commander in chief of the Atlantic Fleet. In 1945 Worthington took command of Destroyer Squadron 57 for duty in the north Pacific, at Okinawa, and in operations off the Japanese homeland. Worthington's postwar assignments included duty as director of instruction and deputy commandant of the Industrial College of the Armed Forces (1946–48); assistant for the Joint Chiefs of Staff and Armed Forces Policy Council (1950–52); and U.S. planner for the standing group of NATO (1952–54).

He retired on 30 June 1954. Rear Admiral Worthington, who lives on Gibson Island, Maryland, is the editor of a compilation of wartime dispatches of the late Admiral Royal E. Ingersoll.

114

The *Benham*'s task force, Task Force 16, commanded by Rear Admiral Spruance, rendezvoused with Rear Admiral Frank Jack Fletcher's Task Force 17 on the late afternoon of 3 June 1942, northeast of Midway. At that time Admiral Fletcher, officer in tactical command, directed Admiral Spruance and Task Force 16, which included the *Hornet,* to remain within visual distance for easy communication.

The idea was to cruise out of range of Japanese land-based planes, to avoid being sighted by their submarines, and when the Japanese started their attack on Midway, to search and destroy their carriers. The element of surprise was paramount in our plans. We believed that the Japanese did not know of the presence of our carriers.

The first report came in at daylight, 4 June, by one of our patrol planes from Midway. The crew had sighted at least two Japanese carriers and a destroyer. Then came another report that many planes were approaching Midway. A little prior to that, Admiral Fletcher had launched his long-range scout planes to cover a sector not believed to be covered by our other search planes.

With these several reports of Japanese units advancing, Fletcher ordered Spruance to attack as soon as the position of the enemy carriers was definitely known and as soon as his force was in appropriate range. Fletcher promised to do likewise as soon as he had recovered his search planes. So about 0900 Spruance launched all the aircraft that could be launched from the *Enterprise* and the *Hornet*. The *Hornet* was now separated a short distance from the *Enterprise,* for this was the custom in battle operations in those days. Our first task in the *Benham* had been the screening of the two task forces and planes guarding the *Enterprise*. Now with the separation of the two carriers, *Benham* continued with the *Enterprise* task force. As soon as all planes had been launched from the *Enterprise,* she assumed position for recovery of any damaged planes or for early recovery.

About noon the *Yorktown* reported her first dive-bombing attack by Japanese planes, and the *Benham,* together with two cruisers and another destroyer, speeded at about thirty-two knots in the direction of the *Yorktown*. Evidently she had suffered serious damage from that first attack, for she was showing great columns of smoke. We arrived in her vicinity and immediately joined the screen about her. She was only making about five knots. We were just getting into position when another report came of a pending attack. *Yorktown* launched what remaining planes she had as soon as she could get up any speed. Actually she increased her speed to about fifteen knots and then seventeen before the Jap torpedo planes came in.

The *Enterprise* also launched what planes she could get into the air. Then, together with her combat air patrol and planes from the *Hornet,* she tried to fend off the oncoming Japanese attack. They did extremely well against the attacking aircraft except for about a dozen torpedo planes flying very low, as close to the water as they could. Most of them were shot down by our fighter planes or by our guns. Even so, two torpedoes struck the *Yorktown* from planes that had got through the screen.

The *Benham* was on the side apparently bearing the brunt of the attack and was shooting with everything she had. One five-inch shell from the *Yorktown* went through the stack of the *Benham* and killed one of our officers and wounded others. There was no way to dodge the shells of our carrier as she fought in desperation. It is one of those acts of battle that can't be helped.

The attack by the Japanese lasted roughly ten minutes. With the two torpedo hits on her, the *Yorktown* took a very strong list. I thought it was something like twenty-five degrees, but when a carrier deck lists it might look a lot worse than it is. At any rate, the captain of the *Yorktown* gave an order to abandon ship. Officers and men slid over the side, climbed down nets, and went into the water.

Now the normal thing to do was to go alongside and take off as many men as we could, but this time it was not thought wise to go alongside the carrier. The men were already in the water and near the ship. We could very easily have hit some of them as a result. Also it seemed to me there was great danger of the ship capsizing.

We and two other destroyers in the screen tried to pick up as many as we could from the water. Other ships continued to serve as antiaircraft screen and antisubmarine screen, for there was still danger. A ship dead in the water is a lovely target for the enemy. We were making real progress with the recovery when the commodore directed those of us loaded with survivors to pull out into the screen around the *Yorktown* and to send in other ships to pick up more survivors. The *Benham* couldn't respond to the order. There were too many survivors in the water around our propellers. We were close to the stern of the *Yorktown* and when people went over the side of her they tended to crowd at the stern.

Then a third attack on the *Yorktown* was reported. The screen was getting into antiaircraft position, and I tried to join them as soon as I could get the ship clear of the people in the water. But by that time, fortunately, the attack was beaten off by our fighters and none of the Japs got into this mass of humanity.

We had taken aboard about 725 survivors. Other ships in the screen had as many as five hundred, four hundred, three hundred. We had far more than capacity, but if there are people in the water you have to pick them up. You don't question where you'll put them. We just picked up everybody in sight, including a fighter pilot while we were steaming away from the *Yorktown*. He was some distance from the ship and just by the grace of God we spotted him in the water.

116

We steamed eastward during the night and the following day in company with the *Astoria* (flying the flag of Admiral Fletcher) and five or six others of the screen. The *Hughes* was finally ordered to return to the *Yorktown* to observe and, I think, primarily to get some confidential publications still thought to be in the ship. Also it was feared that there might be somebody trapped below decks who could be rescued.

In daylight we were ordered to transfer a group of about thirty to the *Astoria* for eventual transfer to the USS *Hammann*. That ship was going back to the *Yorktown* to attempt a salvage operation. After that we were ordered to transfer all remaining *Yorktown* survivors to the cruiser *Portland*. So we rigged four breeches buoys, and by using an airplane crane, we transferred in about four hours what remained of the 725 we had taken aboard. Some of them were badly wounded and they were transferred by stretcher, swinging the ship in close each time and thus allowing the airplane crane in the *Portland* to take the stretcher aboard. It was a slow and tedious procedure, but we kept the four buoys going continuously.

During all this the executive officer of the *Portland* asked how many men we were transferring. I said, "Oh, about four hundred."

And he replied, "We already have four hundred by actual count."

So I said, "Well, that is about half the number that are coming, so we will take your count."

And he replied, "What do you think this is? The Grand Hotel?"

I must say that the *Portland* showed what a ship can do when the crew is properly trained. They not only handled the breeches buoys, the stretchers, and the ambulatory cases, but they also launched and recovered planes for antisubmarine patrol. Fortunately the sea was calm and they were able to get the planes in the air and then pick them up by what they called the dog method, on a sled. Now all this was going on simultaneously, and we were fueling the *Benham* as well.

When we had completed the transfer of those rescued, we were ordered back to try and help with the *Yorktown*. When we arrived there the next morning, the sixth of June, a little before daylight, the *Yorktown* was in tow of the ancient fleet tug *Vireo*. They were making one or two knots, not very much. The *Hammann* was alongside delivering power to the salvage pumps and providing light.

The *Yorktown* salvage crew had been put back aboard. By that time they had corrected the list considerably. Things were looking in much better shape. There were now four destroyers in the screen, plus the *Hughes* and the *Hammann*. We started a circular screen. We were steaming in a tight circle with our sound gear in operation—it wasn't good for more than one thousand or two thousand yards—thinking we were making real progress on the recovery of the *Yorktown,* when about two-thirty that afternoon we heard a report over the voice circuit that torpedoes were approaching the *Yorktown*.

I am convinced they were fired from over six thousand yards, maybe more. It was a glassy sea, visibility was perfect, and there was a target dead in the water. There was nothing easier for a submarine than to stay way beyond a destroyer screen and fire her shots.

We were still steaming in a circle when the warning came. The *Benham*, as near as I can figure, was on the port beam of the *Yorktown* and in her circle clockwise had reached the *Yorktown*'s bow. As we got around the bow all that we saw was the bow of the *Hammann* sinking fast by the stern. We were ordered to attempt rescue operations at once and all other destroyers were to continue their screen against the Jap submarine.

As we discovered, there were several torpedoes fired. They went under the *Hammann* and got the *Yorktown*, but when they exploded they set off the *Hammann*'s depth charges and her torpedoes. There was a horrible mess. I'm not positive, but I think most of the damage was due to the depth charges going off.

At least three torpedoes hit the *Yorktown*. There might have been more. I know one full salvo got her.

I had to proceed into this scene of destruction very cautiously. We had no life rafts left, no boats left; the five-inch shell that had hit the *Benham* two days before cut the falls, so that when we were directed to get out of the area after the rescue operation we had to cut loose the last boat. It had been holed by shrapnel. The only thing to do was to put men in life jackets and volunteer swimmers in life jackets and use lifelines. We got in as close and carefully as we could with the ship to rescue these people in the water, many of them horribly wounded. Then gradually we pulled them back to the ship with the swimmers and lines and put them on stretchers down on the water level and hoisted them aboard. This time we recovered nearly two hundred.

The *Hammann* had a complement of about 235, I believe. She had heavy loss of life. We delivered to the Pearl Harbor hospital about one hundred stretcher cases and about seventy-five ambulatory cases and we buried twenty-seven of them at sea. She suffered fearful losses.

As we went in among the debris from the explosion, one of our condensers became fouled, so that we had no backing power on one engine. Fortunately, it was not forward power. We were finally satisfied that we had picked up everybody, and then the *Balch* signaled us that they had picked up the captain of the *Hammann*. He was unconscious and had with him two bluejackets who were also unconscious. He was clutching each of them with an arm. Captain True, Arnold True, was a good swimmer and apparently had swum way off from the scene. That is how the *Balch* and the screen had happened to spot him.

We were then ordered to proceed to a certain area in the rear where a submarine tender, acting as a hospital ship, would take all these people back. But as soon as I talked with our doctor, he said, "We can't transfer these

118

people again. They won't stand another transfer; they are in that bad a shape."

So I reported to the commodore, "Urgently recommend taking these survivors to Pearl where they can get medical attention. I believe we can save some lives."

He didn't hesitate but said, "Proceed." We did proceed back to Pearl. I checked with the doctor on what speed we could make without affecting these patients' comfort. We got up to about twenty-seven knots in the calm waters on the two-day run back to Pearl Harbor. Of course, every bunk in the ship was used as a hospital bed.

There were still Japs around, though we didn't know where their submarines were.

Everybody on board helped with first aid and looked after the wounded. When we got back to Pearl, we went into the harbor much faster than I had any business going. I had neglected to take off steam early enough. We had one of those fast landings because by that time I'd forgotten I only had one backing engine. But we made it all right. The crew came to the rescue.

Admiral Nimitz was on the dock, members of his staff were on the dock. Ambulances were lined up to take care of all the wounded. This was the first combatant ship returning to Pearl Harbor after the Battle of Midway.

Rabaul, a valuable port in the northeast sector of New Britain in the Bismarck Archipelago, was part of an Australian mandate between 1920 and 1941. The Japanese took it on 23 January 1941 and very quickly made it into a highly effective naval and air base.

The capture of Rabaul was an early result of the success the Japanese had in overrunning Allied positions in the Malay Peninsula, the Philippines, and the Netherlands East Indies. Their easy victories encouraged the Imperial High Command to speed up the timetable for the basic war plan under which it was operating. Victory disease, a term applied to the more impatient and aggressive of his fellow war leaders by Rear Admiral Chuichi Hara, Japanese carrier commander in the Battle of the Coral Sea, was rampant at the time. To them the next logical step was to take the island of Tulagi in the Solomons and Port Moresby on the tip of New Guinea. That would give them mastery of the Coral Sea.

Japanese attention to the lower Solomons became apparent as early as January 1942, when bombing raids were initiated on Tulagi and its satellite islands. The Australians maintained a squadron of Catalinas in Gavutu Harbor and had a small contingent of infantrymen and native police to defend the base and the headquarters of their Solomon Island protectorate.

Further evidence of enemy interest in the area came on 8 March, when the Japanese landed at Lae and Salamaua in New Guinea. This move proved easy, for the Australians, even though the enemy advance threatened their homeland, offered only token resistance. Two months later, on 2 May, the Japanese made an approach to Tulagi and once again met with little objection. In fact, the Australian authorities saw that defense was hopeless and quickly evacuated the island. The Japanese, so confident were they of their occupancy, withdrew their supporting naval units immediately after the island was secured. Even then they paid no attention to Guadalcanal, the big island but eighteen miles from Tulagi. It was said, however, that they did send small parties over there to kill some of the wild cattle that roamed the island. That could not have been the most delectable food for Japanese troops.

When the Pacific war broke out most islands in the Solomons—Tulagi was an exception—were bush country, still a part of uncharted terrain. Only a few enterprising men had ventured to the fringes of the less inviting islands, where they usually planted coconut trees for financial profit. Missionaries had established stations on some of the islands, including Guadalcanal, but even for them disease and climate proved to be fierce deterrents.

Back in Washington, Admiral King saw Tulagi as a possible Allied base. He considered it a strategic checkmate to any further Japanese expansion into the area bordering on Australia. He also saw it as a military base of use when the Allies should attempt to wrest Rabaul from the enemy and launch an offensive against the southern perimeter of his island bases. But King's persistent efforts at the highest level of Allied planning were steadfastly resisted. A firm Allied strategy had been established. The Pacific war would remain something of a holding operation while the Allied powers concentrated their limited resources on securing victory against the Nazis in the Atlantic theater.

The roadblock to any Allied move after the indeterminate outcome of the Battle of the Coral Sea on 8 May was suddenly broken in late June. Aerial reconnaissance revealed that the enemy had landed military personnel, laborers, and materials on Guadalcanal. Work began forthwith on an airstrip near Lunga Point. This was an alarming development. A Japanese air base on Guadalcanal would threaten the U.S. Navy's forward base at Efate in the New Hebrides as well as one that was planned for Noumea in New Caledonia.

The immediate result was seen in an operation order from Admiral

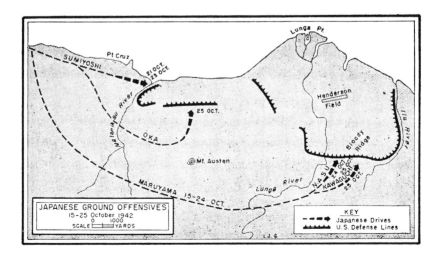

Nimitz, then commander in chief of the Pacific, to Admiral Robert Ghormley, commander of the South Pacific Area, for the seizure of both Tulagi and Guadalcanal. The date assigned was 1 August, but Ghormley had to push that up to 7 August to assemble an expeditionary force. That was gathered in a midocean rendezvous about four hundred miles south of the Fiji Islands. After a dress rehearsal of the amphibious units, the force set sail on the last day of July. There were nineteen transports escorted by forty-three warships. Admiral Richmond Kelly Turner was in command of the transports. They carried two combat teams of the First Marine Division under the command of Major General Alexander Vandegrift, who later confessed that he had not even known the location of Guadalcanal when the operation order first came. The official name given the operation was Watchtower, but after intelligence reports were gathered on the malarial jungles and the humid climate on Tulagi and Guadalcanal, the general began to call it Operation Pestilence.

Since this was to be a dual operation, the transports divided and were escorted into two landing areas, one at Lunga Point on Guadalcanal and the other off Tulagi. This was the first amphibious assault of the U.S. Navy in the Pacific campaign, and the Japanese were taken by surprise. Their intelligence source had failed to give warning of an impending invasion. That paid off initially. An American journalist who rode one of the first transports into Tulagi Bay could hardly believe that his transport had almost sailed past the Japanese shore batteries before a shot was fired. The marines took the small settlement on the island before noon, but later opposition was met on a tip of the island, and it was not completely secured until the following day. On Guadalcanal the first two marine battalions landed without firing a shot. The only enemies they encountered were Japanese laborers without guns. By the next afternoon eleven thousand marines were ashore and in possession of the partially completed airstrip.

But all this was only preliminary. On 9 August the Battle of Savo Island, one of the worst defeats ever inflicted on the U.S. Navy, was fought. It placed the occupation of Guadalcanal in the greatest jeopardy. The long and bloody struggle for the island, and especially for the airfield (later named Henderson Field) had only begun.

The excerpt that follows covers the time when the marines thought the U.S. Navy had abandoned them. Paul Moore was a part of that initial amphibious operation in the Pacific. On the first day he landed with the part of the First Division assigned to Tulagi, but after the island was secured he was sent with others to Guadalcanal, where he was involved in heavy fighting. His account of his experiences is vivid, unvarnished, and perceptive.

Most of the other excerpts in this volume are from men who were trained in the navy. They grew up accustomed to military discipline. Moore did not. A youthful volunteer in the marines who joined the service just months before this searing experience in the South Pacific, he was typical of many thousands of young American volunteers and draftees. As he freely admits, he was inept as a recruit in boot camp, but under the "bludgeoning of chance" he rapidly developed into a responsible, zealous marine with personal courage equal to the best. His change was psychological as well as physical, an experience he shared with the many young Americans who became part of the unifying force that converted an entire nation to the war effort.

THE MAKING OF A MARINE ON GUADALCANAL

THE RIGHT REVEREND PAUL MOORE, JR.

PAUL MOORE, JR., was born in Morristown, New Jersey, on 15 November 1919. He attended St. Paul's School in Concord, New Hampshire, and was graduated from Yale University in 1941. In 1949 he graduated from the General Theological Seminary in New York.

From 1941 to 1945 Moore served in the U.S. Marine Corps. As a platoon leader of the First Marine Division in the Tulagi-Guadalcanal operation of 1942, he was seriously wounded. Later he served as officer in charge of the marine V-12 program at the University of Washington Command and Staff School and as company commander and operations officer at Guam. He left the service in the rank of captain and is a member of the Manhattan District of the 369th Veteran's Association.

Moore was ordained as a priest in the Episcopal church in December 1949. He was consecrated as suffragan bishop in the diocese of Washington, D.C., in January 1964, elected as bishop coadjutor of New York in December 1969, and installed as thirteenth bishop of New York on 23 September 1972.

Moore was part of a delegation that went to Moscow in 1982 to discuss nuclear disarmament with Soviet leaders. He cochaired a special advisory committee on church and society that was charged with the development of social policy and programs for the Episcopal church. Currently he is chairman of the New York governor's Council on AIDs. The relationship of the ministry to psychiatry and the plight of the cities are two of his deep and unflagging concerns. On this latter subject Moore has expressed himself forcefully many times. He is the author of two books, *The Church Reclaims the City* (1965) and *Take a Bishop Like Me* (1979), as well as innumerable articles.

Moore resides in the Bishop's House, Cathedral of St. John the Divine, New York City.

Somebody told me about the marine corps. I knew so little about the marine corps that I thought it was just like the navy except you had a prettier uniform. There was a young marine corps officer at Yale who drove around the campus with his blues on, in a convertible car with whitewall tires, and I thought he was the best thing I'd seen in a long time. I wanted to be just like him. So I enlisted in the marine corps.

I was accepted by the marines and spent the summer waiting to be called to the officers' training class, which was the thing I'd enlisted in, and on the first of November I went down to Quantico. I underwent that very rigorous and rather humiliating basic training; although it was for officer candidates, the basic training was identical to that for any raw recruit. I soon got a very different idea of the marine corps.

I wasn't very good at the things you do in basic training. I couldn't get the hang of close-order drill. I remember one time I just couldn't figure out how to do an about-face. Everybody else learned it except me, and I was very tall and whenever I didn't do something right I stuck out like a sore thumb. So the drill sergeant had me practice about-faces all by myself in the middle of this huge parade ground. By the time I learned and went back, they'd been taught another maneuver—"to the rear, march"—and of course I couldn't do that, so back again I went. And I couldn't undo weapons. I remember wrestling with a machine gun, trying to take it apart. It suddenly came apart and I hit myself in the forehead and blood streamed out of my head all over the classroom. The lieutenant turned around and said, "There's an example of a man who cannot follow orders." No sympathy. In any case, the first marking period I was tenth from the bottom of a class of four hundred and way below the qualification level for an officer.

I went in to the lieutenant and asked him what I could do about it. He just put his head in his hands, then shook his head and said, "Moore, you just don't look like a marine and you never will." You can imagine my disappointment at that. Luckily, we went out on the rifle range shortly after, and I did very well at rifle shooting. I'd had a little bit of experience. We used to do it in the Adirondacks. Not much. I just happened to be able to do it, and for the marine corps, if you do well on the range, it covered a quantity of sins. So I did pass and qualify and get my commission.

126

Then we went down to New River, where Camp LeJeune was, as it was later called. It was just a tent city. Now it's a huge barracks. I was given a rifle platoon, which actually I'd applied for, again because I didn't have enough technical competence to get into the artillery. By this time I'd learned what the marine corps was about, and I thought being a rifle platoon leader would be a sort of basic thing to do. I was excited about it.

Again I made a damned fool of myself. We were told in the marine corps that you should always act quite tough, especially when you first took over your unit, so I was inspecting my rifle platoon as harshly as I could, and I made the mistake of calling down the sergeant in front of his men, which you never do. Then I bawled them all out for not having their brass on their rifles shined up properly, and after I was all through the sergeant said, "Excuse me, Lieutenant, but in combat we're not allowed to shine our buckles." I was humiliated. Finally I got the hang of it and we went overseas, on the first of July 1942.

We went down the Atlantic coast in a converted oceanliner. I had come back from Europe in 1939 in one of these ships, traveling first-class, and when I got back in the ship in the marine corps it was the most incredible deja vu, because the murals were still on the walls; it was still the same ship but it had been converted into a troopship with five thousand people aboard.

We didn't know the destination, not at first. It was very secret. Somebody had leaked the Solomon Islands, but we thought it was Solomon Island off Maryland. That was a place a lot of people had been on maneuvers. We were under submarine alert several times. We went through the Panama Canal, which was a great thrill, and on across the Pacific. We had some protection, but not much.

We continued to train our platoons, each of us, verbally or using blackboards. One very amusing thing happened about a week before we came to our final destination, which was Wellington, New Zealand. We were then told where we were going. Obviously there could be no security leak, and they were very concerned about this first landing of American troops in a foreign country (one of our allies). They wanted us to behave ourselves. The New Zealanders were happy to have us because of our willingness to protect their islands, but also a little nervous. All of their young men were away fighting in the desert, and to have twenty thousand marines piling into a rather old-fashioned Victorian English city, with all the young women there, I think made them a little nervous. Understandably! So we were given this very elaborate cultural lecture to deliver to our platoons about how conservative English society was. We said, "You never speak to a young woman in New Zealand, whoever she is, without being properly introduced. You don't go out without a chaperone." Well, we landed in New Zealand. I had duty so I didn't get off for about an hour. By the time I walked up the main street of Wellington, every marine had a girl on his arm. Sans introductions.

The trip across the Pacific was a great thrill to me. I'd never been in the Pacific. I was a little bit of a bird-watcher, and we had albatrosses following the ship. We went through a few tropical storms. It was really a fascinating voyage. We came into Wellington Harbor, which is one of the most beautiful harbors in the world. The entrance has two green mountains on either side. As we came in there was a rainbow across the entrance to the harbor, and we sailed under the rainbow. I'll never forget that.

We went out to a little old army camp called Paikakariki, a Maori name. The officers of our battalion occupied little wooden huts, which happened to be on the edge of a rather steep cliff. We had a kerosene lamp or two with those glass globes and a tin basin to wash in, and I also had a couple of bottles of bourbon, which we'd gotten as we went through the canal because it got very cold in New Zealand in the middle of summer.* One night I was sound asleep in my skivvy drawers—as they used to call your basic underwear— white underpants, and white T-shirt, and I woke up, thinking I was having a nightmare because I heard this incredible rumbling, which wasn't thunder. The tin basin, bourbon, and glass lamps crashed to the floor. I came awake and the whole hut started weaving back and forth. I thought I was drunk or having a dream. Without knowing what I was doing, I woke up fully, finding myself running as fast as I could across the parade ground. We were in the middle of a New Zealand earthquake.

After only two or three weeks they called us back into Wellington itself, and we went aboard a troopship there and unloaded the transports onto the dock so we could combat load them, putting what we wanted to get out of the ship on top, just like trying to pack your trunk. None of us had any training, but we had to direct this loading. I remember I was in charge of loading the front hold of a transport and showing them how to use the crane that lifted the guns and ammunition and all into it. It was pouring rain. I had a terrible case of dysentery, and I don't think I've ever had a more miserable time in my life for two or three weeks. Then, having combat loaded one way or another, we took off for the Fiji Islands for maneuvers.

In those days they did not have the LSTs and other landing craft whose bows were able to come down on the beach so you could walk ashore. They had Higgins boats, which were white lap-streaked wooden power boats about twenty-five or thirty feet long, each of which could contain a platoon. The way you used a Higgins boat, you'd drive into the beach, jump out of the cockpit over the side, and unload, which of course left you much more exposed to enemy fire than keeping underneath the sides of an LST and having the bow go down as you were ready to come in. We had been trained, thank God, very thoroughly on how to get out of a Higgins boat. One of the

*It was indeed the middle of summer for American marines—but the middle of winter in New Zealand, which is in the southern hemisphere.

128

things you had to do was to hold onto a rail around the gunwale until you found your footing, because you had on about eighty-five pounds of equipment. We came in to the Fijis and hit the coral. Half the Higgins boats were wrecked. Their propellers were crunched. The maneuver was total chaos. Some people damn near got drowned when they went over the side into twenty-five feet of water because they didn't hold on to the gunwale.

All we had was one or two days in the Fiji Islands. Then we got back on board, and as we were steaming toward our next destination, they told us where we were going and what the battle plan was to be. Our battalion was to join a Raider's battalion* and attack Tulagi, which was a small island across the gulf from Guadalcanal. The rest of the division disembarked on Guadalcanal.

As we went on our way we were protected by a few destroyers and a couple of cruisers, but each morning as we got up and looked across the sea we'd see more and more naval vessels. It was the most incredible experience, to look out at these battleships, aircraft carriers, destroyers, cruisers, transports, AKs—this enormous fleet of I suppose a hundred ships. It seemed like a thousand. It felt like the Greeks going to Troy or something. You'd read about this kind of thing. You'd studied it. But to actually see these enormous vessels, these airplanes overhead—you felt totally invincible.

There had been no attack by United States troops before this time. This was the first.

Finally, the night before the landing arrived. By this time we were anxious and excited and tense. Dawn broke. We got up in the darkness and got ready to go over the side. In those days you went down a sort of landing net, a webbing made out of stout rope which they would otherwise use to load cargo. They'd put these nets over the side and we'd use them as a rope ladder to go down into the Higgins boats. Even with a fairly medium-sized sea the Higgins boat would go up and down and the ship would go up and down, and to try to get down that swaying cargo net with about eighty pounds of equipment on your back without killing yourself or getting jammed between the Higgins boat and the ship was quite a stunt.

Each company had a rendezvous area some several hundred yards away from the troopship, into which each Higgins boat as it was loaded would come. So finally you had a group of six or eight or ten boats, a platoon each plus your weapons and your supporting platoons, going around in a circle. We were about a mile from shore, and the little rendezvous areas would be maybe half a mile from the troopship. We would be circling at different places around the ship, so as you were looking down on the ship, there's the troopship and then there are these circles of boats going around and around

*This was a battalion of marines specially trained for difficult landings in the Pacific.

129

and around, boats chasing one another's tails, in different spots around the ship. At this point it was probably H-hour minus sixty or H minus ninety minutes.

When the signal was given the navy ensign in command of the Higgins boat would take off and the boats would go in a preordained pattern towards the beach. All during this time, from dawn on, the cruisers and destroyers had been shelling the shore. We'd never seen a shot fired in anger before, and we didn't see how any animal, much less any human being, could live under this enormous barrage. On Tulagi there were very few major fortifications; it was more like a base than an armed camp. In any case, as we were coming in to the beach under the heavy explosive of shelling from the ships and bombing from the dive-bombers, the whole island was going up in smoke with enormous explosions. About five or ten miles across the gulf the same thing was happening on the shore of Guadalcanal.

Apparently we did catch the Japanese by total surprise, because we found half-eaten meals left. We were in the first wave at Tulagi. Our battalion was to go down to the jungle end of the island and cover that, while the other two companies of the Second Battalion of the Fifth Marines were to land on the settled part, which was an old British colony where the governor-general of the Solomon Islands lived in the good old days. The governor-general's residence was a rather attractive white clapboard house with lovely porches and breezes going through them. You could sit on the porches and look across the sea through the islands of the Solomon archipelago. There was a cricket field there and even a golf course. You had this strange feeling of having combat, not on the cricket fields of Eton, but on the cricket fields of Tulagi. Amazing.

Our company went down to the jungle with no resistance whatever. We heard firing in Tulagi proper, but we didn't know much what was going on. I remember walking along the jungle path. The scouts in my platoon happened to be in the lead when I heard a couple of shots go off, and as we walked along the path following them I saw this dead Japanese soldier. It was the first dead soldier that I had ever seen. That was a pretty traumatic experience. He looked to be about fifteen years old, like a nice little kid, and to see him dead there was pretty bad.

We camped that night, and we had our two-way radios and were in touch with the company headquarters and the battalion headquarters. We could hear the guns going off through the radios as well as with our ears, because we were only about a mile or two away. I could hear some of my buddies, whom I'd gone through officers' training school with, giving orders to their men to fire and talking about so-and-so being wounded and so-and-so being killed, and it was a very strange experience. Total darkness, in the middle of the jungle, hearing this battle going on where some of your friends were involved, then also hearing strange jungle noises for the first time. Whether these were birds squawking in the middle of the night or some strange reptiles or frogs, I don't know, but we were terrified by any noise whatsoever because we'd been told that the Japanese signaled each other in the jungle by imitating bird calls. So we knew we were being surrounded by them, and once in a while our men would fire. We lost two or three men in the company by that kind of tragic mistake.

In the morning we received orders to come back and to counterattack in the Tulagi area and relieve the front-line troops of the night before. By the time we got back, things were fairly secure. We passed through the front lines right by the governor-general's house, and that was the first time I saw dead marines, which was even more traumatic than seeing dead Japanese. I remember seeing a body in marine corps combat dress lying on a stretcher, and I thought he was wounded, but then I saw a fly crawling across his ear. The ear didn't move. The head didn't move. So I knew he was dead. That was my first experience of that kind.

I wasn't in any immediate combat while I was there, except when we ran into a few people in our cleanup operations.

We stayed there about two weeks. My platoon sergeant and I occupied the same poncho at night, which wasn't exactly an attractive place to sleep but nonetheless was warm. Even in the jungle it got sort of cold, at night with the rain and all.

During the first night it was pouring rain. We were on this hill, and we looked across the ocean and saw these tremendous explosions. We could even hear them. They must have been twenty or thirty miles away. This was a very intense naval battle, the Battle of the Solomons. We didn't know who was winning. We just saw the explosions. It was a little like hearing a football game without being able to see it, the roar of the crowd but not knowing who was cheering for whom.

Sunday came several days after Tulagi had been secured. It may even have been the third day, when we were still very dirty and still terribly upset by our first experience with death. The whole outfit, those who were not on duty, came down to the cricket field, and the chaplain celebrated mass. The only clean thing on that entire island was the white linen, which he had salvaged to put over the makeshift altar, and perhaps his vestments. I remember having—it sounds sentimental—but a feeling, you know, about the world being broken, sinful, full of horror, terror, filth, but God being still pure. I had a real sense of reassurance.

Every morning, as we sat there getting over being damp and wet and eating what little food we had, a Japanese submarine would take its place offshore and lob shells on Tulagi. The heaviest thing we had was an eighty-one-millimeter mortar. Every morning our gunnery sergeant, Gunny Diamond, would fire mortars at the submarine. Of course he never hit it.

In about two weeks they decided they wanted to get most of us over onto

Guadalcanal, and the ships that took us across were those APDs, destroyers converted into transports. We went over in the middle of the night, again with submarine warnings, and that was a rather scary business. We did get across, landed on the beach in the middle of the night. And I came ashore and asked about my best friend, George Mead, who roomed next to me at Yale and with whom I'd gone into the marine corps, and found out that he'd been killed. This was a particular shock because I'd understood that there was hardly any action at all. Actually, he was one of the first people who was killed. So that was another very deep blow. First you see a Japanese dead, then you see a marine dead, then you hear one of your own friends is dead. It was sort of a deepening of the hurt, if you will, of war.

As I remember, it was not just our company but the whole battalion which was the mobile reserve for the regiment. Our particular outfit was on the move all the time—first we were on Tulagi, then we were moved over to Henderson Field, and then within a few days there was a counterattack by those Japanese who were still there, on so-called Bloody Ridge, where a Raider battalion was dug in. It was the first big battle of Guadalcanal itself, and our troops resisted it, but the Japs almost broke through to Henderson Field and so our battalion was rushed up the second night to support this unit.

One thing I noticed was the relationship between being in one place and emotional stability. Even though our platoon hadn't had as many days of combat as some of the other outfits, we were always on the move. We never had a chance to really make our foxhole our home. If a marine can dig his foxhole, and dig out a little shelf for his canteen and another little shelf to put a photograph of his girlfriend on, have a little shelter of palm trees to keep the sun off, and make a little home for himself, it makes a tremendous difference to his emotional stability. Again, I remember some of the shock. People were surprised at the My Lai Massacre. Well, I was not surprised.

There was a very senior officer who decided that one of the best ways to keep the Japanese from attacking us was to put Japanese bodies in foxholes in front of our lines, so as the Japanese troops came up the hill they would see the bodies of their friends, dead, facing them. If a body is dead twenty-four hours in the tropical sun, it begins to become bloated. Well, that's pretty hairy. And even worse, in a way, was the glee with which this officer did this.

The second night the Japanese did attack again and we were thrown into combat, which merely amounted to holding the line against some fairly light Japanese fire. Our artillery company did a fantastic job. The artillery almost sounded like machine guns; the rapidity with which the company was able to cover up our front with fire is something I shall never forget. The strange thing was that after the battle was over, one of my men flipped and went into total hysterics, screaming and yelling in the middle of the night. We were not allowed to have any lights when we were occupying the jungle. There was no moon that night. There were no stars either, so there was absolutely impenetrable darkness. You literally couldn't see your hand in front of your face. The only way I could inspect the lines during the night was by the use of a line along the front, just behind the barbed wire. I had to follow the line with my hand in order to find my way and whisper to where I thought my men were to make sure they were okay. Well, right in the middle of such a night, dead silence except for these weird noises from the animals—a *wa-wa-wa* kind of sound—you heard this man screaming, obviously in hysterics. I didn't know whether a Japanese had snuck through the wire and knifed him to death or what. It turned out this guy went absolutely out of his mind. He got over it and is now a very successful businessman in the Middle West whom I see from time to time.

There was a similar incident later on. We had a weapons platoon attached to my rifle platoon to reinforce our line. Each squad had an automatic rifle, so we had three BARs and some rifle grenades. Otherwise it was just the 1903 bolt-action Springfield. I had a .45 Colt myself. I just read in the paper the other day they're no longer to be used. About forty-five years later. In any case, I didn't know the men in the weapons platoon because they weren't part of my own outfit. But in the middle of the night the sergeant in charge of the platoon went crazy, and he continued that way during the daytime. He had a hand grenade from which he'd already pulled the pin in his hand, and he said, "If anyone comes near me, I will throw this grenade." So there he was, I can still see him, a rather Slavic face, sitting down with his back against a tree, holding his hand grenade very tensely, and a very demented expression on his face. He said, "Furthermore, if you report me to headquarters, I will let the grenade go." So there I was and two or three of my men, surrounding this guy, not allowed by him to report. After a while I made some lame excuse, which I wasn't sure he would accept, but he was too upset to be thinking very clearly, and I slipped out, back to the company phone, and phoned in. His own platoon leader and sergeant came up, and finally we persuaded him to surrender the grenade and give himself up, and he went to the aid station.

This kind of thing happened all the time. There was a high incidence of it. I had three or four men who went crazy in my platoon, which was fifteen percent, you might say, and this was true of the other platoons in my company. A much higher percent even than those troops had that had been in more combat. And though it was not a scientific experiment, it seemed to me there was a direct relationship between this and the fact that we were moving all the time.

After Bloody Ridge we were put into another emplacement at the other end of the line. We had a position on the semicircle reaching from one beach around Henderson Field and anchoring itself on the shoreline at the other end. By that time malaria had begun to take its toll, and we were trying to get our men relieved because the high fever means you're not very competent or alert. In those days you were taking quinine, which made your ears ring and therefore you couldn't hear well. I tried to get some of my men relieved, and the word went out that unless somebody's temperature was over 105 degrees they would not be relieved. So you had these men in the foxholes, shaking with fever, ears ringing, trying to hold the line in total darkness, with strange sounds coming out of the jungle. It was really an incredible situation, morale-wise.

One of our experiences was being subjected to the shelling of the Japanese battleships. They had these huge guns. Being shelled by naval gunfire to me was far more terrifying than being bombed or being shelled by artillery. You would hear these shells going overhead just like a subway, with an enormous roar and rattle, and you would just roll out of bed and cling to the floor. By the time you got to a foxhole it would be too late. Also, every day at noon a flight of high-flying Japanese bombers would come over. At about eleven o'clock we would see our F-4Fs, Grumman fighters, go up to fight the Japanese bombers. Then at twelve you'd look up and you'd see this flight of bombers, barely visible in the sky, almost slipping through the clouds. Then you'd see puffs of smoke and this aerial battle, right over your head, between our planes and the pursuit planes that were covering the Japanese bombers. They'd drop these bombs, not very accurately, but when they hit the ground the whole island would just shake up and down.

I remember one day sitting on a hillside far outside our home lines, and we could see the entire coast of Guadalcanal from where we sat. At Cape Esperance there were troopships unloading without anybody interfering with them—five or six, it seemed. You could see the little boats going back and forth to the shore with Japanese troops. We saw Japanese naval vessels sailing up and down the harbor, Iron Bottom Bay, between Tulagi and Guadalcanal, shelling at will. Then I looked up—I heard a plane going along strafing across the top of the jungle—and I looked up and saw this great red circle on the plane. So at that point we thought we had had it, totally, completely, because we'd heard the navy had been sunk. The evidence was before us. Henderson Field was out of operation. We'd read about Bataan, and the orders were being drawn up at that time for us to go off into the jungle for another Bataan, if indeed we did lose, if the battle fell to the Japanese.

I was in one of the battles at the Matanikau River. It was a jungle river about two hundred yards wide where it emptied into the bay. The Matanikau was outside our lines, and for a long time there was sort of a seesaw between the Japanese troops and our own—sometimes the Matanikau was ours, sometimes it was theirs. So from time to time troops would be sent out to try to secure the river. I went out there on patrol, coming at it from inland with our company. I was responsible for leading seven hundred men single file through this impenetrable jungle, with machetes and a compass. Compasses are fine, but if you can only focus on about ten yards ahead of you, you don't find one of much value. I pictured myself going in a slow concentric circle at the head of the whole line. (One time that did happen. A friend of mine got shot by one of his men because his part of the line had doubled back without realizing it.) When we got within maybe a tenth of a mile of the coast, we heard this battle going on, because another unit had gone up the beach, tried to cross the Matanikau, and was being thrown back by the Japanese.

Lieutenant Colonel Lewis ("Chesty") Puller was in charge of this operation, and his tactics were to send one platoon after another across a totally exposed sandspit which closed off one end of the river. The river came down toward the ocean, to the sandspit, and then branched off toward its left bank, while the sandspit ran parallel to the shore. The order given to each of these platoons was to run across the sandspit until they were opposite the bank, wade across the river, and attack the Japanese battalion, which was dug in with automatic weapons and hand grenades and mortars in the bank. We in turn would get support fire from machine guns and mortars from our own troops. Well, one platoon went over and got annihilated. Another platoon went over and got annihilated. Then another. We were lined up just behind the shore, ready to go. Ours was the fifth platoon to go over, and you know, we all realized it was insane. We heard what had happened to the other platoons. But if you're a marine, you're ordered across the goddamn beach and you go. So we went, and we ran across this in defilade on the ocean side of the sandspit, zigzagging and running as best we could so that we wouldn't be exposed, and finally we lined up along the ocean side of the sandspit, just peeking over the top, with our weapons trained on the embankment across this little river. And the idea was that you would send scouts to draw fire and show where the weapons were. Then you would cover your own attack with your two automatic rifles, which were at either flank of this deployed line of fire. You would call for fire from the machine guns and mortars from the other side of the river, and then you would have a frontal attack on the Japanese. The intelligence was that we could wade across. Well, our two scouts went out and found the water over their heads. So here you had these two guys swimming across the river against a battalion of Japanese soldiers.

Art Beres, one of my corporals, got to the opposite bank. I remember him holding on to a root, with the bank about a foot over him, and when he turned around I saw his whole face had been shot away. Two other guys had been killed at that particular moment, and I went across to get Art so he could be brought back. He was swimming. But by that time I'd called for us to attack (even though we were swimming we were told to attack, so we attacked). First of all I retrieved Art, who was there with his face bleeding, and got him back so that he could get behind the sandspit and be protected until he could be taken to the aid station. Then I turned around to continue swimming across the river with the rest of my platoon, and I remember—this sounds absolutely impossible but it actually happened—looking up and seeing mortars and hand grenades going over my head and the water as if it were raining, with bullets striking all around us. I guess we got almost to the opposite bank and at that point realized two or three people had been killed, two or three others wounded, and there was just no way we could do it, so I called for retreat. We ran back, we swam back, and when we got to the bank I found two men who were unconscious on the beach. I and another fellow looked to see how they were and found out both of them were dead. So we just left them there and ran back to the protection of the sandspit. I remember when I was leaning over trying to bring one of my men to safety seeing bullet marks in the sand around my feet and thinking, you know, if I get out of this, maybe it means I should do something special. There was a feeling—I don't know if it's very good theology, whether it's superstition or what, but certainly I felt that I had been extremely fortunate, and that I was, in a sense, living on borrowed time, and that this was another good reason to give my life to the Lord, and it seemed that being a priest was the way.

Well, the ironic thing to me was that when I got back, I asked if I could see Colonel Puller, just to report to him what had happened. I wasn't particularly proud of the fact that we had retreated, but it seemed to be the necessary thing to do. Otherwise we would all have been killed and the emplacement still would not have been taken. I can still see him. He had a fat belly. He was sitting under a coconut tree. I came up to him and said, "Lieutenant Moore reporting, sir." I saluted and told him that I'd just started the platoon across and what had happened, what I saw of the Japanese emplacements. He not only didn't answer me, he didn't even turn his head to speak to me. It's as if I hadn't been there. After a while I just left.

We did not get across the Matanikau River at that point. We fell back to our lines on the perimeter of the airfield.

My old friend Jerry Knapp from Yale came up to the lines to visit me, and he was full of excitement because he was going to be sent home in another week. He flew a torpedo bomber. We envied him because he told us we were about to go into another attack, and he was sympathetic. But it turned out that the next day he was shot down.

We took off the next morning and went up again to the Matanikau River, but this time we went across way up in the headwaters where there wasn't any resistance. The idea was to go around the enemy's flank and then come down to the beach and cut off the rear of the Japanese, who were entrenched on the bank of the river.

Morale was very bad. But there was something about marines—once we were ordered to attack we decided we damn well were going to do it, so we did get ourselves together, and by the time we took off we were all right. You're very nervous before you go in, of course, like before a football game or whatever. But once you get in it—at least as far as I was concerned, and apparently this was true of a lot of other people I've talked to—your psyche gets sort of numbed, and therefore you can do acts of bravery, so-called, without necessarily having to be very brave. You just do them because in the excitement of combat you see this is the thing you're supposed to do, and you do it. It isn't making a decision that requires an enormous amount of courage. Those platoons that were not very well disciplined in that way were the ones that fell apart. Also, once you get into the excitement of the action you tend to forget about being vulnerable. When the machine-gun nest needed to have a hand grenade, I got up and threw the hand grenade, without timidity, though obviously it made me very vulnerable. I'm fairly tall even on my knees, and I got up and threw it, and as I threw it, got shot.

I received the Navy Cross for that, my part in that operation. But it really wasn't any great act of bravery. Some of the more extraordinary heroic actions that take place in combat, I think, are understandable. You read about them and say, "Oh, my God, I would never do that!" But when you get in combat you do it without thinking too much about it. You do it automatically. And the flip side of the coin is the brutality, the imperviousness to killing other people, even brutally; some of the people, I think, become sort of sadistic. Also the fact of being fairly impervious to the death of your colleagues—not that you don't regret it, and not that you aren't trying to prevent it and care for them, but you don't burst into tears when you see this guy you've worked with for a few months lying there dead. "So he's dead. I wonder who I'll get to replace him, to take his place on the line?"

To get back to the Matanikau, we did get through to the ocean right behind Point Cruz without much resistance. The Japanese were clustered up around the Matanikau, and there were reinforcements down in the other direction, but there was a very thin line between these two clusters of troops, so we came down to the river that first day without any resistance. That was a very weird day. It was extremely hot. We'd run out of water. There wasn't enough wire to have a forward observation post for the artillery where we were, so part of our assignment was sitting out in the very hot sun, guiding the shelling of the Japanese position by the artillery.

There was a road going along the beach, and next to that road was a foxhole. I remember the artillery would fire and I'd spot where the shell landed, on either this side or that side of an artillery piece which I could see set up on the road about 250 yards down from where I was, and I'd wait until the shell landed, jump out of the foxhole to see where the explosion was, and then jump back in again and relay through word of mouth, all the way up to where the observation post for the artillery was, that it had landed to the right or left of the target, or whether it was short or what.

As soon as I popped back down in the hole, there would be an explosion just where I'd been standing, because the Japanese artillery would have fired on me. But they would get there too late. So you'd hear the whistling of your own artillery shells going over and wait till they got so close to the Japanese that they had to go into their foxhole. The explosion occurred. You jumped out of your foxhole to see where the explosion was and then jumped back just in time to keep the Japanese from landing theirs. Playing Russian roulette. So that was a rather exciting day. Oddly enough, one became quite immune to danger. I remember having left my cigarettes out in a rather exposed area. Nobody else had any cigarettes; they were a very precious commodity at that point. And running out to get the cigarettes totally exposed to enemy fire. Just for a silly pack of cigarettes, an absolutely crazy thing to do. Everybody thought I was out of my mind. But not much. I also remember having to drink out of a stagnant pool of water. I think we had fresh water back at the camp but our canteens were dry.

We went back that night and camped again up the hill, and the next day we got ready for a full-fledged attack to establish a beachhead rather than just coming down and withdrawing as we had.

This was on the third of November 1942. We came down the line of skirmishers. One person would walk abreast of another, not actually walking but crawling and then some jumping up and running and hitting the deck behind a log or in some protected place—the front platoons would advance in that fashion. We had some supporting artillery before we went down, some mortar fire, and then we had automatic weapons giving us fire cover as we advanced toward the beach. We got within a hundred yards of the beach, just short of the road I've been talking about, but this time we were advancing against heavy enemy resistance. It was a rather open area, with just a log or two here or there, and so my men started getting lacerated by machine guns, Japanese machine guns. I lost four or five men and two or three others were wounded, so the platoon was down to about seven men at this point, and the platoon sergeant and I were still going.

Finally it became clear that we had to do something about the machine guns, so I got up and threw a hand grenade into the machine-gun nest and, as I ducked back, got shot. Although I was shot I was not unconscious. The bullet—it turned out to be a .25-caliber bullet, so it may have been a rifle shot, not a machine gun—came through my chest between two ribs, slightly shattering them, went past my heart, as the doctors later told me, when it must have been on an inbeat instead of an outbeat, and then missed my backbone as it went through the other side of my body about an inch. So it was a very close shave. In any case, I was conscious enough to make sure the platoon sergeant knew that I was wounded and out of action. I gave the command over to him, and I sort of slumped down on the ground. The air was going in and out of a hole in my lungs. That didn't mean I was finished, but I thought I was dead, going to die right then, because I thought if that happened you were gone. I wasn't breathing through my mouth but through this hole. It felt like a balloon going in and out, going *pshhhh*.

I was thinking to myself, Now I'm going to die. And first of all it's rather absurd for me, considering where I came from, my early expectations of a comfortable life and all the rest, sort of absurd for me to be dying on a jungle island in combat as a marine. That's not me. I thought that was sort of funny. Then the next thought was, What are you supposed to be thinking about when you're dying? You're supposed to be thinking about your whole life. It's supposed to go before your mind. And I couldn't summon up much of my life. Then I thought, Oh, my goodness, I'd better say my prayers, because that's also what you're supposed to do, so I made a confession, as it were, in my mind. I may even have said a prayer or two, asked God's forgiveness, commended myself to God. And then I also was still concerned about what was going on in the battle around me.

To say what did happen, the skirmishers went on down to the beach and wound up in a bayonet fight with the Japanese, whom they finally pushed back into the sea. Others were killed. There was a terrible slaughter of Japanese and the battle was finally concluded.

Shortly, a wonderful corpsman crawled up and gave me a shot of morphine, and then a couple of other people got a stretcher and started evacuating me. The morphine didn't put me out but it deadened the pain. I was by that time in a sort of semishock. Luckily by that time the mouth of the Matanikau River had been secured and a bridge built, and the road was open along the beach back to our regimental headquarters, so I didn't have to be carried by stretcher back over the hill. If I had, I probably wouldn't have made it. I was bleeding pretty badly. At Henderson Field they had deep dugouts for the wounded. During the daytime, when there was little air activity, we were put in tents, which were rather pleasant, on bunks and relatively comfortable army cots, and we had good first aid, medical attention, enough morphine to keep us out of pain. I spent the night in a dugout, then the next day I was flown out. That night I'll never forget, because in this dugout, which I remember was about ten feet deep and about twenty feet square, the wounded were packed just like sardines, and it was terribly hot, there was bad ventilation, terrible smells, and these poor guys were yelling and screaming all night. That was a real horror story. The next morning a plane was able to get in, and they put us aboard and flew us back to Espíritu Santo, a navy medical hospital. I think it was called Mob 4.

One of the problems was that we had to fly at the highest possible altitude so that we would not be an easy target for Japanese planes that might see us go by and come up off the ground to get us. I had a terrible time because I was only operating on one lung at that point. I remember that flight as being very painful and also a little bit frightening, because we were in a transport and an easy target for attack. I don't remember how long it took, probably two or three hours, and I was put in a medical hospital at Espíritu Santo, which was really very luxurious compared to where we'd been for three months. There were nice Quonset huts. There was a lot of air, good medical attention, a sense of security, so it was a tremendous relief to be there.

We'd been there about two weeks waiting for the USS *Solace,* the hospital ship, to come, and we'd heard these perfectly marvelous stories about how comfortable the hospital ship was. You'd get ice cream and decent food and a bath and all that sort of thing, and we were all enormously excited at the prospect. The *Solace* came on my birthday, November the fifteenth, 1942—I guess it was my twenty-third birthday—and I thought, what a wonderful birthday present, to have the hospital ship come! You could actually see it, through the end of the Quonset hut, anchored in the harbor. And they came and started taking the guys out one by one, down to the hospital ship. Well, they called the different names and one after another left, and there were only half of us there, then just a third of us, then just two or three of us, and finally I was the only one left—and they never came and got me. And I looked out of the window and saw the *Solace* sailing away without me, on my birthday! That was the worst birthday I ever had. I never really found out why. I think there were only two possible reasons. One was, they just made a mistake and forgot me. That's possible. The other was that my wound was such that they wanted to keep me there. But I don't know why a ride out to the hospital ship, where I would have gotten excellent care with medical equipment and all, would have set me back. So I was there another ten days or two weeks and a whole bunch of guys came in, and the next time the *Solace* came, by God, I was on it, and they took me out. I think if they hadn't they would have had a mutiny on their hands.

They took us out on an LST, a rather large tender, and then we were lifted on board by a crane. It was lowered and a rope like a pulley came down from a crane or a winch and fastened around our stretchers, and then we were lifted through the air and put onto the deck. That was quite a terrifying thing. But we were so glad to get on board that it didn't really matter. Then we had a few days of total luxury on the *Solace.* Meanwhile I was beginning to feel a little bit better. By the time we got down to Auckland, New Zealand, I was really recovering. I don't remember whether the wound had totally healed, but they plugged it up anyway and I think it was beginning to heal over.

The worst thing that happened was that after I'd been there a few days I got a lung abscess, and my temperature shot way up again and I became very, very sick. I was on the danger list. I know I was put in a room by myself, in what we call intensive care now.

My doctor apparently hadn't had the sense to have me get rid of the abscess fluid. It began to fill my lungs, and when his boss came in he was horrified that this fluid had been allowed to stay in my lungs. He said he would either have to operate or I'd have to cough it up, so I opted for the latter, and I had this terrible experience of coughing up all the fluid. Not a very attractive story. Once I got rid of that, they gave me some sulfa because I was allergic to penicillin, and that, plus getting rid of the fluid, put me on the road to recovery.

140

And the next event I remember was Christmas, when we were shown Bing Crosby's "White Christmas," the movie, and that was a real tearjerker for people thousands of miles from home, believe me. And then some nice ladies came in and sang Christmas carols to us and brought us flowers and candy and shaving cream, and I remember the first time I cried a little bit was when I heard those Christmas carols.

The story of the coastwatchers in the Pacific should rightfully be presented in two chapters. In the early part of the war, it was the coastwatchers in the Solomons whose activities had a bearing on the outcome of the conflict, whose heroic efforts led Halsey to exclaim after the American victory, "The coastwatchers saved Guadalcanal and Guadalcanal saved the Pacific." Later on, it was the men in the Philippines who made their own special contributions to the war effort. Their work and complexion differed from those of their Solomons forebears.

Who, first of all, were the people in the Solomons? They were Australians and Americans, they were British plantation owners and missionaries, they were friendly natives and adventurous volunteers from wherever—people who lived and worked in the islands before the war engulfed them. All were engaged to differing degrees in a network that gathered intelligence on the movements of the enemy, his whereabouts and strength, the status and number of his ships and planes. They often gave advance notice of pending raids by Japanese planes flying down "the Slot" from Rabaul to Guadalcanal and the southern islands in the chain.*

The coastwatchers in the Solomons lived with few creature comforts and without most of the modern means of communication, but they were more than willing to share their meager supplies and equipment with downed pilots or shipwrecked sailors. For the most part they were hunted people, under imminent sentence of death if discovered. But danger only seemed to enhance their courage and heighten their purpose. The tales of their successes and failures are legendary. The one most familiar to Americans is the role they played in the rescue of John F. Kennedy in the Solomons. He was participating in motor-torpedo-boat

---

*The seven large islands of the Solomon group, which runs southeasterly from Rabaul for about six hundred miles, form two columns. Between these columns there is a wide, deep-water channel that Japanese warships and planes traveled down on their way to Guadalcanal. U.S. sailors came to call this channel the Slot. Coastwatchers stationed on various islands along the Slot would radio the progress of Japanese vessels and aircraft to U.S. military authorities.

actions in the New Georgia campaign (23 July–2 August 1943) when his boat was rammed by a Japanese destroyer and cut in two. He and some of his crew found temporary safety on a small island. Friendly natives delivered a message for them on a coconut shell to the coastwatcher on another island, and he in turn dispatched a native war canoe to rescue them. Kennedy and his surviving men eventually reached the motor-torpedo-boat base on Rendova Island.

The coastwatchers in the Philippines were equally heroic, but they were different in purpose, makeup, and mission. Not all of the many islands of the Philippines were occupied by the Japanese invaders, and on some of the unoccupied ones there were guerrilla coastwatchers, often with a "liberation army" of native Filipinos serving under them. Their existence was not as lonely or destitute as that of their counterparts in the Solomons. They had radios and were better equipped with weapons and food. But one thing was not different. The coastwatchers of the Philippines were under just as severe a threat of discovery and instant death.

Some of these people were well-educated American businessmen and military personnel stationed in the Philippines before the war began—people who had, by some miracle or ingenious application of wit, escaped through Japanese lines and established themselves in outlying areas, where they were in position to help the Allied cause. In many instances their ranks were swelled by native Filipinos willing to risk their lives for the independence of their homeland.

Often their needs were supplied by U.S. submarines under the overall command of General MacArthur and Admiral Thomas Kinkaid of the Seventh Fleet. MacArthur in particular had an intensely personal interest in their efforts. He may well have been influenced by his earlier knowledge of the work of the coastwatchers in the Solomons, where he also had a command. While his headquarters were still in Brisbane, Australia, and he was contemplating his campaign to regain the Philippines, he recruited a highly skilled, knowledgeable American with years of experience in the Philippines, Charles Parsons, to act as liaison between his command and the coastwatchers in the islands. These men often received specific instructions about the kind of information needed by the fleet. Often they were asked to report on the passage of Japanese naval vessels or on their use of island harbors.

At any rate, we have in the following excerpt a sample of the deeds of some of the coastwatchers in the Philippines. The story is told by Rear Admiral Arthur H. McCollum, who after a number of years in the Office of Naval Intelligence in Washington became intelligence officer in the southwest Pacific with additional duty on the staff of Admiral Kinkaid, Commander in Chief, Seventh Fleet. McCollum served in the southwest Pacific from November 1942 to April 1945. He had direct relations with many of the coastwatchers in the Philippines. In fact, he often trained them to provide the kind of information the naval forces wanted badly. Sometimes he recruited men established in the various islands, especially the strategic ones, whose presence and willingness to serve came to his attention. He had great praise for what these people contributed to the effort of liberating the Philippines.

COASTWATCHERS IN THE PHILIPPINES

REAR ADMIRAL ARTHUR H. McCOLLUM

ARTHUR HOWARD McCOLLUM was born in Nagasaki, Japan, on 4 August 1898. He graduated from the U.S. Naval Academy in 1921 and was selected for three years of study in Japan, where he concentrated on language and Oriental history and culture. In 1925 he attended the submarine school in New London, Connecticut.

McCollum was proud of the fact that during his career he served in almost every type of naval ship; he commanded a submarine, a destroyer, and a heavy cruiser as well as groups and squadrons of ships. His primary career was, however, in naval intelligence. He served as head of the Far East section of the Office of Naval Intelligence; as assistant naval attaché to the American embassy in Tokyo; and as fleet intelligence officer on the staff of Commander in Chief, U.S. Fleet (1936–38). He developed the concept of fleet intelligence centers and designed and assisted in the installation of the first one at Pearl Harbor in 1942. From November 1942 to May 1945 he was director of Allied Naval Intelligence, Southwest Pacific; assistant chief of staff for Intelligence, Seventh Fleet; and commanding officer of the Seventh Fleet Intelligence Center. Starting with no assistants, he developed an intelligence organization for naval campaigns throughout the Pacific and collaborated closely with General Douglas MacArthur and Allied forces. After World War II he was assigned to duty with the Central Intelligence Group, later called the Central Intelligence Agency. Following duty at sea he was ordered to New York to organize and later command the Military Sea Transportation Service in the Atlantic.

146

McCollum retired in 1951 as a rear admiral but was recalled to active duty as a consultant to the Central Intelligence Agency, which he served until 31 October 1953. He lived in Arlington, Virginia, until his death on 1 April, 1976.

This coastwatching is a funny thing. You have to pick out the places that are valuable from a naval point of view so that you can observe what is going on and report. The observing and reporting are crucial. If your watcher gets involved in something like guerrilla warfare he quickly spoils his usefulness as an observer and as a reporter.

It was precisely this situation that developed on the island of Mindoro.* It is strategically situated at one of the edges of the Apo East Pass. The pass goes round the northern end of Mindoro, skirts the southern coast of Luzon, and flows into what is called the Sibuyan Sea. It is a fairly narrow passage and a rather crooked one, not suited for the passage of a large number of large ships. Most of the time they go around the southern part of Mindoro, come up north into the Sibuyan Sea, and then go across to the San Bernardino Strait, between the islands of Samar and Luzon. In the old days, before the war, our transports going to and from Manila nearly always went through the San Bernardino Strait.

We had a number of places in the area that needed to be covered by coastwatchers. It was necessary to have a rather intimate knowledge of the geography there. The ocean or the sea is by no means a smooth stretch of blue water. The ocean floor's got all kinds of wrinkles, and some of those wrinkles will take the bottom out of a ship quite easily. So in a place like the South China Sea or adjacent areas you have what amounts to traveled highways.

The Palawan Passage has to the left of it a rather large area that is known as Dangerous Ground, about fifty miles or so in diameter. It is uncharted, full of reefs. Our people said the Japanese knew all about it. They didn't. They avoided it just as we did. They routed their commercial traffic and their naval traffic up from Singapore along the north coast of Borneo. They would refuel at places like Brunei Bay or Miri on the north coast. Then they would swing up through the Palawan Passage, which is narrow, only twenty to twenty-five miles wide. The Japanese didn't go into the so-called Dangerous Ground any more than we did. All this bushwa about how the Japanese had better charts

---

*Because McCollum had duty both with the Southwest Pacific Force (MacArthur) and with the U.S. Seventh Fleet, it is difficult to pinpoint his location at any given time during the period of events narrated. MacArthur's headquarters advanced north as the campaign in the Solomons progressed, and Admiral Kinkaid had headquarters in his flagship as well as a separate command headquarters at sea.

is sheer nonsense. They didn't. Our charts were as good or better than theirs. We compared them.

So you had to tell the coastwatchers what to watch for and where to watch. You had to prep them.

The Apo East Pass was observed from the island of Mindoro. Now, we had sent in at least one coastwatching party there and the Japanese butchered them, largely because these people, instead of tending to their knitting and observing, had found it much more fun to raid villages and do a little murder and looting on the side. This business of just counting things and reporting was pretty dull, you know. The other was much more fun. If these people got to be too much of a nuisance, the Japanese, occupying the island, would knock them off.

When you sent in a party for the purpose of watching and reporting, you had to depend on the local population. They knew these coastwatchers were there, and if any of the locals reported to the Japanese, the party you sent in was certainly in danger. It was as simple as that. So if your people made the locals mad, or if the locals got the idea that the presence of the watchers was likely to call the Japanese down on them for harboring the enemy, the coastwatchers would not last very long. That was what happened to the first party we put in there. They got into the guerrilla business and were boasting about how hot they were and how many Japanese they had killed. We kept telling them, "Don't kill the Japanese." But they continued to do just that and as a result were shot down by a Japanese patrol.

A lot of the men who volunteered as coastwatchers had been in business in the Philippines and were anxious to get back. We had a fellow named Powers, a lieutenant commander in the reserve, who had landed on Mindoro under strict instructions. I briefed him myself. I said to him, "Lay off this business of going back to Manila. Your job is to watch that Apo East Pass. Develop an observation network and give us the information. That is all that is required. I don't want you to go anywhere near Manila."

The guy had a Filipino wife. That I found out later, but I did not know at the time or I would not have sent him in. His one great desire was to get back to the little woman, who lived in Manila. As a result of that, instead of covering the Apo East Pass, as he should have been doing, Powers was fooling around with the Verde Island passage up north. That passage was of little consequence to our cause. But it is not very far from Manila, and his whole purpose was to get to Manila. Of course, all he did when he got there was to compromise the people. He and his group caused our observers in Manila to be murdered by the Japanese. Agents of the Japanese turned out to be friends of some of Powers' friends, and the result was disastrous.

The difficulty is that these fellows we sent to the Philippines were there on the ground and on the spot. Rightly, I suppose, they felt they knew more about the actual situation than we did, sitting back at some remote headquarters in Australia. In a sense they were right.

There was a Filipino sergeant who was a career soldier in the Philippine army, the old Philippine Scouts. His name was Corpus. His native place was Palawan Island, and he was picked for the job of watching there. He was a very dedicated person. We put him ashore with instructions to keep the Balabac Strait, at the southern end of the island, under observation and to report. He had a radio and other equipment with him.

He had not been there very long, was just in the process of getting himself set up with his communications, when the *Robalo*, one of our submarines that was running the Balabac Strait, was sunk. We knew the strait had been mined. We had charts showing the minefields. They were contact mines and were rather widely spaced. The *Robalo* hit one and was sunk. She went down with all hands except the bridge personnel, which was typical of submarine losses. Captain Kimmel (son of the admiral) and two or three others on the bridge at the time survived.

Corpus heard about the sinking and reported it to us. Then he took off to see if he could rescue the survivors. But the Japanese patrol got to them first. After a certain amount of torture the patrol executed the men. Corpus was extremely upset. Judging from his radio messages to us, he just kind of went off the beam. He had been given this challenge and he failed. I sent several coastwatchers and together we tried to tell him to calm down. But the guy committed suicide. It was a typical Asiatic reaction. "I have failed in my trust and all I can do is to offer my life in exchange." So he did. And of course we lost our outlook on the Balabac Strait.

We sent another coastwatcher down to an island in the Sulu Archipelago called Tawitawi. It has a beautiful natural harbor. I've never been there, but I had read about it at the Naval War College. It was thought we might do something with it some day. So we put an observer on Tawitawi. Day after day he'd sit up in the top of a coconut tree and look out on this beautiful harbor. Day after day he would report nothing in the harbor. Finally it was evident that the guy was going downhill. He was getting stir crazy. At last he said, "Get me out of here. I can't take it any longer. Get me out of this place. Nothing is happening here." It was just at the time that MacArthur was about to land at Hollandia. I was telling the operations officer on the staff to rush a submarine up to observe the entrance to Tawitawi and at the same time to pick up this observer and get him off the island, because he was going slowly nuts. And then the next thing we knew, the coastwatcher's radio blew with, "My God, the whole Jap fleet's in here." The whole Jap fleet was in the harbor—aircraft carriers, battleships, the works.

The Japs were moving into the harbor at Tawitawi as we were taking Hollandia and getting ready to go to the next objective up the line, which was

Morotai. Their move was an ideal one for them, because from Tawitawi you can come down along the north coast of New Guinea. Our submarine very fortunately had got on the scene, and so he was able to report this development.

Some time before this, as preparation for the movement of this step-by-step operation, we had landed the Forty-first Army Division under a very fine general on Biak Island. As frequently happens in the first blush, this army had overrun the Japanese defenses. We didn't know it at the time, but one of the things they had overrun was a Japanese navy cryptographic-distribution station on Biak. Our troops didn't know what they had run into, but the Japanese lieutenant in command of this station reported to Tokyo at once that all of the codes and ciphers had been compromised because they had been overrun by American troops.

Well, in May 1944 this Japanese fleet came steaming down from the north and stopped in the harbor of Tawitawi. There wasn't any question in my mind that they were heading right for us, so we girded up our strength and sent four cruisers and six destroyers to meet the whole damned Jap fleet. That's all we could do. All of a sudden that Jap fleet was heading right for Hollandia—there was no question about it—and then as suddenly they turned and headed north. In reconstructing the pattern of events, we know that Spruance's naval forces had struck at Saipan, and as a result orders had been changed by Tokyo. I suppose that we in the New Guinea area were saved by the timely attack on Saipan.

By this time there was a babble of plain-language Japanese on the radio waves. These plain-language messages could be said to be an intelligence officer's dream, but there were so many messages you didn't know what to think about them. Japanese ships were at sea when Tokyo stupidly ordered a change in the cryptographic system so that they would not be using the one compromised at Biak. But most of the ships already at sea did not have the new cryptographic system. So you had the Japanese command trying to give orders in a cryptographic system that nobody knew. The result was they broke down and went into plain language. That was what led to the so-called Marianas Turkey Shoot.*

I remember a contact we developed on the southern end of the Legaspi Peninsula. This peninsula is the prong that comes down from Luzon to cover the north side of San Bernardino Strait, near the island of Samar. There are a couple of other islands in there. We finally made contact with this man, who had been trying to make contact with us. His name was Julian Flor. He had been a machinist's mate, first class, in the navy and had duty at the Cavite

---

*See the accounts of this action given by Rear Admiral Carl J. Moore (page 214) and Vice Admiral Bernard Strean (page 218).

Navy Yard. He was a Filipino, an enlisted man who apparently was quite good as a machinist's mate. I thought this was a gold mine. Here was a guy, navy and so on, who would take orders and obey them.

We began to send messages to him and he would reply, "Nothing to report, sir." The message would be signed "Julian Flor, major general commanding the Legaspi Liberation Army, machinist's mate, first class, U.S. Navy." It so happened that after the Japanese had occupied the Philippines they frequently turned Filipinos like this man loose. Flor's brother had been the governor of Legaspi Province, so Flor went down there and organized a little army—a liberation army, they called it. They didn't do much fighting and they didn't intend to. But Flor did a beautiful job of reporting. And there is a sequel to his story.

After we had landed at Leyte and gone in there, we established a sort of naval base command ashore. The Filipinos were flocking in. We had a fellow who was an old, old-timer. He was probably a retired chief yeoman who had been filing papers for years and was very good at it. The reserve officer commanding the naval base ashore stood in awe of this old salt.

I had assigned an intelligence officer to Leyte to help out with the distribution of maps and charts there. He came to see me and said, "I know that you've been worried about the lack of reports from the Legaspi Peninsula." He was right, I had been, for Flor had not been in contact for some time. And then he said to me, "Do you know where your man, Julian Flor, is?"

"No," I responded, "but I would wring his neck if I could catch him."

"Well," said he, "he is right over here in the naval base. He's repairing motor launches. He is a machinist's mate, first class, so he has been assigned to repair motor launches."

And then I exclaimed, "For goodness sake, what the hell is all this nonsense?"

Then the intelligence officer told me he had talked to the commander at the naval base and told him about Flor's services for me. The commander said he couldn't do anything about returning Flor to Legaspi. They had to get all the papers signed. They had to make certain about his identification and so on and so forth. It was a personnel matter.

I said, "Well, I want him to get the hell back up to the Legaspi Peninsula and report from up there."

My intelligence officer said he had told the commander that Flor should get back up to the Legaspi Peninsula, but it didn't make any impression. "Perhaps," said he, "you can come over and spring this character."

I went over and talked to the commander. He had graduated with me at the Naval Academy but had not been commissioned because of bad eyes, so he had become a banker and was quite successful. He was really in awe of the one-time chief yeoman, who had to sign the papers, and wouldn't help me.

I went myself to talk to the old salt, the chief, about Flor. He said, "Captain, we can't spring this fellow. We have got to have papers made out."

And I countered with, "Well, make the damned papers out and get rid of him. I need him now."

"I'm sorry, sir, I can't do it. When they come in here they have got to have a white paper, a pink paper, and a green paper. I have to make out all three of them. And I don't have any green paper."

So I said, "Suppose I give you an order to have this guy report to the flagship, to the admiral. I can give you that verbal order now."

"No, sir, I would have to have a radio dispatch or something."

I was so mad I couldn't see straight. I finally got into the skimmer, this little fast motorboat, and went back to the ship, where I sent an urgent priority dispatch to have Julian Flor report to the admiral at once. He showed up along with my intelligence man from the naval base at Leyte. Julian began apologizing for his lack of military panache. I couldn't make out what in the world was bothering him. He kept apologizing for not being properly clad. Finally my intelligence man said, "He needs sidearms, he needs to be armed. He's a general, you know. He's got to have sidearms, pistols, and things like that."

I said, "My God, that's simply done." So I told Al Granum, who was commanding the *Wasatch,* the flagship at the time, that I wanted the works. I wanted a .45-caliber pistol and a number of rounds of ammunition, a canteen, a bayonet, and all the fierce-looking knives he had. "Send it all down, will you please, right away?"

And I got this plaintive note back from Al saying, "Do I get these back?"

And I said, "Hell, no."

Julian Flor was at the naval base at Leyte because he had picked up three or four downed aviators, put them in a banca, paddled them down, and reported at the base. He had gone to headquarters—the correct thing to do—to say that he was there. With that they nailed him and put him to work.

Well, Al Granum got me all the items I had asked for, and I gave them to Julian Flor. He was so tickled. He put on his belt; he flung his pistol around and strapped it to his leg. He was all set, and then he said, "Now, Captain, what can I do for you?"

"You don't need to do anything for me. You just go up there to the peninsula and start reporting."

Then this intelligence officer of mine said, "I'll tell you what you do, Flor. When you get back up there and get everything set, send the captain down a Japanese sword."

"All right."

I didn't think anything more about it. But about three or four weeks later the harassed officer of the deck sent word to me, "One of your Filipino friends—he's a pretty ragged-looking fellow—claims that he is adjutant of Major General Julian Flor, machinist's mate, first class, U.S. Navy."

"Send him down," I said.

This guy came down to the *Wasatch,* one of the early command ships where we had quite an elaborate setup with television and things like that. He came down and the door opened and revealed a guy with the most ragged pair of shorts I've ever seen, a worn-out pair of shoes, his toes sticking through. With a flourish he presented a sword to me and said, "I am so-and-so, adjutant of Major General Julian Flor, machinist's mate, first class, U.S. Navy. He has sent me to present this to you with his compliments." And I have still got the sword.

I think one of the most amazing jobs a coastwatcher of ours did was on the island of Cebu. We had a fellow there named Cushing. He had been promoted to lieutenant colonel in the reserves. I think actually he was part Filipino. He was a very nice chap but was running a so-called guerrilla movement on the island.

You know, Admiral Isoroku Yamamoto had been killed in the Solomon Islands on 18 April 1943. The man who relieved him was Mineichi Koga, whom I'd known in Japan. He was a very fine person. The Japanese at that time had their main base in the central Pacific at Truk. It was their headquarters. Well, we made Truk too hot for them. Spruance's aircraft carriers were bombing Truk periodically, so Admiral Koga and his staff shifted their headquarters to Palau. They had hardly gotten ashore at Palau when Spruance struck that place and we were landing a marine division there to take it over. Thereupon Koga hastily loaded himself and the principal members of his staff into a seaplane and took off for the Philippines.

Well, they got lost. We knew something was up because, my Lord, the Japanese had planes out searching the ocean all over creation and we were listening in on their communications. We didn't know what was going on, but we knew that something very important had happened.

And all of a sudden we got a message from this guy, Cushing, on Cebu: "I have captured a Japanese general, his entire staff, and all of his headquarters papers." We didn't pay too much attention to that, because none of these guerrilla people ever seemed to capture anybody of lesser rank than a general. But it turned out that the guy's name was Koga. Then we realized that he was Admiral Koga, commander in chief of the Japanese fleet.

Well, the Japanese found out that Koga was ashore. His plane had crash-landed off Cebu and fallen into the hands of these guerrillas. Through the grapevine the Japanese garrison learned of it, so they started pressing the guerrillas, and Cushing, I thought smartly, compromised. "Lay off and I'll give up the bodies." MacArthur was incensed. He had visions of having Koga in a cage to display in Australia—you know, that kind of thing. But Cushing made a deal with the Japanese. He would give up the bodies and call it quits if they'd take the heat off. And they did. Koga died right on Cebu. He was badly hurt in the crash landing.

Cushing got all the papers. So we sent in a submarine to pick up the papers. They were the staff papers of the commander in chief of the Japanese fleet. They were loaded in our submarine, but since I thought they were so hot, as soon as the submarine got clear enough we had it met at sea by a flying boat. The papers were then taken off and sent, without being translated, to Admiral Nimitz, who was on Saipan by this time. We knew enough about the plans to know that they belonged now with Nimitz. It was quite a feat to get the papers of the commander in chief of the Japanese fleet, who had been captured by Cushing on the island of Cebu—to get a submarine in there to pick them up and later to have them transferred to a flying boat at sea for quick delivery to us. I don't know whether the Japanese who made the deal with Cushing knew that there were papers on the plane. I do know that we received several sacksful.

That is where we got the complete dope on the Japanese strategic plan for the war, the so-called Sho Operation. It was the plan they put into effect at the Battle of Leyte Gulf. I would not have called it a campaign plan, but it was what you might call a strategic concept. In other words, you have a decoy fleet up here and your main fleet would come through here. You would pinch in there and so on and so forth.* It was called the Sho Operation, for *sho* is an alternative pronunciation of the Japanese character meaning "victory."

This kind of island watching does pay off. You can win, you know, in this business.† But the ball also bounces two or three different ways sometimes. I give you some illustrations.

As you come into Leyte Gulf from the northern entrance, there is an island that sits almost in the center of the strait called Suluan. We had an observer on Suluan Island. He was a naval officer who had been with the PT boats in the Philippines and had escaped capture somehow or other and had set up shop in the Leyte Gulf area. He was instructed to make sure that the strait had not been mined. He did. He actually went out and towed armed boats up and down to sweep for mines, but there weren't any.

Our landing plans for the Leyte Gulf operation called for the initial landing to be made on Suluan Island to secure that end of the strait and clear it of the enemy. They went in there and did that. I had reported that there were no mines at Leyte, for we had swept the channel. They sent back a message, "Sure, there are no mines there, but just to make certain we'll do

---

*Here McCollum is illustrating with gestures the Japanese naval strategists' belief in dividing forces to confuse the enemy as to which is the main force.

†Koga's papers influenced Admiral Raymond Spruance's plan for the Battle of the Philippine Sea. For further information, see Rear Admiral Carl J. Moore, p. 210.

our usual three days of minesweeping." So they spent three futile days sweeping for mines that were not there. This is how the ball bounces sometimes. Sometimes you can't win in this intelligence business.

The next big operation after Leyte Gulf was up there in the Lingayen Gulf. From Leyte we went down and landed on Mindoro to establish air bases. After Leyte had been secured and the back of the Japanese army's operations had been broken at Ormoc, on the western side of the island, the inland side, the next big jump was to put the Sixth Army ashore at Lingayen.

There was a fellow named Volckman who was a captain in the U.S. Army and who had been stationed in the Philippines when the Japanese came in. Somehow or other he had not been captured. I think he had been on a hunting trip when the war broke and he got isolated up around Lingayen Gulf. There he had organized quite a respectable guerrilla outfit. As soon as we were able to make contact with him, we sent in supplies and that sort of thing and instructions as to what we would like him to do. He started reporting that the Japs had nothing in Lingayen Gulf. Well, I knew that the Japs had mined the gulf because we had people over there who had spotted these mines and located them. I duly reported that Lingayen Gulf was mined and where it was mined. Well, our forces went in and of course swept for mines and found only three or four. So American intelligence was perfectly lousy. Yes, lousy! That was the verdict our people passed on it.

Later on we got a very high mark in intelligence. Those waters in the Philippines are pretty constricted. It's not a good place to operate aircraft carriers because there's not enough sea room and, of course, when you put battleships and cruisers in there, the ships' captains have visions of the place being ringed with Japanese airfields whose planes are going to pounce on them. So we adopted a practice of putting an intelligence officer on the flagship of the task groups that moved in there, a man who knew what we had in the way of reporting stations and so on. One of the more successful ones was a fellow named Williamson. He was a lawyer in Chicago, a very fine chap. The admiral that I had assigned him to was commanding a division of battleships, and he was rather dubious about going in through these narrow waters and being bombed out of hand. Williamson held his hand very nicely.

When the admiral came back, he couldn't speak highly enough of Williamson. He said, "I want that guy on my staff permanently."

And I said, "Well, all his value is because of his local knowledge. This he has learned. He has been trained for this job. His value to you was that when he got a report from a coastwatcher up here he could say, 'Forget that, that guy can only count to three anyway. And when he says thirty, it might be three, it might be three hundred, and so on. He's a savage so you can't take all he says for truth.'" Our man was able to give the admiral an offhand evaluation, and this was very important.

"Our withdrawal from Guadalcanal is regrettable," the Japanese emperor said to the Japanese army chief of staff, General Hajime Sugiyama, when that officer came to inform him on 31 December 1942 of the decision of Imperial General Headquarters. Weeks later the propaganda machine of Radio Tokyo broadcast news that the imperial forces, "after pinning down the Americans to a corner of the island" of Guadalcanal, had accomplished their mission and departed to fight elsewhere.

That departure came early in February 1943 and was so secret and cleverly executed that Major General Alexander M. Patch, in command of American marines on the island, was not certain of the event until his men found empty boats and abandoned supplies on the beaches of Cape Esperance, in the far corner of the island, on 8 February. But the departure did not mean that the Japanese had withdrawn their attention from that unfortunate island. They launched nightly air raids that were bothersome and left the American command on uncertain footing. It would have to make a desperate move to secure the island once and for all. This is the background of the situation on Guadalcanal as we see it in graphic detail in the excerpt that follows.

On 1 April 1943 Rear Admiral Marc Mitscher was suddenly named Commander, Air, Solomon Islands, to relieve his predecessor, who was ill. After establishing his headquarters near Henderson Field, the redoubtable Mitscher decided he must do something spectacular to recall the first anniversary of the Doolittle Raid on Tokyo. He had strong feelings about the Japanese treatment of some of the American pilots who had been captured on the mainland of China after the raid. Mitscher did not have to wait long for an opportunity. It was revealed through an intercepted dispatch that came to the attention of Admiral Nimitz in Pearl Harbor that Fleet Admiral Isoroku Yamamoto, commander in chief of the Combined Japanese Fleet, was to make a visit to Japanese bases in the upper Solomons. There he intended to inspect defenses and bolster troop morale. His itinerary was set forth in minute detail. Mitscher concocted a plan to be carried out on 18 April, an auspicious date, as it was the anniversary of the Doolittle Raid.

A member of Mitscher's staff and his personal friend, Rear Admiral Augustus Read, USNR, not only lived through the Japanese bombings but also was privy to the conception of Mitscher's plan. In the following excerpt Read tells his story of Guadalcanal.

CONDITION RED ON GUADALCANAL, AND THE SHOOTING DOWN OF ADMIRAL YAMAMOTO

REAR ADMIRAL WILLIAM AUGUSTUS READ

WILLIAM AUGUSTUS READ was born in Rye, New York, on 21 August 1895. He was a graduate of Pomfret School in Connecticut and of Harvard University in 1918. He served as a private in the First Massachusetts Field Artillery on the Mexican border and as an ensign in the aviation corps of the U.S. Naval Reserve in 1917–18.

Read, a banker by profession, was with Dillon, Read and Company in New York City from 1919 to 1929, becoming a partner in the business in 1921 and serving as vice president from 1922 to 1929. He was a vice president of Central Hanover Bank and Trust Company, New York, from 1920 to 1940, and after the war, from 1949 to 1951, and senior vice president of Hanover Bank from 1955 to 1962.

Read continued in the naval reserve between the wars and went on active duty in 1940. He served for a time in the Bureau of Aeronautics and then had duty in Pearl Harbor. In 1942 he joined the staff of Admiral Marc Mitscher on Guadalcanal and was with that staff during Mitscher's later command of fast carriers in the Pacific. Read became a captain in 1943 and a commodore in 1945 and retired as a rear admiral.

Admiral Read occupied the Read family home in Purchase, New York. He died on 14 September 1976.

The whole course of our lives was completely changed in a matter of just a few hours. On April 1, 1943, Admiral Mitscher returned from the daily Halsey conference in Noumea and told us that Rear Admiral Charles Mason, who had the title Commander, Aircraft, Solomon Islands, had been stricken with a serious type of malaria and would have to be evacuated. Admiral Halsey had ordered Mitscher to proceed immediately to Guadalcanal and relieve Admiral Mason. Mitscher left Noumea at once with his flag lieutenant; that is, he stayed in the camp just long enough to have his bags packed and was on his way within the hour. He told me before he left that he would send for me as soon as he was settled. This seemed to me to be an incredibly lucky break. I had hoped after a spell of duty in New Caledonia to break out of there and get duty in a more forward area. Now all of a sudden, without me having to ask anybody for favors, Santa Claus came down my chimney with the ideal assignment. I was with an officer I liked and respected, and everything appeared rosy.

The next day we were ourselves detached and ordered to Cactus, the code name for Guadalcanal. Upon our arrival we were to report to Commander, Air, Solomon Islands, for duty on Mitscher's staff. We motored up to Tantuta Airfield and waited on the runway for the Scats flight which would take us north to our destination.

We left about ten in the morning and arrived off the southern tip of Guadalcanal early in the afternoon, where we were ordered to orbit while an air raid was in progress at Henderson Field. The weather was deteriorating and clouds shrouded the high mountains, the highest peak of which rose to an altitude of eight thousand feet above the sea. We landed at four at Henderson Field and boarded a jeep for our trip to ComAirSol's camp, where we reported.

Upon arrival at the camp, which was about a half mile from Henderson Field on a low cliff that overhung the Lunga River, we were assigned to our quarters in tents on top of this little ridge. We met our new chief of staff, Brigadier General Field Harris, USMC, and were assigned desks in Admiral Mitscher's hut down at the bottom of the ravine.

The admiral told me that my assignment was assistant chief of staff for administration. He expected me to get after the paperwork, and he was sure that I would find plenty to do.

Down in the ravine the camp was a real sea of mud. In spots it was deeper than shoe height, even the height of the high marine shoes that I had drawn before leaving Ile Neu, the seaplane base. And of course it stuck to socks and trousers like glue. Most of the officers were in tents with board floors. Only the admiral had a hut. The mess hall was a large screened building, with a galley at the far end. There was no electricity in the camp, no telephone switchboard, no service whatsoever in the early days.

At supper I met the junior officers of the mess and immediately after supper went back to the office to see what was to be done. The admiral suggested that we all turn in early, as the weather was clearing and air raids were expected later. I managed to draw a steel helmet and a .45 Colt before going back to my tent. Commander Daniel Gallery, USN, who shared the tent with me, showed me the location of our dugout, just outside our screen door, and warned me that it was a low bridge entrance and exit. He also explained the mysteries of the mosquito net over my cot. We talked for a while and then turned in. I was fairly tired and fell instantly into a sound sleep.

After what seemed to me to be only a few minutes a terrific uproar arose in the camp, somebody beating a large-caliber shell case with an iron rod down in the ravine and calling out, "Condition Red!"

"Come on," called Commander Gallery, "here we go again."

I got into my shoes and pants and stumbled out to the dugout entrance behind him, where various scantily clad figures in pajamas and underwear were running from all directions and disappearing within. By this time searchlights were sweeping the sky and the antiaircraft guns had actually opened fire. Their shells were bursting near the mountain across the river from us. It was quite a spectacular sight, so much so that since it was my first experience watching combat, I decided to stay outside the sandbag shelter and see the fireworks from the trench.

Suddenly one of the searchlight beams picked up an airplane, crossed it, and swung back. In the searchlights the plane looked like a little silver bug drifting slowly our way. I realized it had considerable altitude. Someone came out of the darkness and looked up. Shells were bursting all around the Japanese plane but it continued steadily along. The guy who had just come out of the darkness called out, "Hit the deck!" and disappeared.

Then there were two distinct tearing sounds, as if someone was ripping a linen or canvas sheet, followed by a couple of brilliant flashes and very loud reports in the vicinity of Henderson Field, which was over the next ridge from us. Our whole ridge was lit up as though by lightning. There was quite a roar from the explosions and then comparative quiet.

"Well, that's two," somebody inside the dugout remarked, and somebody else said, "And two to go." The Jap had succeeded in slithering out of the searchlight beams and was not again picked up. The firing ceased and the lights were extinguished. People began coming out of the dugout. Lights were lit in the tents. My tentmate spoke out, "Old Charley's got a couple more, but we'd better turn in. Lord only knows when he's going to drop them."*

---

*Charley was the name American fighting men gave to the nightly Japanese marauders who flew over U.S. camps and installations on Guadalcanal and elsewhere. Washing Machine Charlie was another name applied to the enemy visitors, especially when they were involved in aerial spotting.

161

This was just an intruder mission. If the enemy did any damage it was pure luck. He was only down there to keep everybody awake and to make them get out from under their mosquito nets and expose themselves to malaria. Annoyance was the principal purpose of his raid and it was mighty successful. It annoyed the daylights out of everybody and it did expose them to malaria. Even if you could go to sleep you had the feeling that you might have to jump for the dugout any second, and that just about ruined your rest. Of course, for the fellows who had been on the island this was old stuff. They got right into the dugout. They didn't care two cents about watching anything. They thought I was crazy to be standing around out there, staring goggle-eyed at this spectacular business.

Every night, unless the weather was really bad, there was a Jap intruder over our camp. Certainly there was one over Henderson Field and the other fields operating on the island. The Japanese had a regular operation set up. They'd drop one or two bombs early in the evening and fly around for a few hours and pretty soon, when everybody had settled down, they would come back and do it again until it was daylight or close enough to daylight that they had to get rolling to escape fighter interception. Of course, by the time this intruder disappeared it was very nearly dawn, and I noticed that everybody was tired and disgusted. Only the anopheles mosquitos appeared to enjoy the show; all the dugouts were unscreened and most of the people in them were scantily clad. It soon struck me that the Japanese were really pretty smart to conduct this type of operation on a regular basis. I noticed that a great many of the men in our camp had malaria.

I noticed too, at breakfast, that most of the men were rather downcast because they had been going through this business for months. At the same time they had no enthusiasm for the food being served. It certainly lacked variety. The admiral's steward, who was a magnificent cook, cursed the galley and the food; nevertheless he managed to combine Spam, a monotonous canned meat, with various fancy sauces and gravies that helped disguise it. The doctors had arranged for a dose of Atabrine, the only malaria suppressant available in sufficient quantity for general use at the time, to be taken with the food. After a few days on this I developed some very disagreeable symptoms which the doctors attributed to the drug. They then put me on quinine, two tablets a day and once a week three additional tablets before going to bed. This was called a surge, and while its effects were unpleasant—a loud ringing in the ears and a feeling of lightheadedness bordering on dizziness—the prescription was nevertheless effective.

For the first week or two we suffered only nuisance attacks at night, but rumors were soon going around that increased activity was being observed up the Slot. The Japanese were said to be making definite plans to throw a Sunday punch at Guadalcanal. After about a week—on April 7 to be exact—we received word at lunchtime from our Australian coastwatchers up the Slot that a sizable formation of enemy aircraft, including bombers and fighters—a total of approximately 150 planes—was heading for our area. My appetite promptly disappeared, but everyone else seemed quite unconcerned and the meal went on unhurriedly. Some of the more casual members even sat around for a few extra cups of coffee and a cigarette after dessert, so I tried to appear nonchalant too and remained with them.

It was a bright sunny day, with beautiful white cumulus clouds making up over the high mountain to the west and drifting across the channel between Guadalcanal and the Florida Islands. In the direction of Savo Island the sky was clear and blue and the water stretching toward the shore of Santa Isabel in the distance was the typical brilliant blue of the Solomon Sea. It was hard to realize that this serene and beautiful spectacle would soon be interrupted.

Eventually the camp went to Condition Red and people began to congregate near the various dugouts and shelters. Suddenly there was a brilliant flash way overhead, and immediately a trail of black smoke thickened as an enemy plane, hit by one of our fighters, began to fall. It dove and spun crazily downward, burning fiercely, and long before it reached the eight-thousand-foot altitude of the big mountain a wing ripped off and cartwheeled away, flaming from the root, while the other wing and the fuselage plummeted and crashed near the river with a roar.

In a few moments a tight formation of dive-bombers dove past the shoulder of one of the big cumulus clouds and streaked over our camp, then headed for the shipping in the channel and towards the Tulagi Naval Base on Florida Island. Our antiaircraft guns opened up and soon there was a hail of antiaircraft fragments all over the place. People began filing into some of the dugouts; it seemed kind of silly to be hit by a fragment from your own fire.

I must say these Japs certainly flew a beautiful formation. They came right down, disappeared over the tops of the high trees along the shore of the island, and went over the open water, where the AKs and oilers were trying to take evasive action in the channel.

Within a few moments there was a loud explosion and a huge column of black smoke rose above the bomb-fringed shoreline right off Lunga Beach. The Japs had made a very damaging hit on a tanker that was operating out there. Some of our fighters now appeared, diving to the attack from the general direction of Savo Island and visible until they too got down to such a low altitude that they disappeared behind the treetops along the shoreline.

It was all over in a comparatively short time, and the fighting swung north, beyond our visual range. The alert continued, of course, until all enemy formations had evacuated our area. Then the all-clear was sounded and things went back to normal in our camp.

When the various action reports came in, the early estimates were that the Japanese lost thirty-six planes, the Americans half a dozen, from which we had rescued all but one pilot.

All this occurred within a week of Mitscher's assumption of his new command. Immediately following this show he remarked to me that he intended to do something special on the eighteenth of April, which was the first anniversary of Jimmie Doolittle's raid on Tokyo. In his quiet intense way he told Commander Morton Ring and me that he would beat the enemy to the punch on that day. He said he was sure the Japs would probably have some special plans to celebrate the emperor's birthday later in the month, on the twenty-ninth, but he proposed to hit them first, on what he called "our anniversary," and partially settle his score with them for having executed some of the Doolittle pilots who had been forced down in Japanese-held territory on the Chinese mainland. For this atrocity he never forgave the Japanese, and because of it he never referred to them as the Japanese but always as the bastards.

I do not know what plan might have been adopted if fate had not taken a hand in the situation at this particular point. We were notified by the intelligence community that Admiral Isoroku Yamamoto, commander in chief of the Japanese Combined Fleet, intended to visit our area on the day we were planning to go on the offensive. Admiral Yamamoto, as the original planner of the attack on Pearl Harbor, had achieved a reputation as an outstanding Japanese naval officer, not only in Japanese circles but internationally as well. Our own home-consumption propaganda had attributed to him a remark to the effect that he expected to dictate the terms of peace in person in Washington. This, though completely false, was widely believed to be a fact, and Yamamoto was hated accordingly in our forces. Consequently, if Admiral Mitscher had been asked to nominate a top target, Yamamoto probably would have been first choice. And now that our intelligence sources had furnished us with what amounted to a complete itinerary of the admiral's proposed inspection tour, we were in a position to take action.

According to the information in our possession, Yamamoto was due to land at Bougainville's Kahili Airport at 0800 on 18 April. From Kahili he was to fly to Biak Island, thirty miles or so away, and he was to proceed from Biak by ship to Fasi Island, off the entrance of Shortland Harbor, where he was to arrive at 1040. After an inspection of the Shortland installations he was to leave at 1145 by ship, returning to Biak and thence taking off by air for Kahili, arriving at 1240. Thus for a period of some four and a half hours the leading figure of the Japanese navy would be a clay pigeon for our fighters, if they could seize the initiative and execute what was officially suggested as appropriate action.

Admiral Mitscher and his chief of staff called in the operations office for consultation and various schemes were discussed, but because Kahili was well beyond the maximum range of all navy and marine fighters, the final decision was made to asign the mission to Major John Mitchell's squadron of P-38s.

In order to reduce the chances of premature detection by visual or radar observation, the interceptor planes were ordered to fly a course well west of the islands at an altitude of fifteen feet above the surface of the sea. They were to turn around a seven-thousand-foot peak on Bougainville, which was an active volcano, climbing at full throttle as they neared the coastline, so as to be in the best possible position to make an interception out of the sun if their expected quarry was sighted. This whole operation was carefully worked out, based on split-second timing and the assumption that the Japanese commander's aircraft would be exactly on schedule.

Personally, I was inclined to doubt the accuracy of the information. I asked whether it might not be possible that the detailed itinerary was a hoax designed to suck us into exactly the type of ambush we were so carefully preparing for Yamamoto. I, of course, did not realize or know that at this time the information we had received was based on the interception of Japanese coded radio messages. So when I asked this question, Admiral Mitscher looked very seriously at me for a moment and replied that the answer was negative. Nevertheless, it seemed odd to me that our intelligence could have obtained access to this type of information. My work was always on the administrative end. I made a particular point of trying to steer clear of operational matters because I felt that was the proper field of the trained regular officers. However, I did know that if this information was correct the job of knocking off Yamamoto ought to be just about as simple an undertaking as shooting sitting ducks in a rain barrel, and that if it turned out to be incorrect, a few of our pilots would have nothing to show for a long, hazardous flight the next morning.

Before going to bed that night I had a talk with Admiral Mitscher about our prospects. He told me that he expected this mission to be successful and that, in fact, what he was trying to figure out now was what the Japanese reaction would be. He said he had convinced himself that it would be both prompt and violent—as violent as they could make it. He thought they were probably planning some offensive action for the emperor's birthday anyway, and that any further provocation would simply add fuel to whatever they planned to do. This opinion he seemed to relish.

Our only chance to hit the Japanese hard was when they came down to our area. Our fighters were so short-legged that in spite of many superior attributes, they just did not have the range to get out much beyond the New Georgia area or to fight for any length of time and return to base. The Zero, on the other hand, was a long-range fighter, excellent in performance but short on protection. Consequently, if we could provoke them to come down in force to the area where our fighter planes could get a real whack at them with full gas tanks, the odds were in our favor. That was what Mitscher was hoping to do now.

The admiral said to me that if Major Mitchell shot down Yamamoto, it would be the most deadly insult we could offer to the Japs. He said in that case he wouldn't be at all surprised if some of the senior people at Rabaul had to commit hara-kiri. He wound up, considerably pleased, saying that he was sure it would provoke them into taking immediate and maximum revenge.

The next morning conditions were perfect. The eighteenth was a bright clear day, with little or no wind. The interceptor flight took off on schedule and was due back well before noon. The very few people who knew the plan for the day kept an anxious watch for any signs of P-38s, but to the majority of the personnel it was just another working day. I did not have the opportunity to observe the return of the flight because my routine business took me elsewhere that morning, but when I got back to our camp, Commander Ring was jubilant.

"This is top secret," he told me, "so keep it to yourself. The P-38s have shot down two transports and three out of six Zeros escorting them. They also got another transport later, but they think it was a training plane. We lost one plane but the pilot may turn up. The boss wants everybody to help cook up a dispatch, so if you have any suggestions, let me know."*

It occurred to me that perhaps a good opening line for Mitscher's dispatch might be, "Pop goes the weasel," and I made the suggestion to Commander Ring, who took it to Admiral Mitscher, who approved it. I still have a copy of that dispatch. For some odd reason the yeoman who typed it spelled weasel *weazul.* At any rate, the admiral got his dispatch off and received congratulations promptly from higher authority, particularly from Admiral Halsey.

Once the results of the flight were known and the pilots were back on base,† I was instructed to prepare recommendations for all the survivors for the Congressional Medal of Honor and for spot promotion. I know that later they all did receive the Congressional Medal, but I have no personal knowledge of the outcome of the recommended promotions, as these pilots were

---

*The dispatch was intended to disguise the top-secret results of the effort to shoot down Yamamoto and at the same time communicate those results to King and others in Washington.

†Yamamoto's plane and an escort arrived over Buin at 0935, as scheduled. Major Mitscher's Lightnings of the 339th Fighter Squadron from Henderson Field arrived at the same time. Captain Thomas Lanphier, USA, flashed under the Zekes (Zeros) just as the two bombers were about to land. Lanphier shot down the first plane, which carried Yamamoto. It crashed in a jungle north of Buin. The second plane, with his chief of staff, Vice Admiral Ugaki, spiraled into the sea and sank. Yamamoto and five of six staff officers were killed; Ugaki was critically injured. The American Lightnings retired after nipping three of the Zekes and losing one P-38.

Captain Yasuji Watanabe of Yamamoto's staff, who had been delayed by unfinished business at Rabaul, recovered Yamamoto's body in the jungle, cremated it, and carried the ashes back to Tokyo, where there was an impressive public funeral on 5 June. The departed admiral was held up to the youth of Japan as a model.

merely assigned to the Solomons Air Command and administrative handling of promotions for them was an army air forces matter.

Somehow or other a *Time* correspondent on Guadalcanal got the true story of this episode, and very shortly thereafter that magazine printed an accurate account of the Yamamoto attack. We soon heard that Admiral King regarded this as an extremely serious breach of security and was very annoyed. In fact, we had the inspector general of the navy visiting our camp, in short order, questioning various officers, including all of us and Admiral Mitscher himself. Of course, in our camp the word spread like wildfire, whether from the pilots involved or how, I don't know. Everybody in the place knew about the mission in a few hours and the effect on morale was simply miraculous. This was the first time we had any success of major proportions against an enemy force. The Guadalcanal command had stood off attacks and stuff like that, but they had never had a really successful offensive operation. What this did for all the poor mechanics and enlisted men who had been stranded there from various sunken ships and not been relieved truly had to be seen to be believed.

We actually picked up a Radio Tokyo broadcast on May 21 announcing the death of Admiral Yamamoto due to an operational accident in the forward area. Apparently this had also been picked up and published back home.

To have the credit go to the Solomons Air Command seemed only right to most of our force. I have often wondered how the *Time* correspondent got that story and had it printed. To this day I don't know.

For a while after this it was very difficult to find out what the time of day was in our camp without having to furnish all kinds of fingerprints and special passes and other intelligence blocks, but eventually conditions returned to normal.

By the time of the initial attack on the Gilbert Islands, 20 November 1943, Guadalcanal had been secured by the Americans and General MacArthur had won his initial campaigns in New Guinea en route to his final objectives, the Philippines and the home islands of Japan. Allied strategists, having long realized that MacArthur's approach to the enemy from the south was slow and cumbersome, had planned a central Pacific drive as well. The attack on the Gilberts was the first step of the long westward trek across the Pacific to the Japanese homeland.

No navy had ever attempted an advance of this magnitude, across a huge ocean dotted with far-flung, enemy-held islands. To undertake the task, the most powerful naval force up to that point in history was assembled under one flag: by fall of 1943 Admiral Raymond Spruance's Fifth Fleet comprised six large carriers, five light carriers, eight escort carriers, twelve battleships, fourteen cruisers, fifty-six destroyers, twenty-nine transports and cargo vessels, and a great many landing and beach craft. Along with this unprecedented offensive force came the need to devise new methods of amphibious assault.

The invasion of the Gilberts, larger and more complex than any previous Allied operation in the Pacific, was to be carried out by Task Force 50, the Fifth Fleet's fast carrier force. The Northern Attack Force conveyed troops of the Twenty-seventh Infantry Division to assault Makin Atoll, and the Southern Attack Force brought the Second Marine Division from New Zealand to assault Tarawa.

Admiral Spruance, in command afloat for the Gilbert Islands operation, flew his flag in the cruiser *Indianapolis*. Rear Admiral Richmond K. Turner, in the battleship *Pennsylvania*, commanded the Northern Attack Force; Rear Admiral Harry W. Hill, in the battleship *Maryland*, commanded the Southern Attack Force.

Admiral Hill once said that Tarawa "was a little Gibraltar, and the most thoroughly prepared beach defense of any objective assaulted throughout the . . . war. It was defended by some of Japan's elite troops. The Japanese admiral in command had been quoted as saying that 'a million Americans could never capture Tarawa in a hundred

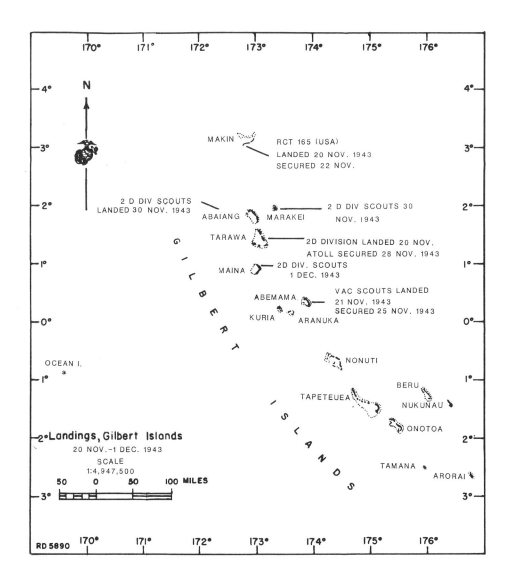

years.'"* It was against such a defense, in the first step of the drive against the central Pacific, that America's untried doctrines of amphibious warfare had to undergo the crucial test of battle. Many of the Japanese defenses on Makin and Tarawa proved too strong for destruction in the bombardment time allotted. But gradually the courage, initiative, and drive of the Second Marine Division mended the initial failure and drove the U.S. forces to victory in the Gilberts.

*Interview with Admiral Hill by John T. Mason, Jr., in Annapolis, Maryland, 1966, for the Oral History Research Office of Columbia University.

170

American losses in the Gilberts were severe and came as a shock to the public. Casualties from the assault on Tarawa totaled approximately twenty percent, a figure exceeded in several later operations in which the marine corps participated as the westward movement proceeded.

In the following section Rear Admiral Carl J. Moore, Spruance's chief of staff when the invasion took place, gives us an account of the assaults on Tarawa and Apamama. Another perspective on the invasion of Apamama is provided by Rear Admiral William D. Irvin, skipper of the *Nautilus* at the time of events narrated. That submarine carried a force of sixty-eight marines and ten bomb-disposal engineers of the Fifth Amphibious Reconnaissance Company to the island, which was occupied by a small Japanese garrision. The marines captured Apamama on 21 December.

ASSAULT ON TARAWA AND APAMAMA

REAR ADMIRAL CARL J. MOORE

CHARLES JOHNES MOORE was born in De-
catur, Illinois, on 19 December 1889. He
graduated with the class of 1910 at the U.S.
Naval Academy and saw sea duty in various
capacities during World War I. Between the
wars he had duty as executive officer in the
Altair, a destroyer tender, and the battleship
New York, and he commanded several destroyers as well as Destroyer Division 5. His
shore duty during these years included tours
in the Navy Department and the Naval War
College. From 1937 to 1939 he was on the
staff of Commander, Battle Force, U.S.
Fleet.

The outbreak of World War II found
Moore in command of the cruiser *Phil-
adelphia*. From that command he reported to the Navy Department and served until
1943 with the Joint Chiefs of Staff as senior member of the Joint U.S. Strategic and
Joint War Plans committees. From August 1943 he had duty as chief of staff to
Admiral Raymond Spruance, commander of the Fifth Fleet. He was with Spruance
throughout the campaigns in the Gilbert, Marshall, and Mariana islands. He then
returned to Washington and was again with the Joint Chiefs of Staff as deputy
secretary. In that capacity he took part in the Potsdam Conference of 1945. He
retired in the rank of rear admiral on 1 January 1947.

After his retirement, Admiral Moore became a fellow on the staff of the
Brookings Institution in Washington and worked there with the international studies

172

group until 1955. He lived in Chevy Chase, Maryland, until his death on 4 February 1974.

The trip down from Pearl Harbor was peaceful enough and I had time to rest and start work on the upcoming operation. Rear Admiral Richmond Kelly Turner ran the force we traveled with and did a very good job of training.

The day before our arrival off Tarawa, Jap search planes came snooping around but were promptly shot down before they were in sight of the ships. I doubt they had a chance to report us. At any rate, as we passed south of Tarawa, Jap searchlights were signaling as if to aircraft. I feel fairly sure the Japanese didn't expect the deluge they got the next morning.

To quote from my notes written after I returned to Pearl Harbor on December 13, 1943,

> I think the most amusing part of this show has been Admiral Raymond Spruance. He is the most wonderful boss I have ever known. But he has exasperated me no end a good many times. I can understand what Mrs. Spruance means when she says he is a bear when he doesn't get his exercise or his sleep or his coffee. He never gets ruffled or excited, never gets exasperated with me when I am disagreeable; but when he doesn't want to do business he just pretends not to hear and goes to bed or walks off and doesn't answer. That is enough to aggravate anybody. He eats quantities of raw sliced onions for his health and walks me for miles up and down the fo'castle with no shirt on to get me brown. Never mind stacks of work to do. This goes on until I insist that the war has got to be won and my tan is really of no importance. He turns in about eight and doesn't like to be disturbed except for something most important. He won't sleep in his emergency cabin because it is stuffy. He has read dozens of books and doesn't like to be interrupted. I refer almost nothing to him except matters of vital importance, and he lets me strictly alone except on these matters. He is most appreciative of my efforts and says, "I don't know how I could have gotten along without you, Carl." As long as I will stay and do the work and he can walk and read and sleep, he'll be contented. I expect no reward. In the presence of rank I am ignored, which is as it should be, I suppose. He'll chat for hours with a visiting friend when he knows I need only a minute of his time to get ahead with my work. The staff is fine. They work hard, take my ill humor, and all do their stuff.

By this time our flagship [the *Indianapolis*] had moved from Turner's force to Admiral Harry W. Hill's. Turner's force broke off and went to Makin, and we continued on down and rejoined Harry Hill's outfit, which was meeting to the east of Tarawa, where some of his troops, equipment, and ships were. Hill had come in with his battleships and transports from Efate and joined us there.

As we were steaming along to the westward, south of Tarawa Atoll, we sighted the running lights of a ship. There was much chatter over the TBS telephone about these lights. Everybody seemed to think it was probably an innocent Jap ship, passenger vessel or something of the sort, running down the channel and not expecting to see anybody. Therefore she had her lights on.

It bothered me considerably, because I thought the vessel might be the submarine *Nautilus*. In our plan we had directed the *Nautilus,* with a company of marines aboard, to move eastward within a certain band of Tarawa, where she had been taking pictures during the daylight hours. She was ordered to proceed to the little island of Apamama, where she would land the marines and take over. I had it fixed in my mind that the submarine would pass to the south of a string of islands that we were north of. I think I probably overlooked the fact that this ten-mile band in which she was permitted to travel also extended north of the string of islands. Anyhow, I dismissed the idea that it might be the *Nautilus*.

Of course we had distributed our orders to everybody in the outfit, and we had told them about this expedition of the *Nautilus*. Well, it turned out that Harry's outfit didn't get that particular annex, for it was mailed later and was apparently a correction to our original orders.

Harry Hill was in on this discussion over the TBS, about the ship we had sighted. One of our destroyers and a cruiser commander were also in on the conversation. Since the ship remained unidentified, both the destroyer and a cruiser opened fire on it.

We were all watching the lights of this ship when our bridge quartermaster reported that two green stars had been fired from the vessel. That was the identification signal for our submarines that night. The first shot fired by our cruiser went straight through the conning tower of that submarine (as we learned later), and the shell dropped down into her body. It proved to be a dud and didn't explode. The submarine immediately submerged. Admiral Russell Berkey, the cruiser commander, promptly said over the TBS that he had hit the submarine. Well, the submarine had gone, her lights had disappeared, and she had vanished from the radar screen.

Then some of us began to worry. We knew it was the *Nautilus* by that time. We'd seen those green stars. We knew she had submerged but didn't know if there was damage. I was particularly worried, because these were my orders and I should have recognized the situation. Others on the staff were on the bridge too, but it didn't occur to them that this might have been the *Nautilus*. Of course, Spruance didn't know or care what was in the orders. He never read them.

Well, the aftermath was that we tried to get the *Nautilus* and one of the repair ships stationed around the area together. The only way we had of communicating with the submarine was through Commander, Submarines, Pearl Harbor. He would get on the *Nautilus* wave length and radio down to her. This was fairly difficult. And we were still under radio silence so we couldn't say anything at the time. We had to wait until the next day before we could act.

The *Nautilus* kicked around for two or three days, landed her troops on Apamama, and then went to sea in order to find the repair ship. But they never got together. There was some communication error. Nothing serious happened, except that Admiral Charles Lockwood in Pearl Harbor was growing frantic over the situation. He knew about his damaged ship. I've always felt very chagrined about that.

Now to go on from my notes made at Pearl Harbor. The particular job of the *Indianapolis* was to bombard suspected gun emplacements and ammunition dumps on the east side of Tarawa Atoll, while the rest of Harry Hill's outfit bombarded Betio, at the south end of the atoll, and while the troops disembarked from the transports. We made a run the length of Tarawa's east side and along the south coast, firing at lookout towers in the beautiful palm groves and at Japanese barges. We started a few fires, one of which burned for a couple of days.

By the time we reached Betio it looked like a shambles. It had been bombarded and bombed for two hours. Fires were burning everywhere. The coconut trees were all blasted. It seemed that no living soul could be on the island. Then we joined with Hill's ships in the bombardment of Tarawa and the troops approached the beach. It looked like the whole affair would be a walkover.

We saw the first wave reach the beach. Then we saw the next two or three waves get stuck on the edge of the reef that fringed the island. We saw the troops disembark and advance for about four hundred yards in water that was waist deep. It was in this phase that we had our greatest losses, for with all our bombardment the Japs had not been routed out of their beach pillboxes. For the next twenty-four hours they made it hell for the marines.

The destroyers remained in close support and the big ships continued to bombard all the next day. Finally, by ingenuity and by taking advantage of the breaks, the marines managed to beat down the opposition on the main beaches and to land on a couple of others. By the night of the second day we felt pretty secure. The fighting continued hard, however, for a few days longer. It must have been awful tough on the men ashore and those in the boats waiting to get ashore. We couldn't see much from the flagship except the raging fires, the shells and bombs falling, and the destroyers and small boats maneuvering about the harbor. We had to keep moving because of the threat of submarines. But the destroyers did a fine job and good luck kept us all safe from the enemy subs. Through it all we on the flagship kept in pretty close touch with what was going on and had a general picture of the situation.

While we were maneuvering for the next two or three days we saw two destroyers attacking a submarine. Captain Burton Biggs, skipper of the *Indianapolis,* saw a submarine surface and a destroyer fire into her hull. She sank eventually. He was a witness to this action because the *Indianapolis* was only about two miles from the scene. The enemy submarine was certainly put down.

Harry Hill did a wonderful job. He is an inspiring leader, knows his stuff, and does everything with vigor and initiative. I had one chat with him on the phone and he was as cool as a cucumber. He asked permission to go ashore. I didn't want to bother Spruance about it so I told him to go ahead. He wanted to see how things were and learn any lessons he could for the next time they had to tackle something like this. Spruance didn't object when I told him. He never did when I took action of that sort.

Kelly Turner ran the job at Makin. It was of less magnitude and the opposition was milder. He finished according to schedule and cleared out. He was himself, Kelly Turner, all the way through. He tried to run our job but didn't get away with that.*

Throughout the assault there was not much for us to do. We lay low and let the men we had put in charge do their stuff. It was afterward that our job began, and we became busy readjusting the forces, issuing new directives, and guiding the next phases.

Admiral Charles A. ("Baldy") Pownall, in command of one of our carrier task groups, also performed wonderfully. We only heard from him twice, and then only when he had something to say. His job was to attack the Jap airfield at Mille, an island just north of Tarawa, and then interpose his aircraft between Mille and Tarawa to prevent the Jap planes from coming down and attacking our ships off Tarawa. He did that job so well. Not only that, but he made repeated attacks on Mille and kept their planes in trouble all the time, so that they only got down to us once or twice.

One week after the first assault our flagship entered the lagoon at Tarawa. Raymond went ashore to meet Nimitz and his party, who had come out from Pearl Harbor. Raymond got separated from them and didn't find out the things I had hoped he would. I went ashore for an hour that afternoon but had to hurry back, because Raymond and I couldn't both be away long.

The place was swarming with marines. I had never known that men could look like they did—dirty, burned, ragged, hot, a week's growth of beard, tired, hungry, thirsty. They were about as fine a lot of men as I ever have

*Rear Admiral Richmond Kelly Turner was known as an irascible leader who tried to direct everything.

seen. What they had been through during that week! I have never seen such a shambles—coconut logs everywhere, sheet iron, guns, ammunition, smashed tanks, equipment, shot-up cars, bicycles, carts. In fact, everything that goes with war was scattered all over—pillboxes, tanks, traps, slit trenches dug up through concrete strongpoints in such numbers they couldn't be counted. Some were smashed to smithereens. Others were still good and had contained live Japs just the day before.

When I was ashore that day, all the dead marines had been properly buried and most of the dead Japs had been thrown into bomb craters and bulldozed over. There were many Japs lying about though, all in an advanced stage of decomposition. I contented myself with smelling them and gave up the pleasure of a closer examination. Some of the strongpoints were still full of hundreds of them. No one had an idea that the place was so thoroughly defended. The defenses didn't show in the photographs, as they were so well camouflaged. I had seen the defenses of our own islands on my trip in August, and I was sure that our own devilish contraptions would be exceeded by the Japs—as they were. Only battle-tested marines could have taken the place. They were wonderful.

TRIALS OF THE *NAUTILUS*

REAR ADMIRAL WILLIAM D. IRVIN

WILLIAM DAVIS IRVIN was born in Mt. Carmel, Pennsylvania, on 4 June 1905. He graduated from the U.S. Naval Academy in 1927. Shortly thereafter he had duty in several cruisers of the Asiatic Fleet. In January 1932 he reported for training at the submarine school in New London, Connecticut, and after qualifying for submarine duty he spent three years in S-boats. He took a course in communications at the U.S. Naval Academy and had duty in the submarines *Nautilus* and *Narwhal*. This was followed by his first command, the submarine *Spearfish*, in 1940. He then spent two years as an instructor at the submarine school in New London.

In August 1943 he became skipper of the submarine *Nautilus,* which he commanded on three war patrols in the central Pacific. In April 1944 he joined the staff of Commander, Submarine Force, Pacific Fleet. Irvin's duty then shifted to the East Coast of the United States, where from 1945 to 1947 he commanded several different submarine divisions. Next he spent two years in command of the service school at the Great Lakes Training Center, followed by a year of study at the National War College in Washington. His duty shifted once again to the Pacific, where he was assistant chief of staff for operations to Commander, Submarine Force, Pacific Fleet. Then came two years of unusual duty in Salzburg, Austria (1950–52) as liaison officer between Commander, Naval Forces, Mediterranean, and Commanding General, U.S. Army Forces, Austria. (Austria, still emerging from World War II, was

178

occupied at this time by the Allied powers.) In 1953 Irvin commanded the USS *Northampton,* a new type of tactical command ship. In November 1957 he became deputy director of communications on the Joint Chiefs of Staff, and in 1960, the first chief (later director) of the newly established Defense Communications Agency. From 1963 to 1965 he had command of the Service Force, Pacific Fleet. He instituted some significant reforms in that service that govern its efficiency to this day. His final duty was in command of the Military Sea Transportation Service, Pacific Area.

Irvin retired on 30 May 1967 in the rank of rear admiral.

I was called into Submarine Command, Pacific, and told that I was to be part of the force that was going to make the attack on the Gilbert Islands. It was the first of the great moves across the Pacific and had been planned in considerable detail by Admiral Nimitz. It was to be conducted for the most part by the newly created amphibious forces of the Pacific Fleet. The Southern Attack Force in that operation (as distinguished from the Northern Attack Force under Admiral Richmond Kelly Turner, whose objective was Makin Atoll) was under the command of Admiral Harry Hill. Its objective was to open the attack on Tarawa Atoll and capture it. After gaining control of Tarawa, it was to take the island of Apamama, lying about seventy-five miles southeast of Tarawa. Apamama sits almost on the equator. As quickly as possible after its capture an airstrip for fighter planes was to be built there.

The *Nautilus* was assigned to a manifold part in the operations of the Southern Attack Force. First, we were to be a weather station making reports for the preparation of the assault; second, we were to be a lifeguard station immediately south of the Tarawa beaches to pick up any aviators who were shot down. The aviators made a terrific attack on the island called Betio, a long narrow strip along the south part of the triangle-like atoll of Tarawa. The Japanese on Betio were concentrated at the western end, although they occupied the whole of the little atoll. The eastern end of it was supposed to be fortified, but no one was very sure about what was on this island.

The next part of my operations plan was to make close observation of the beaches of Betio after its bombardment by both the carrier groups and the surface groups. In addition to the pounding it got from the carrier units, cruisers and destroyers had marched up and down the north-south line to the west of Betio for a whole day, pouring thousands of salvos into the Japanese works. The island was very heavily fortified, we found. There were a great many impediments installed in the shallow water right off the beach. My job was to stay as close as possible to the southern shore during this bombardment and then get in as close as possible to the western end of the island to make observations. After getting out I had to report by radio the conditions of the beach after all this hammering.

The only charts we had dated from 1845 and were poor at best. But we had done some work on an earlier reconnaissance trip and were fairly certain of where we were at all times.

Since another part of our plan was to capture the island of Apamama after taking Tarawa, I had on board the *Nautilus* a reconnaissance company which consisted of seventy marines and interpreters. We were really jammed. Our crew had been cut down to a number smaller than our normal 110 officers and men. I believe we had eighty aboard at the time plus seventy-nine of these marines. We were packed tight, and during the course of the day I could permit the smoking lamp to be burned only ten minutes out of every hour because in just a few minutes of smoking the air would become so polluted that it seriously depleted our oxygen. Meals were also a problem. We started serving breakfast at four in the morning, and there was one continuous meal going until ten at night in order to get to all the people. By the time breakfast was finished we'd be starting on lunch, and the same was true with the evening meal.

While we were waiting before going in to observe the beaches at Betio, we were hanging out (and I use the expression hanging out because in truth that was what we were doing) at the eastern end of the island. Through the periscope I observed what looked like some gun mounts—very much like the eight-inch guns on a cruiser—in the sand piled up on the eastern end of the island.

My executive officer was Ozzie Lynch. I have never met a better exec. He was always polite. He said, "Yes, sir, no, sir, Captain," to the extreme. He deferred to my judgment in everything, and he never argued about anything I said to him.

So I was running on the surface and permitting groups of five and ten marines to come topside to get some air and watch the show. We could see on the horizon these heavy lines of ships marching up from the south and bombarding the western end of the island. Then another group would follow. There was quite a show of fireworks.

Lynch kept popping up and down from the conning tower, where he was checking our position. He stuck his head up through the hatch and said, "Captain, you're too close. Turn away." I was running in a general north-easterly direction with the idea of not getting too close to the island but not too far away when the sun went down so that we could dart in and out for our observations. Each time Lynch would say we were too close I'd ask him to check again. So we had this regular back and forth thing going on. I did think since he was making so much fuss about it that I'd better send the marines below. Then I was on the bridge with only my sailor lookout and with Lynch popping up saying, "You're too close, turn and roll out." Finally, in desperation, he called out, "Captain, I beg you, you're too close. Roll out just a little."

180

So I told him that I'd turn away for just a short time but we must stay in close to the beach so that when the sun went down we could do our observation without having to run too far. I called down to put the rudder over and we started swinging from our northeast course to the north. We had just started to get into the swing when all of a sudden it sounded like two racing freight trains were colliding. It then dawned on me that these shore buggers had opened up on us. I screamed, "Dive, take her down fast!"

And with that Lynch stuck his head through the hatch and said, "You stupid bastard, I told you we were too close."

The shells went over the top of us. I'm convinced they were eight-inch. They were certainly hollering when they came over. So we stayed down until dark. Then we maneuvered toward the island again, getting in as close as we could possibly get, not more than a thousand yards offshore at most. We were so close that we passed a ramshackle lookout tower of bamboo on the beach. I could see, through the periscope, two Japanese on the top of it and one pointing to my periscope. I was so close that I felt I could almost hear those Japanese talking to each other.

We found that the day-long bombardment plus the two days of bombardment by the air forces hadn't done much damage.

Since the landing was to take place the next morning, the amphibious forces and the huge task force would be moving in from the east towards the west through this fairly narrow slot between Betio and the next little atoll to the south. This didn't leave a great deal of room for maneuvering. Several days before I had been amazed at the considerable amount of current in this slot from the east and the west. In fact, I perceived the current to be about three to three and a half knots.

As I said, our job was to observe the beaches on Betio, go out and surface, and then report on the radio what we had seen. After looking at the beaches, we could see that the guns were still there and seemed to be in apple-pie order. We had to make sure that we went well out before we could surface, and since the current was running at three knots from east to west, there was little or no hope on my part of turning and running against it. And my submerged speed would be only three or four knots at most, so I would be just a sitting duck until I could get out of there. It was certainly imperative that I leave that slot before the task force came in. There was no question in my mind that everybody in the task force would be trigger happy, and I was in no position to tangle with anybody.

I'd been specifically prohibited from going out west because the cruisers and destroyers and carriers were still milling around in that direction. So I had to open out south from the Betio shore in this slot, get on the surface, run east along the base of the southern atoll, make a turn, and get down to Apamama, doing it all in the dark. And it was imperative that I get off my report on the beaches, because they were going to land the next morning.

I sent off my message even though it was considerably later in the evening than we had anticipated. We were well into this slot between the atolls. We had a long way to go to get out of it on our way to Apamama. As we were running out in the dark and running into the face of the oncoming task force, I knew that I had to stay on the surface as long as possible in order to get the speed up to escape this mousetrap. And I had to be sure that I ran undetected.

I knew that recognition signals from the oncoming fleet were different light signals for different times. We had a Buck Rogers–type gun that fired a pistol-like cartridge with different color signals for different times. Now for the time period we were in, the signal was supposed to be solid green. I had an officer, Red Porterfield, standing by my side on the bridge while we were clunking along as fast as we could, trying to get out of this slot. I told Red to check and recheck the time, and if I slapped him on the back and said, "Fire!" to be sure to get the color signal right. He went down to the conning tower to check the time, and sure enough, it was supposed to be green.

We could just barely discern the form of what we thought was an oncoming destroyer to the north of us. We didn't like the way he seemed to be nosing around. So there was nothing we could do except to keep running to the east and hope that we'd get out of the slot before anything untoward happened.

A few minutes after this there was a terrific explosion astern. It was a hell of a bang. My first deduction was that I was running so close to the atoll to the south of us that I had run over a mine. I could actually hear the pounding of the surf on this atoll. We were that close to it.

Shortly after that we saw this destroyer, and it seemed to be turning towards us. I watched it for a second and I slapped Porterfield on the back and said, "Fire that recognition!" And he fired. Out went the most vivid red light you have ever seen. As I said, the signal was supposed to be green. Red was the unfriendly signal. Well, this cartridge went up into the air and then broke into a brilliant green light and dropped, but it had been red all the way up. I think everyone in that task force saw this—first red and then green—and was convinced we were unfriendly. With that the destroyer opened fire. We could see red flashes as the guns went off. A split second later we got a hell of a jolt on the port side, immediately below the conning tower. I knew that we had been hit.

I screamed to dive. I also screamed to my executive to see if we'd taken any water in, because there had been an awful impact on the port side. He reported some small leaks, nothing to be concerned about. There was, however, a hell of a lot of water coming down from the conning tower into the control room. Lynch was shouting up to the conning tower that we must have a leak up there, and we did. We had a dilly. A voice tube ran from the bridge into the conning tower, and in the conning tower there was a big gate valve which was supposed to be pulled shut when we dove, closing off the voice tube to the bridge. It was part of the diving procedure for one of the crew on the conning tower to swing the valve on this voice tube when we dove. But this time the impact of that shot on the port side had upset things sufficiently so that when they pulled the valve, it jammed and wouldn't close. So we had water pouring through a two-and-a-half-inch or three-inch hole into the conning tower. It was an awful lot of water and it accumulated as we went down. In no time at all we were fighting to keep our equilibrium.

We managed to stop the water through the foresight of the machinist's mate who was on duty in the conning tower. When he saw that he couldn't close the valve, he rammed his elbow in it. So we made the dive with this machinist's mate's elbow in the voice tube. The boy at the dike. That's what kept the water flow down.

It had been pouring into the conning tower and control room in such quantity that it was spilling over the gyro switchboard, which was not very far from the ladder. We had an electrician's mate whose name was Hector. He was a quiet little fellow and he was really good. He tried putting canvas over the hatch to stop the flow. He eased over to the executive officer, who had taken the dive and was controlling, and said, "Mr. Lynch, if we can't stop the water from coming in, you could just put a list on it so that when the water comes down the hatch, instead of flowing on the switchboard it will flow over to the side and we can save the gyro and the auxiliary gyro." So good old Ozzie went to work, not only to keep the ship afloat but also to put a list on it so the water wouldn't flow onto the switchboard.

We used a bucket brigade to carry the water from the motor room to the engine room and the next compartment forward. We wanted to lighten the stern because we'd used practically all of our trimming water to get control. In time we found the leak and controlled it to a degree, and we began to fight our way back up from 225 feet. Now our control depth was only 200 feet, and we had such an angle on that our stern must have been down close to 300 feet. The *Nautilus* had a riveted hull, and from the time we hit 200 and below, the rivets would squeal as they reset themselves. There'd be a hell of a whine and then a leak would develop. A rivet would reset itself under pressure.

We finally got the ship under control and up to 200 feet. By this time the task force had passed us, and fortunately we hadn't gotten into a sonar attack. That would have messed us up. I didn't have any idea where in the world we were other than that we were damned close to the atoll to the south of us. I thought I was so close that the flow of the current was going to put me up on the beach. But we hadn't touched anything so far. Then we eased back up to 150 or 100 feet.

The marines we had aboard were concentrated for the most part in the forward torpedo room. They didn't like any part of this. I thought I'd better go forward and talk to them. They were scheduled to be landed the next day and to take the island of Apamama, which was the next part of our operation. I went up into the torpedo room and tried to joke with them about everything being in hand. We were getting out of our hole, I told them, and so there was nothing to be concerned about. One of the men was a sergeant. I said to him, "You haven't been worried about this, have you?"

"No, sir," said he, "not in the least."

I told him I was glad to hear that, and then he said, "The only thing I've got to say, Captain, is that this is a hell of a place to have to dig a foxhole."

Now we got back to periscope depth and swung the periscope around in the dark but couldn't see anything. So we decided to ease up, surface, then get the hell out of there. We blew our ballast tanks until they were dewatered to a degree, and then we cut in the turbo blows, which were high-volume low-pressure machines. Low-pressure turbo air evacuated the rest of the water in the ballast tanks. (If too much air went to one side or the other, the ship tended to list.)

Well, we finally got to the surface and shifted the turbo blowers. I was at the hatch calling down, "Too much to port, blow more in the starboard." And I kept screaming, "Blow more to the starboard."

Finally my exec called up and told me to go down again. I asked what in the hell he was talking about, going down again. I said, "Blow more to the starboard."

He said, "Well, we've only been blowing in the starboard. There's something wrong in the port side."

So I sounded the diving alarm and we went down again. I almost had a mutiny. Here were these sailors who'd just come out of this situation where we'd almost hit the bottom. Now they were being taken down again in this crazy thing with everything going haywire.

But we got down and buttoned up and found that we were tighter when we were submerged. And Ozzie Lynch got on his thinking cap again with two or three others and tried to locate our trouble. He finally decided that the high-pressure lines which went directly to the ballast tanks were intact, because when we blew we came up all right. The low-pressure lines, the turbo-blow lines on the port side, must be parted, he said. There must have been some holes in them, because when we blew the starboard tanks the air didn't seem to be going into the port tank. Consequently, the air we were putting in the port-tank blow lines was doing nothing. So we must have had holes in the blow lines, which, incidentally, ran along the outside of the hull and could have been damaged by the explosion.

As it turned out, that was exactly what it was. The low-pressure blow lines on the port side had been torn out by the first hit in the vicinity of the conning tower. When we put air into them, of course, it escaped without blowing the ballast tank. So we decided that the only thing we could do was to surface the submarine completely by blowing with high-pressure air. We did that and we went aloft. In the interior we closed off certain individual valves so that we could hold her dry. Now we were in a bad position to dive again because we'd have to do it by opening these hand valves. Normally the whole thing is done with a hydraulic mechanism that opens and closes the valves.

After we got to the surface we sized up our damage. We found the low-pressure blow lines on the port side were definitely open. There was no question at all that we also had some very sizable cracks in the hull on the port side and in the periscope well, because we'd taken a considerable amount of water. The water that we'd taken through the conning tower we deduced had come from the valve, and fixing the valve would take care of that problem.

Now we had to devise some means whereby we could dive, because if we sat on the surface we would likely be attacked by a plane, probably one of ours. There was every reason to expect that would happen, and then we would be in real trouble. Normal diving time on the part of a fleet submarine is fifty-eight to sixty seconds. Our diving time in this condition was at least a minute and a half or two minutes, but with the condition of our blow lines and with the hand operation of the valves, it would take anywhere from four to five minutes to dive. Well, by that time we could have really been in trouble—we would have had it!

We had already missed a day trying to get to Apamama to capture the island. I decided to place men by the hand valves on the port side and develop a procedure whereby they would turn and open the valves when we sounded the diving alarm. By doing this, we could get down in two and a half to three minutes. It was a touchy damn thing, but it made it possible for us to run on the surface.*

So we got down to Apamama about twenty-four hours late. Apamama was another atoll, much smaller than Tarawa, in the form of a triangle, with a string of small islands on the south side, several larger islands along the east side, and a whole string of very small islands on the west side. According to our intelligence, the island was being held by Japanese marines.

Now we had this seventy-nine-man marine outfit with us, and we figured that if they could land on the south shore of Apamama and work their way around and up the east shore, then they could drive out these Japanese marines—liquidate them, if possible, and take the land, hopefully in two days.

After we got to the surface that night, I told the task force commander about our condition. I didn't say that we were incapable of carrying out our mission. I only said that we were delayed but proceeding. On the basis of

---

*The hand-operated valve method reduced diving time. The submarine was so vulnerable to air attack that if it took four or five minutes to dive she would have had to stay down, which in turn would have prevented her from maintaining her schedule. As Irwin says earlier, submarines could only make a reasonable speed on the surface.

what I said, he felt we were able to do the job. But the next day he began to have misgivings and asked questions about this, that, and the other thing. He knew that our main induction had been leaky and that for the most part we had gone down with it flooded. This, together with the complications of our tanks, caused him to reconsider. After three or four days he decided to pull us out of there. We were in no position to play around. But to get out we would have to have an escort. That was a big task, to find one that could lead us home. There was no hope of getting repairs in that theater.

In the meantime, the marines would go ashore from the *Nautilus* in rubber boats and would land and work their way along the south shore. The plan was that they would put up panels in the trees that would tell us where they were and what they needed. We would provide them with more ammunition, more food, and other necessities and take off any wounded men. So we put them ashore the next night and they got off in the rubber boats.

I recall saying to Captain James Jones, USMCR, who had been with me on our first patrol in the *Nautilus* and who was in charge of the seventy marines on board, "Now be damned sure you keep us informed where you are, because I'll be totally in the dark out here and submerged all day long. When we come up at night we have a flat battery and we have to make early contact and then get back out to charge our batteries so that we can be in a survival state for the next day."

We let them off during the night. The next morning we took up our patrol along the south shore of the atoll and there was nary a sign of anything—no panels, nothing. We couldn't see a damn thing. We stewed all day long about where they were and how they were making out. Then I began to have misgivings about the opposition on the island. Perhaps it was much greater than we anticipated. They might very well have been ambushed and wiped out.

So we went through a long, hard day looking for them. We came up that night and searched as close as we thought was possible to the beach. There was no sign of anything. No lights, no fire, nothing. We left and charged our battery and went back toward the beach early to try and discern something before the sun rose. We got nowhere. It was the second day and we'd still had no contact with them, absolutely nothing. By the end of the second day I was really upset. The whole thing had blown up. I was trying to make up my mind about what we should do. We had a few rubber boats left. I knew that I could get some volunteers who would be willing to go ashore and look for the men, but I thought I might lose them as well.

We drew off the second night and came back the third day to search again. We saw a panel. It indicated that the marines were far short of the progress we thought they would make. Later on during the day we saw another panel that indicated they wanted to return that night for ammunition. (Different panels hung up in the trees meant different things.)

So we positioned ourselves that night and Jones came up in a rubber boat with two other men. One man had been badly shot by an automatic rifle and the other had a hernia. Jones wanted ammunition badly and more food. He said their progress was all right, and that he hoped he would make it around the southeast corner that night and up along the eastern shore. His men had made a reconnaissance up there and found that they had to get across a stream that ran from the ocean into a lagoon. They were pretty certain they could see Japs entrenched on the other side of this stream. There was a coconut grove and they saw the Japs under the coconut trees in this grove. Jones' thought was that he would line his people up along this stream and face the Japs from the north side, because he thought they were entrenched there. He said that if I surfaced off this point and opened up with our guns on this coconut grove, our guns would be able to blast the Japs out.

Well, we were equipped with some superquick fuses that went off on palm fronds. We arranged a fire-control staff with a walkie-talkie. We were to work into a position just off this stream, as close as possible to the beach. After establishing communications we would open up and shoot into the palm trees—also shoot down if we could. We were close, however, and the trajectory of the fire was so high that it was extremely difficult to bring it any closer to the trees.

With this makeshift communication system worked out, we opened up and fired. The shell hit the palm fronds and fell onto the ground below. Jones radioed back to me that that was fine, but to aim the next shell a little bit to the right, or lower, or to the left, etc. A couple of times he shouted, "You stupid jackass, I said to the right. You shot to the left and almost hit me." We had that kind of exchange going.

Both of our guns went off but only one was working. They were made so that when they fired one would squat. The breech would go down and the brow would go up and the shell would go way over into the center of the atoll. Our elevating mechanism had gone haywire on one gun; when it fired it would slip and throw the barrel up into the air and project the shell way out—miles away.

It wasn't very long before Jones thought that the blasts had combed out practically all the coconuts, and he didn't think there were any Japs left. He told us to cease firing. His men were going to try and get across the stream. In a very short period of time he called back and said they were across. There was nothing but debris and dead bodies—Japs all over the place, all dead. We had agreed that if he did succeed, I was to go off and do the next thing I was told to do. I was still supposed to go to Nauru Island and do a lifeguard mission down there.

In the meantime I had been told to withdraw to a particular spot south of Apamama, which was supposedly out of the action area. The surface task force command had become awfully leery of Japanese submarines. The carrier USS *Lipscomb Bay* had been sunk during the action at Tarawa. As a result, practically the whole area was untenable for us. All our people would shoot first and ask questions afterwards. In our condition we were fair game for anything and everything that came by.

I had been screaming to Pearl Harbor to send somebody to take off the casualty I had on board. I also asked for a welder and some plates so that we could try and patch up the holes in our port side.

During the course of our bombardment of Apamama, the quartermaster touched me on the sleeve and said, "What do you want me to say to him?"

I said, "To whom?"

And he replied, "To the hospital ship that's lying out here. He wants to know if he can pass." I told him to tell them to get out of there, and fast. So the ship went south and around the atoll, out of our sight.

After he had gone I thought to myself, "Why in hell didn't I give him this injured man?" One of the two men who had been returned to us the night before had died. He had been shot up pretty badly. The other man with the hernia condition was in bad shape, and there wasn't anything we could do other than get him to a doctor who could operate. So we had requested the task force commander to send a vessel down to this spot with a medical man. This is what they had done.

After finishing our bombardment, I pulled off to the south coast of Apamama with the idea that somebody would come and help us. There was a salvage vessel that had been in the area between Apamama and Tarawa, and when the going had gotten rough with shells flying all over the place, the vessel thought the better part of valor was to get out of there, so she pulled down around the southwestern corner of this atoll. Here I was fussing around in the same area. I came charging down, thinking this was the ship that was going to take care of my problems. I was on the surface, flashing my light and trying to tell the vessel to close. But instead she put her tail to me and ran to beat all hell. So I began to chase her down. The more I chased the more she tried to get away. Finally she did read my message and slowed down, but she kept her tail to us.

She put a boat in the water and sent a man over to us. I asked him if he had a welder and some plates. He didn't know anything about a welder and plates. I told him that we had a sick man we wanted to get to a doctor fast. He said they didn't have a doctor on board, so I shouted, "What the hell are you doing down here?"

And his reply was, "The captain didn't tell me."

So I told my men to put the sick man on a stretcher and send him back to the ship with instructions to get a welder with some plates to patch up our holes—also telling the captain to get this man to a doctor.

We found out later that the crew of the salvage vessel had thought they were running away from air raids. The vessel had been sitting offshore on the eastern side of the atoll when somebody ashore started shooting at her. The crew couldn't figure out where the shooting was coming from. Actually, it was my faulty gun shooting all the way across the atoll and landing near the ship. And, remarkably, the gun's range, though incorrect, was so consistent that we came close to the vessel every time. So she started running.

She couldn't do anything for the sick man, and it also turned out that she didn't have a welder on board and she didn't have plates.

At this point I decided to go south and stay there until I received further instructions. Instead of sending someone to do the welding so I could continue with the mission, SubPac was fussing about getting an escort to bring me home. They sent another salvage vessel, the *Grapple*. She came and escorted me back to Pearl.

In his drive through the Solomons toward the formidable Japanese base at Rabaul, one of Admiral Halsey's most important objectives was Empress Augusta Bay, on the west coast of Bougainville, the largest of the Solomon Islands. The operation there (1 November 1943) was considered a dangerous one because Cape Torokina, at that end of the bay where the landings took place, was about 210 miles from Rabaul. Halsey's memory of what the Rabaul-based forces had inflicted on the troops landing at Guadalcanal, more than 560 miles away, was painful, and for this reason his subordinate commander, Rear Admiral Theodore S. Wilkinson, planned the operation with the greatest care.

Wilkinson, commanding Task Force 31, a collection of attack transports and cargo ships carrying the Third Marine Division to the landing area at Empress Augusta Bay, wanted quick and efficient landings so that his vulnerable transports could hastily retreat before the Japanese counterattacked and wreaked havoc on them. That he achieved, despite the difficulties of unloading his transports. Unloading a ship that carries not only assault troops, but also the equipment, supplies, and vehicles they will use on shore, is a complicated art. Everything must be stowed on board so that it can be taken off in the order in which it will be needed on land.

In the following selection Vice Admiral Felix Johnson tells his story of the *President Adams,* one of the eight transports under Admiral Wilkinson's command. Johnson, her skipper, was an extremely efficient commander. He was aware of the difficulties involved in the landing at Empress Augusta Bay, and he took all the steps necessary to overcome them. At the same time he was concerned for the welfare of his crew. His comments show that in even the most dangerous actions in the Pacific commanders could have the compassion to look after their men.

INITIATION
IN AN ATTACK TRANSPORT

VICE ADMIRAL FELIX JOHNSON

FELIX LESLIE JOHNSON was born in Aberdeen, North Carolina, in 1897. He attended schools in that state, including the University of North Carolina, before entering the U.S. Naval Academy. He graduated in June 1919 and served thereafter in a number of destroyers and in the USS *Penguin* of the Yangtze Patrol. In 1926 he returned to the Naval Academy as an instructor. In 1928–31 he again saw duty with the Asiatic Fleet. After his return to the United States he had duty in several capacities on the East Coast, ending with a tour of two years with the naval mission in Brazil.

His first command was the USS *Lang* in 1939. In 1941 he returned to the Naval Academy as secretary to the academic board and as aide to the superintendent. Early in 1943 he was given command of the USS *President Adams*, a military transport. After participating in the amphibious landing at Cape Torokina, Bougainville, he left to become assistant chief of staff to Admiral Halsey, Commander, South Pacific. He retained that post until he returned to the United States in June 1944 and took command of the USS *Springfield*. She provided escort for President Roosevelt's trip to Yalta in January 1945 and then joined Cruiser Division 17 for the Okinawa campaign. Johnson returned to Washington to become assistant chief of the Bureau of Personnel in June 1945; director of public relations for the navy in 1946; and Commander, Destroyers, U.S. Atlantic Fleet, in 1948.

His final active-duty tour came in 1949, when he was appointed director of naval intelligence, in which capacity he served until his retirement in September 1952. Vice Admiral Johnson was recalled to duty in 1954 to serve as chairman of the Naval Reserve Evaluation Board and then as chairman of a board to evaluate the promotion system for naval reserve officers. He resumed retirement in 1956 only to be recalled to active duty as chairman of the Naval Reserve Evaluation Board until June 1962, when he retired once again.

Admiral Johnson died at his home in Leonardtown, Maryland, in 1981.

The *President Adams* was what was called an attack transport. She had been one of the Dollar Line ships that went around the world, and was about eighteen or twenty thousand tons. She could carry up to two thousand troops. She had been commissioned as a navy transport about a year before I took her over, and her first effort had been participating in the Guadalcanal operation.

When I took command I discovered that my crew was all reserves. I don't think I had a single regular on board. We had around six or seven hundred men and around sixty-five officers and I was the only regular among them. They were wonderful. My executive officer was a New York broker, the first lieutenant was a Sears Roebuck salesman, the engineer had worked for a stationary power plant in southern California, and my navigator was an ROTC lad from Yale.

As it turned out, I had a very short cruise on the *President Adams*. Initially I made two or three runs to Guadalcanal and New Georgia with New Zealanders as replenishment troops. We always had about six destroyers with us on such trips and sometimes we had air cover, especially when we got close to Japanese-held islands in the area. The Japs were reported to have submarines around as well, but I did not see one the whole time I was there.

On these trips we carried the maximum number of troops—about two thousand. It was very crowded. They had their own equipment but we had to feed them. They also had their own chaplain, a New Zealander named Burragwanath. He was the biggest man I've ever seen in my life. His size almost brought him to grief one day when we were having a practice landing on New Georgia.

To embark in the boats that would take them ashore, the men had to go down a cargo net, hand over hand. These nets were strung alongside the *Adams*. Our big chaplain, who had been ashore with his men, was coming back to the ship. Apparently he was quite tired and was one of the last to get out of the boat that brought him to the transport. He climbed and climbed and got almost to the top of the net but then couldn't go any further. All he did was just hang on, and you could see his hands begin to loosen. Fortunately the fast-thinking coxswain in the boat gunned his engine and dashed

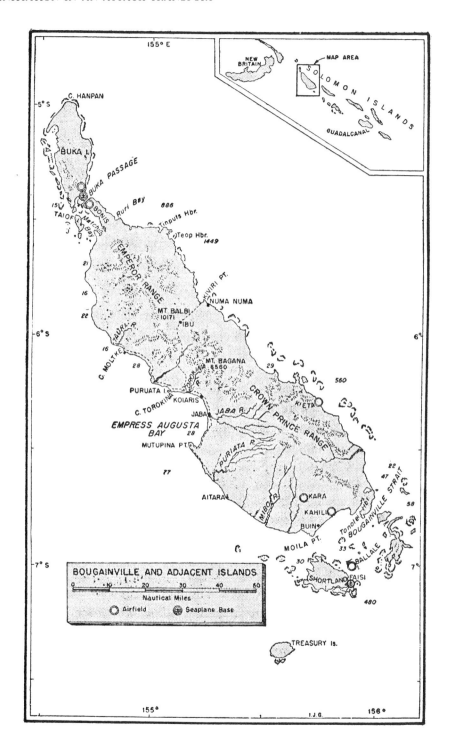

ahead just as Burragwanath fell from the net. He hit the water behind the boat. He would have been killed if he had hit the boat, but as it was he was just knocked out and he soon recovered.

One day before the U.S. marines were to land at Empress Augusta Bay on Bougainville (1 November 1943), I had eighteen hundred troops on board. They had been cooped up on the ship for several days. It was hot and very uncomfortable. So we decided to run over to a neighboring island that was not occupied by the Japanese. We had a practice landing in preparation for Bougainville and all eighteen hundred marines went ashore. It had been suggested by somebody—maybe my New York broker—that we send about fifty cases of beer ahead and put them on a mound in the middle of the island. When the men hit the beach they stormed forward and captured the beer. Each man got his reward, a couple of beers. Then we brought them all back on board ship and sailed the next day for Bougainville, where the *President Adams* got involved in two separate engagements.

A month or two later I was down in Noumea walking through the hospital grounds. There I met a very tired-looking marine sergeant. His clothes were all messed up. It was obvious he had been through some action. He was sort of drooping along. Then he saw me and gave a very sharp salute and said, "May the sergeant address the captain, sir?"

"Certainly, Sergeant, what is it?"

And then he said, "The sergeant would like to observe to the captain that the *President Adams* is the best damn transport in the South Pacific. It gave the marines beer before they landed in Bougainville."

About the twenty-eighth of October we had loaded marines at Espíritu Santo. After that we had sailed for our date in Bougainville at Empress Augusta Bay. The landing was to take place just inside Cape Torokina. We had thought that landing was going to be worse than it was, but it turned out we had some very effective air cover flying in from Guadalcanal. The distance was such, however, that our fighters could only come up and stay over the Bougainville area for about an hour before dwindling fuel made it necessary for them to turn back. This called for a constant replenishment cover of fighters.

Our landing was scheduled for about seven-thirty in the morning, but somewhere around two o'clock that night we steamed toward the bay. (There was an active volcano just back of Empress Augusta Bay and it was belching forth flames. It was an eerie sight.) We were part of a flotilla of about five troopships and we had an escort of perhaps eighteen destroyers.

We had no sooner reached our designated spot and anchored than the lad who was the gunnery officer—I think he was a senior lieutenant reserve—called up to the bridge and asked if he could commence firing. We had only six three-inch fifty-caliber guns as armament. But it was quite a thrill, nevertheless. For the first time in my life I called out "Commence firing!" when there was an enemy on the other end firing in turn.

Then we began sending our men ashore, load after load after load. Of course it was the first time in combat for most of these men and there was some apprehension. I had a wonderful young Baptist chaplain from Texas on board, a junior lieutenant. Before the men landed he had something like twelve hundred men to give communion to, so he was up the whole night before they debarked. I remember that he came up on the bridge about four o'clock saying, "Captain, would you like to have communion? I can give you four minutes' worth." That was the most impressive communion I ever had.

The men had a pretty rough time when they landed on the beach; thirty-one were killed. But it wasn't nearly as bad as we had expected, because our planes had strafed the beaches and done a good job for us. A flock of Japanese Zeros came over of course. At one time I saw eight of them that had crashed and were blazing.

There were no Jap warships in the area. I think Tip Merrill had had a very successful night action with his cruiser division and that might have accounted for the absence of the Japs. Arleigh Burke had also been operating in the area with his destroyers, the Little Beavers. It was on one of his night engagements that he had been alerted to the fact that there was a Japanese force coming down the Slot and been told to intercept it. He began sending messages down to the headquarters at Noumea: "Burke making thirty-one knots to intercept the enemy, Burke making thirty-one knots to intercept the enemy." The operations officer down there finally sent one back: "Thirty-One-Knot Burke, you've got to get up off your rear and make thirty-three if you're going to catch those boys." And he did. That's why he has been designated ever since as Thirty-One-Knot Burke.

After that first landing of troops on Bougainville our mission was to go back to Espíritu for more troops and return. We did, and one week later we made our second landing on the beach. This time around we had more difficulty from the air. However, I didn't lose any men.

After the first landing a tragic thing occurred. I had thirty-one dead on board. Now that had a very depressing effect on the men, to have corpses lying around. Also I was afraid they might begin to decompose. It was going to take us two and a half days to get back to Guadalcanal. It was the first time this had ever happened to me, so I decided I'd bury them at sea. I thought that was my prerogative as the skipper, but it didn't turn out to be. I had the bodies all laid out on the fantail with weights attached to take them down. The chaplain was poised. I hoisted a general signal which said that I was preparing to bury the dead. Immediately I got a signal back: "Negative, cancel." It came from my division commander, a senior captain. He said the bodies would be taken back to Guadalcanal. Later he told me that their families had a right to the bodies if they could be returned.

The *President Adams* had been a passenger steamer and had made trips around the world. She had large cold-storage spaces aboard. I should have thought of this before I made plans for burial at sea. Now we put the bodies in the storage spaces until we got back to Guadalcanal. They were taken ashore and buried there. The families could make arrangements for reinterment later.

After landing the troops the second time we were ordered to New Zealand. That was to provide some rest and recreation for the crew, but it was also to fetch more New Zealanders for the Solomons. We stopped at Noumea for an overnight, and early the next morning I heard four bongs, meaning a four-striper was coming aboard. I went back to the gangway to meet him. A captain I'd never seen before came over the side and saluted, saying, "Good morning, Captain, I'm your relief."

"Oh?"

And he said, "You've got to get your things in a hurry and get off because we sail in an hour. Here are your orders." And he gave me my orders. They were to join the staff of the commander in chief of the South Pacific, Admiral Halsey. Nothing more was said.

I rushed around and flung things in my bags. At that point I did a very dumb thing. I forgot the golf clubs that I had brought with me when I got command of the *Adams*. (Originally I had thought that when I was in Australia and New Zealand I'd be able to get some golfing in. That showed how little I knew about war!) I guess those clubs went wherever the *President Adams* did after that.

When General MacArthur's drive on the island of New Guinea and Admiral Halsey's battle for Guadalcanal were concluded, both commanders had substantial springboards for their push farther north, toward the Philippines and the Japanese homeland. Their objectives for the advance were decided in March 1943 at the Pacific Military Conference in Washington, D.C. At that conference Rabaul was not set up as a principal target, but it was assumed to be such. Both Admiral King and General MacArthur regarded the port town as important. MacArthur was anxious to have it as a base to implement his return to the Philippines, from which he had been driven a short time before.

In April 1943 Admiral William F. Halsey was ready to start his drive through the Solomons towards Rabaul. There were two big thorns in his side. First, the Japanese were at work fortifying their positions in the forefront of the apparent Allied offensive. Their "Tokyo Express" (the name for supply forces that operated at night) went into high gear down the Slot in the central Solomons. Second, there were two Japanese airstrips at Munda, on the southwest tip of New Georgia Island and at Vila on Kolombangara Island. Both were in an area that interfered with South Pacific naval operations. Halsey loosed a number of raids against them and had mines laid in their approaches. He also sent cruiser task groups under Admirals Stanton ("Tip") Merrill and Walden ("Pug") Ainsworth to intercept the components of the Tokyo Express and to engage in shore bombardment.

When Halsey began his preparations for the landing at Empress Augusta Bay on Bougainville, the largest of the Solomons, he ordered a round of air and sea strikes on various airfields and ship targets. The campaign went on during the closing days of October 1943 and into the early part of November. Naval gunfire was provided by Admiral Merrill's task force, of which Arleigh Burke's Destroyer Squadron 23, known as the Little Beavers because of its eager application to tasks at hand, was an active part. The actual landing at Empress Augusta Bay took place on 1–2 November. It was then that Burke proved himself an aggressive, omnipresent leader and earned the lasting sobriquet Thirty-One-Knot Burke, by which Admiral Halsey addressed him in dispatches.*

One of the most notable exploits in this series of actions came on 25 November, when the Japanese ran a Tokyo Express of destroyers ferrying troops to Buka, an island just north of Bougainville and Empress Augusta Bay. American air patrols intercepted five of the destroyers, and when the ships steamed into the narrow Buka passage, Burke's Little Beavers sank two of them and chased the others almost all the way back to Rabaul. That was the last Tokyo Express to traverse the Slot.

The following incident, an excerpt from Burke's oral history, occurred during the Bougainville campaign of November 1943. It highlights both the daring and the integrity that made Burke a legend in the U.S. Navy. The story also underscores the spirit of comradeship that enables men of the sea, even former enemies, to sit down together when the business of war has ended and find their common ground.

*For the story of how Burke earned his nickname, see Admiral Felix Johnson, "Initiation in an Attack Transport," p. 196.

A POSTWAR REVELATION

ADMIRAL ARLEIGH BURKE

ARLEIGH ALBERT BURKE, born in Boulder, Colorado, on 19 October 1901, graduated from the U.S. Naval Academy in 1923. He earned a master of science degree from the University of Michigan in 1931.

Persistent efforts on his part took him from a billet at the naval gun factory in Washington early in World War II to the South Pacific, where he commanded four destroyer divisions successively. In March 1944 he became chief of staff to Admiral Marc Mitscher, commander of Fast Carrier Task Force 58, and remained in that job until June 1945. In 1949 Captain Burke directed the efforts of the navy in the controversy over unification of the armed forces. At the outbreak of the Korean War he served as deputy chief of staff to Commander, Naval Forces, Far East, and later he served as a member of the United Nations Truce Delegation in Korea. He was director of the strategic plans division of the Office of the Chief of Naval Operations from December 1951 to March 1954, when he took command of Cruiser Division 6. Admiral Burke was appointed chief of naval operations in August 1955 and was twice reappointed, serving in that capacity longer than any other naval officer.

Burke retired from active duty on 1 August 1961. He has made his home in Bethesda, Maryland, since retirement. One of his major accomplishments has been the founding of the Georgetown Center for Strategic Studies.

Rear Admiral Kinichi Kasaka, who had commanded Japanese army and navy forces at Rabaul, was the head of an organization called the Rabaul Kai. It is a veteran's organization of Imperial Japanese Navy people, all people who fought from Rabaul against what they called the Southwest Area, which was the Rabaul area, the Solomons. I got a letter after I was retired asking would I please come to Japan, that they would like to have me join the Rabaul Kai in a ceremony. I wrote back and said, "Admiral, I don't think you want me there. I don't think your organization understands. I fought as hard as I could against your whole organization, and I don't think you really want me. I wouldn't want to go in there under any false pretense or anything."

He wrote back and said they knew all about it. "We know all about you and that's why we want you."

So I went over there. I went through this whole big Shinto ceremony at the Yakusumi Shrine, complete with cleansing, saki toasts, and palm leaves, and became a member of their society. I had to make several speeches, of course. The Japanese love to make speeches and they love to have other people make speeches too, so I had to make many speeches to this organization at the ceremony, at the dinner, at a meeting that they had. I became a kind of blood brother!

It wasn't until that ceremony was over that I understood why I was asked. The reason was that one time during the war, in November 1943, I made a sweep with my squadron of destroyers, DesRon 23, north of Rabaul, north of Kavieng, and I came a little north of the equator some place, to the shipping lane between Kavieng and Palau. Then I took a formation down the shipping line towards Kavieng, hoping to run into some Japanese ships. Well, we did. We saw a little smoke, saw a ship. I had five destroyers, and we were bow-to, so they couldn't recognize us. We knew that anything we sighted was enemy. They thought we were Japanese.

I thought there would be more than one ship but there wasn't. There was just this one ship and it was a small ship, and here were we with five ships, each one of ours bigger than that one small ship. Well, we were far north of any air cover and we were within close reach of Japanese air cover, so if they sighted and recognized us and got off a report we would have had Japanese air down on top of us right fast. That wouldn't do. If she were going to be sunk, she had to be sunk fast.

So by TBS I told the ships, "Bend on the international signal for surrender." This was a code signal. "And break that signal when I give you the word to break it." That means that the signal is hoisted up to the yardarm, except it's rolled, so that when the halyard is hauled the signal floats out.

The Japanese ship was at a fairly good distance, six or eight thousand yards. I went into echelon formation so that we could open up with all guns, so that all the ships' guns could bear. All I had to do then was shift course just a little bit and let her have it. So everything was in formation. She was probably nervous by then.

Then I said, "Break the signal." They broke the signal but, within thirty seconds, the Japanese ship opened up with this very small gun. She was going to fight instead of surrender. Well, there was nothing to do but sink her, so we sank her, and we probably sank her within fifteen seconds after the first bullets hit, because we just snowed her when we commenced firing. Then we went over to pick up survivors. I had three ships picking up survivors. Most of them would not be picked up, they'd swim away. We'd get one Japanese aboard and give him a cup of coffee and try to persuade the others to come aboard. We got a few that way. So we had three ships picking up survivors and the other two ships searching around for Japanese submarines, because another old trick in war is to get ships when they are picking up survivors. So we picked up thirty, forty, fifty—I've forgotten now.

After all the survivors had either drowned or come aboard, I said, "Let's stop all engines for one minute. We'll have a one-minute prayer service for the gallant captain we just sank." So we did. He was not a survivor.

Apparently one of the Japanese prisoners heard that and reported the incident to Kusaka. That's exactly what the Japanese would have done, which I didn't know. They would have done it, because the battle would be over, finished, and if you fought well, they'd honor you. I found out later that when our planes would crash in Japan, the Japanese would go over and get the people who'd been killed and give them an honorable funeral, hold a ceremony for them—for good warriors, enemy warriors, but good ones. They had done their duty, and the Japanese gave full honor to people who did their duty.

Well, that was a revelation. That revelation came a long time after I had retired, but part of it came before, the realization of the Japanese understanding of life, their way of living together, their understanding of integrity and honor, or *Bushido*. So I understood a little bit about why Japanese are Japanese, and I like them very much now.

The Battle of the Philippine Sea is now considered one of the most decisive encounters of the Pacific war, but when it ended on 20 June 1944,
controversy over the decisions of Admiral Raymond Spruance, commanding the Fifth Fleet, blocked any balanced appraisal of it. Spruance
was criticized for being too cautious and for having lost a great opportunity to smash Admiral Jisaburo Ozawa's Mobile Fleet.

On 15 June the Mobile Fleet emerged from the straits of the Philippines into the Philippine Sea, where it joined other forces and headed
for the Marianas. Spruance's fleet was west of those islands; on the
morning of 19 June his flagship, the *Lexington,* was about ninety miles
northwest of Guam and a hundred miles southwest of Saipan. He was
under orders to defend the amphibious landings on Saipan, Tinian, and
Guam.

A week earlier, guessing that Ozawa was counting on help from
Japanese land-based air forces on Guam, Spruance had suggested that
Admiral Marc Mitscher, commanding Task Force 58, launch a neutral-
ization strike against enemy planes and airfields on the island. On the
morning of 11 June Task Force 58 planes effectively prevented the par-
ticipation of Japanese land-based air in the Battle of the Philippine Sea.

The main phase of the battle took place on 19 June, after Ozawa
launched four massive raids from his carriers. Task Force 58 radars detected the aircraft coming from the west, and 450 Hellcats were sent to
meet them. During the next eight hours of fierce and almost continuous
fighting, a total of 346 Japanese aircraft were destroyed (and in a separate action two Japanese carriers, the *Taiho* and the *Shokaku,* were
sunk), while the Americans lost only 30 planes and sustained one hit on
a battleship. This virtual annihilation of enemy air power has come to be
known as the Great Marianas Turkey Shoot.

At 2000 on 19 June three of Mitscher's four carrier groups started
west in an abortive attempt to locate the enemy. It was not until the next
day that a plane from the *Enterprise* reported Ozawa's position, 175
miles away. Mitscher launched an all-out strike, 216 planes from ten carriers in only ten minutes. By the time they sighted the enemy force it

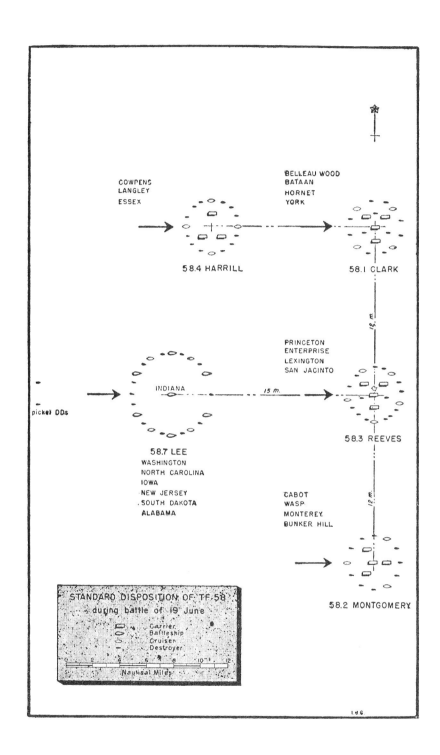

COWPENS
LANGLEY
ESSEX

BELLEAU WOOD
BATAAN
HORNET
YORK

58.4 HARRILL

58.1 CLARK

12 m.

picket DDs

INDIANA

15 m.

PRINCETON
ENTERPRISE
LEXINGTON
SAN JACINTO

58.3 REEVES

58.7 LEE
WASHINGTON
NORTH CAROLINA
IOWA
NEW JERSEY
SOUTH DAKOTA
ALABAMA

12 m.

CABOT
WASP
MONTEREY
BUNKER HILL

58.2 MONTGOMERY

STANDARD DISPOSITION OF TF-58
during battle of 19 June

Carrier
Battleship
Cruiser
Destroyer

0   2   4   6   8   10   12
Nautical Miles

was sundown and they had flown nearly three hundred miles. There was neither the time nor the fuel to organize coordinated attacks, but the strike did manage to destroy the newest Japanese carrier, the *Hiyo*, and sixty-five planes.

On their return flight the American aircraft arrived at a scene of massive confusion. The lights on the ships of Task Force 58 had been turned off to elude enemy submarines, and the pilots had trouble finding their carriers. Almost half the planes landed on the wrong carriers. Eighty planes either crashed or had to ditch in the water for lack of fuel.

The next day Spruance called off any further chase of the enemy and headed for Saipan. Fifty-nine floating aviators were rescued en route.

Despite Japan's staggering losses in the Battle of the Philippine Sea, Mitscher was bitter over losing his chance to sink the entire Mobile Fleet. As for Spruance, he was criticized by many for failing to venture after the enemy. But the commander of the Fifth Fleet had good reason for his actions. His orders, after all, included only one objective, to defend Saipan, Tinian, and Guam. Another factor that should not be overlooked, although many of the histories on this subject do not mention it, is that Spruance had access to Japanese intelligence papers laying plans for a divided fleet, i.e., a decoy and main fleet. With two fleets the Japanese could undertake a flank attack. Rear Admiral Carl J. Moore, chief of staff to Spruance in this battle and a captain at the time, reports in his oral history that Spruance stayed near Saipan because he feared the Japanese might attempt a flank attack and inflict heavy damage on the amphibious forces on the island.

In light of the results of the Battle of the Philippine Sea, it is difficult to fault Spruance for his decisions. In two days of fighting the Americans lost 130 planes and 76 aviators. The Japanese lost three of their largest carriers, 480 planes, and almost the same number of airmen. There was no time for the enemy to replace his losses before the Battle of Leyte Gulf in October 1944, and never again would he recover from the devastating blow delivered to his naval air forces. In the future Japan would have to resort to kamikaze attacks to delay the inevitable American advance to the home islands.

The Battle of the Philippine Sea is represented here in two very different accounts. Rear Admiral Moore presents an overview of the action. His narrative is restrained, concerned with tracing the reasons behind Spruance's various command decisions, including the one to withstand the pressure to pursue a retreating Japanese fleet. In contrast, Vice Admiral Bernard M. Strean, who during the battle was commander of VF-1 on the *Yorktown*, is vivid and personal. Strean was in the thick of aerial combat. His story of dogfights with Japanese planes is exciting and emotional, and his story of returning to the darkened carriers of Task Force 58 after the long sortie against the distant Japanese fleet recalls the desperation and anger of pilots who felt they had been neglected.

COMMAND DECISIONS DURING THE BATTLE OF THE PHILIPPINE SEA

REAR ADMIRAL CARL J. MOORE*

On the seventeenth of June Admiral Spruance issued a dispatch battle plan which he gave to Admiral Marc Mitscher and Admiral Willis Lee. (The battleships of Mitscher's carrier task groups were assembled as a fourth group under the command of Admiral Lee.) The battle plan read as follows:

> Our air will first knock out enemy carriers as operating carriers, then will attack enemy battleships and cruisers to slow or disable them. Task Group 58.7 (Admiral Lee) will destroy enemy fleet, either by fleet action if enemy elects to fight, or by sinking slowed or crippled ships if enemy retreats. Action against the retreating enemy must be pushed vigorously by all hands to ensure complete destruction of the fleet. Destroyers running short of fuel may be returned to Saipan if necessary for refueling.

It is interesting and important to note that Admiral Spruance, a War College expert, talked the plan over with his chief of staff and then wrote the battle plan himself. It was not put in the stereotyped battle plan form. Moreover, it was written in plain language that could be understood by everyone concerned.

Spruance also issued a directive to Mitscher at that time saying, "Desire you proceed at your discretion, selecting dispositions and movements best calculated to meet the enemy under most advantageous conditions. I shall issue general directives when necessary and leave details to you and Admiral Lee." It was that sort of dispatch that helped make Spruance a great naval officer. His whole idea was to give orders, trust his subordinates, and let them

*For biographical information on Moore, see pp. 172–73.

run the show. He would only interfere when necessary. They could look to him for directives in case they wanted them, and he could interfere at any time he chose if he didn't like what they were doing.

At dark on the 17th of June, the situation appeared to be as follows: Enemy forces, probably consisting of five battleships, nine carriers, eight heavy cruisers and a number of destroyers, were at sea east of the Philippines for the purpose of attacking our amphibious forces engaged in the capture of Saipan. The task of Task Force 58 was to cover our amphibious forces and to prevent such enemy attack. The enemy attack would probably involve a strike by carrier-based aircraft supported and followed up by heavy fleet units. The possibility existed that the enemy fleet might be divided, with a portion of its involving carriers coming in around one of our flanks. If Task Force 58 were moved too far from Saipan before the location of the enemy was definitely determined, such a flank attack could inflict heavy damage on our amphibious forces at Saipan. Routes of withdrawal to the northward and to the southwestward would remain open with such a flanking force. The use of enemy airfields on Guam and Rota was available to the enemy, except as our carrier-based aircraft were able to keep these fields neutralized.

That was quoted from the battle report. Spruance's reference to an attack from either flank was something that was very much on his mind, largely because just before we sailed from Pearl Harbor we had received in the mail a Japanese plan of action, which had been captured at Hollandia by MacArthur's forces, and somebody was smart enough to send a copy to us.* We didn't know whether it had been received by Turner and Mitscher or not, but it was very significant as far as we were concerned.

Samuel Eliot Morison later wrote that a flank attack was exactly what the Japanese had done at Coral Sea and in the battle around Guadalcanal, so Spruance had good reason to expect an end run.

I think there was more to the report than a carrier doctrine of end runs and strikes around the flanks. I think the thing encompassed heavy ships as well, with the whole idea being that if they could draw the ships to an attack in the center, and heavy ships or carriers could make an end run and get in behind, they could do the damage they wanted to do. The report indicated to Spruance that this sort of action might be taken. His experience with the Japanese and this word we had from General MacArthur influenced his actions right through the operation.

Spruance sent a dispatch on the morning of the eighteenth to Mitscher and Lee:

*The Japanese intelligence papers, which had been captured by a coastwatcher in the Philippines, included information about a divided fleet (a decoy and a main fleet) that would be capable of launching a flank attack against the American force. For information on the capture of the papers, see pp. 153–54.

Task Force 58 must cover Saipan and all forces engaged in that operation. I still feel that main enemy attack will be coming from the westward but it might be diverted to come in from the southwestward. Diversionary attacks may come in from either flank, or reinforcements might come from the Empire. Consider that we can best cover Saipan by advancing to the westward during daylight, and retiring to the eastward at night, so as to reduce possibility of enemy passing us during darkness. Distance which you can make to the westward during day will naturally be restricted by your air operations, and by a necessity to conserve fuel. We should, however, remain in air-supporting position at Saipan until information of enemy requires other action. Consider seeking night action undesirable initially, in view of our superior strength of all types. Earliest possible strike on enemy carriers is necessary.

In that dispatch he emphasized the fact that he still suspected the possibility of an end run, and he wanted to keep the forces in easy range of Saipan.

The afternoon search from the carriers on the eighteenth was negative, and the eastward position (reported by the USS *Cavalla*) to which ships were proceeding was still outside our area of search. None could be closer than five hundred miles to Saipan if steaming from the position last reported for them. During the day of the eighteenth, between noon and eight o'clock, we only made 112 miles towards the west. This was due to our flight operations, which forced the carriers to head eastward into the wind. The night of the eighteenth, patrol planes of Admiral John Hoover, commanding land-based aircraft in the forward area, central Pacific, searched from Saipan six hundred miles to the west.

At eight o'clock on the eighteenth we got a report from Commander in Chief, Pacific Fleet, stating that a Japanese transmission had been located by a direction finder. It gave us the enemy position and stated it was correct within one hundred miles. Nothing could be more accurate than that—a reported position with a circle of one hundred miles around a dot. About three hours later, that night, we intercepted a dispatch from Commander, Submarines, Pacific Fleet, to the *Stingray*, saying they were unable to receive a dispatch from the *Stingray* because Japanese transmissions were interfering. Since we knew rather accurately the position of the *Stingray*, it would give us another position on the Japanese fleet if this did indeed turn out to be a contact report that the *Stingray* was trying to transmit.

These two reports indicated the presence of a Japanese force there, but the two positions were some distance apart. It showed that there may have been two Japanese forces operating. There was no indication that the fleet was concentrated, though it was heading eastward.

On the eighteenth Admiral Mitscher recommended that Task Force 58 change course to 270 degrees at one-thirty in the morning in order to be in a position to strike the enemy at five o'clock in the morning. Spruance replied to that: "Change proposed does not appear advisable. Believe indications given by *Stingray* more accurate than that determined by direction finder. If that is so, continuation at present seems preferable. End run by other carrier groups remains possibility and must not be overlooked."

Further reasons for Admiral Spruance's adhering to his previous decision to retire eastward were that (a) the position of the force located by direction finder bearings was not definite, being within one hundred miles; (b) the originator of the enemy transmission was not known positively; (c) the size and composition of the enemy force was not known; (d) it was of the highest importance that our troops and transport forces on and in the vicinity of Saipan be protected, and a circling movement by enemy fast carriers be guarded against; (e) there was the possibility that the enemy radio transmission was a deliberate attempt to draw our covering forces from the vicinity of Saipan; (f) the *Stingray* transmission at 2346, in the vicinity of latitude 12° 20′ longitude 1° 39′ east, had been jammed by the enemy, indicating that *Stingray* might have made a contact in that vicinity. The *Stingray*'s position was 435 miles, 246 degrees from Saipan.

Putting us further in doubt as to what the situation was and confirming Admiral Spruance in his decision, we got a report from the USS *Finback* giving the approximate position of searchlights at 2010 on the eighteenth. Direction finder 6, the *Stingray*'s transmission, and the *Finback*'s report indicated three possible positions of enemy task groups at widely separated positions. This further confirmed Spruance in his decision to continue eastward.

It was also indicated, early in the morning, that the enemy was fully aware of our position, because our aircraft reported that we were being trailed by land-based aircraft, probably from Guam. It was again evident on the early morning of the nineteenth that we were being trailed by Japanese planes. A combat air patrol over the carrier task group with the *Belleau Wood* had been vectored southward in the vicinity of Guam and reported that enemy planes were taking off from the airfields in Guam. These planes might have been reinforcements flown in from Truk, Woleai, Yap, or enemy carriers, because nearly all the planes on the Guam airfields had been cleaned up by our fire attacks earlier. At any rate, Mitscher ordered a fighter sweep over Guam to stop the possibility of attack on our forces, and some ten aircraft were shot down at that time.

At about eight-fifty in the morning of the nineteenth, Admiral Spruance and Admiral Mitscher received a long-delayed dispatch from a patrol plane from Saipan that had been active during the night. The pilot reported a large enemy force and gave its latitude and longitude. At the time of the sighting, Task Force 58 was some 330 miles to the east of the reported position. This was still outside the range of our early-morning searches. A supplementary report of the enemy force indicated that it was in two groups, one of about thirty ships and the other of about ten. An analysis of these reports revealed that the force reported might have been a concentration of all the groups of Japanese vessels that were operating to the west of us, or it might have been the concentration of two or more groups. So our information didn't mean an awful lot even then, but it didn't preclude the possibility of a flanking movement, either to the north or south, or a movement in from the west.

At ten o'clock in the morning of the nineteenth, the radar from Task Force 58 picked up a large bogie bearing 265 degress and about 125 miles away, obviously heading in from the west at an altitude of twenty-four thousand feet. Mitscher immediately launched all aircraft on the carrier decks, directed that a search and attack group be sent to the west, and kept his fighters available to oppose the large bogie that was coming in. The search and attack group to the west returned with negative results. They had to remain in the air for hours because of the activity on the carriers, which were launching and recovering fighter aircraft during the heavy Japanese raids that followed and continued until somewhere around three o'clock in the afternoon. Most of the enemy planes were intercepted by our fighters, but some got through. The *South Dakota* was the only ship that received a direct hit, but comparatively little damage was done and battle efficiency wasn't interfered with. There were near misses on the *Minneapolis*, the *Wasp*, and the *Bunker Hill*, but their fighting efficiency was restored promptly. At the end of the raids Mitscher reported that 358 enemy planes were shot down and 25 more probably destroyed. Our aircraft losses up to that point were 25.

A search on the twentieth from Task Force 58 found nothing except for enemy aircraft. We had, however, a report from long-range patrol planes operating from the South Pacific of two carriers and two heavy cruisers and destroyers well to the west of our search area. Shortly after there came a report from the *Cavalla* that she had torpedoed a Japanese carrier of the *Shokaku*-class that had just received aircraft. Obviously the two reports were of the same unit.

Our carriers had to continue on an easterly course rather than a westerly one throughout the day, heading into the wind on account of aircraft operations so that we ended up in the afternoon only about forty miles northwest of Guam. That night Spruance and Mitscher detached Task Force 58.4 for fueling and directed them to make strikes on Guam and Rota on their way to a fueling rendezvous. Spruance sent another dispatch to Mitscher at that time saying, "Desire to attack enemy tomorrow if we know his position with sufficient accuracy. If our patrol planes give us required information tonight no searches may be necessary. If not, we must continue searches tomorrow to ensure adequate protection for Saipan."

A search in the morning of the twentieth made contact only with enemy aircraft, but they were Jakes—patrol floatplanes that obviously had come from enemy cruisers and not carriers. This indicated there were cruisers in the vicinity, and they might have been part of a protecting force for the carrier that *Cavalla* had torpedoed. Of course, we didn't know whether she was sunk or not. Spruance told Mitscher that the torpedoed carrier might be afloat still.

> If so, believe she will be most likely heading northwest. Desire to push our searches today as far westward as possible. If no contacts with the enemy fleet result, consider it indication fleet is withdrawing and further pursuit after today will be unprofitable. If you concur, retire tonight towards Saipan. Will order out tankers of Task Group 58.4 and direct Task Group 58.4 to remain in the vicinity of Saipan. Carrier must be sunk if we can reach her.

(Sometimes in this report we referred to that carrier as the *Zuikaku*, sometimes as the *Shokaku*. We didn't know which one it was. Either name went.)

In the afternoon of the twentieth the carriers launched a search extending 325 miles. As a result, we had reports of an enemy fleet composed of battleships, carriers, cruisers, oilers, and destroyers. They were in three groups, and at least one group was on a northerly course at ten knots. The reports also said there were no planes on the decks of the carriers. Now up to the time of the new reports, we had figured that probably the Japanese force would retire towards the southern Philippines, but this indicated that they were retiring to the northwest, probably heading for Okinawa or the home country. The presence of ships in this area making ten knots suggested that there might be damaged ships, which we had a good prospect of overtaking. There was little chance of ever catching up with any undamaged ships.

When the enemy fleet was sighted, it bore 289 degrees and 290 miles from Task Force 58. Mitscher diverted the course of the task force to the east and immediately began launching planes. Full deckloads from all the carriers took off by a quarter of five. This was about an hour after we first got word that this force had been sighted. They had to fly about 340 miles to reach their target, with our carriers heading eastward and the enemy heading westward. By that time it was about six-forty. They attacked vigorously and as long as they could, but they weren't able to stay with it because of darkness and a shortage of fuel and, of course, the need to head back to their own carriers. According to reports, the damage inflicted on the Japanese fleet was considerable.

Our planes returned to the carriers after dark. A period of about one and a half hours was consumed in completing the recovery. Many of the planes were forced to land in the water because of fuel shortage. As a result of this strike on the enemy, we lost a total of ninety-five aircraft, either shot down by the enemy or forced to land on the water. Quick work by destroyers on the night of the landings, and search and rescue by destroyers, aircraft, and submarines on the following day, saved many aviators who otherwise would

214

have been lost. The final count indicated that we lost twenty-two pilots and twenty-seven aircrewmen only.

After the contact report of enemy ships had been received on the afternoon of the nineteenth, Admiral Mitscher recommended that Admiral Lee's battleships be released to proceed at high speed to the northwest in order to be in position to engage the enemy's fleet after daylight. Spruance replied to him, "Consider Task Force 58 should be kept tactically concentrated tonight and make best practical speed towards the enemy so as to keep them in air striking distance." I had no record of these two dispatches. Evidently Admiral Morison did; he probably got them out of Mitscher's records. The matter could likely have been handled by voice telephone. I probably wasn't on the bridge at the time, for I didn't remember anything about the exchange, nor did Vice Admiral E. P. Forrestel, at the time a captain on Spruance's staff, when I queried him much later.*

At daylight on the morning of the twenty-first, Mitscher launched full deckloads of planes organized for a strike on the enemy. They were directed to turn back if they'd covered three hundred miles and found nothing. He also sent out search planes that were not armed with bombs and had a heavier load of gasoline. They made contact with the enemy groups. They were reported making a speed of twenty knots and trailing oil. They were 352 miles away from Task Force 58 at the time. That was beyond the range that our air groups could reach and still have enough gasoline to return to the carriers. So no further contact was made with these ships. There was still a chance of picking up some damaged ships if there were any left behind.

On the morning of the twenty-second Spruance took the *Indianapolis* from the carrier task groups and joined Admiral Lee in the battleships. They were in advance of the carriers. Mitscher was told to search to the right and left of the supposed bearing of the enemy, looking for damaged ships. But searches during the day were negative, and by the afternoon of the twenty-second Spruance directed the retirement of the battleships and the carrier task groups toward Saipan. That was the end of the battle.

---

*Moore is offering an explanation for Morison's reference to the dispatches exchanged between Admirals Mitscher and Spruance. Moore was a meticulous record keeper and would have felt remiss at not being able to produce the records of the dispatches.

215

A HIGH SCORE
AND A CLOSE CALL
IN THE PHILIPPINE SEA

VICE ADMIRAL BERNARD M. STREAN

BERNARD MAX STREAN was born in Big Cabin, Oklahoma, on 16 December 1910. He graduated from the U.S. Naval Academy in 1933. After flight training at Pensacola in 1935 he was designated naval aviator. Following early flying and instructor duty he became a member of the Fleet Stabilization Board in October 1942.

In May 1943 Strean took command of Fighting Squadron 1, attached to the USS *Yorktown,* and was engaged in the Battle of the Philippine Sea and operations in the Marianas. In 1944 and 1945 he commanded Air Groups 98 and 75. He attended the Armed Forces Staff College in Norfolk, Virginia, in 1949–50. Later assignments included service as head of the technical training programs section of the Office of the Chief of Naval Operations and commander of the carriers *Kenneth Whiting* and *Randolph.* In 1957 he spent a year at the National War College in Washington, and in 1961 he became, simultaneously, Commander, Patrol Force, Seventh Fleet; Commander, U.S. Taiwan Patrol Force; and Commander, Fleet Air Wing 1. After service as assistant chief of naval operations (fleet operations) in 1963 he took command of Carrier Division 2. To this he later added duty as commander of the world's first all-nuclear-powered task group. It was in 1964 that he conducted Operation Sea Orbit, an around-the-world cruise to demonstrate the strategic mobility of the U.S. Navy's nuclear-powered surface forces. From 1965 to 1966 he was deputy chief of naval personnel, and from 1968 to 1971 he was chief of naval training at Pensacola.

Vice Admiral Strean retired in 1971 and has lived in Arlington, Virginia, since then.

Then the First Battle of the Philippine Sea happened. Apparently the Japs had planned to attack us and go on to Oronte Field, on Guam, and areas further north.

I was sitting in the *Yorktown*'s ready room with my harness on. Everybody else had gone out on a mission to Guam except for ten pilots, who were there with me. All of a sudden we received information that there was a large aerial force proceeding towards us. Of course our planes were immediately launched. I think in four minutes we were in the air with no other information than that there was a large force coming towards us.

I got in the air. I had been sleeping and was a bit drowsy. I then began to think, What is this, anyway? What do they mean by a force? It was an aerial force, so they sent us up thirty some thousand feet and then back down to five thousand feet. This is how bad radar was in those days. They couldn't determine the altitude. Then again we were back up to forty thousand feet. By this time I saw the enemy coming in. There was a swarm of airplanes. I reported back that there were three to five hundred airplanes. I thought, My God, ten of us, three hundred or five hundred of them—we won't last very long. But we got up on top and started making our attacks.

Very soon our planes came from other carriers in the fleet and hundreds of them joined us. Then as the enemy formations broke up we got to competing with each other for what was left. I remember seeing one Jap that was doing rolls; he was going around in a turn and he must have had seven or eight of our airplanes following him. I thought they must be awfully bad shots, and I moved in right ahead of these planes, with everybody bitching that somebody was going to get hit. I moved up to the tail of this guy, firing at him all the way. He was still rolling as I pulled away and got out of there. He's probably still living.

Only nineteen of their planes got through to the aircraft carrier.

It appeared that the Japanese (and I believe it was borne out by facts) had shot their whole wad on this one big attack on our carriers, but it was ineffective. At that time we didn't know how much damage we'd done. It was difficult to get an accurate account from a pilot of what he had shot down, for a pilot in combat is quite excited and he gets only glimpses. Speed makes a difference in your recognition and sight.

But we were successful, and upon reflection I think the reason was because of the absolute discipline on the part of the Japanese airplanes. In the past, their fighter planes had always broken away from their bombers and got in a dogfight. Here they would have been more effective if they had made

217

it every man for himself, but instead they stayed right at the same altitude, just weaving over the top of their bombers. I think that rigid discipline on their part, not letting anybody leave the formation, is something that permitted us to work at will on top of them.

So our whole fleet was brought together again with planes back on deck.

We sat all day long waiting for information about where the Japanese ships came from. There had to be a fleet out there.

It was on the afternoon of the twentieth when the word came. The report turned out to be in error one degree, which was sixty miles out of position. They launched us all—everybody they could—and sent us out to attack the fleet. It was four o'clock in the afternoon and the enemy was about two to three hundred miles distant. After we got in the air they corrected the position.

It was going to be well after dark when we got back to the carriers, but we were night qualified and so they sent us out anyway, knowing we would arrive over the enemy before the end of daylight.

I was leading the fighter sweep for the whole of Marc Mitscher's Task Force 58. We had several squadrons of fighters, and we went out first to sweep the area of their defending aircraft. We got there and we saw the fleet. There was nobody to defend them, for there was nothing in the air that we could find. So we continued sweeping the area until our bombers came in.

The Japs had several task groups deployed with destroyers in a perfect circle around their carriers. They had a cruiser or a battleship supporting the carriers with antiaircraft fire. As our bombers came down on them they did a tight circle turn and fired all kinds of colored ammunition. It was quite a sight. It was about dark when our people finished bombing. Then we fighters made an attack on their ships because we were carrying bombs in case we didn't have to fight their cover. I was credited with a bomb hit on the *Taka,* an aircraft carrier, a large converted carrier, one of their important ones.

Then we started back to our carriers. The weather was pretty bad, with towering cumulus. It was dark and difficult to get in formation. I think I could only find about four people to lead back to the carrier, which was about 350 miles away. When we got back there it was drizzling rain.

That was the greatest fiasco the navy ever had. The lights had been turned off on the carriers. Japanese pilots in Zeros were supposedly in the landing circle.

When I first got back I found my own carrier with our direction finder (we called it a Hayrake), but then it was so dark that in making a turn I apparently found another carrier. (It was not possible to recognize a carrier when you got close to it except by its wake and shape.) There must have been about thirty people circling her, when only six were supposed to be there at one time. I got down in the circle nevertheless, for I thought that if they couldn't get aboard I could. But every time I came around to land it was a foul deck and they gave me the wave off.

That carrier turned out to be a light carrier, a small one. They turned off the lights and told us to get away. I thought that was damned unfeeling of them, for here we were about to get our feet wet.

I still had some fuel; I had about thirty gallons. The fighters did all right, but the bombers were going in the water one after the other. This was all part of the confusion. People were saying they were going in the water and the carriers were throwing in float lights as a result. After telling the light carrier what I thought about them, I pulled up and got on the Hayrake again and started searching for the *Yorktown*.

Every carrier was surrounded. You couldn't get lined up unless you were close to the carrier. You could see the deck then and could try to come around and get in position by seeing the wake aft. In looking for my carrier I must have made approaches on perhaps four or five ships. One turned out to be a battleship. I was frustrated and didn't know where to go from there. I was trying to figure out what I would do, so I just continued my approach. Gee, that battleship! They turned on the lights. They fired Very pistols and yelled, "Pilot trying to land on the battleship—get away, get away!"

Well, I pulled up and got again on the Hayrake and found my own carrier. I kept telling them to turn on the lights because too many people were going in the water. Finally they did turn on the lights. Authorities claim that Admiral Mitscher was responsible for this, but I claim I was the one they could hear bitching and asking them to do it. They not only turned on the lights but they turned on vertical searchlight beams. So it was like a carnival out there. I circled my home carrier and finally got aboard. The first question we all asked that night was, "What ship is this?" because you could not tell one ship from the other.

We had a case, which I think is phenomenal, where two pilots went by one carrier, broke up, and came around and got aboard on their first pass— but they landed on different carriers. That's how confused things were. In another case, two people were coming in stacked one above the other, so that the signal officer could only see the fellow below. The top fellow could see the signal officer and was taking the signals that were being given for the other pilot. They both landed on the same carrier without touching each other. One went right over the top of the other.

As I said, everything was pretty confused that night. They were taking planes aboard and, after letting the pilot out, pushing them over the side to sink because the space was needed.

In contrast to the light carrier that had quit operating and receiving homecoming planes, the *Yorktown* took many, many more than she could carry. The next day everybody was unscrambled and flown off to their own ships.

I think the confusion of our return to the carriers that night was part of a calculated risk that Mitscher took, knowing that some of our people couldn't get back. He went ahead with the operation anyway, thinking that maybe if some of them didn't get back, he would pick them up in the water. Next day we did pass through that area where so many of the pilots had gone in the water. Everybody in the *Yorktown* fighter squadrons was picked up.

The afternoon of the next day they decided that we would go in and attack an undefended island—Pagan Island, north of Guam. It had never been hit before. I was to lead the several hundred airplanes that were to make the attack—just one, for the island was supposedly not defended. It was thought there were a few Japanese there.

We went in and of course took the same precautions we would on any defended island. We went in fast, at about 250 knots, and then pushed over in our dive. On the way down I could see that they were shooting at us. There was a ship in the harbor that was also shooting.

Suddenly I heard the word that I had been shot down. I knew it wasn't true, but I wondered why it had been said. It turned out that my wingman was hit with a bursting antiaircraft shell at fourteen thousand feet. They hit him squarely and his plane blew up. That is what they were talking about when I made my dive.

As I went down in my attack I pulled out very low, at a hundred feet or something like that, and I was continuing to fire at the ship in the harbor. It was firing back at me. Suddenly I heard a *boom!* in the wing and a hell of a fire started up in the right wing. It seemed to me about cabin height. There was a tankful of gasoline there, one of the main tanks. All our gasoline was carried in shellproof rubbers bags to protect it from shells, but I had seen Japanese airplanes flame and blow up so I thought immediately, "I've got to get out of here." I had always practiced how to release the canopy. There were a couple of pins holding it and when you hit it, they let go. Well, I gave one hell of a yank. One pin came out all right but the other one didn't; the encloser stayed on and I couldn't get out. By that time I was over the Jap ship, in a position where I could go into a cloud. It seemed to me that the fire had started to die down. I rode it out for a few seconds to see what was going to happen. Apparently it was not a gasoline fire but a hydraulic fire, so I rode on back to the carrier. Because there were no wheels they let me skid in on the deck. At least I had gotten back, but my wingman had been killed. This was the island that was supposedly undefended. Somebody upstairs took care of me.

The telling efforts of U.S. submarines in the Pacific war were approaching a climax in the middle months of 1944. Japan's ships were bearing the brunt of a carnage reminiscent of the savage German attacks on Atlantic shipping in 1941–42. Vice Admiral Charles Lockwood, Commander, Submarines, Pacific, had introduced the German wolf pack to the Pacific and perfected the techniques for its operation. Supplies of oil and foodstuffs imported to the Japanese empire were rapidly diminishing. Japan's supply of escorts had decreased, and Admiral King gave Japanese destroyers priority as targets for American submarines. Something like two hundred thousand tons of enemy merchant shipping was being sunk every month. The shipbuilding yards of the homeland could not make up for the loss. All these factors were beginning to take a toll on the morale of Japanese seamen. Their chances for survival in ships in a convoy were lessened every day.

American sea power was quickly advancing westward and narrowing Japanese sea-lanes. The East China Sea became a favorite hunting ground for U.S. submariners. Named Convoy College, it was a scene of great destruction.

As soon as Saipan was secured by U.S. amphibious forces (June 1944), the USS *Holland* was stationed there as a forward fueling and repair base for submarines. This made the 3,600-mile trip to Pearl Harbor less of a necessity and further restricted the sea channels available to Japanese convoys.

The following excerpt is Vice Admiral Lawson P. Ramage's account of the epic battle, on 30 July 1944, of the *Parche,* a member of the third wolf pack dispatched for operations in the Luzon Strait. Of all the submarine battles in the Pacific, the spectacular attack launched by then-Commander Ramage on a Japanese convoy was among the wildest. It soon became the talk of the entire submarine force, and for his deed of daring Red Ramage received the Congressional Medal of Honor from the hands of President Roosevelt.

WOLF PACKS ON THE PROWL

VICE ADMIRAL LAWSON P. RAMAGE

LAWSON PATTERSON RAMAGE was born in Monroe Bridge, Massachusetts, on 19 January 1909. He received his early education in Beaver Falls, New York, and at the Williston Academy in Easthampton, Massachusetts. A 1931 graduate of the U.S. Naval Academy, he served briefly in destroyers and a heavy cruiser, then attended the submarine school in New London.

After several assignments in submarines and at the Naval Postgraduate School in Annapolis, he became a staff officer of Commander, Submarines, Pacific Fleet in Pearl Harbor, where he was on duty when the Japanese attacked. In the spring of 1942 he was on board the USS *Grenadier* for her very successful second war patrol. His first command was the USS *Trout* in 1943. Later he commanded the USS *Parche* during four of her successful war patrols. For the remainder of the war he was personnel officer on the staff of Commander, Submarines, Pacific Fleet. In 1946 Ramage commanded Submarine Division 52 with special duty in Arctic waters. From 1947 to 1956 he had numerous assignments in the Atlantic and at the Navy Department in Washington, including command of Submarine Squadron 6 and duty as chief of staff to Commander, Submarine Force, U.S. Atlantic Fleet. In that time he also completed courses at the Armed Forces Staff College in Norfolk and the Naval War College in Newport. In 1956 he became director of the surface-type warfare division of the Office of the Chief of Naval Operations, after which he commanded Cruiser Division 2. In 1959 he became director of the antisubmarine/submarine warfare division of the Office of the Chief of Naval Operations. Other assignments followed: deputy chief of naval operations for readiness and fleet operations and, in 1964, command of the First Fleet. In 1966 he was deputy commander in chief of the Pacific Fleet. His final tour was as commander of the Military and Transportation Service.

Vice Admiral Ramage retired on 1 April 1970.

I headed back for new construction at the Portsmouth yard in New Hampshire. Friends told me that I would get one of the new heavy-hull boats being turned out at that yard. Those boats could dive to a greater depth, which would prove to be a big advantage over the earlier boats from New London. The ship assigned to me was the *Parche*. My old friend, Rear Admiral Thomas Withers, was there at the yard, and he, together with the engineers and draftsmen, was very cooperative. Any good idea you had could be incorporated into the design of the submarine. I think that one of the great things we did was to convert the number-three ballast tank into a fuel ballast tank. This almost doubled the total amount of fuel available to the ship. Many other little items we asked for we got as well. We were able to do this much more easily then than we'd be able to now. In wartime most things are a lot easier.

With the new hull we could dive to four-hundred-foot keel depth, as contrasted with the three-hundred-foot ability of previous ships. In these newer boats we also had the negative tank, which was normally flooded when the ship was cruising. It made her that much heavier so that when you dove you went down faster. As soon as you got under you blew the water out of the negative tank to get back to a neutral buoyancy. This additional aid in getting down proved quite significant.

We finally got under way in early January 1944, transited the Panama Canal, and went straight to Pearl Harbor. There we learned that we were going to join one of the first wolf packs formed in the Pacific. We were adopting the successful procedures of the German wolf packs in the Atlantic. We were assigned a wolf pack commander, and he decided to ride the *Parche*.

The thing that upset me at this point was the decision they made at Pearl to paint us a lighter color. I wanted to be the blackest cat out there, but they had got some of those camouflage experts working on the problem. They decided that black, total black, was not the best color, so they painted us in shades of gray and sent us out on a convoy exercise off Oahu. It didn't take any time to convince me they were right. I was amazed at the effect these different shades of gray had on the hull. It just painted the ship into complete oblivion. You couldn't see the submarine at any distance. My anxiety over that was relieved.

The new wolf pack consisted of the *Bang* and the *Tenosa* with Captain George Peterson as the division commander. He and I put together our first wolf pack instructions while en route to Midway and there passed them on to the others. The difference between these new instructions and those for the single submarine was primarily in the positioning of the ships. Two of the submarines in the pack would try to get in position ahead of the target on either side of its bow. The third submarine would trail and take his position astern in case the target was damaged. Then he could pick it off. If it turned or reversed course or eluded the two advance submarines, the third submarine would still be in a position to attack.

One other important aspect of these new instructions had to do with the fact that we didn't want to be patrolling together all the time. We didn't want to be continually on the alert for one of the other submarines in the immediate vicinity. So we divided our patrol area up into sixty-mile squares. That was one degree to a side. Each submarine was assigned a twenty-mile lane sixty miles long. This broadened our front for detecting the target in the first place. As soon as somebody made a contact, word would be relayed to the other two submarines in the pack and they could close in. As soon as the pack got within range of the target, they would naturally pick it up on their radars and then proceed immediately to their assigned stations. In so doing they would normally be out of range of the torpedoes from the other submarines. We never had any submarine sinking another of our own, so I guess the technique was effective.

Then in order to get full coverage of our patrol area we moved the whole formation about sixty miles a night; that is, one degree at a time either to the east, west, north, or south. In that way we made a continuous pattern around the whole area assigned. It seemed to work out very well. We got full coverage and we quadrupled our front. Normally we would join up in a line perpendicular to the expected course of anybody coming through.

It made all the difference in the world in terms of the tonnage sunk. Normally one submarine has to go down at some point, and when he does he loses the picture for a while. But if something is there he can pick it up. More and more attacks were made on the surface at night. It gave everybody much more freedom of action and a chance to engage more targets.

One encounter during the *Parche*'s first wolf pack patrol with the *Tenosa* and *Bang* is noteworthy because of a new technique we used: reloading torpedoes in combat. We had got word of another convoy coming up from the south, and so we rendezvoused to exchange plans. We did that at night. The next morning the convoy showed up, and we tried to trail it on the surface. Before long, aircraft came out from Formosa and forced us down. We were down most of the morning. Then we made another attempt to pick them up in the afternoon but again were forced down. Only after four o'clock, when the planes departed, were we able to get up and start closing in. We were within ten miles of the convoy when a surface escort picked up the *Parche* and started coming in our direction. About this time the convoy changed course due east, so we turned parallel and just kept going full speed on the surface. The escort was closing gradually, but we hung off because it would soon be dark and then we would have a chance to throw him off. This is exactly what happened. Then we turned north to close in on the convoy, but she too turned north. Every time we would start getting on the beam of the convoy it would change course again. They knew we were out there. The convoy went north, then northwest, and finally about one o'clock in the morning it was heading due west, toward the China coast.

I knew it couldn't go in that direction very long. It would certainly have to snap back soon and head again to the northwest. So I decided I was getting tired of this. I decided to close in now and take my chances on getting in position for a submerged radar attack. By the time we got to about four thousand yards the whole formation had changed course right back to where I thought they would go, to the northeast. So instead of being on the starboard bow, I found myself on the port bow. I had to cut across the bow immediately and get back to my side of the formation. As I did, we were in there so close that I decided I might as well go ahead and pick off the first two ships. We fired four torpedoes at the first one, a big transport, and got her. Then immediately we shifted to the second one with the two remaining torpedoes and got her.

I think that *Tenosa* had been on the other side of the convoy earlier in the evening, but there were still four or five ships left. Since I had nothing left in the bow tubes, I had to maneuver into position to get a stern shot off at the third big ship I wanted to hit. I drove in, swung around to bring the stern tubes to bear, and this fellow [the third ship] opened up with machine-gun fire. By the time I got lined up, I was out about one thousand yards. The torpedoes were electric torpedoes. I didn't have too much faith in them to begin with. They were much slower. With these ships fully alerted and zigzagging, I thought it was rather silly to fire an electric torpedo with a slower run. Anyway, I made the second pass around with no success. Then my torpedo officer came up and asked permission to reload the bow tubes with the steam torpedoes. Now this was something that was absolutely unheard of. No one had ever considered reloading the torpedoes while the submarines were on the surface, charging around at twenty knots, in contact with the enemy, and subject to diving without notice. Once you got those torpedoes out of the racks they were just like greased pigs. You could easily lose control of a torpedo in a maneuvering submarine, and if so you could really mash people below deck. I questioned the torpedo officer about it, and he assured me he was ready to reload. He had cleared all the bunks out of the torpedo room. He guaranteed that he could keep that torpedo from getting loose, so I said, "All right, go ahead." While we were in the process of going around again he reloaded two torpedoes forward. Then we drove straight in and let them have it. That took care of the third ship.

Then we saw the *Bang* on the surface. He moved into position and fired his last two torpedoes with very good results. The *Tenosa* was all out of torpedoes, so the two of them immediately departed for home and left me to sit around for another ten days; I still had ten torpedoes, one for each of the tubes. The consequences of my stay were not too pleasant, for the enemy kept that area under complete surveillance the whole time.

I don't think the real impact of our surface reload became general knowledge, but it certainly was a significant first as far as our submarines were concerned. Eventually others like Commander Gene Fluckey adopted that technique. That's how they got their big bag of ships, too . . . It was, of course, the basis of our success subsequently. All the submarines we've built since the war have been able to reload on the surface, but during the war if you tried that you were running a big risk. With a great big ship staring me in the face and wanting so badly to sink it, I was willing to go to any length to get some steam torpedoes reloaded forward. Maybe it was rather foolhardy to take such a chance, but like everything else, if it works out it's fine.

After our first patrol in the *Parche* we returned to Midway for a refit. That first patrol was successful and certainly convinced us that we could reload the torpedoes while under way and also while in contact with the enemy. We had a chance then to reevaluate a lot of our actions and see whether we could get more or less official blessings for them. While in Midway my squadron commander, Captain Lew Parks, was designated to be the wolf pack commander for our next patrol. He decided to ride the *Parche*. We left on the next patrol with the *Hammerhead* and the *Steelhead*. This wolf pack was called Parks' Pirates. I was more inclined to refer to it as the Head Hunters because we had the *Steelhead,* the *Hammerhead,* and the Red Head.*

Our first real contact with the enemy was just south of the Bonin Islands. One morning we got a call about six o'clock that a picket ship had been spotted near us. We swung around and decided to take her under fire. We closed in, I guess, to about thirty-five hundred yards and opened fire with our four-inch deck gun and later with the forty-millimeters. We got a couple of hits almost immediately, certainly by the time we got to three thousand yards. This apparently knocked the boat steering out. It was a ship of about fifteen hundred tons, a brand new steel ship with a nice rounded bridge structure. Obviously it had not been in commission too long. It had armament but the crew never really got organized. We must have surprised them

---

*That is, the *Parche*. Ramage was known to his friends as Red.

that early in the morning. And now with that hit they were completely disadvantaged. We closed in and in short order had the ship on fire. I was rather amused when, right in the middle of this action, our wolf pack commander came on the bridge with all his movie equipment and started recording the scene in color. It turned out to be quite a spectacular show. After the ship had gone around and around in circles several times and then burst into flames, she settled by the stern and went straight down with her bow pointed vertically to the sky.

Then we closed in and saw about five survivors in the water. We were trying to see if we could pick up any of them, though not with any great enthusiasm because we were still on our way out to our patrol area. But none of the people in the water showed any inclination to come on board. As a matter of fact, they swam away from us. We had initially counted five, but then all of a sudden we were missing one. To our great surprise we found that one fellow had pulled a bucket over his head and was looking out through it, trying to keep from being seen and picked up. There was nothing more we could do there, so we continued on our way. Actually we had no place for them on board. If we had to try and keep them under surveillance in a submarine during the patrol, it would have been a difficult problem. We would have had to turn them in first.

Then we got out on our patrol station. It was what they called Convoy College, an area south of Taiwan, north of the Philippines, and out to about the Pratas Reef. It was an operational area and was right across the convoy route of the Japanese. Usually there were three wolf packs in this area, which was divided into three sections. Each wolf pack patrolled a section for a certain period and then moved to the next section. The times were all laid out for us before we left, or they were given to us by radio at various times so that we didn't interfere with each other.

This procedure continued for the first week of our patrol without our sighting anything. It was pretty discouraging. This was the most lucrative patrol area of any in the Pacific, and here we were all ready and waiting. Then one evening, shortly after dinner, we got a call from the conning tower that there were targets on the radar out about twenty miles. I went up to take a look. I saw those three pips that looked like targets, so we changed course toward them and went ahead on four engines. Then they disappeared. We wondered what could have happened, but shortly thereafter they appeared again. They had gone into a rain cloud or something that broke up the contact on the radar. We went to general quarters and got ready for a night surface attack when all of a sudden there were flashes on the horizon. Meanwhile the wolf pack commander had come in to see what was going on. The flashes looked like searchlights, so Parks said, "What was that?"

"Well, they're shooting at us." My reply came almost at the same time that we heard a *ka-boom! ka-boom! ka-boom!* and water splashed all over the sub. Obviously, at that range they had us on radar and their gunnery was damned good. It was far better than I would have believed possible on an opening salvo. I turned and said to Parks as he began to move away, "Where are you going?"

"I'm going below. You can do whatever you want."

After considering for a moment, I decided maybe that was the better part of valor, especially if they were going to continue that sort of gunfire. Certainly they weren't going to steam anywhere near us if they knew we were there, so there wasn't any point in pursuing this any further unless we could do it submerged. We dove and they sent one destroyer over in our area pinging around, but then they continued on.

Apparently there were two cruisers and a destroyer and they were fast. This was the first indication we had that they did have pretty good radar on these ships. I say the range at which they opened was about fifteen thousand yards, about seven and a half miles. It was a pretty good range for their guns too.

That was the only thing that happened for a while. Our patrol was getting very dull. Then we got an intelligence report that a Japanese submarine was returning from European waters loaded down with German radar. It would be coming through Bashi Channel at noon on a certain date. So I suggested to the wolf pack commander that we join the other wolf pack down in that channel. By putting six boats in there we would be damned sure that we got this submarine. Parks concurred in that idea and said, "Can you contact the other wolf pack commander?"

And I said, "You just write out your dispatch and I'll have him on the horn in about five minutes." He wrote the dispatch.

The other commander, who happened to be senior, said, "Okay, come along. We're glad to have you." And he laid out the respective positions for all six submarines in the channel.

The next day we got there, dove into position, and then began waiting. At noon we were just holding our breath expecting to see this Jap submarine any minute. Nothing happened. Nothing happened at one o'clock or two o'clock or three o'clock. We were getting very discouraged about this time. Four. Then about four-thirty or five o'clock, there was a *ka-boom!* A big explosion. We looked through our periscope and saw a big column of smoke going up. Then we knew that one of the submarines in the other pack had gotten that Jap boat. If he had got by them, we'd have been next in line. We just missed out on it, on our chance. But at least that Jap submarine was running through on the surface and they got him. He had been delayed but he was pretty much on course. It's amazing how all this intelligence worked out as well as it did.

We had been getting a lot of other intelligence reports about convoys coming north and coming south. Usually they were outside our particular area. So our wolf pack commander decided we had better get over on their track in each case. As a result we were running back and forth on the surface during daylight practically all the time. And we were getting more exasperated as time went on. The Japs must have had planes up spotting us. Then we got word back from Pearl Harbor, "For God's sake, stop charging around on the surface. They're spotting you." Every time we got into position on the track, the convoy would be diverted. We were just giving away the whole show. They were intercepting the Jap's messages in Pearl while we were playing a losing game out in the convoy routes. So we finally had to give that up. And our time ran out. Our thirty days on patrol had expired and we hadn't really had a shot at anything except that small gunboat off the Bonins. The *Hammerhead* had to leave because she had to continue down to Perth. Now the wolf pack commander asked for an extension of our time for another five or ten days. We certainly didn't want to go home empty-handed after all this.

We surfaced one night about the third day out on our extension, on 31 July 1944, and got a message from the *Steelhead* that a convoy had been contacted and he was trailing it. We were given the course, the speed, and the position of the convoy. So we immediately went on four engines and proceeded on a course to intercept. The commander kept working out the maneuvering board diagrams and correcting our course down to half a degree or a quarter of a degree every ten minutes or so.

Our chase began about eight in the evening. We weren't getting any more information from the *Steelhead* and we weren't getting any contact with the convoy. I was greatly agitated and kept insisting that we had better contact the *Steelhead* and ask what was going on. He should have been relaying messages to us unless the convoy was still on its initial course and speed. Had it been, we would surely have been making contact by now. I was convinced that the convoy had changed from a southwesterly course, the one we were on, to a southeasterly course, heading more or less into the islands around the northern end of Luzon.

Parks was reluctant to open up and query the *Steelhead*. I kept insisting. Finally he said, "If we haven't heard anything from them by twelve-thirty, we'll go ahead and ask." So twelve-thirty came, no message. We called the *Steelhead* and asked where he was, what was going on, and where the convoy was. Sure enough, it had changed course shortly after the *Steelhead*'s initial message and was heading southeast. So we were way off in right field. We were about thirty or forty miles from the convoy. We had to make that up. So we swung around and headed in. It wasn't until about three in the morning that we finally made contact with the convoy. Finally we were coming more or less straight up from the stern or off the Japs' quarter. We saw they had an escort on their beam and one a little further forward on their bow, on the starboard side. We did not know where the *Steelhead* was but presumed she was over on the port side, which is where she should have been according to regular patrol doctrine.

As we came up we noticed that there was another escort moving in our direction from the head of the convoy. This gave us two escorts about parallel to and about a couple hundred yards off the beam of the convoy. Another escort was directly ahead of us. So we were the fourth ship in this particular square. I decided there was no point trying to go in around these escorts, so I made a reverse spinner, turned outboard, and then came around and under all of them to get inside the escorts. No sooner had we made this turnaround and come on a course heading into the convoy than we found that the convoy had changed course ninety degrees to the southwest. Now we were dead ahead of them and closing fast, so fast that we hadn't really had time to get a setup on them. One of the ships was right on us. Before we could do anything we were alongside and going by at twenty knots at about one hundred yards.

So I said, "Okay, we'll swing around and get her." She saw us, so we bore off to her port. We came around and let fly a couple of torpedoes, but she was still turning and we were turning, so that wasn't a very well-organized shot. Apparently both the torpedoes missed.

About this time we saw what looked like two carriers off to the west or southwest and we said, "Let's go get those two big ships." We headed that way, took aim on the leading one, and let go four torpedoes. Every one hit—one, two, three, four, right down the side of the ship. We were firing now to kill with every shot; we weren't firing spread. The ship turned out to be a tanker and she went straight on down.

The torpedo officer was following the other ship, which had got away. As we turned around now she was on the stern, and he said we had a good setup on the stern tube. I said, "Let her have one torpedo of the stern." We had cleared all the torpedoes out of the forward tubes—six of them—so we swung around and brought the stern to bear on the second ship. That happened to be a tanker also. We let three torpedoes go and all three hit, but the ship only went down by the bow and had a small fire going. The two tankers were light and apparently had been going south for a load.

That took care of all the torpedo tubes. We had fired ten torpedoes. Now we saw a transport dead ahead of us. Someone called up from below and said two torpedoes were ready, reloaded forward. I said, "All right." So we fired those two torpedoes at the transport and we caught her well on the bow and the beam. She went down.

Then we decided that we had better go back and get the tanker that was down by the bow. Of course, we had no torpedoes forward. We were busy reloading aft. As we came under the stern of the tanker we cut as close as we could to keep out of the way of her depth gun. She couldn't train it down on us; she was well down by the bow and the gun was practically pointing straight into the air. We came tight under and crossed her stern. We were heading out to what we saw was another ship, a good-sized ship, on the other side of this group. All of a sudden the tanker began shooting. The whole place was alight with gunfire. Everybody was shooting at everybody and anything, but we were invisible, I felt, except for the rooster tail we were laying out as our boat went through the convoy at twenty knots. When the tanker began shooting right down our wake it began to get a little bit hot. So we decided we had best put her out of her misery. As soon as we got enough distance, seven hundred yards or so, we fired three torpedoes out of the stern and sank that tanker. Now we had two tankers and a transport down and a hit on the first ship.

Just as we got to this point we saw one of the escorts trying to ram us. We called for all the speed we could from the engine room and got across her bow. Then I turned right to come parallel with her and throw our stern out from under her way. We passed each other at about fifty or one hundred feet, close enough so that we could have shouted at one another.

There was another escort just beyond. I didn't want to run into her, but she was closing fast. As soon as we cleared her we saw another big transport dead ahead. They reported from below that torpedoes had been loaded again, two forward. So I said, "Give this fellow [the transport] one right down the throat." We were lined up directly with her and we let two torpedoes go. One of them didn't hit, but I think the other one did. Anyway, we held fire for a minute to get a better bearing, then fired another torpedo. In all we got two torpedoes into her, which put her down by the bow. Then we passed her and there was another ship. We fired down the throat of this ship and got her down by the bow and then continued to the left to bring our stern to bear on her starboard side. Then we let one more go and that hit her directly amidships. It put her down.

Now we had four ships sunk and one damaged, and it was beginning to get a little bit light, a little bit too light. We couldn't see any other ships that were of consequence. There were mostly escorts now, just charging around and firing flares and shooting whatever small arms they had. So we decided to pull clear and get ready to dive for the day. We needed to get some distance between them and where we were going to dive. As we maneuvered we saw them signaling to each other and trying to make a reading of what had happened. One of the quartermasters said, "I guess they have a lot of reports to fill out, too."

When this whole thing started the wolf pack commander was up on the deck and there just wasn't room enough for everybody there, so I said, "Clear the bridge." I got rid of everybody, including the lookouts. I had just one quartermaster with me, two of us on the bridge. He was keeping a look aft as I kept a look forward. But the whole operation went by so fast it's hard to reconstruct everything that we saw happen in such a short time.

231

According to the record, forty-six minutes elapsed, but that is from the time we got up and made the first turn and started in. I think actually that from the time of shooting it was about thirty minutes.

There had been about nine ships in the convoy. We picked out the five that were of any size. Of course, the *Steelhead* had been working on them all night. She got credit for a couple, but she was given credit for two of the ones we got. According to the book, we both got credit for the same ships. She had been firing from a distance of three thousand yards or so. She never got into the midst of the convoy.

The return to Pearl Harbor was uneventful. The day we arrived Admiral Lockwood came down. He was very pleased and congratulated all of us. But in due time the patrol report was reviewed. Then the chief of staff usually wrote a little note to the commanding officer and summed the whole thing up—whether it was good, bad, or indifferent. Commodore Merrill Comstock wrote a note to me and said, "This was foolhardy, very dangerous and an undue risk." But he added, "I guess it's okay as long as it came out all right. You got away with it but don't do it again. That isn't exactly what we expected you to do."

But at least it set a precedent. From then on the other submarines, notably Gene Fluckey on the *Barb* and Dick O'Kane on the *Tang*, followed the same procedure and got many more ships as a result. Both Gene and Dick were awarded the Medal of Honor for similar tactics. FDR gave me the award back in Washington on 12 January 1945.

On 12 March 1944 the Joint Chiefs of Staff made the decision to proceed with the capture of Saipan, Tinian, and Guam, three of the southernmost of the Marianas Islands in the central Pacific and the only ones of the group that had any military or economic value.

Admiral Richmond Kelly Turner, by this time the veteran amphibious commander in the Pacific, was named to command Admiral Raymond Spruance's Joint Expeditionary Force, which would undertake Forager, as the operation came to be called. Turner lost no time drafting the overall objective of Forager: to secure control of sea communications through the central Pacific for the support of further attacks on the Japanese.

There were other, more specific objectives in the grand design. The navy had plans to develop both Saipan and Guam into advanced naval bases (Admiral Nimitz would move his headquarters to Guam almost immediately after it was secured by the American invaders), and the army air forces wanted bases for its Superfortresses in the further development of efforts to bomb the Japanese homeland. A less tangible motive may have been the knowledge that an attack on the Marianas was perhaps the greatest challenge to the Japanese so far. The islands were one of the links in the enemy's defense perimeter. Moreover, after Japan had been given a mandate over the Marianas by the League of Nations in 1920, she had begun a colonization and agricultural program there. The Marianas were regarded by Japan as part of her homeland.

The Allied operations against the Marianas were fraught with difficulty. Pearl Harbor was thirty-five-hundred miles away and Eniwetok, the nearest advanced American base, was over a thousand. Eniwetok, moreover, was not much more than an anchorage. Only great advances in logistics, the advent of reefers, tankers, and refrigerated food ships, plus new methods of refueling and supplying warships at sea made it possible to overcome the physical obstacles built into an operation the magnitude of Forager.

Saipan was invaded on 21 June 1944 and secured by 9 July, after bloody fighting that resulted in over sixteen thousand American casual-

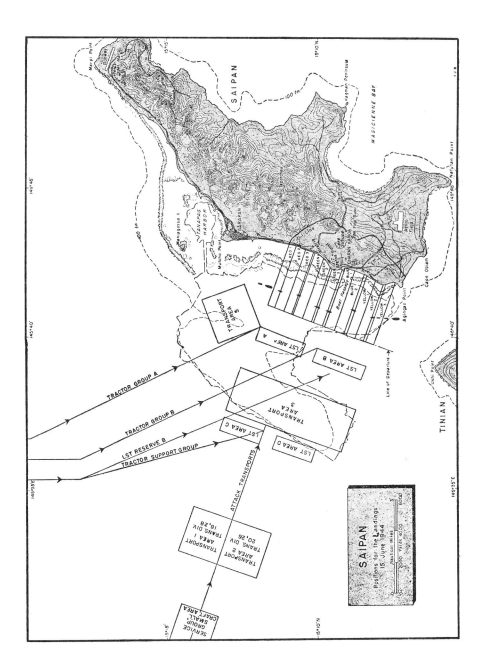

ties. The one encouraging aspect of the assault was the success of the UDTs, which were being used for the first time in the Pacific theater. Their story, told by Rear Admiral (at the time Lieutenant Commander) Draper Kauffman, vividly illustrates the imaginative techniques developed by an adventurous group of young pioneers. These were men who had passed through a demanding selection process and one of the most

234

intensive physical training programs imaginable before joining their UDTs.

Little time elapsed before the next offensive, against neighboring Tinian, began. On 5 July Admiral Turner announced that he had designated Rear Admiral Harry W. Hill to command the naval attack force for the capture of the island, which commenced on 24 July. It is Admiral Hill who speaks to us in the second excerpt, a detailed yet personal account of the planning and execution of the second phase of Operation Forager. His meticulous preparation may have been one of the reasons Admiral Spruance, in a lecture to a British military audience after the war, was able to say of Tinian, "It was the most brilliantly conceived and executed amphibious operation of the war."*

Indeed, the operation worked, and in a matter of only days. On 2 August Tinian was declared secured. Eight days later Guam had been taken. On 12 August the Japanese general's command post was stormed and he and all his men were killed or committed suicide.

*Thomas Buell, *The Quiet Warrior*, p. 302.

THE UDTs COME OF AGE AT SAIPAN

REAR ADMIRAL DRAPER KAUFFMAN

DRAPER LAURENCE KAUFFMAN was born in San Diego on 4 August 1911. He graduated from the U.S. Naval Academy in 1933 but was forced to resign from the service because of poor eyesight. Until 1940 he was employed by a steamship company. Then he joined the American Volunteer Corps with the French army. He was captured by the Germans and released in August 1940, when he made his way to England and joined the Royal Navy Volunteer Reserve as a lieutenant. He served there in bomb disposal work for a year and resigned to accept an appointment in the U.S. Naval Reserve in 1941.

In January 1942 he set up a bomb disposal school in the Washington Navy Yard. In June 1943 he organized the first navy demolition teams. In April 1944 he had duty with the Pacific Fleet and became commanding officer of the UDT that took part in the assault on Saipan. Later he took part in the assault on Iwo Jima and Okinawa. Kauffman transferred to the regular navy from the reserve in 1946. In February 1946 he joined Task Force 1 to conduct the atomic bomb tests at Bikini Island. Later he established the navy's first radiological safety school. From June 1951 to 1953 he was a member of the strategy and tactics staff at the Naval War College. Then he had duty in the Navy Department and served for two years as aide to Secretary of the Navy Thomas Gates. In 1963 he set up a new department in the navy, the Office of Program Appraisal. In 1965 he was appointed superintendent of the Naval Academy and in July 1968 was made Commander, U.S. Naval Forces, Philippines. In June 1970 he became commandant of the Ninth Naval District, Great Lakes, Illinois.

Kauffman retired as a rear admiral on 1 June 1973 and died on 18 August 1979 in Budapest, Hungary.

Admiral Turner decided for the next amphibious operation in the Marianas he wanted five full-blown underwater demolition teams, three for Saipan and Tinian, two for Guam. He also assigned five APDs to underwater demolition for the Marianas operation.

When I arrived in Hawaii the base at Maui was already established and I became commanding officer of UDT 5. Maui was an advanced base and it was used to organize one-hundred-man teams, whereas Fort Pierce (the training center in the States) was still organizing six-man naval combat demolition units.

Very shortly after I arrived, I think it was April 1944, I was sent for by Admiral Turner in Pearl Harbor. He drew a rough outline of what turned out to be Saipan, showing a reef about a mile off the beach with a lagoon in between. Then he said, "Now, the first and most important thing is reconnaissance for depth of water, and so I'm thinking of having you go in and reconnoiter around eight."

I had been in the navy long enough to know that when you say "eight" you mean eight in the morning, not eight in the evening, but it just never occurred to me that he meant the operation to take place in the daylight. So I gave him the asinine answer, "Well, Admiral, it depends on the phase of the moon."

"Moon? What in the hell has that got to do with it? Obviously by eight o'clock I mean 0800."

I sort of gasped and said, "In broad daylight? Onto somebody else's beach in broad daylight, Admiral?"

"Absolutely. We'll have lots of fire support to cover you."

I had great respect for Admiral Turner but I didn't believe this was even close to being possible. I'm sorry to say that my answer was negative. I said, "I do not see how you can do it in broad daylight," and suggested a night operation.

He said, "Well, there's one major difference for reconnaissance. You can see in the daytime and you can't see at night."

That was pretty basic. We discussed it some more and he told me that was what we were going to do. I gave him an aye, aye. I can't say I gave him a cheery aye, aye. I left his office and went back to Maui with the idea that this was really one hell of a problem.

Then, of course, we changed a lot of our training methods. We'd never contemplated swimming that far. It was a mile in and a mile out. So we inaugurated the one-mile swim before breakfast seven days a week, which went on for the rest of the war and which I hated. I said no one could go on this operation who couldn't swim a mile. Long-distance swimming had never been one of our requirements in training—had been four hundred yards before, or something like that—and everyone blamed me.

Incidentally, when we got on the ship en route to Saipan and I explained the operation to the team—my team—they immediately figured out that if the lagoon was one mile wide, that was one mile in and one mile out, so you had to be able to swim two miles. I was asked that question right away, and I said, "Well, I assumed that if you could swim the mile in, there would be a sense of urgency that would enable you to swim the mile out."

We decided that we would use two teams for reconnaissance at Saipan, matching the two marine divisions, and we would keep one team in reserve. So I got permission to pass on to Commander Dick Burke, who was commanding officer of team 7, the intelligence I had received from the admiral. We collaborated a great deal in our training, but still the two teams trained on their own and used different techniques. This doesn't sound very orderly, but it was beneficial because we were able to try out different ideas.

It was not until two days before we left Pearl Harbor that Admiral Turner changed the op order and put me in command of all three teams in addition to my own, which was one of the three. In any case, I had acted all along as a kind of planning officer and I'd had to go back and forth to Pearl all the time from Maui to work with the admiral's planning staff.

I remember one morning doing something that I think only a reserve would have dreamed of doing. I got in to see Admiral Turner and he started out with the usual, "What do you want now, Draper?"

I said, "Well, sir, what I would really like is to borrow just for a weekend a couple of battleships and cruisers and destroyers."

He said, "You want to do what?" I explained it again, and he said, "I heard you, and what in hell would you like to borrow my battleships and cruisers and destroyers for, or perhaps I should say your father's battleships, cruisers, and destroyers?" (My father was then Commander, Cruisers and Destroyers, Pacific.)

I said, "Well, sir, you speak of this very heavy fire support, these guns firing directly over us, and I would guess that this would be a very unusual experience, to be swimming in with eight- and six-inch guns firing almost a flat trajectory right over your head."

And he said, "As a matter of fact, it would be good training for the ships, too. Okay." So he did comply. He sent over for the weekend two battleships, three cruisers, and a squadron of destroyers.

They were used at Kahoolawe, Hawaii. We swam in and they fired over our heads, and I must say it was an extraordinary experience. We really had to get people used to it before they had to worry about shells coming the other way from the beach.

238

I also remember that we had sort of a rehearsal on that occasion, and Commander Peter Horn, who was Admiral Turner's communications officer, listened in on our circuits and decreed afterwards that he had heard many groups in the navy communicate and that easily the first prize for bad communications went to the UDTs. So he sent two of his people over to try and train us in communications discipline in the remaining couple of weeks, with, I must say, not very great success. I think it wasn't until Captain Byron Hall ("Red") Hanlon arrived (a senior regular navy officer named as head of the UDTs after the Tinian operation) that our communications began to improve. Our basic problem was chatting and using slang. For instance, my official call was Blow Gun. I told my exec, "All right, then, you're Blow Pistol." There was no Blow Pistol in the official call signs, you see. I remember Horn telling me that I should not make up call signs for people. I'm sure Horn was right, but he was very much of a purist. I used unofficial call signs in the Saipan operation because I hadn't been able to get a call sign for my exec and I needed one in the interim.

Every day we were dreaming up new ways of doing our job and changing our techniques in the last two weeks before the landings. That could have been disastrous. For example, the Fourth Marine Division commander said that he wanted very accurate plots of water depth because he wanted to send his tanks towards the beach in LCMs. The tanks would leave the LCMs at the reef. They needed a path from the reef to the beach where the depth of water was three and a half feet or less, otherwise they'd drown out. From the looks of the charts, what appeared to be the shallow area in the aerial pictures gave him a line right across the northern beach where his tanks could get in. He based his tank plan on that, but he wanted to be sure of it.

Well, this need to plot a lagoon two thousand yards wide by over two thousand yards long and plot it with accuracy and in detail really worried us, so we developed at the last minute what is called string reconnaissance. That too is still used today. We got empty powdered milk cans, small ones about four inches in diameter, and welded two of them together, end to end. Then we fixed to their ends two large wooden side flanges—round flanges—and then around the milk cans, or reels, I should call them, we wound eighteen hundred yards of fish line. One end of the line was attached to a buoy which was anchored just outside the reef. We knotted the fish line every twenty-five yards with a distinctive knot so that you always knew exactly how far you were from the place where you anchored the buoy. Each man (the men swam in pairs) then had four plexiglass slates on which it was possible to write with a pencil underwater. He would write the water depth and other information each twenty-five yards or wherever there was a significant change, such as a pothole. Since the fish line was attached to a buoy anchored outside of the reef, and since the APD took radar bearings on each buoy, we knew the positions of the buoys and were able to have some idea as to how accurately the pairs of swimmers had kept to the line vertical to the reef or the shore. We made a fairly good plot that way.

We didn't think that one up until about a week before we left. When we sent a message over to the supply officer in Pearl Harbor saying that we had to have fifty-five miles of such and such a number or type of fish line by the following Tuesday, we lost a day because the supply officer asked for amplification of our request. He was sure this was an error or that we were crazy. That was a lot of fish line.

We got it. We had to do this special knotting on the way out. We had a day in—I think it was Eniwetok or Roi—and each unit of two men put up posts in the sand twenty-five yards apart, wrapped the line around the post, and got the distinctive knotting done.

Also at the last minute, I'd been complaining because people would come back from a rehearsal and say, "The water is knee-deep," or "It comes up to my chin," or "It's halfway between my elbow and my shoulder." So I made everybody stand up against the turret of the APD, which we duly measured and marked, and we took some ship's black paint and painted a solid black line around each man every foot of his height above the deck and a dash halfway around him every half foot. We did the same thing up the arms from the fingertips. The black paint must have been a special kind because it was forever before we got the darned stuff off.

Now all of this was part of a developing technique, and it was going on until the day we operated. And these ideas were not mine. They came from either the very young officers or the enlisted men.

I'll describe the Saipan operation in a little more detail because it was the first UDT operation, and I'll describe my team's part simply because I know it. The other team, number 7, did every bit as thorough a job.

My team's four beaches were contiguous and ran north to south: Red 2, Red 3, Green 1, and Green 2. Each was seven hundred yards long. The defenses were five trenches about ten yards from the water line with machine-gun positions about every forty to fifty yards. This we had learned from aerial surveys. The marines were very interested in learning more about other apparent emplacements (block houses, etc.) back of the beach line and also about possible exits from the beaches. They assigned a young marine lieutenant, Gordon Leslie, to teach us what to look for in those areas. Incidentally, I also used Gordon as a UDT platoon leader; he stayed with team 5 throughout the war.

The teams were to have had two and one-half hours of fire support, from 0900 to 1130. No additional time was possible because of limited ammunition supply. We also were assigned thirty minutes of air support, from 1000 to 1030, during which time our carrier aircraft would strafe parallel to the water line and about ten yards inland so that we could close from three hundred to one hundred yards during that period.

240

We left the APD at exactly 0900 in our four landing craft (LCPRs), each of which had a platoon with eight pairs of swimmers. We always swam in pairs. Each pair had one of those reels I described, a buoy, and an anchor. The APD conned each LCPR to the point at the north end of its eight hundred yards of beach. The LCPR, paralleling the reef, dropped the first unit off. There was a following buoy one hundred yards astern the LCPR, so the men knew each hundred yards. Every hundred yards another pair was dropped off.

The next idea I'm going to describe, I'm sorry to say, was a Kauffman idea, and it was lousy. I had decided that to do this properly the commanding officer and the platoon leaders should be able to move freely across the front, so they could keep some kind of control over what their swimmers were doing. We got ahold of some rubber mattresses with small electric motors on them. I had one and each platoon leader and assistant platoon leader had one. They were the most magnificent targets. It was the dumbest idea I'd had in a long time—well, one of the dumbest. It always kept us scared because we were under a good deal more fire than the other people were. However, it did enable us to keep control.

I had a young buddy named Page. He was always called my seeing eye because he had very good eyes and mine were no good. But Page was color-blind and I was not, so Page would tell me what I was looking at and I'd tell him what color it was.

We had been given all kinds of scary intelligence about sharks and man-eating clams, or at least clams so large that if you stepped into an open shell it would clamp onto your leg. But nothing like that ever happened, and frankly we had too much to worry about to give it any thought.

To my absolute amazement, all of the men went in at least to fifty yards, and most of them went in closer than that under a great deal of fire. Page and I left our flying mattresses three hundred yards from the beach. We had a little anchor, and we anchored there and swam in because it would have been ridiculous to take a mattress in any further. Also, as previously planned, I turned over command at that point to my executive officer, John DeBold, in the lead landing craft.

The shellfire from the ships worked out beautifully. The bad part was that the air support failed to materialize. I recently reread Admiral Turner's action report on the Marianas and the UDTs. His comments on the lack of air support are definitely not tactful. I really don't know what the reason for the failure was, but in any case most of us got back to the four landing craft. We knew that one man had been killed—his buddy reported that—and two of our men were missing. The fire support for us was to stop at 1130, and so at 1130 I ordered all four boats back to the ship. This was a very unpopular order since two men were missing, but I had all of the reconnaissance information we had gathered in those four landing craft. I knew that one of team 7's landing craft had already been sunk and mortar fire was dropping all around ours, so I could not risk the reconnaissance information. We went back to the ship and started collating all of this material.

We told the fire-support ships to please keep a lookout because we were missing two men. One of the ships—I think it was the cruiser *Louisville*—reported that two men were sighted in the water at such and such a position well inside the reef. After I had written down everything that I had personally learned in the morning, I took three men who had not been on reconnaissance and a boat crew and we went back to pick up the two missing men. Apparently I wasn't the only one with bad eyes that day. All four of us thought we saw the two men in the lagoon, so I said, "Okay, cruise around outside [the reef] and I'll swim in." And I was only fifty yards from the two human heads when I found they were not human—they were coral. Very discouraged, I swam back to the reef. Meanwhile the landing craft was zigzagging up and down outside it. When I got to the reef I saw five men stand up in the landing craft and shake their hands in the air like prizefighters.

What had happened was this: When we first looked for these men we were cruising along the reef, looking toward the shore. However, the men had swum out beyond the reef, and after I had started in toward shore the landing craft spotted them beyond the reef. It picked them up and waited to pick me up. So my swim was absolutely unnecessary.

We lost only one man in the operation. We had seven injured, including one of the two who had been missing. Because of his injuries he had to be towed out by his buddy, which is why we lost track of them.

Anyway, we got back and sent the required message to the task force, telling them what we'd found. Then we spent all night laboriously making up charts, detailed charts, with this string-reconnaissance information on them. When the amphibious force arrived the next morning we had fifteen copies ready to go. I sent an ensign over to Admiral Turner's and Lieutenant General Holland Smith's flagship, their joint flagship, expecting that the ensign would turn his charts over to some lieutenant. The young man arrived aboard and was taken immediately up to Turner's cabin. He stood there fascinated while the big men— Turner and Smith—discussed their plans. I took my copy over to Admiral Hill, because he was in command of that specific beach's landing, and I sent my marine to General Thomas Watson, in command of the Second Marine Division, who was on the same ship. I also sent officers and charts to the tank battalion and the LVT companies and the LCM groups.

I had sent to the tank battalion commanders the only route we could find that they could use to get to the beach safely; it went from Red 3 diagonally down to the middle of Green 2, which was a hell of a long way from the landing spot General Watson, the division commander, had planned. After I had seen Admiral Hill, General Watson came in and said, "What in hell is this I hear about your changing the route for my tanks?" I explained and he said, "I know, Leslie (the marine) has explained all this to me, but I want my tanks to go in across the Red 2."

And I said, "General, they'll never, ever get through there."

And he said, "Well, all right," and turned to his ops officer (it seems to me he must have been Wally Greene, later commandant of the marine corps) and started dictating a message, a fairly lengthy one, to his tank commander.

With that I spoke up. "Sir, you don't have to send that. Just tell your tank commander to follow demolition plan Baker."

Once again Watson flared up and turned on me and said, "And who the hell's tanks do you think these are?"

I had to apologize. Then he said, "Furthermore, young man, you're going to lead that first tank in, and you'd better be damned sure that every one of them gets in safely without drowning out."

So at about H plus thirty minutes we led the first tank in. What I did was borrow an LVT to take the lead. It was very interesting. We had a lot of buoys ready. We dumped them in the LVT so that we could drop them along the shallow lane into the beach. Thank heavens none of the tanks drowned out. My skin was saved. From north to south, parallel to the beach, the bottom varied in depth from three to eight feet. Obviously it varied in depth as you went in towards the beach.

In the morning I had also suggested to General Watson and Admiral Hill that we blow a channel through the reef deep enough for landing craft. They decided to wait and see how the resupply went using just the LVTs. About eleven-thirty that morning, just after I'd got back from the tank operation, I got a message from Admiral Hill telling me to go in and contact the shore party commander on the subject of where he would like a channel blown through the reef.

So we turned our LVT around and toddled in to the beach. When we had led the tanks in, we hadn't gotten out of the LVT. But this time we actually went on the beach, the marine and I. Well, we were huddled down in the LVT with a piece of stub pencil and scratch paper, trying to figure out how much explosive we'd need to use on a channel about three hundred feet long, forty feet wide, and six feet deep, when the LVT touched down on the beach and we jumped out. It wasn't until then that we realized how we looked. We had on our swim shoes or coral shoes, which had originally been white and we'd had to dye blue. They had ended up a sort of baby blue. We had on swim trunks, a face mask around our necks, and that's about all—no helmet, nothing like that. Of course, there on the beach were the marines, carrying on as they normally do, digging holes in the ground, shooting at people and people shooting at them, and the damnedest racket. And boy, let me tell you,

Gordon and I started digging fast. I ended up between two marines. One of them gave me a startled look and called across to the other, "We don't even have the beachhead yet and the so-and-so tourists have already arrived."

Well, the hour and a half it took to find that damned shore-party commander—we were hopping from hole to hole, scared and conspicuous in those weird outfits—was one of the scariest times of my life. But we found him and he told us where he wanted the channel. He said, "Furthermore, I want it very, very badly and very, very quickly."

So that night we started laying it, and we had a very difficult time. We ultimately needed 105,000 pounds of tetrahol in twenty-pound packages. Each package had to be secured firmly to the coral reef, which was very hard to do with the surf constantly pounding over it. Then the five thousand packs all had to be connected with explosive cord or primer cord so that when we fired they would all go simultaneously. Incidentally, we had to triple the cord as we were afraid it would be cut by the combination of sea and coral. Of course, the fact that we were doing this on a dark night didn't help. We were supposed to be finished by dawn but were not ready to fire until about 1000. The Japs finally figured that something was going on with this group of swimmers all working together in a group on the reef, and they made our last hour or so miserable with mortars. Of course our worst worry was that one of their mortars would hit a pack or a section of primer cord and set the whole shebang off along with all of us.

We finally finished wiring the mess together. I pulled the nine fuses, three for each of the three circuits, and then we swam out to the landing craft and got the hell out of there as fast as we could. The fuses were set for ten minutes, but you could never be sure that none of them would fire early. Of course, the area had been cleared of all other craft for over an hour.

We had no idea what a spectacular show would result. When the shot went off, it produced a base surge of a type that I have only seen with a nuclear underwater test at Bikini. I had neglected to tell Admiral Hill specifically when we were going to pull the fuse, and suddenly on his flagship he saw this wall of absolutely black water go straight up for a quarter of a mile and then start spreading outward. It completely covered four of five LSTs and then came over his flagship. The water wall made every ship it went over filthy dirty because of the residue of the tetrahol. It certainly accomplished the task at hand, but I got sent for immediately. I can remember going into Admiral Hill's cabin and dripping black water all over his fine rug. Admiral Hill and I discussed the advisability of letting the task force commander know the next time I was going to fire a shot like that!

It took us another twelve hours that night to make the channel usable, because the initial blast did not get rid of all the shallow areas. But I think the explosion turned out to be useful. At least, it was commented on very positively by Admiral Hill in his action report and by Admiral Turner.

244

To go back to the pre-D-day reconnaissance for a minute, one thing I did not appreciate at the time and actually not until some time later was how conspicuous we were. Here we were swimming in to the beach. This was unusual. It was almost as though we were putting on a show for the support ships. Here was a total of, I guess, four battleships, six cruisers, and sixteen destroyers, all circling around, supporting us and watching us, and listening in on our communications system. They all had copies of Turner's op order. To make matters worse, all of them knew that the Kauffman who was in command was the son of Commander, Cruisers and Destroyers, Pacific— their boss, so to speak. I didn't realize all of this until I ran into some of these people later and they started quoting me things from my communications. I think what was quoted back to me most often was what I said when I thought that our fire support ships were firing short. Instead of firing onto the beach, they were firing into the lagoon. So I had my little crackerbox radio and called Johnny DeBold, my exec, and said in an excited voice, "For God's sake, tell the support ships they're firing shorts."

Then came Johnny's very slow, very calm reply. "Skipper, those aren't shorts; they're *overs*. They're not ours!"

And according to my friends, I replied, "Oh!"

In retrospect, the daylight operation of the UDTs there was vastly superior to nighttime activities. Admiral Turner was right in every respect. My anticipation of casualties being over fifty percent was wildly wrong. I had team 6 in reserve, thinking they would have to do a lot of the night demolition because we wouldn't have much left of the two teams that went in in the morning. But our casualties in this operation and in every operation were always less, percentage-wise, than the casualties of the marines involved in the operation.

There was one fact I hadn't realized, and that is how very difficult it was for the Japs to hit the men's heads in the water, particularly as they were bobbing up and down and zigzagging between bobs. The swimmers came up for air, went down, swam in one direction, came up for air, went down, and swam in another direction. It's amazingly difficult to hit men in the water, especially if you have five-, eight-, and fourteen-inch shells wandering in your direction.

After the Saipan operation we had adequate air support, and it made a considerable difference. At Iwo Jima I think it made the overwhelming difference. Air support was very valuable during the half-hour period when the swimmers would close from about seventy-five yards to about thirty yards. The gunfire support was fine, but it never really got down to the water's edge. The gunners were always scared of hitting swimmers, whereas the fighter planes would make run after run, strafing along the beach just above the water line.

245

A PERFECT
AMPHIBIOUS ASSAULT

ADMIRAL HARRY W. HILL

HARRY WILBUR HILL, born in Oakland, California, on 7 April 1890, graduated from the U.S. Naval Academy in 1911. Sea duty followed, and then in World War I he was in the battleship *Texas* operating in the waters of the United Kingdom.

After the war he had duty as flag lieutenant to commanders in both the Atlantic and Pacific fleets; had shore duty in Hampton Roads, Virginia, and at the Naval Academy; served as aide to the chief of naval operations; and commanded the destroyer *Dewey*. From 1938 to 1940 he was war plans officer on the staff of Commander in Chief, U.S. Fleet, and for the following two years he worked in the war plans division of the Navy Department. As commander of the cruiser *Wichita* he operated with units of the Royal Navy in convoy duty to Murmansk, and as commander of Battleship Division 4 he saw duty in the South Atlantic. In 1943 Hill was appointed Commander, Amphibious Group 2, Fifth Amphibious Force, under Admiral Richmond Kelly Turner. In this capacity he participated in the capture of Tarawa and in later operations against the Gilberts, the Marshalls, the Marianas, Iwo Jima, and Okinawa. In June 1946 he established and served as commandant of the National War College, the highest-level educational institution of the armed forces and the State Department. In 1949 he became chairman of the General Board of the navy, and on 28 April 1950 he was named superintendent of the U.S. Naval Academy. Although his official retirement from the navy came on 1 May 1952, in the rank of admiral, he continued to serve as superintendent until August of that year.

Admiral Hill lived in Annapolis, Maryland, until his death on 19 July 1971.

The original directive for the Marianas operation called for the seizurc of Saipan and Guam, and the seizure of Tinian "on order."

On July 2, after being relieved of responsibility for all the beach unloading on Saipan, Turner gave me advance notice of his intention to designate me as attack force commander for Tinian. The date was indefinite. He hoped it would be relatively soon after he and Holland Smith could discuss troop availability. His staff had already made a cursory study of the beaches, but to him there appeared to be only one place to land. That was on the beaches near Tinian Town.

The three divisions at Saipan had taken severe losses and were badly in need of a rest period after more than three weeks of continuous combat. Turner and Holland Smith decided that the Tinian job must be undertaken by the two marine divisions, the second and fourth, after a brief rest and reorganization period. They had suffered over ten thousand casualties in the Saipan operation, and only one small replacement draft of twelve hundred had been received.

On July 5 Turner's official message came through to me: "Rear Admiral Hill is hereby designated to command Naval Attack Force 52 for the capture of Tinian, with reorganization to be effected later. Request proceed with plans subject to approval by originator (Turner) of tactical scheme and allocation of forces."

Tinian is an island twelve miles long with a maximum width of six miles, separated by a three-mile strait from the southern tip of Saipan. Instead of the rugged terrain of Saipan, Tinian is generally open flat country that is under intense sugar cultivation. The six-hundred-foot peak of Mount Lasso rises gently from the northern plain. That was the location of the Japanese primary airfield. Tinian Town, or Sunharon, with a tiny harbor protected by an outlying reef, is in the southwest corner. About two miles east of the harbor the ground rises sharply in a steep escarpment to the height of about 600 feet. To the north there is a gentler rise to 340 feet. These two positions dominate the town and the four beaches. Two of these beaches are within the harbor, and one each is north and south of the harbor. The eastern coast is fringed with cliffs of varying height. That is true also of most of the western coast adjacent to Tinian Town. There are two tiny strips of beach (White 1 and 2) near the northwest corner of the island. They are about a thousand yards apart. On the northeast coast there are two fairly good sandy beaches (Yellow 1 and 2) in a shallow and unsheltered bay.

Our intelligence had given us an indication of the Japanese defense forces on the island. There were about nine thousand army troops. The core of these was an experienced regiment which had arrived from Manchuria in March 1944. Naval personnel manned the bulk of the island's "fixed artillery." This included three British six-inch coast defense guns near Tinian Town, seven 140-millimeter guns covering Yellow Beach, and three covering White Beach. There were also many dual-purpose mounts ranging from 120-millimeter to 25-millimeter. They were in place in the vicinity of the airfield, Yellow Beach, and Tinian Town. JICPOA had passed on their latest intelligence to indicate that the Japs considered Tinian Town the area most likely to be invaded.

Throughout the Saipan operation Tinian had been under continuous air observation and bombing. Naval bombardment had been continuous on all known or suspected targets. By the time we began planning in early July, practically every known fixed defense had been knocked out and Japanese airfields made inoperable. But previous experience in amphibious warfare had taught us that many perfectly camouflaged batteries of all calibers were probably waiting for us. So we continued to maintain air observation operations and ship bombardment right up to D-day.

One of my first actions after learning that Tinian was my job was to send for Lieutenant Commander Draper Kauffman, the senior UDT commander, to discuss the beach reconnaissance. If we used the northern beaches in our landing, it was essential that we not disclose our thinking to the Japs, so a night reconnaissance was necessary. Kauffman told me, however, that the UDTs had not had any night training. Still, he could have two teams ready for the task in a week. We got Turner's permission for Kauffman to use Magicienne Bay on Saipan for this purpose. One week later he reported that his teams were ready.

Holland Smith also wanted one of the marine reconnaissance companies to engage in a night reconnaissance of the area behind the beaches. I was not too enthusiastic about this because of my fear that they might be detected. Smith assured me, though, that they were expert at "seeing without being seen and hearing without being heard" and would bring back some very useful information. So I ordered both types of reconnaissance for the night of July 10.

Holland Smith was very enthusiastic about a landing at the northern beaches. One of his strong reasons was that the area was within good supporting range of army and marine corps artillery which could be put in place on the south shore of Saipan.

As my staff began its study of Tinian and its beaches, all they had to go on was Turner's conclusion that we must land at Tinian Town and Holland

Smith's hope that we could land on the northern beaches. The development of the plan for action was my responsibility alone, subject only to Turner's approval. I had to be sure I could land the troops safely and then maintain them for the period of combat. These two basic requirements have to control any amphibious commander's decision. Of course, he is naturally anxious to meet the wishes of the landing force commander when that is practical and possible.*

Our first impressions of the Yellow beaches on the eastern shore were unfavorable. They were exposed and on a windward shore. There was always a fairly heavy surf in the area of strong northeast trade winds. Heavy surf is a constant hazard to unloading operations. It would have been impossible, or at least extremely difficult, to install pontoon piers in such a place. Back of these beaches the land rose sharply. Landing would be difficult against a well-organized defense. A considerable number of access roads would have to be built before tracked or wheeled vehicles could be used. We knew these beaches were flanked by defenses in good enfilading positions. We also knew that construction was under way on additional defenses.

On the northwest shore were two tiny beaches. They measured only fifty yards and one hundred yards respectively. Both were far smaller than what is required for amphibious landings—at least five hundred yards of beach for each battalion landing team. At Saipan our forces used eleven beaches with a width of at least five hundred yards for the landing of two divisions. One of these tiny beaches on Tinian had a covering of sand, but the approach was badly fissured and might not have been usable by amtracs or DUKWs. The larger of the two beaches was backed by a bank of rough jagged coral ledges. They would have required blasting before any wheeled or tracked vehicles could leave the beach. We did discover that there were no visible defenses at these beaches, but there were fixed coast defense guns in place.

The four beaches at Tinian Town were adequate. Indeed, the two in the harbor were excellent. Of course, here too we had made a study of Japanese defenses. It was apparent from this that the Japs had determined the Tinian Town beaches were of first importance, Yellow beach ran a poor second, and the White beaches were not even in the running.

So we knew that they were expecting us at Tinian Town. From our intelligence sources and from our constant aerial observation of the preceding two weeks, we could tell that their efforts to make ready additional defensive installations there were furious. The high ground to the north and east of the town offered the same opportunity as at Saipan for artillery and mortars to be hidden on reverse slopes, where they could cover every foot of

*This was Admiral Hill's refutation of a statement he read after the war that a previous plan of Turner's and/or the marines' had been prepared for the northern beaches.

the landing areas. This said to us there was a likelihood of our troops being pinned down at the beaches by deadly fire. It also meant that the movement of the troops inland for the first two or three miles would be over areas dominated by the Jap defenses on the high ground. The more we studied the situation, the worse it looked from the point of view of the troops. Playing the game by the Japanese rules would prove very expensive in lives. So our conclusion had to be that landing at Tinian Town should be the last alternative.

As we studied further we concluded that landing on the beaches on the northeast shore would also be both expensive and hazardous. And there were too many dangerous unknowns. Then we began a very careful analysis of the problem presented by the use of the two little handkerchief-sized beaches on the northwest shore. Our thinking began to take a different form: we tried to fit known requirements for our landing into this cramped area. Now there appeared to be a number of problems. Landing two divisions on such a narrow front would require more than one day. What extra hazards would that involve for our troops? What about emergency supplies during that busy troop landing time? What about beach dumps, with no beach spaces available? What was the estimate of the time required to capture Tinian? What minimum supply was mandatory in case of bad weather and poor unloading conditions? How much cargo could be airlifted?

The more we thought about it the closer we came to concluding that with careful planning there was a real possibility of using these beaches. One factor in their favor was their proximity to our base on Saipan. This would certainly aid in the supply problem.

Well, I was armed with these questions and others when I went ashore to talk with General Harry Schmidt. He was to be the landing force commander in charge of the Fourth Marine Division. I met with him and with several others and discussed all phases of the landing problems. The beach reconnaissance I had ordered had not yet been made, but I found the marines' evaluation of the Tinian Town and northeast beaches to follow much the same pattern as ours. They didn't like either possibility. But if the troops could be put ashore on the northern beaches, General Schmidt estimated that his troops could capture the island in eight days. He also estimated that ten days' supply of emergency cargo—food, water, ammunition, and medicine, plus gasoline and oil—would see them through. They could also resort to airlifting cargo in case of emergency. A large number of DUKWs would be available to take cargo over the beach to dumps on the sugarcane fields nearby. The marines were not concerned about security during the actual landings, because they could mass thirteen battalions of artillery on the southern tip of Saipan and this would knock out any Jig-day counteroffensive on the part of the Japs.

I returned to my ship in a very optimistic mood. It had been an interesting

250

discussion. Everybody there had been trying to find practical ways in which to use these two tiny beaches, and it was seen that the White beaches offered a real possibility for our purposes.

My staff and I made a quick estimate of our ship requirements for the operation. The next day I went to see Turner to give him this data and outline our views about using the White beaches. To my consternation he was adamantly opposed to even thinking of the White beaches. He then gave me positive orders to stop planning at once for such a landing. It turned out to be a very explosive conference and placed me in a most embarrassing position. I tried in vain to convince him that we should wait for the report on our reconnaissance of the area and that in the meantime we should continue to explore the situation there as well as the other possibilities. He just wouldn't listen to me outline the problems we had analyzed. He wouldn't hear me describe in detail how we proposed to overcome them so he could get a better understanding of it. I was anxious to do that because I really wanted criticism. With his sound judgment I wanted him to try and pick some of my thinking apart and say, "Well, that plan won't work because of this and this and this. You'd better try another solution." I went over fully wanting his help and assistance and instead I literally got blasted out of the cabin.

I confess that I returned to my ship in a state of perplexity. Here I was, charged with the sole responsibility of planning but now ordered to prepare a plan that neither I nor the landing force commander, General Schmidt, liked. Of course, I could appreciate the fears of Admiral Turner over the proposed use of these beaches, but at the same time I realized that we had considered all angles of the problem much more fully than he had. Because he was indeed a commander of such proven wisdom and judgment, it did bring into question the correctness of my own thinking.

The board ride back to my ship, the *Cambria,* was a long one. In that time I came to the conclusion that we should explore further the feasibility of the White beaches regardless of Admiral Turner's orders to the contrary. I was risking something. I was breaking every rule I was ever brought up to follow. He was my boss and I'd gotten my orders. And I didn't obey them. Well, I did in a way, for I split my staff and I worked on both plans. Something might go wrong at the last minute and that could force us to land at Tinian Town. My op plan contained both plans. So I split my staff into two groups. One was to continue work on the White beaches plan and one was to develop the Tinian Town plan. This would, of course, delay a final decision on our course of action.

One of my concerns about the White beaches was the weather. Fresh in my mind was the heavy typhoon swell that made us stop all unloading on the open beaches at Saipan on the afternoon of D-day. Such a happening could prove disastrous at Tinian with its tiny beaches. To reduce the chances of running into bad weather, we set a three-day limit on getting our troops ashore with equipment and emergency supplies for at least six days. This seemed to be a practical goal, considering our nearness to Saipan.

Meanwhile the night reconnaissance of White and Yellow beaches had been conducted without detection. The well-trained UDT personnel proceeded in rubber boats from the APDs until within about five hundred yards from shore, then swam to the Yellow beaches, where fairly heavy surf was running. Moored mines were found in the approaches, also large boulders and potholes. Barbed-wire obstacles were on the beach, and night construction work was under way on the high ground behind the beaches. Means of egress were limited and would require much improvement before they could be used by vehicles. The report on these beaches was most unfavorable.

On the White beaches the same procedure was followed, but the strong current swept the UDTs north of White Beach 2, so that only White Beach 1 was examined. This small beach proved to be quite satisfactory, with no potholes or boulders, and a gradient suitable for all amphibious craft. The current was a real obstacle; many of the swimmers were unable to find their way back to their boats after completion of their work and were not picked up until after daylight the following morning. None were lost.

The following night White 2 was reconnoitered. The beach was found to be generally usable. They did report, though, that fissures along the outer edge of the underwater reef might be a hazard. The beach itself was poor, with large boulders. Portions of it were backed up by vertical or undercut limestone cliffs, which would restrict passage by LVTs to a rather narrow exit until the cliffs were bulldozed or blasted. The beach gradient was satisfactory, and as a whole the beach seemed about as good as we had hoped for.

The most troublesome item encountered was a string of land mines flanking the desired landing area. The UDT report indicated their positions accurately, so it was decided that in the night of Jig minus one the UDTs would go in and destroy them, even though it might indicate our interest in that beach. But this valuable task was not accomplished, because an unexpected squall separated the rubber boats from the floats carrying the explosives and in the darkness the mines could not be located.

After receipt of the report from the reconnaissance teams, I went again to see Turner and told him about the condition of these beaches. By this time my staff and that of General Schmidt were thoroughly convinced that we should adopt the White beaches plan. This must have been on July 12, not many days before Jig-day. But again Turner would not listen and again ordered me in a very positive manner to stop all White beach planning and to issue my plan for Tinian Town. This had already been prepared, of course.

I then went ashore and explained the situation to Holland Smith. He had always been in favor of the White beaches if we could make a workable plan. Then I went to see Admiral Raymond Spruance, commander of the Fifth Fleet. I outlined my plan to him and explained its many advantages over any other landing point. Then I told him of my two discussions with Turner. Spruance liked the boldness and surprise element in the plan for the White beaches. He said he would call a conference, I think the same afternoon, to settle the matter. At the conference were Generals Holland Smith, Harry Schmidt, Thomas Watson, Clifton Cates, and Admirals Hill and Turner. There we had a full and frank discussion of the advantages and disadvantages of each plan. Then Spruance called for a vote. Five affirmative votes were cast in succession for the White beach plan. Then he turned to Turner. I held my breath but Turner quietly said that he also approved it. What a great relief that was for all of us.

Before leaving the *Indianapolis* I talked further with Spruance regarding the weather problem. The success of the plan depended upon our having good landing weather for at least three days after Jig-day. Most of the west Pacific typhoons spawned in the waters south of Guam and then proceeded to the north and west. Typhoons create heavy ocean swells that radiate from the center at a rate of about four hundred miles per day and for distances in excess of a thousand miles. These swells can be seen from low-flying aircraft. I told Spruance of the typhoon swells on D-day at Saipan that had prevented the use of the exposed beaches. He immediately offered to establish on Jig minus three a daily seaplane patrol extending a thousand miles westward. Each plane would carry an aerographer as an observer. He further authorized me to postpone Jig-day at my discretion if water conditions were not favorable. I was a very relieved man on my return to the *Cambria* that afternoon.

Now, of course, the load on my back was even heavier than before. I had forced the issue with Turner and it was imperative that the plan succeed.

About a week before this, after I had my first unsatisfactory discussion with Turner over the question of the White beaches, I went back to the *Cambria* to find a visitor waiting for me. He was Commander Lewis Mang (U.S. Naval Academy, 1932), who had just flown in from Washington with an interesting motion picture he wanted to show us. I had known him and his father before him at the Naval Academy. He was at this point attached to an army air forces experimental unit in Florida. His film showed a new firebomb the air forces people had been developing. Its base was napalm. Mixed with gasoline it made a slow-burning gelatinous mixture that would flow into dugouts and foxholes while burning. When delivered by a low-flying plane, one bomb would cover a wide area with destruction. We were much impressed with the pictures. Mang said the bomb could be made easily from aircraft wing tanks. The mixture could be made from the napalm the troops used to waterproof their vehicles. He had brought two hundred fuses along with him.

I immediately called Holland Smith and told him I was sending Mang ashore with some interesting ideas. Holland Smith and Harry Schmidt took one look at the film and they were sold. We were all anxious to get it. We knew there were dugouts in back of our White beaches because the reconnaissance team had gotten close enough to hear some Japs talking. This seemed an ideal way of wiping out whatever was hidden under all that brush on the rise behind the beaches. The marines were enthusiastic about trying it out on Tinian. Enough wing tanks were available but they would need more napalm. I got off a dispatch to Nimitz immediately requesting air shipment of eighty-five hundred pounds of napalm.

I'm sure that he and his staff were wondering what in the world we needed that for, but a dispatch from him the next day stated the napalm was on its way. Mang stayed ashore to help with the manufacture and assembly of the bombs and also to instruct the pilots of the Mustang (P-51) planes based at Saipan, for they would do the bombing. If dropped from a high altitude, the napalm bomb makes a large pool of fire, but if it is dropped by a fast low-flying plane the bomb bursts and spreads the flaming jelly over a wide area. It looked ideal for the foxholes and dugouts we knew existed behind the White beaches.

When the bombs were all assembled we planned a trial run for them on Jig-day minus two, selecting objectives at various points on the island so as not to disclose our landing plans. One of the targets was not far from White beach. I invited Spruance, Turner, the marine generals and their staffs, and the press to go with our staff in a destroyer to a position offshore to observe the bombing there.

The effect was awe inspiring. A burst of flame rose one hundred feet or more into the air and then the flames just seemed to flow along the ground. After the landing on Tinian we measured one such strip. It was about one hundred yards long and more than thirty yards wide. This is half the size of a football field. Needless to say, the remainder of our two hundred napalm bombs were used to excellent advantage on Jig-day.

That was the first time in history that a napalm bomb had been dropped in war. After these tests I sent a dispatch to the Navy Department describing them and recommending their development for naval use.

When Spruance and Turner had given their approval to the White beaches plan, work on details proceeded very rapidly. It was completed and issued to all commands on July 17. The Fourth Division was to land on Jig-day, followed by the Second Division. H-hour was set for 0730 on July 24. The control setup, preliminary gunfire, bombing, and use of LCI (G)s to precede the initial waves were to follow the normal pattern. In order to make sure that LVTs could exit from the portion of White 2 beach which was backed by vertical sandstone cliffs, the SeaBees hurriedly designed and constructed an ingenious ramp that could be carried on top of an amtrac to a desired spot. There the landing end of the ramp would be secured to the cliffs. Then the amtrac would back out from under the ramp, leaving it in place at an angle that was steep but still usable. It was a top-heavy rig, but of the ten manufactured, seven reached the beach safely and were used. Amtracs carrying the three others swamped en route.

While troops were landing on White beaches, the Second Division, embarked in transports, was to make a diversionary feint off Tinian Town, deceiving the Japs and immobilizing their troops there. On Jig minus one minesweeping was to be undertaken off the southern beaches with gunfire support. At 0600 on Jig-day a quick sweep of the approaches to White beaches was to be made out to the hundred-fathom curve.

Naturally there had been no opportunity for rehearsals, but there had been very close liaison among all commands throughout the planning period.

The *Indianapolis*, with Spruance on board, had been in the vicinity of Guam for Admiral Richard Conolly's attack on that island. He returned to Tinian in time to join on Jig-day the gunfire support group operating off Tinian Town. Turner, in the *Rocky Mount*, also returned from the Guam operation on Jig-day plus one.

As Jig-day drew near, the pressure built up on all of us, both navy and marine. We remembered the deadly reception we got on Saipan and realized that if the Japs had not been fooled as to our choice of landing beaches on Tinian, they could easily have moved artillery and mortars in to cover those tiny beaches. Then we could be walking into a trap which might prove critical. The pressure was particularly heavy on me in this operation, more so than in any other in the war, because of Turner's lack of confidence in our plan.

On Jig-day minus one our bombardment of Tinian was stepped up. Battleships, cruisers, and destroyers were massed in the vicinity of Yellow beach and Tinian Town, with only one cruiser working over the areas in the vicinity of White beaches. Air strikes increased in intensity and low-flying reconnaissance planes took a last good look for camouflaged strongpoints. These flights resulted in great good fortune. They spotted a well camouflaged battery of three six-inch coast defense guns on a point a couple of miles south of White 2. It was in a wonderful position to enfilade the beaches and create havoc in our transportation area. The *Colorado* was directed to knock it out. She did that promptly and thoroughly.

At 1115 on Jig-day minus one minesweeping and beach reconnaissance off Tinian Town were completed. I am sure that this maneuver was an important factor in lulling any doubts the Japs might have had about our landing point. In the meantime General Harper's shore-based artillery pounded the northern areas of Tinian. Sporadic fire was continued both by naval vessels and artillery during the night. Some of this was focused on the coastal roads leading to the northern portion of the island. There was no enemy response to any of this, and reports from my weather patrol planes had been negative. So I confirmed the designation of Jig-day and the H-hour of 0730.

Jig-day turned out to be cloudy with occasional rain squalls and an east wind of seventeen knots. At 0330 one transport group was under way for the demonstration off Tinian Town. At 0500 Cambria moved down to the White beaches. At 0515 the UDTs reported their inability to carry out their night mission of destroying the land mines on White Beach 2. We warned our troops of this fact. At 0530 the heavy bombardment was begun by our ships. During this period the minesweepers at White beaches promptly and efficiently completed their work. A steady stream of LSTs, LCIs, LSDs, and pontoon barges was now arriving in the area and disgorging their amtracs and DUKWs. Everything was clicking beautifully. However, because of a slight delay in forming boat waves the control officer recommended a ten-minute delay of H-hour to 0740. General Cates had decided to land two regiments abreast, one on each beach. It certainly was unusual to see those two tiny groups of eight LVTs and sixteen LVTs take off at 0717 for White Beaches 1 and 2 respectively. Never in my ken had such an insignificant first wave started a major offensive operation. Many a prayer was said and many fingers were crossed during that critical half hour.

We had anticipated the effect of the strong current and the usual dust cloud from the intensive fire on the beaches, so small guide vessels (LCCs) were assigned to each flank of the two waves. In addition low-flying Mustangs flew the route, for we could not afford an error in locating these beaches. Even so, there was a discrepancy in the timing. The first wave did not hit the beach (White 1) until 0742, and it was eight minutes later when the first wave arrived at White 2. The current and the dust cloud caused them to drift off course, in spite of our efforts with the guide boats and the Mustangs.

We knew that land mines existed on White 2, so our troops had been ordered to disembark at the water's edge until the mines had been cleared. Fifteen mines were removed from the beach. Four amtracs were destroyed in the landing at this beach because of submerged mines. But except for this the landing proceeded like clockwork.

At first, successive waves of troops went in at seven-minute intervals, but later ones went in on order from the beach. Our plan was working even better than we had dared hope. Opposition on White 1 was light and only moderate on White 2. Meanwhile Colonel Kiyouchi Ogata's force of well-trained Manchurian veterans was waiting behind the southern beaches for the assault that never came.

The following day I happened to talk with a young marine who had been nicked by machine-gun fire during the landing operations. I asked him what wave he had gone ashore in and he told me the nineteenth. "But in any more landings I'd like to be in the first wave, for nothing ever happens to them."

That was something of a commentary on the heavy naval gunfire support before the initial landings.

By 1400 the seventy-seven-millimeter howitzers of both divisions were ashore, and all forty-eight tanks were ashore before dark. General Cates, anticipating a night counterattack, had arranged for a large supply of barbed wire to be sent ashore during the afternoon. By 1730 the entire Fourth Division and one battalion of the Second were ashore. Early afternoon waves had landed bulldozers, and UDT blasting teams had made rapid progress clearing the beaches and providing exits to the selected dump areas behind them. This excellent work paid big dividends in the next few days. We realized that maximum opportunity had to be taken of the existing good weather and favorable sea conditions. Even a moderate swell could interfere seriously with unloading on those poor beaches. As it was, two LCMs with embarked vehicles were swamped at the reef edge of White 2, where the fissures were much worse than had been indicated by photographs and beach reconnaissance. After that, all boats carrying vehicles were landed on White 1 or at causeway piers.

By late afternoon supplies were being unloaded and things went well. Our aim was to have a three-day reserve of "hot cargo" ashore by dark on Jig plus two. There were some complications that did seriously interfere with our unloading plans, but nothing really dampened our feeling of relief and satisfaction with the developments of that first day. Three regiments of troops plus a battalion with their equipment had been landed successfully at a cost of only 15 dead and 240 wounded. The great portion of these casualties were occupants of the two amtracs blown up by the mines on White 2.

Now with so many troops ashore in a short time, we knew that our plan was assured of success. Our main worry at this point was whether or not good unloading conditions would continue and to what extent we would have to rely on emergency plans for supplies.

During the night we maintained a fairly continuous illumination of the troop area by navy star shells. At about 0300 the beach area came under heavy enemy artillery fire. Simultaneously, a heavy and well-organized attack was launched with tanks against the south and east portions of our perimeter. Most of the tanks were stopped, but three did penetrate our outer line. The Jap infantry kept on coming. They were obviously making an all-out attack to drive our troops off the beach. In several areas they did break through our outer lines in spite of all our men could offer. It was the decisive battle for Tinian Island. When daylight arrived more than twelve hundred Jap dead were counted in front of our positions. The heavy losses in this offensive drive definitely broke the back of the Tinian defense.

Jig plus one was another day of satisfactory weather. At daylight unloading was commenced. Both beaches, the LST area, and the troops got a considerable volume of mortar fire. It came from the Mount Lasso area. The

Second Division then started landing at 0700, and by nightfall all but two battalions were ashore and the line had been advanced to the edge of the airfield. The night that followed was quiet. At 0800 on Jig plus two the troops began to move behind a heavy gunfire barrage. The airfield was overrun very quickly, and then our construction teams took over to put it in operating condition. The weather still remained good, so unloading went ahead steadily. By nightfall almost all the preloaded cargo of rations, water, and ammunition had been landed. In addition the organizational equipment of the Second Marine Division was on shore. Since most of the distilling units for both divisions of men had been landed now, it took one worry off our minds, for there was little usable water on Tinian Island.

By nightfall also the troops that had been making rapid progress during the day reported that Mount Lasso was in their hands. They reported 1,800 Japs killed and only 159 marines.

It was becoming more apparent with each passing day that the advantage of the initial northern landing was certainly in our favor. It began, of course, with the surprise element that had permitted an almost unopposed landing. But as the troops moved south they overran many gun emplacements and defensive positions that had been constructed in such a manner that they could only be used against attack from the southern sectors. They had to be abandoned by the Japs without a fight as the marines advanced from the north.

Jig plus three (July 27) saw the causeway on White 2 made ready. It was put into operation at once. Jig plus four saw the arrival of the first plane on the Tinian landing strip. This also took a great load off our shoulders. It turned out to be just in time, because squalls began building up in size and by afternoon all unloading had to be discontinued. The surf conditions had become too bad.

By Jig plus five (July 29) weather and sea conditions had grown worse. Our DUKWs continued to do well but the LSTs had trouble. One of them went aground and caused much concern because it had a large number of wounded marines on board. But by daybreak they were all safely evacuated. During this time the ocean swells, caused apparently by a distant typhoon, continued to increase. The causeway at White 1 was torn from its moorings and the pier at White 2 was broken in two and piled on the jagged coral. So by Jig plus six (July 30) our holiday was over and all unloading stopped except for what DUKWs were able to deliver. I then asked for the standby squadron of C-47s on Eniwetok. They were sent to Saipan and began an air shuttle service for us. This handled all our casualties for the remainder of the operation at Tinian.

Meanwhile the troops had been moving fast. By nightfall they had taken Tinian Town and all the island to the north of that. What a wonderful job those two marine divisions had done!

258

But now there was a tough finale before them. The Japs had retired to a strong position on the plateau of a steep three-hundred-foot slope. The high ground was the southeast corner of Tinian Island. There was no way to get at this except by frontal attack up a steep and rocky cliff. The marines decided to give the Jap positions a maximum dose of air, naval, and artillery gunfire. Two battleships, three heavy cruisers, fourteen destroyers, 126 planes, plus eleven battalions of artillery threw the works at that rise from daybreak until the jump-off hour of 1830 on July 31 (Jig plus seven). Marine records state that it was "the most intense and most efficiently controlled of any bombardment of amphibious operations thus far in the Pacific." Even so, it took the troops all day with the fiercest fighting of the whole operation to overcome the fanatic opposition of the Japs.* By nightfall the marines were firmly

---

*To illustrate Japanese fanatacism, Admiral Hill concluded his account of Tinian with an eyewitness report from a member of the Fourth Marine Division:

Actually the most dramatic battle was yet to be fought—without the firing of a shot. It was the battle against military fanaticism, the fight to save Japanese civilians from a ghastly suicide ceremony planned by their own troops. Our only weapon was a public-address system mounted on a jeep and on several naval vessels offshore. From a plateau it was directed toward a two-hundred-foot cliff, where scores of caves held thousands of civilians. Lieutenant Colonel Haas, commanding officer of the First Battalion, Twenty-third Marines, ordered the jeep, a protective screen of tanks, half-tracks, and infantry to advance to the edge of the plain. An interpreter told the unseen thousands that the battle was over, that American troops would give them food, water, and medical care. They came out cautiously, saw our tanks and troops, wondered if it were a ruse. Most of them remained huddled together on the plain a few hundred yards away. A few broke off and wandered towards us. When they came in, we fed them and gave them water. One of them, who had been superintendent of the sugar refinery on Tinian, volunteered to address his fellow citizens. After he had spoken, his wife also made an appeal, telling them they would not be harmed. At this many more streamed out of the caves and came over to us. Then several soldiers joined the civilian group, attempting to dissuade it from surrendering.

As marines watched in amazement, one of the soldiers leaped off the plain into the sea, a sheer drop of more than a hundred feet. In a few minutes another jumped. For half an hour the suicide leaps of the soldiers continued.

In the caves overhead an intermittent puff of grey smoke from hand grenades told of other Japs who preferred that form of suicide. The drama was coming to its bizarre conclusion. Several soldiers had succeeded in gathering a group of thirty-five or forty civilians around them. The marines looked on in helplessness as two of the soldiers tied the group together with a long rope. Suddenly a puff of smoke from a grenade went up from among the tightly packed group. This was only the beginning. The grenade had been used to detonate a larger charge of high explosives. A terrific blast shook the ground. The bodies of the victims were thrown twenty-five feet in the air. Their arms, legs, and hands were scattered across the plain. The remaining soldiers committed suicide with hand grenades.

This seemingly broke the spell. Hundreds of civilians now made for our lines. Japanese fanaticism had lured a few score to their deaths, but American persuasiveness had saved thousands of others. By 12 August 13,262 civilians were safely in stockades. We had literally saved these people from their own protectors.

established on the plateau, and by the next day, Jig plus eight, all organized opposition was over and Tinian was secured. The Stars and Stripes were hoisted that afternoon in Tinian Town with Admirals Spruance and Turner and General Holland Smith in attendance.

After the Americans were driven from the Philippines in 1942, General MacArthur insisted that they return. He felt a moral obligation to liberate a loyal people. He believed also that the main island of Luzon would be a very good place to gather military and naval forces for a final assault on the Japanese mainland. Admiral King, on the other hand, wanted to bypass the Philippines and invade instead the large island of Formosa, near the Chinese mainland. The question was considered at the Quebec Conference in September 1944, which both President Roosevelt and Prime Minister Churchill attended. A decision was made in favor of the Philippines. A final date for the operation was set, determined in part by a suggestion from Admiral Halsey. Having recently conducted air raids over the Philippines, where he had met with weak opposition, Halsey concluded that an early date was feasible.

The initial American invasion of the Philippines was undertaken by General MacArthur at Leyte Gulf on 17 October 1944, and on 20 October there was a landing in force.

Admiral Thomas C. Kinkaid, commander of the Seventh Fleet, General MacArthur's naval arm, is the author of the excerpt that follows. He deals with the short period that was allotted for planning the extensive operation and then tells about the landing in force. Kinkaid expounds the concept he had of his mission as naval commander: he was to transport and establish the landing forces, and to see that they were covered and stayed ashore. He also discusses Admiral Halsey's mission during this operation, which was to protect the fleet and the amphibious forces during the landing and during whatever actions might take place afterwards. Kinkaid understood that Halsey was to guard the San Bernardino Strait and stop any Japanese forces trying to penetrate it from the north to interfere with American actions in the gulf. Halsey believed his primary mission was to annihilate the Japanese fleet, and when he located the enemy north of the strait he set out to accomplish that mission without leaving a force behind to guard the strait. Delayed and misinterpreted dispatches regarding Halsey's move north, in pursuit of what

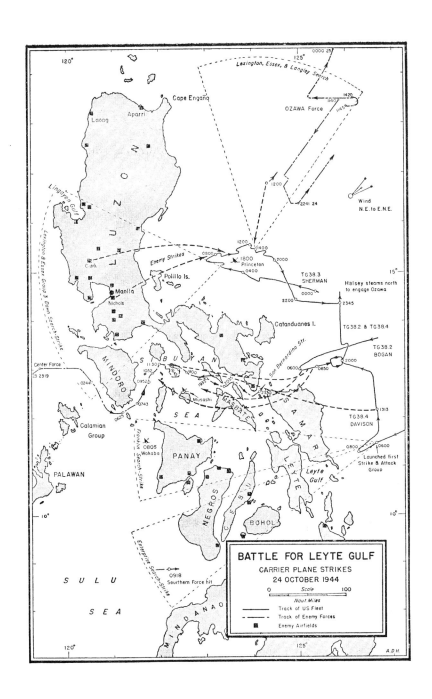

120°

Cape Engaño

Laoag
Aparri

L U Z O N

Lingayen Gulf

Clark

Lexington & Essex Group 3 Dawn Search-Strike

Manila
Nichols

MINDORO

Center Force
23 2319

0244

0743

0925

0952b

1032

1130

1300

1330

1355

Musashi

Calamian
Group

PALAWAN

Franklin Search-Strike

0805
Wakaba

PANAY

NEGROS

CEBU

BOHOL

S U L U

S E A

Enterprise Search-Strike

0918
Southern Force hit

MINDANAO

120°

0000 25

125°

Lexington, Essex, & Langley Search

1420
1140
1145

OZAWA Force

1200

2241 24

Wind
N.E. to E.N.E.

1200
1400

Enemy Strikes   0800   1200

Polillo Is.   1800
Princeton
0400   2000

Catanduanes I.

2200   0000

TG 38.3
SHERMAN

Halsey steams north
to engage Ozawa

2345

TG 38.2 & TG 38.4

San Bernardino Str.

0600   0850   2000

TG 38.2
BOGAN

1313

TG 38.4
DAVISON

0800   0600

Launched first
Strike & Attack
Group

Leyte
Gulf

LEYTE

SAMAR

MASBATE

S I B U Y A N   S E A

15°

10°

125°

BATTLE FOR LEYTE GULF

CARRIER PLANE STRIKES
24 OCTOBER 1944

0   Scale   100

Naut Miles

——————— Track of US Fleet

– – – – – – Track of Enemy Forces

▪ Enemy Airfields

A.D.H.

262

turned out to be a Japanese decoy force, resulted in the well-known incident at San Bernardino Strait.

Certain of the naval and air engagements during the Battle for Leyte Gulf are discussed at some length, especially the Battle of Surigao Strait (24–25 October). Others are dealt with in a more cursory fashion. Primarily, Admiral Kinkaid was intent on making clear his understanding of the situation as it involved his naval forces. To his credit, he saw some justification for Admiral Halsey's interpretation of his overall mission.

COMMUNICATION BREAKDOWN AT THE BATTLE FOR LEYTE GULF

ADMIRAL THOMAS C. KINKAID

THOMAS CASSIN KINKAID, born in Hanover, New Hampshire, on 3 April 1888, graduated from the U.S. Naval Academy on 6 June 1908. After early sea duty in battleships, he enrolled in the postgraduate school of the Naval Academy.

He saw service in World War I in battleships and followed that with three years in the Bureau of Ordnance. From 1922 to 1924 he was on the staff of Admiral Mark Bristol in Turkey. From 1924 to 1930 he had duty at sea; an assignment at the naval gun factory in Washington, D.C.; and duty as fleet gunnery officer and aide to Commander in Chief, U.S. Fleet. Next he took a course of study at the Naval War College. In 1930 Kinkaid became naval advisor to the American members of the disarmament conference held in Geneva, Switzerland, in 1931–32. After tours in the Bureau of Naval Personnel and in command of the cruiser *Indianapolis*, he became U.S. naval attaché to Italy (1938) and Yugoslavia. Early in World War II he was in command of a task force that engaged in the Battle of the Solomon Islands and the Battle of Santa Cruz Island. On Guadalcanal he commanded a task force built around the carrier *Enterprise* and various battleships. In 1943 he was named commander of the North Pacific Fleet for the Aleutian Islands campaign. On 26 November 1943 he became commander of the Seventh Fleet under General Douglas MacArthur. Relieved of that command in November 1945, he returned to the United States where he served as commander of

264

the Eastern Sea Frontier and the Atlantic Reserve Fleet until his retirement on 1 May 1950.

Admiral Kinkaid died in Bethesda, Maryland, on 17 November 1972.

Plans had to be made months ahead of time. In Australia we had a plan worked out, which was to move up the coast of New Guinea to Halmahera and cross over to Mindanao, stopping at the Toland Islands and then going into Sarangani Bay in southern Mindanao. At the head of that bay we were to establish a base and put in airfields. From there we would bomb Leyte Gulf and invade at Leyte on 20 December 1944. We started to carry that plan out. We took Hollandia and we had an expedition under way to Halmahera. General Douglas MacArthur, incidentally, was going along in a destroyer.

Then Halsey, commanding the Third Fleet, reported that in bombing Luzon and the surrounding area he had encountered very little resistance from Japanese air. He suggested therefore that the date of the attack on Leyte Gulf be advanced. It was on the thirteenth of September that he sent that dispatch. MacArthur's chief of staff passed the message to the general in the destroyer. MacArthur approved of it and it was sent on to Washington. At that time the Joint Chiefs were meeting with the British Chiefs in Quebec—the Quebec Conference—and Halsey's dispatch was sent up there. The Chiefs were at dinner when the message arrived. They were called out. They read the dispatch and approved it. So an approval from them came back in no time. It was a remarkable instance of quick response.

General MacArthur immediately turned around and headed back for Hollandia to work on the change in plans. We had about five weeks to make our plans for this new schedule and get them distributed. I figured that it would take us about two weeks for distribution, so that gave us three weeks to make up the plans. Of course, we knew our objective and what we intended to do, so we finished on time. The plans were distributed to all of our ships, and our expedition got under way as scheduled.

In the meantime, the Central Pacific Command had sent us some forces under the command of Vice Admiral Theodore S. Wilkinson. They were to be used for the invasion of Leyte. He came down to the Admiralty Islands with his ships. That was also where the other ships scheduled to join up with the Seventh Fleet reported.

Our three weeks of planning were spent in Quonset huts in Hollandia. Wilkinson and his outfit were in one and my planners were in the other one. We could talk back and forth, as these were open window huts. My amphibious commander, Rear Admiral Daniel Barbey, commander of the Northern Landing Force, was anchored in the bay at Hollandia. If there was any question, the Wilkinson team would call over to us and discuss it. If a decision was needed on something, they could simply walk thirty yards or less to my office and I'd make the decision. So there was no delay over anything. It was a perfect setup for planning. Of course, by that time we knew something about planning and about briefing people. We had a very good briefing shack there, built especially for that purpose. Because of all this we had our plans ready at the end of the three weeks, as we had anticipated.

When we were finished we called a meeting, at which my staff was present and also some of MacArthur's staff, including his chief of staff, his operations officer, and one or two others. People from Wilkinson's outfit flew down from the Admiralty Islands. I suppose we had fifty or sixty people at this briefing. I started the speeches off by calling on the various men in the order of their planned arrival at Leyte Gulf for the operation. First came Vice Admiral Jesse Oldendorf, who had what we called the Bombardment Group for want of a better name. He had battleships which would do the bombarding, but he had a lot of other things of use to us. For instance, the frogmen who cleared the beaches. He had minesweepers and a lot of special groups that went along with him, groups that would start operating three days before the landing. They started operating on the seventeenth of October, and the landing was to be on the twentieth.

After each of Admiral Oldendorf's subcommanders got through talking, we had the next group, that of Admiral Barbey. After him came Wilkinson. He talked about what his group, Task Force 79, was going to do. There wasn't much for me to do in the way of summing up, for it was all clear from the talks of the various participants. We also had a CVE group represented at this planning. I had eighteen CVEs, and they were divided up among the various elements of the convoys.

There were only two or three questions asked during the question period, and they came from MacArthur's staff. But the thing was that all the people connected with this operation had been in on the planning. They had been right there. Oldendorf said to me afterwards, "This is the first time I've ever been in on the planning of an operation that I had to execute, and I have been through many of them in the central Pacific." So when we started off, we knew exactly what we were going to do.

Before we shoved off, I flew up to Seeadler Harbor in the Admiralty Islands and saw Wilkinson and his people. He had a big buffet supper so I could meet the various commanders.

There wasn't any need to harangue the troops or anything of that sort. They all knew what was going to happen and what was to be expected.

Distribution is not a simple thing when you've got a lot of ships scattered around. When Wilkinson's amphibious force came down, the chief of staff of the army suggested that it be sent to Milne Bay, where the transports could be unloaded and reloaded for this operation. He suggested this because we were going to land on sand beaches and this amphibious force had been equipped to land on coral beaches. Well, I figured that if they could get in over coral they could certainly get in over sand, so I said no. The amphibious ships just went with the equipment they had to some other islands where it had been intended they would land before their orders were changed.

We didn't have any problem planning with the army air forces, since here it was all navy air force. The army air forces didn't have any bases close enough to give cover for Leyte. I had eighteen CVEs for cover and escort during the approach, and afterwards they laid off the coast and operated in three different groups. At night they would go out sixty or eighty miles from the coast. In the morning they would go in about thirty miles from the coast and send off their planes to give direct air cover for the army forces ashore. Also to provide a CAP overhead for the gulf. Then, of course, we had the carrier force. The Third Fleet was supposed to hold the Japs off so that they wouldn't be on our necks while we were landing and getting established ashore.

The Battle for Leyte Gulf has been called one of the great naval battles of history. I think it was, considering the forces involved, the area over which the action took place, and the results—the implications of the results. As commander of the Seventh Fleet, I was to transport the landing forces to Leyte Gulf beaches, establish them ashore, and see that they were covered and stayed ashore. The Third Fleet under Admiral Halsey was to give us protection during the landing and during whatever actions might take place afterwards. His was a strategic cover, mine was a direct cover and the protection of the landing forces. It's a very important point that I have brought out frequently, because I had a mission and Admiral Halsey had a mission.

In spite of the fact that we did not have a common superior, I have frequently said that if both Halsey and I had carried out our respective missions correctly there would have been no confusion. It is logical, of course, to have one head, one commander in any action of that sort. But when our two large forces came together, one from the central Pacific and one from the southwest Pacific, there was no time to reorganize the whole setup. It has always been my opinion that that was not necessary in our case anyway—that one commander would not have been better than two where each of us had his mission, I thought, very clearly stated.

We had a rather large number of ships and a rather large force. The first section, the Bombardment Group (which performed a good many tasks in addition to bombardment), was to arrive on the seventeenth of October at the entrance to Leyte Gulf, where first they would occupy Suluan Island and Dinagat Island. The minesweepers would go in first and clear the way. Then we had the Hydrographic Group, clearance groups, frogmen, and so forth.

I was reluctant to give the forces three days of preparation for the landings. (We were not to land until the twentieth.) That would simply mean three days' warning to the Japs that we were coming. But much as I argued the matter, I couldn't get them down to two days. It was all right. Some of them wanted four days, but three days proved sufficient, even though a storm came up the morning of the seventeenth.

At a certain distance behind the Bombardment Group was the Northern Attack Force, Barbey's group. And a certain distance behind him was the Southern Attack Force under Vice Admiral Wilkinson. There were over seven hundred ships in all. Somebody said to me one time, "How did you possibly control seven hundred ships?" Well, I didn't quite do it with my own two hands. It was a question of organization. That's the thing. We had hundreds of ships come to us from the central Pacific, but they came in organizations. If they were combatant ships they came in divisions, with just one man at the top to whom I gave orders.

But the approach certainly was not simple. We had to start with the time of landing, start at the operating end. We had to start with daylight on the seventeenth and work back to see what time the first group, the Bombardment Group, had to leave port to be off Leyte at that time. We did the same thing for the other groups on our one long approach line. Some of the ships started from Seeadler Harbor, some from Hollandia, and all were put on a schedule obtained by working back from time of arrival off Leyte. It was fun. I was fascinated with this thing—the study of times of departure and arrival. On the way the ships had to fuel. We had a fueling group which met each one of the separate groups at a scheduled time and position, steamed along on the course while fueling them, and then dropped off and went back and picked up another group.

Early in the morning of the seventeenth a typhoon came through just ahead of our ships. We had to do something about it because we had three large convoys in line. In addition, we had one or two small convoys that were improperly escorted. I was always concerned that Jap subs would get mixed up in them. If the typhoon had come up while we were steaming toward Leyte Gulf, the only thing we could have done was turn out of the course. We still wanted to keep our zero hour, so if such circumstances had developed, on orders from me each of the convoys would have made a wide sweep to the left, southward; they would have come back on the line at exactly the same place and exactly the same time the next day, so that from there we could go on. In that case the only change would have been in the date but not in the time of the operation.

That's what I thought might happen when I got that first report from Oldendorf saying, "We're in the middle of a typhoon." But fortunately a while later another dispatch came along saying it was clearing up. Now typhoons move rather rapidly that far north. This typhoon had passed ahead of the line and gone on to Leyte Gulf. Oldendorf got there before it had entirely passed. It sank one ship, it ripped the mast out of another one—small ships. Our CVEs had no planes in the air and were not able to operate until the following day.

At any rate, when the Bombardment Group did arrive, it opened up on Suluan Island, on Dinagat, and on Homonhon. We landed a small force on Suluan, found no great opposition there, and landed another on Dinagat.

The entrance was heavily mined. A rather wide channel to the beaches had to be swept and since you have to have an area for the gunfire-support ships there was a great deal of sweeping to do. I forget the exact figure, but two or three hundred mines were swept in the entrance. There were none around the beaches or in the middle of the bay. One destroyer, in the course of sweeping, was hit by a mine and badly damaged. I think a mine hit one other ship, but otherwise the ships all got through undamaged.

Then, while the minesweeping was going on near the beaches, the Beach Clearance Group went in. It found nothing there. The beaches were sandy, but there were few obstacles. Although covered by ship's fire, the Clearance Group was exposed to machine-gun fire and mortar fire and sustained some losses. It was on the seventeenth, eighteenth, and nineteenth of October that these operations were conducted.

Then on the twentieth our convoys arrived and entered the gulf. There had been a minor landing on Panaon Island in the Surigao Strait by a small force which had accompanied the Bombardment Group. One of the groups of CVEs was assigned to give the force air cover while it landed. Barbey's group, the Northern Attack Force, landed in the Tacloban area on White and Red beaches. It had a little difficulty there, again with machine guns and mortars, although there had been very heavy preparatory bombardment. And Wilkinson's group, the Southern Attack Force, landed about ten miles south on the same coast, on beaches Orange, Blue, Violet, and Yellow, near Dulag. There was not a great deal of opposition on the beaches because we had rather heavy gunfire support. The Japs had some pillboxes, but very often if they opened fire you could spot them and knock them out.

Incidentally, on the approach Oldendorf and his Bombardment Group were given twelve of the eighteen CVEs at our disposal. Each of the groups that followed was given two CVEs.

Of course, all the ships were prepared for the occasion. The combatant ships were ready to escort and support our amphibious forces. The old battleships—there were six of them—were filled up mostly with high-capacity ammunition, not with AP ammunition, although they did have some projectiles with the capacity to penetrate armor. The CVE planes had general-service bombs to support the forces ashore rather than AP bombs. So when they actually got into action with an enemy surface force, there was a slight handicap to say the least. They carried a limited number of torpe-does, and all of them were expended before the action was over. Then the planes started making dummy runs which were quite effective. Just at the time when the planes were expected to drop torpedoes, the Jap ships would sheer out of column to avoid them. The dummy runs broke up their formation quite effectively and scattered their ships.

Unloading was very important. The first day, of course, it was a matter of getting the troops ashore. We landed something on the order of seventy thousand or eighty thousand that first day. Then two days later about thirty thousand more went ashore. The army had wanted us to send them up in two convoys, one to land the first day and one to land two days later, but we couldn't do that because we didn't have enough escort ships. They all went together in that first convoy, but thirty thousand of them stayed aboard until A-day plus two.

Then it was a matter of unloading stores. The first thing was to unload enough food and ammunition for the first few days, just to make sure that the troops had what was required. After that, they really started unloading the cargo ships and everything was piled on the beaches. In fact, it stayed piled on the beaches for many days. This is one of the most difficult things to do in an amphibious operation, clear the beaches. When the action started, when Kurita and his force came down the coast of Samar with the idea of going into Leyte Gulf, our beaches were full of ammunition, food, everything we needed. Our army commanders were camped just a few yards from the beach, a hundred yards or so, and were wide open. Just two cruisers loose in that gulf could have done a lot of damage. And yet Halsey said they could only have harassed us. Actually, if they'd destroyed what they found on the beaches and killed some of the commanders, it would have delayed the operation for many months, maybe stopped it altogether.

Our command organization was interesting. Not all of our ships went in that first day, but a very large number did. The amphibious forces were under my command. I was commander of the Seventh Fleet but also commander of Task Force 77, which was designated the Central Philippine Attack Force. Under me were two commanders, Vice Admiral Wilkinson and Rear Admiral Barbey. Alongside each of us was an army commander. As we went into the attack the amphibious force commanders were in command of everyone with them and under them. After the troops landed, the army commander would go ashore, check his communications, and report that he was ready to take over command. Finally, when Wilkinson and Barbey had heard from all of their commanders, they would report to me and then I would turn command of the forces ashore over to General Walter Krueger, the Sixth Army commander.

That worked out very well. I think the last report came in on 21 October, and Krueger elected to stay aboard with me. I told him beforehand I'd be glad to have him stay, utilize my communications and so forth, until he was ready to go ashore. So he stayed until the twenty-fourth. By that time we had news of the Japanese fleet coming up through Palawan Passage, and he decided it was a good time to get ashore, which it was. He was all ready then, with a headquarters set up down the beach, just a few miles below Tacloban.

General MacArthur remained in his cruiser, the USS *Nashville*. He was anchored about five or six hundred yards from me in the *Wasatch*, my so-called command ship. It had a merchant-ship hull that had been altered to have quarters for two commanders, an army and a navy commander. It also had very powerful and diversified means of communication. It was ideal for that sort of thing. We had no more protection, however, than did a merchant ship. We had a few guns, of course, but we always steamed with a couple of destroyers and submarine escorts.

The Battle of Surigao Strait took place on the night of 24–25 October.* In the early morning of the twenty-fifth Kurita came through San Bernardino Strait and made contact with our CVEs about 0700. That was the worst phase of the whole show. Anticipating what might be the situation in the morning, the night before [24 October] I had directed Rear Admiral Thomas L. Sprague to have attack groups ready. I'd directed him to send one attack group down into the Mindanao Sea to get any stragglers or escapees from the anticipated action, which he did. I'd also directed him, at daylight on October 25, to send a search northward toward the San Bernardino Strait. I did that mostly out of curiosity, to know what had gone on up there. I thought that Vice Admiral Willis Lee (Commander, Battle Line, Third Fleet) was there with Task Force 34, and I didn't expect to find anything that we hadn't planned. I was quite wrong about that.†

*The battle plan of Admiral Soemu Toyoda, commander in chief of the Combined Japanese Fleet, called for a pincer movement against American amphibious forces in Leyte Gulf. According to this plan, Vice Admiral Shoji Nishimura's Force C of the Japanese Striking Force was to arrive off Tacloban in Leyte Gulf just before dawn on 25 October and join forces with Admiral Kurita's Center Force for an attack on the amphibious craft and transports the Japanese believed would be there. At 1600 on the twenty-fourth Kurita sent a signal saying he had been delayed by an air battle in the Sibuyan Sea. Nishimura, nevertheless, continued toward Tacloban.

The first phase of the Battle of Surigao Strait was a running engagement between Nishimura's force and American PT boats. Thirty PTs on patrol fired thirty-four torpedoes at the Japanese and obtained one hit, on a light cruiser. Nishimura next met with Destroyer Squadron 54, which launched a torpedo attack around 0300. This was followed immediately by an attack from a second destroyer division. Then ten minutes later Destroyer Squadron 24, on the right flank of the Japanese, released another spread of torpedoes. Meanwhile, Admiral Oldendorf's battleships and cruisers were waiting for the enemy ships to come within range. They did, at about 0323 on the twenty-fifth. The Japanese lost their two battleships and all their other ships except for a destroyer, which escaped. Vice Admiral Kiyohide Shima's Second Striking Force, then in the Mindanao Sea, was speeding toward Leyte Gulf to join up with Nishimura. Shima ordered one torpedo attack, but after learning what had happened to Nishimura's ships he decided to retire. Thus by 0500 on the twenty-fifth the Japanese Southern Force was broken up and in retreat.

†On the afternoon of 24 October Halsey's search planes revealed the presence of the Japanese Northern Carrier Force (a decoy) to the north of the San Bernardino Strait. Halsey

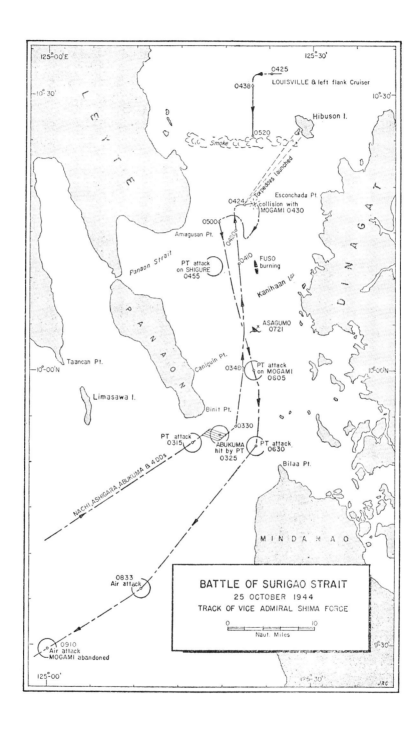

125°00'E

0425
0438 LOUISVILLE & left flank Cruiser

10°30'

Hibuson I.

0520 Smoke

Torpedoes launched

Esconchada Pt.
0424 collision with
MOGAMI 0430

0500

Amagusan Pt.

0420

Panaon Strait

0410 FUSO
burning

PT attack
on SHIGURE
0455

Kanihaan I.

ASAGUMO
0721

Taancan Pt.

Cariguin Pt.

PT attack
on MOGAMI
0605

10°00'N

0348

Limasawa I.

Binit Pt.

0330

PT attack
0315

ABUKUMA
hit by PT
0325

PT attack
0630

Bilaa Pt.

NACHI, ASHIGARA, ABUKUMA & 4 DDs

M I N D A N A O

0833
Air attack

0910
Air attack
MOGAMI abandoned

BATTLE OF SURIGAO STRAIT
25 OCTOBER 1944
TRACK OF VICE ADMIRAL SHIMA FORCE

0   10
Naut. Miles

9°30'

125°00'

125°30'

Well, unfortunately Sprague's search did not get off. At daylight he got off his antisubmarine patrols and he got off an attack group against stragglers from the night action, but by the time he was ready to get off the search our planes had made contact with the Japanese fleet. So we never had the benefit of the search.

I had also directed the PBYs to make a night flight. They had trouble and got no results. In fact, every time they'd get near one of our ships they'd be fired at, and I think they spent most of their time trying to avoid our ships rather than advancing to see what they could find around San Bernardino Strait.

Of course, the mere fact that in the morning we had no report from Admiral Lee and his Task Force 34 seemed to indicate that everything was all right.

In the middle of the night or early in the morning of the twenty-fifth, I called a meeting in my cabin of the staff and everyone connected with the operations to see if there was anything we had forgotten to do or anything that we were doing that was wrong. We went over the whole situation. The meeting broke up about four in the morning. As Dick Cruzen, the operations officer, was leaving, he turned and said, "Admiral, I can think of only one thing. We've never asked Halsey directly if Task Force 34 is guarding the San Bernardino Strait."

I said, "All right, send a message." And that was what we sent out. It took two and a half hours for the message to get to Halsey—which was too bad. But even if I had known that Task Force 34 had gone north, leaving San Bernardino Strait unguarded, I don't know what could have been done about it. Well, we could have moved our CVEs south, where they could have operated with full air strength and attacked Kurita's fleet instead of coming into direct contact with it. But I never in the world would have sent the battleships out of Leyte Gulf to stand at the entrance to San Bernardino Strait.

If Task Force 34 had been there, Kurita would not have been able to come through. He had no air with him, no carriers, only battleships. We had the preponderant strength at the strait. I think we would have sunk the whole

---

gathered the elements of his Task Force 38 and went north to attack that force at dawn on the twenty-fifth. Early in the afternoon of the twenty-fourth Kinkaid had intercepted a Halsey dispatch (not addressed to Kinkaid) in which Halsey said he was forming "Task Force 34 [with four battleships] under Vice Admiral Willis Lee, Commander, Battle Line. Task Force 34 will engage decisively at long range." When Kinkaid learned that night that Halsey was heading north with three groups, he assumed that the Task Force 34 of the afternoon dispatch was being left behind with Mitscher, Commander, Task Force 38, to guard San Bernardino Strait. In reality Halsey, who saw no reason to divide his fleet, took Task Force 34 with him, the strait was left unguarded, and Kurita came through it with his ships undetected. When the Battle for Leyte Gulf was over, Halsey explained his move north, saying "it seemed childish to me to guard statically San Bernardino Strait."

Jap fleet then and there if we'd had Task Force 34 off of San Bernardino. Not only that, but it would have saved a lot of lives and ships in the CVE groups. It would have made all the difference in the world. It was absolutely the logical thing to have done, so when I intercepted that message of Halsey's, I thought, "That's fine." It never occurred to me that it would not be implemented and that there would be a change made. It was not only interpreted that way by me but by almost everybody else who got it—Nimitz and his staff, Mitscher and his staff.

According to that battle plan of Halsey's, there were two battleships to be left with Mitscher (Commander, Task Force 38), who got out orders to those two ships telling them what to do. In other words, Mitscher was interpreting that order exactly as I had and was taking action in connection with the ships that were to be left with him. Nimitz, the next morning, as you know, sent a dispatch to Halsey saying, "Where is Task Force 34? All the world wants to know." Arleigh Burke, who was Mitscher's chief of staff, didn't like it when the order was changed and Halsey was taking all the ships north. He went to Mitscher and suggested he send a dispatch to Halsey recommending that Task Force 34 be left behind at the strait. Mitscher said, "No, he evidently knows something that I don't know." I'm sorry that Mitscher didn't bring it up at that time. It might have changed the situation.

Halsey spent ten years or more trying to justify his action and still sticks to the opinion that it was the correct thing to do.* Some of his efforts to justify it were at my expense. I don't mind that so much, but I don't think his logic was very good.

One historian says that the whole thing was the result of two wrong assumptions: Halsey's assumption that Kurita had been so badly damaged that he couldn't come out from San Bernardino and do any great damage to us, and that even if he did get into Leyte Gulf he'd only harass our forces; and my assumption that the San Bernardino Strait was being guarded by Task Force 34. Well, I did assume that, but I claim I had reason it.

One of the things that will be discussed at war colleges in the future will be our respective missions. As I said before, my mission was to transport troops, to cover them in the landing, to give them cover after they were landed, and to give them air support, direct air support, in their operations. Halsey's mission, to put it briefly, was to keep the Japanese fleet off of our necks while we were doing this.

I must point out that in Nimitz's orders to Halsey giving him command of the Third Fleet there was a paragraph which said that the primary mission of the Third Fleet was to destroy the Japanese fleet. That still remained in effect, and I think that was the thing which Halsey thought justified his move

*This interview took place in 1960.

274

north to attack Ozawa. For Halsey, an aviator, the main Japanese force was the force that had carriers in it. Actually Ozawa's was not the strongest force, but it was the only one that had air power. So I think, combining that with the paragraph in his original orders from Nimitz, he felt justified in taking everything up north after Ozawa, neglecting his obligation to cover and support the Leyte operation.

When the CVEs were being driven south by the Japanese cruisers, I had a dispatch from Sprague asking permission to enter Leyte Gulf. I sent back a negative reply. To enter Leyte Gulf meant that he would be in confined waters and would be an easy mark for Japanese air. If he got as far as the entrance to Leyte Gulf, he would have to be joined by my surface ships for cover. In fact, the message I sent to Oldendorf as soon as we had the report of our CVE under fire was to assemble all of his ships at the northern part of the entrance to Leyte Gulf, get them all there as quickly as possible. That was followed a little bit later by an order to divide his ships into two groups and send one group outside to a buoy—point E, I think. It was a marker buoy to our entrance to Leyte Gulf. I did not want to send those ships outside of the gulf, although at that time the CVEs were in dire need, for the enemy cruisers were just a few thousand yards from them. I couldn't let them be hammered to pieces without doing anything, so I gave these preliminary orders.

Actually, Kurita turned around before the designated half of Oldendorf's outfit started out, so it never got down to the buoy. My thought was to send Oldendorf's ships down where they could join immediately with the CVEs and then hold up decision on the others until we saw what happened. But Kurita turned around just before they left the gulf.

When Sprague directed his escorts in the northern group off Samar to attack the Japanese line, he started something that I thought was the most daring and most effective action throughout the war. Three destroyers and four destroyer escorts made separate attacks on the main enemy battle line in daylight. The atmosphere was pretty murky from smoke, and the destroyers made smoke as they attacked. They broke up the Japanese formation, which is in my mind one of the things that caused Kurita to turn north. Every time torpedoes were launched the Japs would turn out of formation to dodge them. Pretty soon they were spread all over the ocean. Kurita himself, on Monday morning, said that he turned away in order to regain technical control, for he had lost it during the melee.

It has been said that when I sent a series of messages in plain English to Halsey, they had some sort of an impact on Kurita, because he thought them deceptive and felt that a much heavier force was about to appear and put him in grave danger. Shelley Mydans, a correspondent for *Time* magazine, had an interview with Admiral Kurita after the war in which she asked him if the message I sent in English had anything to do with his turning away. He told her that Admiral Kinkaid must have thought the Japanese didn't understand

English, because he sent the message in plain English. He admitted to her that he did think it indicated that there was a stronger force nearby which I was calling into action. He said that had some bearing on his decision, but that the main reason was his desire to go north and join Ozawa.

I've been given credit for being very canny on that occasion, but it is not so. Actually, the reason I sent the message in plain English was my desire to expedite it. I sent a series of messages, you know. It has been referred to as my frantic call for help. I don't think there was anything frantic about it. I was sending all the information I could just as quickly as I got it with the request for immediate action by Halsey. I had finally got to the point where we had to have something done or we'd be in even worse trouble. Richard Cruzen, my operations officer, and I talked it over and decided to sent another message to Halsey, and as Cruzen went out the door he turned to me and said, "In plain English?" I thought for a moment and said yes, because at that time the Japanese fleet and ours were all mixed up. They were all together and there was nothing the Japs could learn about our disposition or what we were going to do. My call for the battleships would get there much more quickly if it were sent in plain English—and it did. There was nothing canny on my part in sending it that way. It was just the common-sense thing to do, that's all.

The Battle for Leyte Gulf was the first time kamikazes were used as an organized force, and it was terrible. They were difficult to stop. The first attacks came on Sprague's southern group of CVEs. They did a great deal of damage there, though I think the attacks were an error of judgment on the Japs' part. They should have been up in the northern group, which was being attacked by Kurita's surface forces. They should have worked with him. But at any rate, these attacks went on for two days.

Then in succeeding weeks they attacked our ships in Leyte Gulf. I kept some battleships and destroyers and cruisers in there as a protective measure, steaming back and forth in the gulf. Every day I could see the faces, from the skippers down to the lowest seamen, getting longer and longer because they just couldn't stop the kamikazes. Sometimes a single plane would come in and dive. Sometimes the planes would come in in small groups, sometimes in a large group—by that I mean three sections of three each. As they approached, one plane would drop behind, as though there was something wrong with the engine; as the larger group went over the ships, all the antiaircraft would be trained on them, and then the plane that had dropped behind would come in in a dive. The kamikazes had a lot of tricks like that. But their attacks were effective. They did a great deal of actual damage.

The morning after the naval action in Surigao Strait, October 26, I sent a dispatch to General MacArthur inviting him to join me in the *Wasatch*. General Krueger had gone ashore and his quarters were available. I added in my message that I needed his cruiser, the *Nashville,* to join the cruisers at the mouth of the gulf. Well, I didn't hear from him at all—no reply—but we kept an eye on him. Pretty soon we saw boats going ashore from the *Nashville.* MacArthur went ashore to his quarters in Tacloban. Then I sent the *Nashville* down to join up with Oldendorf's group.

The night action in Surigao Strait was perfectly carried out, I would say, but it was a rather unusual thing. At the Naval War College we had all been taught for years about "crossing the T." The old theory of crossing the T applies when two battle lines are steaming parallel to each other. Ours, say, has a higher speed than the other and crosses ahead of the enemy line so that all of our guns can bear on the enemy's leading ships and the ships in the rear of his line cannot bear on ours. That is crossing the T. It was said that at Surigao Strait we crossed the T. Actually, we did nothing of the sort. We put the cross up there and the Japs walked into it in confined waters and completed the T. It was just a trap laid for them and they walked right into it. All of our ships could bear on their leading ships. We didn't cross the T in conventional style, but that's all right. It makes a good story.

I think I have said before that communication starts in the head of the man who's sending the message. It doesn't start at the key where the message is being transmitted. A person sending a message has got to know what he is doing. He has got to use proper wording, use as few words as possible. The message must be clear and concise. Then it's turned over to the coding room and they turn it over to the man who's going to transmit it, the radio operator. When it is received it goes through a reverse process at the other end. But the human element is involved all the way through the message's movement. When a circuit gets jammed with three or four messages to go out, in an emergency such as we had at Leyte Gulf, the communications officer should report immediately to the senior man and ask, "Which one do you want to go first?" If that had been done at Leyte Gulf, it would have saved some headaches. One of my very important messages to Halsey didn't get to him for about two and a half hours.* I would have sent it in plain English if I had realized.

We landed on the twentieth of October.† On the twenty-second our submarines, the *Darter* and the *Dace,* which had been stationed westward with the idea of reporting any advancing enemy, made contact with some ships headed north towards the Palawan Passage. They lost contact. They said there were three ships they thought were cruisers, but they couldn't get

---

*The message, which Kinkaid refers to earlier, asked Halsey if Task Force 34 was guarding San Bernardino Strait.

†At this point Kinkaid is summarizing the operation at Leyte Gulf, beginning with the landing of 20 October and continuing to the end of the engagements with units of the Japanese fleet. In the earlier part of his narrative Kinkaid was outlining his mission as commander of the Seventh Fleet and Halsey's mission as commander of the Third Fleet. Now he goes on to mention actions he deemed pertinent to the total story.

in position to fire or identify them. The next night they did make contact with what turned out to be Kurita's force from Singga Roads, heading north in Palawan Passage. The submarines used their heads. They didn't just barge in and fire their torpedoes; they paced Kurita's force through the night, up through Palawan Passage, so that before daylight they knew the enemy course accurately and they knew the enemy speed accurately. The enemy was in two columns. One of the subs took each column and they made their attacks. The two cruisers in one column were sunk, or rather one cruiser was sunk and one damaged.

In the other column one cruiser was sunk. That was a very well-conducted attack, and it meant a good deal to get the reports from these two submarines, for they gave us a pretty good idea of what was going on. I passed that information to everyone who needed to know. An extremely important result of the attack was that the cruiser *Atago*, Kurita's flagship, was sunk. He transferred from her to a destroyer, then later from the destroyer to a battleship, but in so doing he lost many of his communications personnel. That was a great handicap.

Now that was the morning of October 23. The evening of the same date I thought we had enough information to put it all together and send it on to everybody who needed it. So I sent off a dispatch referring to all the reports we had and giving our estimate of what was going to happen. That went to MacArthur, Halsey, Nimitz, and King.

It was evident then that the Japs were coming in. So the next day, the twenty-fourth, we had all day to study the thing in Leyte Gulf. First Halsey sent out search groups from his carriers, and they made contact on the morning of the twenty-fourth. The southern group, coming up through Mindanao Sea for Surigao Strait, was attacked by Jap search-attack planes—that is, a couple of fighters and a bomber in each of two or three groups. Our planes reported fairly heavy damage, which proved to be wrong. The Japs actually made only one hit, on the forward turret of one of the battleships, and it didn't do very much damage.

Before that Halsey had had his carriers disposed in three groups outside of my CVEs, which were operating in three groups: the southern group, southeastward of the entrance to Leyte Gulf; another group off Leyte Gulf, perhaps fifty miles; and still another group about thirty miles to the north of that. So Halsey's carriers were placed outside of these groups, and when I got his plan, his operations order, I said to myself, "Well, that's exactly what I would do if I were stationing these carriers myself." I couldn't have been more pleased with what he had done.

Rear Admiral Shoji Nishimura's outfit was picked up in the morning as it entered the Mindanao Sea, something before eight o'clock. Around that time Halsey directed his three carrier groups to join up off San Bernardino Strait with the middle group. Rear Admiral Ralph Davidson, who had command of the southern group, sent a message to Halsey pointing out that

that would take him out of range of the ships [Nishimura's] that his search groups had picked up and bombed. But Halsey still continued this concentration off San Bernardino. So Nishimura's outfit was not bombed for the rest of the day, or at all before the Leyte Gulf action. That didn't bother us very much because we felt we had plenty of strength to meet Nishimura from the reports we'd gotten, which we thought were reasonably accurate. There were two battleships, a heavy cruiser, and four destroyers in Nishimura's group. So we sent everything down to Surigao Strait.

We had all day to think about it, to make up our disposition. We had six battleships going back and forth at the head of the strait, and cruisers and destroyers on the bow and stern of that formation. The cruisers and destroyers could go down both sides of the strait and attack. And then we had PT boats—the exact number I don't know, but the fleet had forty or fifty in all. When we had first sent out a call for PT boats, only about twenty replied that they were ready for operations. But then they found out what was going on, and they scurried around and got their engines put together again. We ended up having thirty-nine that could go. We had them divided into thirteen three-boat sections, spread out all the way from the southern part of Surigao Strait as far west as the island of Bohal. They were to cut off the ocean entrance to the southern part of the strait and check a few designated places. They were to attack and report.

The group off Bohal made contact about ten-fifteen at night and fired their torpedoes, I think without effect. They were taken under fire and two of them put out of commission, but the third one, although it had its radio damaged, used its head and headed eastward. There it made contact with the next group, enabling it to get off a report to Oldendorf. So he was informed that Nishimura was heading up to Mindanao Sea for Surigao Strait.

At that time we did know that Halsey had gone north with a group, but I thought that Task Force 34 was being left to guard San Bernardino Strait, for about three in the afternoon I had intercepted a message saying that Task Force 34 would be formed of four battleships and other types taken from Task Force 38. It was later in the evening that Halsey said he was going north with three groups. I knew that he had left before the action in Surigao Strait started. I think I had good reason to assume, however, that Task Force 34 was there guarding San Bernardino. Instead, he took the whole force with him. He never actually separated Task Force 34 from the other group.

Halsey said that the message I intercepted was a preparatory signal, a battle plan. All right. In fact, we took it as that. We didn't intercept anything later.* But it was such a logical, perfect plan that I couldn't believe he'd not carried it out.

---

*Kinkaid refers here to a message Halsey sent later to the Third Fleet indicating that his *whole* fleet, not just part of it, would go north in pursuit of the Japanese Northern Carrier Force.

We had figured out by counting noses that Ozawa couldn't have more than two battleships up north with him, and they were the old ones which had been converted, with a ramp on the stern for flying off planes. We always counted noses when we could. We tried to figure out where the battleships were. We had reports on the battleships with Kurita, on the two with Nishimura, and the only two left were the two up north with Ozawa.

When the Battle of Surigao Strait took place it was well executed. The PT boats sighted and reported Nishimura's force, and then as they closed in they attacked. They got a few hits with torpedoes but not many. I was a little disappointed in that respect. I thought they would get more because they are fast on the surface and hard to stop. When Nishimura got into the strait, Oldendorf ordered the destroyers to attack. Those from the western side went down the strait first, then those from the eastern side. Still later another group came down from ahead. The torpedoes from our destroyers did a great deal of damage before the battleships opened up. The battleships did not open at extreme range because they wanted to conserve their armor-piercing ammunition. They did open up, I think, at about twenty-one thousand yards, but by that time Kurita's flagship had been sunk and the other battleship was pretty well battered up. Then a little bit later Vice Admiral Kiyohide Shima came up the strait with his force. He was a little late, but he got there in time to experience a collision between his flagship and the *Mogami,* which had turned and was heading south. A remarkable event!

The one thing that went wrong for us was during the attack by Destroyer Squadron 54, which was coming down from ahead. Its orders were clear enough. When the destroyers had fired their torpedoes they were to turn east and hug the shore on their way back north, so that they would be clear of the gunfire from our battleships and of the Japanese gunfire. For some reason or other one destroyer, the USS *Grant,* didn't comply. She turned and went directly north, and she got in the line not only of Japanese gunfire but of ours. She was very badly shot up. It was quite remarkable that she didn't sink. She was eventually towed to the gulf with an enormous number of dead and wounded in her. But that was the only mistake among the screening vessels that I know of.

In the battle line there were a few mistakes too. One ship misunderstood a signal and might have had a collision, but she managed to get out of the line. And then another ship, because of her outdated fire-control system, couldn't get on the target and didn't fire a single round. One of the others fired only one salvo, right at the end of the action. Nothing ever goes perfectly, you know.

Manus, the largest of the Admiralty Islands, is only fifteen miles long and twelve miles wide. Together with Los Negros Island it forms a cradle for Seeadler Harbor. That harbor, with its varying depths of from twelve to twenty-five fathoms, proved to be one of the finest anchorages in the South Pacific and one of the most important staging points for the Allied fleets in the last fifteen months of the Pacific war. Manus was one of those air and naval bases like Saipan and Okinawa whose possession by the Allies rendered the defeat of Japan inevitable.

The Admiralty Islands were seized by the Japanese in April 1942 and recaptured by the Allies in March 1944. Almost immediately after the islands were secured work began on the Manus naval base. Admiral Halsey planned the layout for the base and furnished naval forces to construct it. This was the last cooperative effort of the South and southwest Pacific commands; as U.S. forces advanced toward the Japanese homeland, the South Pacific area was left behind and gradually reduced to garrison status.

After Los Negros and Manus were captured the Japanese stronghold at Rabaul was boxed in. The formidable defense there—troops numbered almost one hundred thousand—could now be bypassed by the Allies in their move toward Japan. Already MacArthur was planning a westward leap of four hundred miles to Hollandia. After that he would blaze a trail of islands that would lead him eventually to Leyte Gulf and the Philippines.

Manus was important to the U.S. Fleet. A single statistic underscores that point: almost half the units involved in the invasion of Leyte Gulf were assembled beforehand in the anchorage at Manus. From the base there naval aviation units were able to range as far as New Guinea and the Carolines. And as long as the Japanese held positions in the South Pacific, Manus served as a base for the highly effective motor torpedo boats.

As a communications center for all dispatches passed between the forces of General MacArthur and Admiral Halsey, this facility became a part of the story of Leyte Gulf. The message traffic was so heavy at one

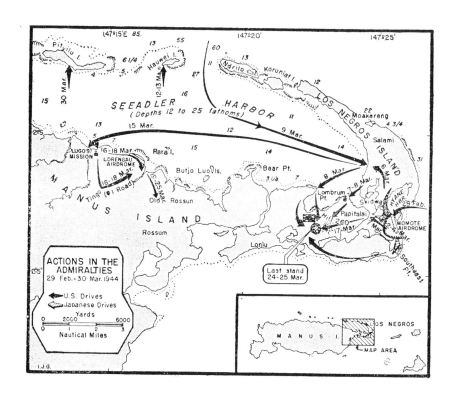

point that dispatches from both Admirals Halsey and Kinkaid were delayed in delivery and caused some anxious moments for Kinkaid's Seventh Fleet.

In the latter stages of the war the facilities of Manus were available to units of the Royal Navy that came to assist the U.S. Navy. They had arrived in the Pacific after the fall of Germany to augment the U.S. effort for the final assault against the Japanese homeland. Initially they had been based in Sydney, Australia. The base there was not completed, nor was it close enough to the scene of action for effective operation with the U.S. Fleet, so Admiral Nimitz made Manus available to the British ships.

The brief excerpt that follows, from an interview with Rear Admiral Ralph Kirk James, gives the reader a glimpse of one of the facilities at Manus—a graving dock capable of handling one of the largest of ships in the navy, the battleship *Iowa*.

282

CHRISTMAS IN THE *IOWA*

REAR ADMIRAL RALPH KIRK JAMES

In 1906 Ralph Kirk James was born in Chicago, Illinois, where he attended various schools, including the Armour Institute of Technology, before entering the U.S. Naval Academy. After graduation in 1928 he transferred to the Naval Construction Corps, and in 1933 he received a master of science degree from MIT. Subsequently he served at the Puget Sound Naval Shipyard and then aboard the tender USS *Whitney,* attached to the destroyer forces of the Pacific Fleet.

James was on duty in the Bureau of Ships in 1942 when he was named a member of Admiral William Glassford's State Department mission to French West Africa. On that mission James surveyed the Allied shipping interned in Dakar Harbor, reviewed damaged ships in Casablanca's harbor, and surveyed Allied ships in the port of Algiers. In January 1943 he accompanied Admiral Glassford to the Casablanca Conference, where he recommended the disposition of French naval ships in Allied hands. In 1943 he was given duty with the commander of the South Pacific Fleet. At headquarters on Espíritu Santo he was responsible for the coordination of all fleet repairs in the area. In 1944 he was transferred to the staff of Commander, Service Squadron 10, headquartered at Manus in the Admiralty Islands. There he became the maintenance officer responsible for repair work on damaged ships. In 1945 he returned to the United States and became commanding officer of the new Ships' Parts Control Center at Mechanicsburg, Pennsylvania. From that wartime command he went to the Bureau of Ships as comptroller and then in 1955 became commander of the Long Beach, California, Naval Shipyard. He was promoted to rear admiral in 1956 and returned to the Bureau of Ships as assistant chief. In April 1959 he was named chief of the bureau. He served in that capacity for four years and then retired in June 1963.

In retirement James became executive secretary of the Committee of American Steamship Lines, representing shipping to the major ports of the world. One of his major contributions in retirement has been to help develop the navy's first hovercraft.

I reported to Captain Alexander Early, in command of the base at Manus, and said, "I have this message from Admiral Halsey about preparing the dry dock for the *Iowa* on the twenty-fifth of December, Christmas Day, 1944." It was the twenty-second when I got the message. I had three days, first, to make it possible to float two destroyers and the *Canberra* off the dock so they wouldn't sink; second, to pump up the dock again and reset blocks for the *Iowa;* and third, to receive and dock the *Iowa,* which had shafting trouble.

It was the worst seventy-two hours I spent in the South Pacific because I was getting no cooperation from my commanding officer. He frustrated me every step of the way. I finally said, "Sir, I must advise Admiral Halsey that I am getting no cooperation, that you will not do this, that, or the other thing."

But we got the *Canberra* off the dock. It was first necessary to put large steel plates over the holes on the sides, where she had been opened up and cleaned out so the hull could be patched permanently. We had to do a temporary job to get her off the dock, because this message from Halsey was not a "can you" message, it was a "you will" message, and I never argued with my big boss. To make a long story short, we got the *Canberra* off on the afternoon of Christmas Eve.

We then got to work setting the blocks for the *Iowa,* not knowing at this time what her troubles were. We were observing radio silence and there was very little communication to indicate what was wrong. I had gotten the word of shaft troubles, so I brought one of my repair ships—which had a greater ability to do shafting work—and laid it alongside Battleship Dock 1. Then we started to make our preparations. I hadn't left the dock in seventy-two hours, hadn't gone to bed, and about four o'clock in the morning I got the message from my people that the dock was all set. I piled into my little skimmer and proceeded outside the nets to board the *Iowa.* She came roaring in just at dawn. I boarded her and went up on the bridge. There was Captain Jimmy Holloway, the commanding officer, and Admiral Oscar Badger, the Battleship Division 4 commander. He had been my boss down in Espíritu Santo, so we had a little conversation. Then I told Captain Holloway the plan for receiving the *Iowa.*

He said, "Where is your dry dock?"

I pointed way up the bay and said, "It's about eleven miles straight up this way."

Our instructions to all vessels docked was to bring the *Iowa* in fair to enter the dock. Then at a prescribed point, where small boats with lines would be stationed, the lines would be taken aboard and the ship towed into dry dock. According to navy regulations, I would then become the conning officer of that ship. We had a prescribed maximum speed which would be observed at various checkpoints as we proceeded.

Jimmy Holloway was charging up the harbor with this big battleship, the biggest I'd seen, and I was getting more and more nervous. Ships were moving all about as the *Iowa* passed through the mooring areas. I finally had to say, "Captain, you've got to slow her down. You're going much too fast."

"Oh," he said, "that's your dry dock?"

"Yes, sir."

He said, "I'll bring her right in on the line."

We passed two boats with the lines going about seven or eight knots, which doesn't sound like much, but with sixty, seventy thousand tons of ship behind you that's a hell of a lot of momentum. He hadn't stopped or backed engines at all.

We got to the point where we had less than a hundred yards to go and I said, "Captain, you've got to back her down. You're going to wreck my dry-dock block setup."

"Oh no," he said, and with this he eased the *Iowa*, still going four or five knots, into the dock. He got the ship just about halfway into the dry dock when he ordered full speed astern. The *Iowa* shook like a damned destroyer and stopped just where she was supposed to be. But I was absolutely shattered because I knew what damage he'd done. He'd swept the dry-dock blocks out from under his ship by reversing his engines full, inside the dock. I had warned him of this.

"I cannot dock you now. We've got to sit here until I find out what's happened below," I said.

I called my divers and held an emergency consultation. We put divers into the dock, and my instructions to them were, "Don't try to reset blocks. If you see any block that is out of place and that might punch a hole in the *Iowa*, just knock it out, dog it down so it won't float up, and we'll dock her on what's left."

That's exactly what we did, and finally, about three hours later than it should have been, we sat the *Iowa* down on the blocks. We overlooked one misplaced block. It punched a hole right through the ship.

Then of course we attacked the problem of shafting. It was now Christmas afternoon. Finally we found out what the problem was. A cap on the end of the barrel staves that line the strut-shaft bearing had come adrift and staves

285

had worked out. We had all the parts we needed and repairs proceeded. After seventy-two hours of no bath, no shave, no rest, with a pot of coffee always at my elbow, I decided to get in my little skimmer, which I drove myself, and head back at twenty-two knots to the *Sierra,* where I was then headquartered. Just as I came alongside the *Sierra,* a boatload of officers from the ship were getting into the officer's motorboat.

They spied me and said, "Hey, hurry and clean up and come over to the Lorengau Officers' Club. There are two hospital ships in; there are women aboard. We're having a Christmas party."

I said, "I haven't gone to bed in three days. I'm going up and take a shower and go to bed."

"Aw, you're a sissy. This is Christmas Day and when have you last seen a white woman?"

That was too great an inducement. So I went up to my stateroom and started with a bath. I could smell myself coming in. After I had showered I came out and started rubbing down, then I looked in the mirror at my hair. There was still a lot of soap in it so I went back in and reshowered and came back out again. Then I discovered that I hadn't had soap in my hair after all; I had a grey streak that was born in that seventy-two-hour period. I can tell you the moment it was born: when Holloway pulled his high-speed throttle-jockey stunt on me.

That episode will live on until they lay me away, because the grey streak in my hair is a perpetual reminder. It is also a perpetual reminder of my very dear friend, Admiral Jimmy Holloway.

The assault on Iwo Jima in the Volcano–Bonin islands was a matter of pressing necessity once American B-29s began their bombing missions against the Japanese mainland in late November 1944. They flew from bases in Saipan, and the distance to Japan was formidable. A forward base was needed for emergency landings and for the use of P-51 fighters. The Joint Chiefs decided that Iwo Jima in the Volcano Islands must be seized. Iwo Jima, a tiny island that lies only 660 miles south of Tokyo and 625 miles north of Saipan, fulfilled the military requirements.

Discerning military strategists in Tokyo had estimated that after the Americans took Saipan their next landing would be on Iwo Jima. Consequently, the Japanese organized the 109th Infantry Division and dispatched it to the island. A keen-minded lieutenant general, Tadamichi Kuribayashi, was placed in command and given a mission to make the island impregnable. Kuribayashi planned to repel an amphibious attack on the beaches and to provide a determined defense in depth. He had two airfields built on the island and a third under construction at the time of the American invasion. Many of his preparations for the defense of Iwo Jima became known to the American planners through extensive photoreconnaissance. Rear Admiral Harry W. Hill, one of the planners of the Iwo Jima campaign and second in command to Vice Admiral Richmond K. Turner of the Northern Attack Force, said that of all the data he had sifted through for other amphibious campaigns in the central Pacific, the data on Iwo Jima was the most detailed.

Plans for the assault went forward rapidly, but there were delays. Two major considerations affected the timetable. A target date, January 1945, was twice postponed until mid-February because the necessary support craft were tied up in amphibious operations being conducted simultaneously in the Philippines and the central Pacific. The logistics for their transfer and relocation was formidable. Another matter requiring urgent consideration was the typhoon season. With the war moving rapidly toward a climax, the big island of Okinawa stood as a final hurdle before the assault on the mainland of Japan. The first of April was the latest possible date such a campaign could be conducted without running into the typhoon season. Military men had learned through bitter experience that this weather phenomenon was an inexorable foe of men and ships and must be avoided at all costs. These two factors forced planners to sandwich the campaign for Iwo Jima between the MacArthur campaign in the Philippines and the prospective assault on Okinawa.

Originally it had been thought that the campaign for Iwo would take only five days, but once the signal was given to land troops there, many unexpected obstacles arose and the fighting dragged on for almost a month. Admiral Hill's account of the campaign makes it clear that volcanic ash on the beaches and the vagaries of wind and weather at times presented almost insuperable problems.

The capture of Iwo Jima cannot be measured only in terms of the lives lost, the bodies maimed, the planes and ships destroyed, though in that regard the price of the struggle was dear. It must also be considered in light of what it contributed to the total war effort. Iwo Jima gave Allied forces a strong strategic position for the ultimate attack on the Japanese homeland. It gave the army air forces an intermediate base of inestimable value. Before the war ended, about twenty-four hundred B-29s carrying more than twenty-seven thousand crewmen landed safely on the island. They were saved the ordeal of having to ditch in the open sea. And ultimately, the evidence seems to confirm, the capture of this island so near Japan proper finally convinced the Japanese high command that the end was near.

THE LANDING AT IWO JIMA

ADMIRAL HARRY W. HILL*

Turner and I wondered what the next assignment would be for us—Formosa, Okinawa, and the Volcano Islands were all possibilities. I had some interesting discussions with Turner on this subject. He had given considerable thought to the possibility of bypassing all of these objectives and making a direct assault on the Tokyo Plain with nine divisions. Such a plan was feasible from an amphibious point of view, but the great distance of the Tokyo Plain from our nearest base would mean that for all air support, except that from the long-range B-29s based on the Marianas, we would be dependent upon fleet carriers. The nearest base would be Guam, which was just in the process of being developed.

I was not too enthusiastic about Turner's idea, although I often wondered if I was opposing a bold plan with too little consideration, just as he had done with my Tinian proposal.† I am sure he urged this plan on Spruance but do not know if he discussed it with Nimitz. I know that neither of these men thought it would be necessary to invade the homeland of Japan. Our naval blockade was rapidly strangling the Japanese economy and could prove to be a decisive factor for an early peace. Both of them, as well as Admiral King, vigorously opposed the later decision of the Joint Chiefs of Staff to invade Japan. In any case, it never developed as a plan until the attack on Japan was studied later.

When Turner and I arrived at Pearl Harbor, we learned that Spruance had recommended to Nimitz that the next operation for the Fifth Fleet be

*For biographical information on Hill, see pp. 246–47.
†See p. 251.

Iwo Jima, followed by Okinawa. In September Admiral King conferred with Nimitz and Spruance in San Francisco and finally approved of Spruance's suggestions. The Joint Chiefs quickly followed with their concurrence. On October 3 they issued a timetable for MacArthur's invasion of Luzon and for Nimitz's seizure of "one or more positions in the Bonins-Volcano group on January 20, 1945, and one or more positions in the Ryukyus with a target date of March 1, 1945."

Things moved rapidly as soon as the directive was issued. Within four days we received a JICPOA study of Iwo Jima and were told to go to work. The organization setup was very similar to that used for Saipan. Spruance was in overall command and Turner was to command the Joint Expeditionary Force. I was second in command to Turner and also Commander, Attack Force, for the landing operations. A new idea of Turner's was to name Rear Admiral Henry Blandy as Commander, Amphibious Support Force, to conduct the preliminary bombardment, the minesweeping, and the UDT work. Lieutenant General Holland Smith was again named as commander of the expeditionary troops, and under him Major General Harry Schmidt commanded the Fifth Amphibious Corps, consisting of the Fourth and Fifth Marine divisions.

Also under Spruance's command was the newly organized Service Squadron 6. This was a seagoing group of tankers, supply and ammunition ships, and jeep carriers. New methods to transfer ammunition and heavy stores had been developed. The rather short duration of the Iwo campaign was to give the service squadron a good trial. It produced some outstanding results, as the records show. Our fleet was no longer dependent upon overseas bases for its logistic support.

Iwo Jima is situated almost on a line between Tokyo and Saipan. It is 660 miles south of Tokyo and 625 miles north of Saipan, a desolate-looking little island dominated by the 550-foot dome of an extinct volcano, Mount Suribachi. In shape it has been likened to a pork chop: it extends from the narrow tip at Suribachi for a distance of four and two-thirds miles in a northeasterly direction, and has a maximum width of about two and one half miles at its northern end. North of Suribachi the ground rises from either flank of the beaches like a dome and ascends gradually to a plateau about three hundred feet high in the central portion, where the airfields and the town of Motoyama are located. From this plateau the ground falls in jagged gorges and ridges to the shoreline. Steam and smoke emerge from several hot volcanic spots on the island, the source of the sulphur that is refined there.

The available charts for Iwo Jima were extremely small and of little military value. However, we did have a wealth of photographic material from the aerial strikes that had been made. We had, as well, considerable data of great value regarding Iwo and its defenses. This had been found in the

Marianas. I can say that it was far and away the finest coverage we had for any of my Pacific operations.

On the eastern shore a shallow and continuous beach extended from Suribachi in a northeasterly direction for six thousand yards, at which point the coast turned eastward in high jagged cliffs and sheltered a small boat harbor. These cliffs, with Suribachi at the southwest, made for excellent artillery positions. Actually the island was so small that all beach areas were within easy gun or mortar range of all enemy installations.

The beach itself was reported to be of black volcanic ash or sand. Behind the beach the ground rose gradually, but wind or water had formed a series of rather steep terraces which might cause early trouble for wheeled vehicles. Except for three small rocky outcrops about three hundred yards off the center of the beach area, the approaches were clear, with deep water extending close inshore. The western beach ran almost north from Suribachi, and the usable portion of the beach proper was approximately the same length as the eastern beaches. In the northern portion the beach rose more gently, although it was scarred by several terraces of varying width. A submerged bar similar to the coral reef at Saipan ran the full length of the island about three hundred yards offshore. We had no data on the depth of the water covering it, but there were many indications that it was too shallow for passage by LSTs. No usable beaches existed on the northern half of the island.

The meteorological data we had indicated that the winds in February usually came from the north to west sectors with a force of about fifteen knots. Typhoons were very rare at that time of year.

We considered all of these factors and arrived at a unanimous decision that the assault landings must be made on the eastern beaches. They were used regularly by the Japs for amphibious craft similar to our LSTs. They brought supplies and equipment from Chichi Jima, 150 miles to the north.

Our first reports indicated that the Japanese defense force was in excess of thirteen thousand army and navy troops. We also knew they were working hard to strengthen their defenses. Our reconnaissance disclosed eight coast defense guns, sixteen double-purpose mounts near the airfield, many pill-boxes and machine-gun positions, open and closed artillery positions, one blockhouse, and miles of antitank trenches and fire communication trenches. Caves at the base of Suribachi were very probably sites for gun installations, as were the cliffs on the north flank of the eastern beaches. The whole island was particularly suitable for mortar installations of all sizes. These could be easily mounted in caves and foxholes and be made secure from any form of naval gunfire.

One of the photographic studies disclosed a line of partly buried objects along the waterline of the eastern beach which appeared to be a string of

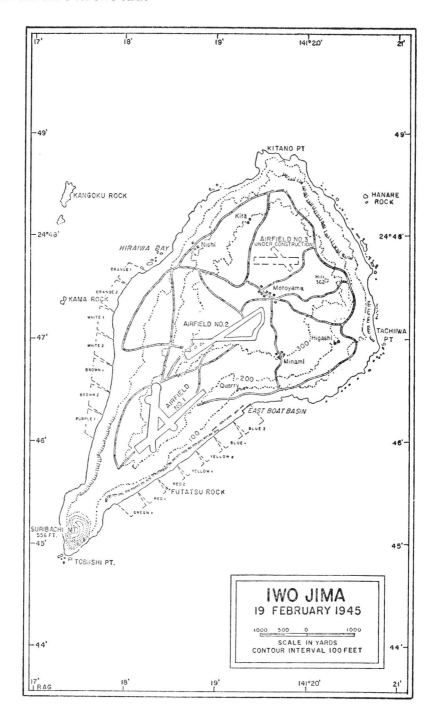

KITANO PT

KANGOKU ROCK

HANARE
ROCK

Kita

AIRFIELD NO. 3
UNDER CONSTRUCTION

HIRAIWA BAY

Nishi

ORANGE 1

ORANGE 2

KAMA ROCK

Motoyama

Hill
362

WHITE 1

AIRFIELD NO. 2

WHITE 2

Higashi

TACHIIWA
PT

BROWN 1

Minami

300

BROWN 2

Quarry

200

PURPLE 1

AIRFIELD
NO. 1

EAST BOAT BASIN

BLUE 2

100

BLUE 1

YELLOW 2

YELLOW 1

RED 2

FUTATSU ROCK

RED 1

GREEN 1

SURIBACHI MT.
556 FT.

TOBIISHI PT.

IWO JIMA
19 FEBRUARY 1945

1000 500 0 1000

SCALE IN YARDS
CONTOUR INTERVAL 100 FEET

gasoline drums. Our intelligence information had previously indicated that the Japs had been experimenting with gasoline which could be ignited to make a wall of flame at the time of landing. This line, regular enough to give it the appearance of an engineering installation, caused us considerable worry as we started our planning.

The planning setup was very similar to that used for the Marianas. My plan was restricted to the landing and all the problems connected with the beach and unloading operations. We had about six weeks to prepare. That seemed easy, in that we were working with old friends in Generals Schmidt and Cates.

Harry Schmidt concurred, as had the others, in the selection of the eastern beaches, but to take care of unforeseen conditions we designated the western beaches as an alternative and prepared plans for each which dovetailed without much conflict.

When Spruance and Turner began their detailed study of available shipping, it became apparent that the dates set for the Luzon operation and for Iwo Jima would have to be changed, because there was not enough time to allow for reallocation of amphibious and support shipping from one operation to the other.

This calls attention to a phase of the Pacific war I think is rarely understood. MacArthur was moving northward into the Philippines with several army divisions. Nimitz was moving westward from Pearl Harbor with several divisions. But there was just a limited number of ships available to form the striking and covering forces, transport the troops, land them, and deliver supplies. Identical combatant ships operating under the alternating title of Fifth Fleet and Third Fleet formed the striking force and cover for both MacArthur's and Nimitz's operations. However, they always remained under Nimitz's command. But the transports and cargo ships and amphibious craft such as LSTs were shuttled from one theater to the other as the tempo of assault operations required. There were just so many ships to go around, and they had to be juggled continuously. Naturally any delay in one operation caused a postponement of the release date of the ships involved and immediately affected the timing of succeeding operations.

This was the situation early in 1945. The Okinawa date had been deferred until April 1, but as a study of Iwo Jima turned up greater difficulties than had been anticipated, Holland Smith asked for a further delay so that a ten-day preliminary bombardment of the defenses could be made. Spruance denied this request. One of his main reasons was the fact that the schedule was now being squeezed from the other end. The typhoon season at Okinawa was approaching. The lengthy operation predicted there had to be completed before a typhoon could strike the huge armada of ships that would be assembled. Any further postponement would create an extremely serious hazard to the Okinawa program.

From the start of planning we were concerned about the soft volcanic sand rising in terraces behind the shallow beaches. We explored this problem by making a series of tests on a very soft beach on the western shore of Oahu. Here we beached an LST with tracked and wheeled vehicles and found that the vehicles stalled. A good-sized sand sled was manufactured and tried out. It proved quite satisfactory when towed by a tracked vehicle, so a large order for these was placed immediately with the navy yard.

About this time one of my staff called my attention to a strange development shown by successive air photographs which were being received. A Jap LCI-type vessel had been disabled by air bombing while discharging on the east beach. Successive photos showed that the shoreline was rapidly extending seaward near the stern of this vessel. That indicated a beach much softer than normal. Now this meant real trouble, if even the wet portions of the beach were too soft for trucks and wheeled equipment.

I think it was Commander Squeaky Anderson—the almost legendary beachmaster for many of the operations in the central Pacific—who first came up with a solution to this. We asked the navy yard to take sections of Marston matting—thin steel matting in sections of ten by one and a half feet, used for laying temporary airstrips—and hinge enough of these together to make a length of fifty feet. They were hinged on alternate edges—an accordion pleat—so that a tractor by pulling one end of the compact package could quickly extend it and presto, there was a usable section of road.

We made another test at the soft Oahu beach with a few of these sections. Various marine representatives were present. The LST again landed and a small tractor disembarked, trailing a sand sled loaded with three packages of matting. A spike was driven through the end of the first section of the matting, and within one minute we had a 150-foot road over which the wheeled vehicles moved without difficulty.

We were much pleased with the effectiveness of this scheme and the ease with which it could be laid. So the navy yard went to work, and by the time of our departure from Hawaii we had over eight miles of matting with small tractors and sleds ready for use. They were loaded in LSTs and LCIs, and they were to be the first vehicles to debark in the assault.

This proved to be invaluable. The first sections were laid on rough and unprepared routes, and they became badly twisted and bent, which in turn created additional problems on an already cluttered beach. But as soon as bulldozers were able to prepare a smooth path, the matting became a foundation for all beach outlets.

This small item of planning, which resulted from a smart evaluation of air photographs, played a vital role in our operation. I regard it as one of the greatest and most unpublicized contributions of my staff to the success of our Pacific campaigns.

It was more than fortunate that D-day was delayed because it gave us time to get this equipment ready. When we landed on the beach at Iwo, we found not sand but a fluffy volcanic cinder so unbelievably soft that a man would sink to his shoetops. Even tracked vehicles had great difficulty negotiating it. Several tanks and many LVTs were among the beach casualties that morning.

We had a continuous flow of excellent air photographs and other intelligence during our planning. Now we knew there were at least fifteen thousand troops on Iwo, so the marines estimated it would take two weeks of intensive combat to capture the island. Not much new construction was appearing in these later pictures, probably indicating that much of the Jap defensive buildup was going underground.

It was not until after the capture of the island that we realized the tremendous strength of its interconnecting defense system. Lieutenant General Tadamichi Kuribayashi had arrived the previous summer and made Iwo into the most impregnable fortress in the Pacific. Observers who had inspected German fortified areas in both world wars testified that they had never seen a position so thoroughly defended as Iwo. Not only were ground-level pillboxes and gun positions protected by heavy concrete, but all adjacent positions were connected by spider-trap tunnels. Within Suribachi the caves extended at least thirty-five feet into the mountain with vast abutments of concrete. The caves had angles inside of ninety degrees to protect against flamethrowers and demolition charges. Near the north end of the island, control centrals for communication artillery were in deep excavations at five levels, the deepest as much as seventy-five feet underground with more than five hundred feet of tunnels. General Kuribayashi's headquarters were here, in concrete warrooms, and near the eastern shore similar headquarters had been built for his subordinate commander.

Turner brought to Pearl for the planning sessions two transport squadron commanders with their staffs. Our first estimates indicated little difficulty with the actual landing operations except on the beaches. They would be under constant gun and mortar fire, which would badly damage landing craft and beach party equipment as well as result in heavy casualties.

Squeaky Anderson, our beachmaster, recommended that salvage craft be provided and crews be trained in beach salvage. Also a huge LeTourneau crane was included for one of the early deliveries on the beach. It was a great asset in the hectic days that followed. We also had seven diesel fire pumps to handle any serious fires that might start on the beaches. But one of the most valuable additions to our equipment was several armored bulldozers. Squeaky had made this a special project of his. He told of his ideas for placement of twenty-pound sheets of steel to protect the driver and the engine. The SeaBee battalion that would accompany us on the invasion completed this project, and the cabs of the tanks were the safest places on the beach. During the actual operation Major General Keller Rockey's Fifth

Division found the going tough on the rugged terrain of the northern tip of the island. His bulldozer operators were being knocked out about as fast as he could replace them, so he sent me an urgent request for a couple of armored bulldozers. They quickly became the pet of that fine division. I am sure that Rockey echoed our recommendation that armored bulldozers be made standard equipment for assault shore parties.

The use of LSTs as casualty-evacuation units had been effective at the Marianas, and the number provided at Iwo was increased to four. The marine estimate of casualties was about ten percent of the troops ashore in the first two days, so we knew it would be a critical problem. The LSV *Ozark* was to carry fifty loaded amphibious trailers to Iwo and after their discharge was to function as an auxiliary hospital ship at the anchorage. In addition, three hospital ships and one hospital transport would be available. These ships, together with departing transports, were to evacuate nearly fourteen thousand casualties from Iwo during those thirty-five days of combat.

My gunnery officer and I spent much time considering prelanding fire support. On our way home from Tinian, General Cates and I had discussed the possibility of putting a rolling barrage of fire ahead of the troops for a short period after they landed. (At Saipan the Jap defenses had stayed quiet during the prelanding naval gunfire, but the moment it stopped, when the troops hit the beaches, they opened up with a deadly barrage.) Cates and I discussed another point: If the naval gunfire did not stop abruptly, but just lifted progressively to a few hundred yards in the rear of the beach, would the Jap guns still stay quiet? It sounded like a worthwhile try. Cates was enthusiastic about it. I think these conversations I had with Cates were actually the basis for the fine gunfire-support plan that was prepared by my gunnery officers and those of Turner and Holland Smith. The support lasted for about sixty minutes after the troops hit the beaches. They also had three hours of additional barrage fire on call in case the advance needed it. On D-day the plan definitely seemed successful. Enemy fire on most of the beach area was light until approximately H plus thirty minutes. By that time several waves of troops had gone ashore fairly cheaply and got pretty well clear of the beach.

Our final plans were ready and distributed in late December. On January 11, 1945, Harry Schmidt and his staff embarked on the *Auburn* and established a corps headquarters there. The next day all the assault vessels sortied from Pearl and conducted five days of very useful rehearsals at Maui and Kahoolawe. Just before we departed, word came from the *Auburn* that Admiral Turner was on the sick list, and I was ordered to take command of the force.* By the time the rehearsals were over he was back on his feet. On

*The *Auburn* was Hill's flagship at Iwo Jima. Schmidt, in command of the marine division, was also on board this ship. Hill was off in Hawaii for rehearsals when word came from his flagship that Turner was ill.

February 5 all of our ships entered Eniwetok for logistic replenishment and then went on to Saipan, where further attention was given to rehearsals. Mr. Forrestal, secretary of the navy, arrived at this time and was the guest of Turner on the *Eldorado*.

Just then Turner again came down with a virus, had a very high fever, and was threatened with pneumonia. I begged him to take it easy and obey the doctor's orders. We had an adequate attack plan, experienced commanders and troops, and we could carry on successfully till he was able again to take the helm. The navy just couldn't afford to lose him. He said he would be careful but would be all right in plenty of time—and he was. Before D-day he was back on his feet and carrying on as usual.

We sailed from Saipan on the afternoon of the sixteenth. That very morning, at daybreak, Admiral Spruance, with Marc Mitscher's heavy carrier force, struck the Tokyo area with a great air attack and followed it with another the following day. They inflicted heavy damage on shipping, aircraft factories, and airfields in the coastal areas and destroyed, according to our reports, over five hundred planes. That was good news for us, because Iwo was in easy striking distance for many types of Japanese planes. At the same time, Admiral Blandy's striking force began a slow systematic bombardment of all known targets on Iwo. He had eight battleships, six cruisers, fourteen destroyers, some escort carriers, and some smaller craft. On D-day two fast battleships and the *Indianapolis*, Spruance's flagship, joined the force.

Through my knowledge of the called gunfire over Turner's circuits—they were monitored by my staff during the bombardment—I decided that most of the targets suitable for destruction by naval gunfire were eliminated. Others that remained were promptly knocked out by called fire after they disclosed their positions.

Perhaps the best informed comment on the accomplishments of Blandy's three days of shore bombardment comes from the enemy. General Kuribayashi sent a dispatch to the chief of the Japanese General Staff in Tokyo during the course of the assault. He said, "We need to reconsider the power of bombardment from ships. The beach positions we made on this island [with] many materials and great efforts were destroyed within three days. . . . The power of the American warships and aircraft make [it possible for them to land on any] beachhead they like. Preventing them from landing means nothing but great damages."

On the evening of February 17 we got radio news of a successful minesweeping operation. We also got word on the UDT operations, which were contested by a well-camouflaged and undetected battery in the cliff area at the north end of the eastern beaches. The premature disclosing of this powerful battery was most fortunate for us; it was quickly put out of action by battleship gunfire. If it had still been undetected on D-day, it could have raised havoc with the advancing boat waves.

The report of the UDT reconnaissance was favorable. They detected no underwater mines or obstructions, no rearranged gasoline-fire curtain at the beachline. Our fears on that score had proved ungrounded.

All was routine with us as we steamed toward the objective, and all ships arrived on time at the transport areas about seven miles offshore. It was a fine clear day with a ten-knot breeze. H-hour had been established for 0900. At 0630 Turner signaled, "Land the landing force." All proceeded with remarkable precision, and promptly at 0830 the first wave left the line of departure, hitting the beaches at exactly 0900. There had been practically no gunfire in the offshore areas. Only light casualties were suffered by the first waves of troops as they landed. The heavy fire and the rolling barrage seemed to be quite effective in holding back enemy fire, except on the northern beaches, where the mortar fire began to take a heavy toll.

Then the LCTs and LCMs carrying tanks were called in. They all beached and discharged successfully, in spite of the heavy gunfire now covering all the beaches. The tanks began to encounter difficulty moving inland on the soft cinders. Several of them lost their treads. We began to get reports from the beaches indicating trouble, much trouble. Many LVTs had also encountered difficulties, and several were casualties. About noontime both divisions called for some of their reserve units, which were sent in.

Then the wind changed to southeast and increased in velocity, creating a medium but sharp breaking surf. The beach was very steep. As the small ships landed, their bows went up sharply and their sterns dropped. Many of them were swamped. The current running parallel to the beach caused many others to broach. By nightfall the beach was a chaos of wreckage and this, of course, slowed the whole unloading operation. The beach and shore parties managed to supply an adequate amount of "hot cargo," ammunition, for the troops nevertheless. Here again the amtracs and DUKWs proved their worth.

Squeaky and his four assistants were everywhere and must have had charmed lives, for in spite of heavy casualties among the beach parties they came through without a scratch. A Royal Navy liaison officer later said, "On the beach was an extraordinary character, almost as wide as he was tall, wearing the insignia of a navy captain, but delivering his commands in amazingly blasphemous language with a strong Scandinavian accent. He managed to get things done."

By the next morning the wind had shifted again to the west. This gave our people a chance to improve the beach situation. But this was all short-lived. In early afternoon the wind shifted and there was quite a heavy surf on the beaches, greatly hampering both salvage and unloading. Even the larger craft, the LCTs and LSMs, had considerable trouble on the beaches because their stern anchors failed to hold fast in the soft bottom. Dropping those stern anchors was like dropping a spoon in a bowl of soft mush. Underwater wreckage caused considerable damage to some of the ships' hulls and propellers. I really feel completely inadequate trying to describe the mess on those beaches.

D plus two came with showers but with better wind conditions. So I ordered the launching of a section of pontoon causeway to determine whether it could be safely moored at the beach. All efforts failed. The soft volcanic cinders simply wouldn't hold the anchors. I also ordered the launching of seventeen pontoon barges to take advantage of the favorable change in weather, for I felt we had to take every break we could get. But the weather changed again and made me regret my decision; these craft simply could not hold fast on the beach. As with the pontoon causeway, no anchors would hold in those soft cinders. Some of them went adrift when their engines failed. On the whole those barges did not help solve our problem. They only succeeded in aggravating it.

Meanwhile the troops were inching their way forward, but the going was tough on all fronts. The Fifth Division had crossed the island and turned north, leaving a detachment to take care of Mount Suribachi defenses. Both division command posts were established ashore. That afternoon a unit of the Third Division that had arrived on D-day from Guam had been landed successfully, and it took a position on the left flank of the Fourth Division. The weather had really deteriorated now, with strong winds blowing directly on shore. That afternoon I ordered Squeaky Anderson, the beachmaster, to take a look at the western beaches and advise me on the practicability of shifting to them.

Now a shortage of manpower for handling supplies had developed similar to that at Saipan. The shore party was largely composed of men who were ultimately to be used as replacements for the combat divisions. With the heavy casualty rate and the tough opposition, the replacements were being rapidly withdrawn from the beach to move into the front lines. This depletion seriously slowed down the beach unloading. The longer our craft remained on the beach, the higher the rate of their broaching or disablement became. Again, as at Saipan, it demonstrated one serious defect in the marine landing organization.

Squeaky encountered heavy sniper fire as he and his assistants looked over the western beaches. They were found usable, but the steep rise behind the southern portion, the only portion not under heavy gunfire, would require considerable bulldozing and road construction first. Also, a channel would probably have to be blasted through the off-lying bar to permit the use of LSTs. So for the time being action had to be deferred on this project.

That night, while Admiral Turner and his force were going to their retirement areas, they were attacked by about fifty Jap planes. The CVE *Bismarck Sea* was hit by suicide planes. She sank rapidly, with heavy loss of officers and men. Two other ships and one LST were also hit by kamikazes but escaped major damage. That same night four suicide planes struck the carrier *Saratoga* and caused such serious damage that she had to proceed immediately to Pearl Harbor for repairs.

D plus three (February 22) proved to be the worst day so far, with a cold rain and onshore wind of twenty-five knots. No small craft, including the old reliables, Amtrac and DUKWs, could be used. But the LCTs and LSMs continued to discharge steadily on the beaches, where conditions had improved. They were now becoming the workhorses of the supply train.

On D plus four (February 23) the force of the winds diminished. I was increasingly concerned about my Amtracs and DUKWs. One-third of the cargo LVTs were wrecked by this time or inoperable, and the percentage of damaged DUKWs was about the same. They had been victims of the same difficulty that confronted some of the smaller vehicles on the steep beach. When their front wheels took hold, their sterns dropped and they swamped. So the only possible procedure was to try and ride a wave in and get clear before the next one broke over them.

I talked to General Schmidt about the desirability of starting work at once on the western beaches. He agreed and ordered his corps of engineers to undertake preliminary work with Squeaky Anderson. The complications of shifting from east to west beaches were many, and we hoped we would not have to change. Yet we were barely keeping up with the urgent demand, particularly for ammunition. Our beach party was too small to man both sets of beaches at the same time, so it was imperative that alternative means be provided. Actually, we did not use any western beach until D plus eleven.

About ten-thirty a big cheer went up from our flag bridge. Someone had pointed to the top of Mount Suribachi. Our flag was flying there. It was the sign that troops of the Fifth Division had finally fought their way to the top. The *Auburn*'s captain passed the word over the loudspeaker and a great cheer went up from all hands. I can't really express the great feeling of pride that surged through me. It was pride in our marines and pride in our country. I have the same feeling now every time I pass that beautiful Iwo Jima Memorial in Arlington.

The remaining units of the Third Division were landed that day without incident, and Major General Erskine established his command post ashore. Then on the following day General Schmidt left the *Auburn* and took over tactical command of the troops ashore. It had been a real pleasure to have him and his staff on board. With such excellent communications on the *Auburn* they had been able to follow closely the troop movements and the numerous requests for fire support and air support.

The presence of the Third Division at the front lines eased the pressure on the other two divisions, and the troops progressed slowly but steadily against main enemy defensive installations. As the Fourth Division on the right flank pushed past the rugged cliff formation flanking our beaches, we were able to utilize some small craft on the two northern beaches, which were in a partial lee. On southern beaches, now fairly clear of wreckage, some of the island command group were already ashore and by D plus ten (March 1) had taken over the unloading on three beaches there. By that same date thirteen of the transports and many LSTs had been released to their bases to reload for Okinawa, where operations were due to begin in a month. The airfield on Iwo, now partially repaired, was reported usable for emergency landings of carrier-type planes.

On D plus eleven the west coast beaches were opened to LCTs and DUKWs. The next day the western beaches were in full swing and several of the unloading ships were shifted there. Conditions were fine for two days, then the winds shifted and for four succeeding days unloading was again confined to the eastern beaches.

Early in the operation, as the bad beach conditions forced us to depend on the larger craft for unloading, the commanders of the LSTs, LSMs, and LCT units and their staffs transferred to the *Auburn*. When their craft came alongside the heavier ships, they took a real beating. Our normal supply of fenders and Manila rope was exhausted. Most of the boats were using wire, and that had no resiliency. As they surged back and forth alongside the rolling ships, there was considerable hull damage and minor flooding. Occasionally crews were knocked off their feet as their boats reached the limit of their mooring wires. I can assure you there was never a dull moment for those fine young officers and men. They were working a twenty-four-hour day and had to catch rest whenever they could. They did a marvelous job. I don't think anyone not there could realize the tough problems these youngsters overcame so magnificiently.

On March 4 (D plus thirteen) we got a big thrill when a damaged B-29 made the first emergency landing on number-one airfield, which was still being lengthened. The wheels touched down early, but B-29s required a long run, and as that plane neared the end of the runway, we thought it might nose over the steep bank of the new fill. But it stopped within a few feet of the bank and a big cheer arose from the anchorage area. A few days later several damaged B-29s returning from attacks on the Jap mainland landed without difficulty. I am sure that General Henry Arnold in Washington was gratified to have his wish come true. He had wanted that field on Iwo, and it was to save many air forces bombers and their fine personnel.

One of the truly remarkable things during all these assault operations was the rapid follow-up made by SeaBees to improve operating facilities for our use. This was particularly true of airfields.

Under constant but decreasing gunfire as our troops advanced, the SeaBees had made number-one field ready for fighter planes by March 5 (D plus thirteen), and the very next day twenty-eight P-51s and twelve P-61s arrived. Two days later two more squadrons of P-51s and a squadron of marine TBMs arrived. They gradually took over combat air patrol and air support tasks. This permitted the release of most of our CVE force to Ulithi, where they were to rearm and hurry back to Okinawa. The target date there was creeping up fast.

Spruance came back to Iwo and remained there until March 5, when he sailed for Guam. I had a good visit with him before his departure.

On the eighth Turner asked me to come over to see him. He said he was turning over command to me when he left for Guam the following morning. With that, Holland Smith transferred to the *Auburn*.

At that point there were few remaining combatant ships at Iwo—one big carrier, four CVEs, four cruisers, and about twenty-five destroyers. Most of them left by the eleventh. I felt rather naked, for only two cruisers and eight destroyers remained, not a very formidable force for a position only six hundred miles from the Japanese mainland. My only attack power lay in those squadrons of planes at Iwo. Nevertheless, it was real thrill—and a big challenge—to take over command of the operation in its closing moments. Relieving Admiral Turner at any time was tough. He had such a comprehensive grasp of every detail and had a ready solution for every problem that developed.

That day, patrols of the Third Division reached the water at the northeast end of the island. The Fourth Division was still facing heavy Jap resistance at two strongpoints in the broken terrain at the eastern side of the island. About one thousand yards from the northwest tip the Fifth Division was moving very slowly, for it was still encountering resistance in the steep gulleys traversing that portion of the island. In that area they later found General Kuribayashi's command post with its five levels of tunnels.

By the evening of March 11 (D plus twenty) the Third and Fourth divisions had reached the shoreland. A dawn strike of twelve P-51 planes loaded with five-hundred-pound bombs was made on the planes, airfield, and shipping at Chichi Jima. Similar strikes were made on that island nearly every day from then on to prevent its use as a staging point for attacks on Iwo.

On March 14 the flag-raising ceremony was held, although the Fifth Division was still clearing Japs out of numerous pockets in the small north corner of the island. It was a simple ceremony but an impressive one and expressed heartfelt thanks to the many brave men who had lost their lives in making it possible.

Reembarkation of elements of the Fourth Division commenced that morning. Later in the day Holland Smith flew to Guam. Three echelons of the garrison force had been unloaded, and two airfields on Iwo were operational. Already a total of thirty-six B-29s had utilized the Iwo field for emergency landings. This staging point was to prove more and more valuable in the succeeding months.

During my talks with Turner and Spruance before their departure for Guam, I told them of an idea that might be helpful in diverting the attention of the Japs for a few days. I was certain that they were most fearful of the damaging attacks that had been made on the homeland by our carrier planes. They had been powerful attacks and were impossible to defend against. A great force of about one thousand planes had come from nowhere, without warning, and after devastating the strike area had disappeared back into nowhere. The Japs had no way of telling where the carriers were or when they would strike again. I had devised a simple plan to capitalize on their fears, and both Spruance and Turner approved.

The Japanese had established a picket line of small trawler-type ships extending eastward from Tokyo for a couple hundred miles. They were to warn of pending attacks. On March 14 I ordered the destroyers *Dorch* and *Cotton* to make a wide sweep to the east, circling into that picket line during darkness. They were to locate at least two of the vessels and sink them, but only after giving them time to report the attack to Tokyo. That night I had a special listening watch set on all Jap circuits. It was manned by Jap interpreters.

Shortly before 2300 one of our destroyers contacted one of these vessels, illuminated it with star shells, and opened fire. A few minutes later the other destroyer opened fire on another picket ship. On the radio circuits bedlam arose, with uncoded reports to the effect that the ships were being attacked by a large force of battleships, cruisers, and destroyers and were sinking. Moments later all hell broke loose in Tokyo. Messages, most of them uncoded, warned of a prospective carrier attack at daybreak. All shipping in coastal areas was ordered into port. Planes in coastal airfields were ordered inland, and all military installations were alerted to the forthcoming attack. It really was wonderful. I wished we had a bottle of champagne to open for a celebration.

At Iwo the only noticeable effect was the absence of our daily snooper attacks. But I have often wondered whether the ruse might have forestalled a last-ditch effort to interfere with our Iwo occupation. Only three weeks after that, the Jap high command did make such a decision; they ordered the superbattleship *Yamato*, with a cruiser and eight destroyers, to make a desperate banzai attack on our forces at Okinawa. En route, she was sunk by Mitscher's planes. Had the Japs made such a move at Iwo, we would have had little with which to stop them. Of course, it would have been too late to affect the final outcome, but they could have inflicted considerable damage on our shore supply dumps and our garrison forces.

In setting up this operation I had given it the code name Sockem. A couple of weeks later a gentle tap on the wrist came in the form of a general dispatch saying that hereafter code names should not in any way indicate the type of operation involved. Perhaps the instruction was initiated by Admiral King, but I am sure he sent it with a grin on his face, for this type of offensive operation, which keeps the enemy off balance, was always much to his liking.

On March 22 an LST broached on Yellow Beach. Two tugs, greatly hampered by rough seas, failed to get her off. The seas quickly formed a bar of volcanic ash seaward of her, so that she was resting in a little inland pool.

The following day Nimitz arrived for an inspection of Iwo Jima. I showed him the LST in its little private lagoon and told him that I expected to have it off the beach very shortly, when tugs were available. He smiled and said that would be fine, but I'm sure he was convinced that this was just the wishful thinking of a Pollyanna. We took steel hawsers to her; a few days later two tugs took a strain and, slowly but surely, aided by the wave erosion on that bar, she came off, with no major damage. The next day I took great delight in sending Nimitz a message reporting LST 27 was afloat and proceeding under its own power to Guam. That soft treacherous beach had paid at least one dividend!

The Japanese defenders fought stubbornly and well to the end. On the twenty-first a message to Chichi Jima was intercepted. It stated, "We have not eaten or drunk for five days but our fighting spirit is still running high. We are going to fight bravely till the last." On March 25 the final pocket of resistance was reported eliminated as the troops of the Fifth Division reached the water. But in spite of their search-and-destroy tactics they did not find all of the enemy troops; at daybreak the following morning two hundred to three hundred Japs moved down the west side of the island and attacked marine and army bivouacs near the western beaches. A confused battle raged for three hours, with the Seventh Fighter Command hard hit but recovering from its initial surprise to fight back. The enemy force was well armed with both U.S. and Japanese weapons. Forty of them carried swords, an indication that a high percentage of them were officers or senior noncoms.

It is believed that General Kuribayashi died somewhere in those last four days of fighting at the northern tip. His body was never found. As he prepared to die he wrote a note to his emperor expressing most profound apologies for being forced to yield a strategic point to enemy hands and asking his emperor never to lose faith in the supreme and everlasting destiny of the Japanese people.

After that final melee on March 26 (D plus thirty-five) the capture and occupation phase of Iwo Jima was declared completed. It should be noted, however, that during April and May the garrison force, on aggressive patrols, killed 1,602 more Japs and took 860 prisoners.

On March 28 I flew to Guam and the *Auburn* departed for Pearl Harbor.

The seizure of Iwo cost the lives of 4,891 marines and 639 navy men and a wounded total of nearly 16,000. More than 15,000 Japs were buried, and it was estimated that about 6,000 more were sealed in underground tunnels. Less than 200 Jap prisoners, mostly wounded, were taken during the combat period. It was a vicious struggle between brave men and will always stand as one of the great military epics of all time. Admiral Nimitz summed it up perfectly: "Among the Americans who served at Iwo Island, uncommon valor was a common virtue."

For me and my staff Iwo will always be a nightmare. The beach problem, aggravated by the vagaries of weather, created almost unbelievable difficulties, and for several days we were greatly concerned about our ability to keep the flow of hot cargo to what ultimately totaled over eighty thousand troops ashore. With a beachmaster less determined than Squeaky Anderson, we might well have been in serious difficulty. During the action a correspondent asked Squeaky the secret of his success, to which he replied, "Success, hmph! I get so much hell from the admiral, I just pass it on. Then we always get things done."

That is a wonderful story, but I can assure you that Squeaky got no hell from me during those bitter days. Never have I been so thankful to any one man, and I gave him all the encouragement, praise, and assistance it was in my power to give.

A salvage force serves a vital function. If the ordinary facilities of a harbor have been destroyed by a retreating army, it is the task of this force to clear debris and repair damage before the conquerors arrive in full strength.

Great strides were made in salvage operations during World War II, primarily because of new equipment. For the first time electric pumps and winches, as well as other devices designed to make emergency operations efficient and speedy, were installed on salvage ships. Such innovations were the fruit of experience in various parts of the world. When Allied forces drove the Germans and the Vichy French out of North Africa, many of the harbors there were in a deplorable state. They had to be quickly cleared to maintain the schedule of the Allied advance into Sicily and Italy. Supplies had to be poured into these ports, and they had to be handled without delay. As the Allies continued their advance similar problems were encountered in places like Palermo and Naples.

Urgency likewise attended salvage operations in Pacific ports. Again there was the need for hasty and effective action so the juggernaut of the Allied forces could make an unimpeded advance. Sunken and disabled ships immobilized Pearl Harbor, Tarawa, Saipan, Tinian, and Iwo Jima as the Americans pushed through the central Pacific toward Japan. The mess had to be removed before the advantages of newly won island bases could be utilized. General MacArthur faced huge salvage problems as he made his gigantic hops up the chain of islands from the Solomons and New Guinea to the Philippines. Everywhere the lessons learned through bitter experience were quickly applied in the next leap forward.

The U.S. Salvage Force made great contributions to the final Allied and American victories, and yet its efforts went unapplauded: its ships were only auxiliary vessels—the ARSs, the tugs, the workhorses of the fleet. Still, the tasks they performed were of utmost concern to top commanders in both the Atlantic and the Pacific. Eisenhower, MacArthur, Nimitz—these high-ranking officers knew how essential the demanding work of the Salvage Force was to the success of the war effort.

Admiral William Sullivan's account of the clearance work performed at Manila from March to August 1945 is a graphic example of what was accomplished in all the theaters of war. In Manila the Japanese had done all they could to block the use by advancing Allies of a harbor that was both magnificent and crucial to their cause. It was from Manila that the final assault on the Japanese homeland had to be launched. That last push, the invasion of Japan, would require a tremendous amount of supplies, and they would have to be staged through Manila. Both General MacArthur and his naval commander, Admiral Thomas Kinkaid, were aware of the problems involved in clearing a harbor that was littered with some five hundred wrecked vessels. Both of them cooperated with Sullivan in his efforts.

Sullivan reveals the innovative character of a salvage master, and he does it with disarming candor. There was a job to be done, under great pressure and in a minimum of time, and despite the odds he was determined not to fail.

HEADACHES
AT MANILA HARBOR

ADMIRAL WILLIAM A. SULLIVAN

WILLIAM ALOYSIUS SULLIVAN was born in Lawrence, Massachusetts, on 27 August 1894. He attended Phillips Andover Academy and graduated from MIT in 1917, being commissioned in the navy the same year.

From 1917 to 1937 he had varied assignments in ship construction and repairs at navy yards from Portsmouth, New Hampshire, to Cavite, Philippine Islands, including three years as supervising constructor in Shanghai. In 1938, while at the model basin of the navy yard in Washington, D.C., he began a study of problems connected with ship salvaging. That was followed by two years as assistant naval attaché in London for ship salvage matters. He directed salvage operations on the East Coast of the United States during the enemy submarine campaign of 1942. That same year he went to Casablanca, organized a harbor clearance force, and supervised work there and in Port Lyautey. He joined the staff of Admiral Sir Andrew Cunningham, RN, Commander, Allied Naval Forces, Mediterranean (1943), became chief of U.S. navy salvage the same year in the rank of commodore, and proceeded to open blocked ports on the North African coast. He commanded Task Force 84 during the Sicilian landings and the later landings at Salerno, directing salvage operations simultaneously. He cleared the port of Naples after its occupation by Allied troops, commanded Task Group 122.2 during the Normandy landings, entered Cherbourg with the occupying troops, and directed harbor clearance there as well as at

LeHavre, Rouen, Brest, and other French ports. In February 1945 he was in the Pacific, where he reported to Admiral Thomas Kinkaid, commander of the Seventh Fleet, and to General MacArthur. He entered Manila with the army troops and assumed the task of harbor clearance there, leaving that job in August 1945.

Admiral Sullivan retired in the rank of rear admiral on 1 May 1948. He died in LaJolla, California, in September 1985.

In January 1945 I went to Leyte, where I reported to Admiral Kinkaid, who was in command of the Seventh Fleet. He could not tell me much about the situation in Manila, but he said that reports from the air indicated the Japs were blowing up the city's waterfront and we would have a lot of work. He said the army spearhead was at the gates of the city then.

I missed the plane that day and so I stayed another night at Kinkaid's naval headquarters. Early the next morning I left in a two-engined cargo plane. We flew over Cavite and across the bay but were too far away to see much. I did note a mass of sunken ships in the bay and the harbor and some fires burning in the city. I also saw the old dry dock *Dewey* sunk in the middle of the bay. We flew on and landed on a beach near some ships that were moored offshore and unloading supplies in DUKWs and landing craft. Quite a sizable amount of cargo was coming ashore. I assumed that this was Lingayen. A jeep with a trailer was waiting for me. I offered a lift to three young army officers who had come over with me and who had been told to hitchhike to their destination. It was about a three-and-a-half-hour ride to Armac, where General MacArthur had his headquarters.

I reported and was told I had an appointment with the general in the morning. The next morning I reported to him. He asked about my status and my orders. I told him I had been on temporary duty in various harbor-clearance operations in Europe and that I had similar temporary-duty orders for Manila. Verbally I had been instructed to get the operation organized in Manila as quickly as possible, so that Commander Wroten, who was to follow me, could take over and carry on. I told him about the men and equipment sent out from the States for this operation. So far I had not seen any salvage officers or men, but Commander B. S. Huie (Commander, Salvage and Rescue Group, Service Force, Seventh Fleet) had been sent out some months before and was in charge. He was operating with Vice Admiral Daniel Barbey (Commander, Task Force 78) offshore with the combat salvage force.

I told the general I hoped to use some Philippine labor. I also learned that many of the old American supervisors and foremen of the navy yards at Cavite and Olongapo were still in Manila. They had been prisoners of war. I hoped to get some of them to work with me and organize Philippine labor. I

310

explained the organization we had in Europe and how absolutely necessary it was for our salvage force to work as closely as possible with the army engineers and army transportation. I told him about Naples, where I thought things could not have been handled more efficiently than they were. I told him about Cherbourg and some of the troubles we had had there with the unintelligent interference by both army and navy higher-ups.

MacArthur said he did not think I would find any of the former civilian internees in good enough physical shape to stay on and help with harbor clearance. He thoroughly approved of my idea of using Philippine labor, for he thought there would be a tremendous amount of work to do. Had I seen anything of the harbor from the air? I told him I had flown over the bay—too far out to see much of the harbor but close enough to see the masts of many sunken ships. He wanted to know how I compared this work with that done in Europe.

I told him it would take many days of study before I could answer that question. There seemed to be as many big ships sunk in Manila Bay as in any European port. The great range of tide which had helped in places like Cherbourg was absent in Manila Bay. Here in Manila we wouldn't have the help of British lifting craft, which we had had in Europe. Here we would undoubtedly have to rely on patching and pumping, compressed air, derricks, and improvised lifting arrangements. Much would depend upon the degree of efficiency exercised by the Japanese when they had placed demolition charges. I told him about our great luck in Europe—the Germans had only blown holes to get the ships to sink. They did not try to make them difficult to raise, and undoubtedly the Japanese had.

The general went on to say that he thoroughly agreed with my idea of the closest degree of cooperation between the army engineers and navy salvage. He said I should work closely with his engineers, especially his chief engineer, General Hugh Casey, and the chief of the engineering troops, Major General Leif Sverdrup. He also said something to the effect that I would find his army different from the army in Europe. I would find one-hundred-percent cooperation in the Philippines and no difficulties. (As it turned out, the cooperation I got from the army couldn't have been better.) He told me that he himself would keep in close touch with the work. If I had any problem I was free at all times to come and see him. In fact, he thought it would be well if I made a point of coming to see him once a week. He would have his secretary arrange a convenient hour.

Later that morning headquarters moved to a house in the northern suburbs of Manila. A group of about twelve Cub planes was used to fly the staff. I shared a Cub plane with an engineer officer who was a pilot.

I must say that although I had never met General MacArthur before, I felt confidence in him such as I had never felt in Europe, except with people like Admiral Sir Andrew Cunningham or Admiral Jimmie Hall. He was far better than any of the commanding generals I had run across in Europe. Oh, there's no comparison!

The next morning I went to the waterfront with an engineer officer. We went only to North Harbor, a recently built addition to Manila Harbor. A number of small piers had been built here to accommodate interisland shipping. The port of Manila in ancient times had consisted of some piers built on the banks of the Pasig River, about three-quarters of a mile from the mouth of the river. A small island at the mouth had been used by the engineers who had developed the modern harbor. This was called Engineers' Harbor. A breakwater something like a flat V started out from Engineers' Island, running south and west. A second breakwater in line with the first ran further south, providing shelter for a couple of miles of the waterfront. In the shelter of these breakwaters, some large piers had been built to take modern oceangoing ships. The area inside this breakwater had been dredged, of course. This was called Manila Harbor. But we called it Manila South Harbor to distinguish it from the new development north of the Pasig River, which was built for interisland ships.

The Japanese were still holding out in the Intramuros and in the areas between the Intramuros and South Harbor. They occupied the left bank of the Pasig and as far as the Luneta on the other side. The buildings or whatever had been on the waterfront of Manila's North Harbor were completely demolished. There was a great amount of debris there and it had to be moved away. The piers in this section did not appear badly damaged, but we couldn't get near enough to see much, for if we tried we would be visible to the Japanese on the other side of the river. We could see, though, that the slips between the piers were almost chock-full of sunken barges, interisland ships, harbor craft, and the like. The river itself was dammed up in a number of places with wrecks. They were mostly small ones. We could see larger ships that had been sunk in Manila Bay just outside the breakwater forming South Manila Harbor. Beyond that we could see nothing of the condition in South Harbor.

When we arrived some army personnel were on the scene with a bulldozer and some trucks. They were trying to clear away some of the debris in the area and were working in a place where the Japanese on the left bank of the Pasig could not see them. But as soon as they began work, snipers on the breakwater off North Harbor opened fire and killed the bulldozer operator. The truck drivers then opened up with rifle fire, but that only drove the Japanese to cover on the side of the breakwater. So a Cub plane was obtained and a man was sent up to toss hand grenades on the open breakwater. The grenades drove the Japs off the breakwater, but they swam to a sunken ship about fifty feet offshore. Five or six of the men reached the wreck. The army then called for some mortars to open up on the wreck. The engineers got to work but were soon again under fire. So finally the assault party got an LCVP and were covered overhead by a couple of planes with men in them tossing grenades. When they got to the wreck offshore they used a flamethrower and with this killed the Japanese on board.

During the night more Japanese swam out from Engineers' Island to the wreck. I think that particular ship had to be cleaned up ten times, on ten successive mornings. I wasn't around to see all of that, but it was reported to me by the engineers. I know that our salvage people did kill over five hundred Japanese on the wrecks around Manila before we were through with the job of clearing the harbor. For thirty days after our work started we had to carry guns every time we went out to do a job, because it wasn't possible to tell when a Jap would pop up. There were no Japanese army troops in Manila at that time. This was all the work of some crazy Japanese sailors and marines. The Japanese general in command at Manila had ordered Manila declared an open city, but the Japanese navy wouldn't take orders from the general.

I did not stick around North Harbor very long that first morning. I wanted to find out something about conditions in South Harbor, for it was in this harbor only that Liberty ships could be unloaded at a pier. It was the most important area for military supplies. The map of the Manila area showed a number of bridges over the Pasig River, but the Japanese had blown up all of them.

The army had landed some airborne troops south of Manila, and these troops had reached the city's south side. I was anxious to get around there to view the situation in the main harbor from the south. That first day I didn't get anywhere.

It was becoming evident that when we got into South Harbor we would find the destruction so great that larger ships would not be able to discharge supplies there for a long time. The army was now existing on supplies being trucked in from Lingayen and from Subic Bay over very bad roads and over very make-do bridges. We had to start bringing in supplies at Manila. So our first priority was to clear away the wrecks in North Harbor and the Pasig. As soon as the minesweepers were through cleaning up Manila Bay, the army would bring in Liberties to moor off the breakwater of Manila's North Harbor and discharge into barges, landing craft. These in turn would discharge at the piers in South Harbor and on the banks of the Pasig.

A large slip on the south side of pier 2 in North Harbor was earmarked for use by LSTs. A combat engineer regiment had been assigned to clear away the debris of the buildings. In Manila the army followed the same procedure that it had in Europe. Combat engineer regiments started port clean up and continued until the regular port construction regiments came in with heavy equipment. Here the engineers had noted that the slip was intended for use by the LSTs. A concrete wall at the foot of the slip had to be cut down so the ramps of the LSTs could be dropped. They had started work on the project when I arrived one morning. They were going to demolish the wall with explosives planted in the ground behind the wall. They were using charges, I noted, with several times as much dynamite as necessary. As a result, chunks of concrete were being blown fifty to a hundred feet out into the slip and into the sunken craft, which I would have to clean up.

There were two fine steel barges that had been sunk at the base of the wall. I had looked these barges over on a previous visit and saw they were in pretty good shape. As soon as they were floated we could fix them up with permanent patches and put them back in use. If I could get at these barges it would not take more than two or three hours' work to float them. In a half a day's work we would have two excellent barges for use in discharging supplies. But the chunks of concrete blown loose by the engineers had ripped big holes in the sides of both barges. Salvage would be much more difficult now, and repairs seemed out of the question.

I brought it up with the brigadier in charge. He looked like a harassed man, and I had difficulty getting his attention. But he finally sent word to the men to reduce the size of the charges. They did by perhaps ten percent, but the chunks that continued to fall would have to be salvaged. That night I asked General Casey to get these combat engineers out. I told him I would clean up the place with our salvage crew when they arrived in Manila. So he arranged to have the regiment given some other work.

When we had men and facilities available to work in North Harbor, we started to clear up the wrecks so that the LSTs could be brought in. We found more than sixty wrecks in the slip in Pier 2. However, we ran into an obstacle. Our diver reported a large water main running right across the slip and only about eight feet below the surface. The main would have to be cut out to permit LSTs to use the slip. The engineers then investigated and found that it was a working main that provided water to North Harbor. They did develop a plan to relocate the pipe, but during my time in Manila I never saw an LST use the slip.

After lunch in the general's mess on the first day, I was standing outside watching a battery of heavy guns firing on the walled city. It had been firing all night and had interrupted my sleep quite a bit. What I was really looking for at that moment was some transportation. At that time General Sutherland, the chief of staff, came along and asked what kind of transportation I had. I said I was looking for some. At that he called an officer from a military transportation unit that was passing by and said to assign me a jeep with a driver. I kept this jeep and the driver as long as I remained in the Philippines.

I told a friend of mine, a Filipino businessman, that I wanted to see something of the situation around South Harbor. He did also, so he came with me and we made a wide loop around the central portion of Manila. At one or two places we passed infantry engaged in street fighting with Japanese barricaded in places only a block away. When we came within a few blocks of the old Army-Navy Club someone started shooting at us from a tall building on the righthand side of the street. We turned the jeep around in a hurry and went back, looking for shelter. We left the driver with the jeep and worked our way down to the waterfront and along the waterfront to the club. The building had been pretty well burned out, but the walls were still standing and so was the second floor. The stairways inside were gone, but it was possible to get to the second floor by a ladder. There was a company or so of infantry stationed in and around the building with marksmen firing at Japanese in the Manila Hotel.

We went up the ladder to the second floor to see what we could of the waterfront. A colonel had just been killed while he was looking out of one of the second-story windows, so we were warned to keep out of sight of the Manila Hotel. We tried to get an angle view but we didn't see very much. So we thought of going out on the jetty, where we thought we could see more. But this area was exposed to snipers in the hotel windows, so we decided to crawl out on the riprap side of the slip, which juts into the Army-Navy Club. If we could get out on this sloping bank we could keep below the top and the Japs wouldn't see us.

We crawled out. It was pretty difficult, because the riprap was heavy and there were a dozen or two stinking corpses of Japanese we had to crawl around. We finally got out to the end of the slip and we could see the south side of pier 7. This is the largest pier in Manila Harbor. We could see wrecks of three large ships on this side, but crouching down below the level of the roadway, as we had to do, we saw very little. Since we were far enough away from the Manila Hotel at this point, we thought we were safe and we stood up to see more. Within a minute there was a *swish!* and a projectile of perhaps three or four inches passed over our heads and landed in the water about fifty feet away. It was a dud, but we lost no time trying to crawl back to the club.

I was told that the MacArthur headquarters were being moved again. As a result I was to move into the Admiral Hotel on Dewey Boulevard. It was now taken over by the engineers. There I was assigned to an apartment on an upper floor. The elevators were working with current supplied by a diesel generator. The hotel, I found, had not only been wrecked but completely looted. All the furniture was gone, as well as many of the doors, the bathroom fittings, the hinges, even the moldings. Native Filipinos had done this. My apartment had a large living room, a couple of bedrooms, and a kitchen. There was no furniture of any kind except for two old armchairs from which the upholstery had been cut off. I did have my cot and a mosquito net. The sergeant in charge of the place gave me a couple of boxes, a small one to sit on and a big one for a desk.

A shell had made a hole in the wall at the end of the living room. It was a large hole, so large that one could walk right through it and fall five or six floors to the courtyard.

There was a gruesome decoration on the white plaster of one of the long

315

side walls. It was an outline in red of the back of a peacock fan chair. The sergeant told me that a Japanese officer had sat in the chair and committed hara-kiri with a hand grenade held to his belly. Later the Filipinos had looted the apartment, but they had not bothered to remove the body of the Japanese or the smashed-up chair. I now understood what the smell was that invaded the place.

That night I got word that Vice Admiral William Farber was at Olongapo, so I left by first light of morning. It is only a hundred miles to Olongapo, but in the jeep it took us until eleven o'clock at night to make the trip. The roads were in terrible condition and the detours were many. Only a few walls were standing in the town, enough to show where it had been. Admiral Farber was with Admiral Barbey, trying to cut short his stay in the Philippines. He had heard something about the missing salvage personnel and equipment. What did I know about this matter, and how much harbor clearance work was needed in Manila? I told him what little I knew about the salvage matters.

The admiral decided that he wanted to come to Manila with me. Perhaps we could get two Cub planes in the morning and get a look at South Harbor, after which he could return by Cub plane to Olongapo. Barbey had arranged for a navy plane to transport him the next day to Leyte, where he was to see Admiral Kinkaid. Barbey told me that he would send for Huie if I could return to Olongapo with Admiral Farber.

The admiral left with me by jeep and we arrived in Manila late in the afternoon, heavily covered with dust. That evening he paid his respects to General MacArthur, and General Sutherland loaned us two staff Cub planes for use the next day. As soon as we got into the air we had a view of South Harbor. It was a mess. The piers were pretty well demolished. The Japanese were evidently blowing up everything that was not already smashed by bombing. Pier 7, the largest in Manila, was lined on both sides with sunken ships. Only a detailed survey would indicate the amount of time that would be required to put this pier back into use. It was a major job. The wrecks were too numerous to count from the air. It was still early in the morning and the rays of the sun were coming at an angle, so I thought I could detect some wholly submerged craft. We saw four such craft laying in line across the main harbor entrance. Later we found there were five in this position.

We flew across the bay to Cavite. There I noticed one side of the sunken dry dock *Dewey* was completely smashed in. This ended my hope of putting it back into service after some repairs.

Back at Olongapo we boarded Admiral Barbey's flagship and found Huie waiting for us. He had very bad news. Over half of the enlisted personnel doing salvage work had been lost in transit, apparently. They had never reported to the Seventh Fleet Service Force. Those that had reported had been shipped to various places and assigned to other duties. The personnel officer was not going to have any unemployed naval personnel hanging around waiting for Manila to be captured. He would put them to work. He said that when harbor clearance work became necessary he would assign the personnel needed. As for special training required for harbor clearance work—nonsense!

Huie said that a large quantity of salvage equipment designated for the Manila Harbor clearance force had been sent to Hollandia. The crates had been marked USN Salvage. The storekeeper who handled it had thought this was equipment turned in by our salvage units. He had set it aside as a result and invited anyone to come and help himself. Huie got there in time to get some pumps and miscellaneous gear, but he said the other stuff that had been left was not usable because of missing parts.

Huie had been ordered to organize a combat salvage force, so he managed to find thirty-five men and some officers. It was no trouble getting the officers, but he had a lot of trouble finding men. He gave me a very frank account of his argument with the Service Force staff. They had been quite disagreeable and arbitrary. That had been my experience when I arrived in the Philippines. I was very disappointed at his news, but I was glad he had spilled the beans in front of Admiral Farber, for at last Farber had some idea of the kind of trouble I'd encountered almost every place in this war.

Barbey told Admiral Farber that he was not surprised. In fact, he knew already about what had happened. He doubted that the present commander of the Service Force knew the real situation. He thought the matter should be brought immediately to Admiral Kinkaid's attention, for it was a subject of much concern to General MacArthur. Admiral Kinkaid would want to inform General MacArthur himself before anyone else did so. Barbey offered to release Huie and his salavage unit at once so I would have something to start the job with. It would take a few days, however, for Huie to get his people together and move to Manila.

We flew to Leyte and arrived early in the afternoon. Admiral Kinkaid was shocked at the news. He said he would give the matter personal attention. Any salvage personnel or equipment that could be located he would move at once to Manila. He felt sure that he could find the personnel in question. He asked me to return to Manila directly and tell General MacArthur the whole story.

Admiral Farber decided I should remain in Manila and get the place organized.

I left Leyte at once. It was long after dark before I arrived at Manila. I went directly to headquarters. MacArthur came out in a bathrobe and we sat at the end of a mess table with a dim lantern. I told him the story. He did not show any emotion or disgust but simply said such things must be expected in a big organization in time of war. Then he asked me what I was going to do. I said that Admiral Farber had instructed me to remain in Manila until the harbor clearance work was well in hand or finished. "Good," said MacArthur. "Now we'll see what the army can do for you. What do you really need?"

I said we first needed some good divers to start surveys as soon as we could get into Manila's South Harbor. We would need a few floating cranes, more divers, and some salvage mechanics to start work on North Harbor and the Pasig. I would need barges, floating cranes, a few land cranes, some trucks, salvage pumps, compressors, diving equipment, miscellaneous tools to start. When we knew what the actual situation was in South Harbor I would need a pretty big organization, but by that time Admiral Kinkaid should have been able to find some of our missing personnel and equipment.

General MacArthur roughed out some messages for various army units that night. He ordered them to send to Manila any officers or men who had had any experience in underwater work, and any large pumps or compressors not in active use.

General Sverdrup was the army representative who would give me the priorities the army wanted me to follow for harbor clearance work. He was a well-known consulting engineer in civilian life. I found him a very fine officer, a highly qualified engineer, and one with whom it was pleasant to work at all times. He had command of all the engineering troops of the area and developed the overall army plan of rehabilitating the area. It was quite a satisfactory arrangement. Instead of having to deal with army transportation and the army engineers I had only one officer to deal with.

I had been keeping my eye open for a place that would be suitable for a salvage base. I wanted something on the waterfront, something not needed by the army for discharging supplies. I wanted a place where we could load or unload salvage equipment from barges or small craft, a place where we could repair salvage barges or convert salvage craft into salvage units. I wanted an area big enough so we could store salvage gear and build sheds for valuable equipment. In addition, it had to have enough dry ground to make a tent colony for our personnel. That was asking a lot and I knew it.

Finally I located a spot on the south bank of the Pasig River. I asked General Sverdrup for permission to use this area. He considered my request, and meanwhile I went ahead and got one small building cleaned out. I started to use it as a classroom. Within twenty-four hours of my meeting with General MacArthur, two army officers reported with a couple dozen men. All had some diving experience in inland waters on various industrial or construction projects. None of them had any experience with ships or boats, or knew anything about salvage. So I started to give lectures to these officers and men on ship construction, what a ship looked like, the difference between the bow and the stern, how we put on salvage patches, how we rigged pump suctions.

Now before we received any salvage gear or any personnel to start organizing a salvage base, the army found urgent need for all the land on both sides of the Pasig River. I was asked if we could use a slip in an area adjacent to the Manila Hotel for our salvage base. This area was every bit as good for our needs as the one we had chosen on the Pasig River, so I agreed immediately to a swap.

I had only given a few lectures when one of my officers, who had some experience and was a graduate of the salvage school, showed up in Manila and relieved me of the task.

As soon as I had returned from Leyte I looked up the army air forces photographic representative at general headquarters. I told him of our need for information on the wholly submerged wrecks in the harbor and bay. It would be some time before the harbor and bay could be swept of mines and a hydrographic survey could be made to determine the location of wrecks. I thought perhaps the air forces could save us a great deal of time by taking photographs of the harbor. The water in the harbor was cloudy but not excessively so. I suggested the photos be taken between seven and eight in the morning, when there would be good strong sunlight coming in at an angle to show the shadows on the bottom—the shadows of the wrecks. In the afternoon a pronounced swell developed , causing ripples on the surface and obscuring any shadows of ships on the bottom. I also suggested that the photos be underexposed and overdeveloped.

The army air forces were glad to try and help me but apparently thought my suggestions on the ideal time for photos were those of a fussy old man. Within twenty-four hours I obtained from them some splendid enlargements of the harbor and the bay. They were conventional aerial photos, however, and apparently were taken in the middle of the day, when every ripple on the surface showed. They did give us a good idea of the wrecks that were sticking above water in South Harbor. Then I started a study of harbor clearance problems by marking up one set of these plates in ink. I did get another set of aerial photographs, from a *Life* photographer, Carl Mydans, who got them from some army photographer. When they were pasted together they gave a pretty good bird's-eye view of all the wrecks. They were useful to me in my office which I finally got around to fitting up on the waterfront.

By that time we had access to South Harbor, for the Japanese had finally been cleared out of the walled city. Things began to move. Huie arrived from Leyte with some of his men. Admiral Barbey released a couple of ARSs which had been assigned to his force. His ships could not move into the bay directly until it had been cleared of mines, or even into the harbor until the entrance had been cleared of the sunken ships. About the same time our old reliable, Doc Schlesinger, arrived with some corpsmen and with the hospital facilities that had been sent out for our harbor clearance boys.

Before I could start setting up a salvage base, the area had to be cleared of dead Japanese. The bodies of at least a couple dozen were floating around the ship in front of the Manila Hotel. A couple dozen more were lying in the roadway or in the high grass of the Luneta. I asked a military unit to clean up this area, and they did so at once.

The first thing we erected on the salvage base was two tents for Dr. Schlesinger's hospital. Each tent had twelve beds. Schlesinger said we would need more hospital facilities; he did not think the naval base as it was presently organized would do anything but send us more patients. He was particularly concerned about the health of our salvage people. He warned me not to drive the men as I had driven the others in Europe because of the tropical conditions in the Philippines. I would have to work the men less and I should see what could be done about better rations for them. He also cautioned me to take things easier myself.

A day or two after Huie arrived from Leyte, the last of our salvage personnel started to trickle in from other assignments throughout the Pacific. They came in by twos and threes, and it was two or three months before the last of them arrived. The men were all discouraged and demoralized. Some of them came up from New Guinea and brought jungle itch with them. It proved to be contagious. I got it all over my face and nothing could be done to stop it.

Very little valuable equipment for our needs turned up in the first shipment from the Seventh Fleet Service Force. That which did come was lacking important parts such as generators, carburetors, and fuel pumps. We finally used most of the shipment as spare parts for what we already had. Two more shipments of equipment had been sent to the Philippines, but due to problems it was some weeks before we got it all. When we did get it we had more than we needed.

To start the harbor clearance job we depended on what the army supplied us as a result of General MacArthur's messages and what Huie brought with him from his combat salvage teams. The commander of the Service Force came up to see me as a result of Admiral Kinkaid's investigation into the missing salvage personnel and equipment. He was very sore and bawled me out for going over his head directly to Admiral Kinkaid. He wanted me to understand that now I was part of the Seventh Fleet Service Force. I waited until he said what he wanted to say and then called his attention to the fact that Admiral Farber was my boss, and it was Farber who had gone to Admiral Kinkaid. I told him I did not give a damn who got credit or discredit for anything. I was out here to get Manila Harbor cleared, and I was going to do it and not cover up for anyone. We parted without a meeting of minds.

Later I got orders to report every week the percentage of work done and work remaining to Commander, Service Force, so he could inform the army of what we were doing. So I told Huie, who had set up a records office, to send in a progress report once a week, for I would certainly forget to. I told him to start off with one and a half percent the first week, two and three-quarters the next, and so on. He should always give the percentage in fractions. A dumbbell would think we had given the reports careful consideration. But Huie should never jump a week's report by more than two or three percent and never let it get above fifty percent without seeing me again. Well, I never heard any more about these reports. I do know, however, that they were being sent in for some time.

As soon as there was access to South Harbor I went over. I started at pier 7, for this was the one the army wanted cleared most. There I found my pet combat engineering regiment ahead of me. The Japanese had wrecked all of the dockside cranes on both sides of the pier. Some of the cranes had been blown into the water. Some were hanging suspended over the water by wrecked steel structural members. My pet engineers were clearing away the sides of the pier by cutting away the structural members supporting the cranes and thus permitting them to drop into the water. I christened the regiment the Grenade Tartars, and again I asked to have them sent to a combat area where they belonged. This was my last gripe with the army. These combat engineers were replaced by the port construction regiments, who worked very efficiently. We enjoyed the greatest degree of mutual cooperation.

There were two ships sunk on the south side of pier 7. At the end of the pier was a ship of moderate size. Its main deck was underwater. To remove the ship would have required the construction of a complete cofferdam, and there was a serious shortage of lumber. A complete cofferdam would require a very great deal. It would also require a great deal of labor, so I decided not to do this job if we could get by without it.

The second was a big ship of ten to twelve thousand tons. It had been hit by at least four bombs. Its name was the *Kinka Maru*. We found it had been a combined transport and freighter. At the amidships waterline there was very little structure left, for at least two bombs had hit in this area. Another bomb had exploded in the number-one hold and a fourth in the after section of the ship. Removing the ship would be a major job, for it would take a large crew to cut it up and remove it piecemeal. It would also involve many months of work; we soon learned that because of prevailing weather conditions divers could not work well in this area in the afternoon. It would be much better, we figured, if we could bring the ship out whole. That, of course, was questionable.

As soon as possible, we started doing night work whenever it was practicable.

Weather conditions were another factor. Every day a wind blew up and by two o'clock there was a very heavy swell in the bay. The south side of pier 7 was not protected by a breakwater. Two sections of a breakwater existed, but the third had not been completed when war came.

On the south side of pier 7 there was a space filled with the wreckage of port facilities, railroad cars, and miscellaneous objects dumped overboard by the Japanese. They had completely cut across the pier structure in two places. They had stretched some floats under the pier, lashed them together. The floats carried sea mines. Then when they were detonated they wrecked a section of the pier about thirty feet across and right through. This showed much, much more imagination than anything the Germans did in Europe.

On the north side of pier 7 we found a sunken Japanese tanker and another smaller ship sunk outboard. The remaining north side was blocked by the debris of port facilities, railroad cars, motor vehicles, and all kinds of other stuff. In fact, the clearance of this pier was the most interesting clearance job I supervised during the war.

The army loaned us mobile cranes, and we used them to clear up the miscellaneous wreckage alongside the pier. Our crew of divers were split into teams of mixed naval and military personnel. We had as many military personnel as we had naval at the beginning, but later on we had many more naval personnel.

I undertook to provide five berths at pier 7. I felt that five berths there were as many as could be worked at any one time.

We discovered a huge hole in the bottom near the forefoot of the *Kinka Maru*. In order to plug it, we would have to make an enormous wooden patch and work it into place under the ship. That would involve much tunneling and dredging, but if we wanted to float the ship out it was imperative. We did not know whether there were other holes of any consequence, and that would not be known until we had made a pump test. That could not be done until we had the big hole patched. So I ordered a timber patch constructed, even though there was a good probability it would be wasted effort. Amidships no lost buoyancy could be recovered. The sides and the main deck were too badly smashed to be made tight. The double-bottom structure appeared to be intact, but when we tried to remove the ship there was a question as to whether it would hold. The damage was not so bad aft, but we did have to build a cofferdam about sixty feet long and four to six feet high along the rail forward.

We found that we had difficulty fitting the cofferdam. We had to get a section down and well braced in the calm of the forenoon, because the afternoon swell washed over the deck. Whenever we sent divers down they disturbed the rotting cargo of grain—a bomb had exploded in a ship's hold filled with grain—and the air in the whole area became so contaminated with the foul gases that work had to stop. We left an air compressor running during the night to aerate the hold spaces, but sometimes the air carried the smell ashore. The other units working in the area complained strongly.

I knew this was going to be our biggest job, so I gave it first priority in men and equipment. We started the job in early March and worked through April and May. By this time we had cleared up North Harbor, the Passig River, the main entrance harbor, and all of the other wrecks along the South Harbor piers—everything except this wreck and the wholly submerged wreck ahead of it.

As much of the topside structure as possible was cut away to reduce the weight topside. The machinery and anything that was not needed to stiffen the ship's structure were removed. Some heavy trusses of scrap metal were built across the midship gap at the main-deck level. And on the sides of the ship the anchor chain was run back and forth across the fracture and secured on each side by welded clips.

When we pumped the ship, we were going to have all of our recovered buoyancy in the extreme ends, and then there would be a tendency for the ship to buckle amidships. If it did that we would probably not be able to move it, for the bottom amidships would buckle toward the harbor bottom. We did not intend to pump the extreme ends of the ship dry, for this would certainly increase the tendency to buckle. We would have to maintain a maximum amount of free surface, but then would our ship capsize when it came afloat?

We were afraid this ship would turn out to be another job like one we had in Casablanca Harbor, where the double-bottom structure had been permeated with numerous fragmentation holes. We could not tell about the double-bottom status of this ship until we lifted it out of the mud. It was lying in a couple of feet of fine silt.

When we got ready to make a serious attempt to float the ship, I arranged to get on it or on barges alongside it as much pumping power as possible, not only to dewater the ship but to overcome a good deal of uncorrected leakage. To offset any tendency to buckle or capsize because of free surface, I borrowed cranes from the army and hooked them into the ship's structure amidships. I hoped that the pull of these cranes would help the ship's structure carry the unbalanced loading, and that by varying the pull of the cranes we might correct any tendency to list.

The water level dropped fast when we started the pumps. After that it dropped rather slowly, as more uncorrected leaks started to develop. I had plumb bobs erected in a few places and stationed men to report any changes where the bobs contacted some ruled-off white paper; I wanted to see whether the ship was coming up as a unit or whether the two sections were acting independently. And soon the men working these marks reported movements. They confirmed my fears. The extreme ends of the ship were beginning to lift; the middle was staying put. A lift to starboard was indicated on one side of the fracture and a list to port on the other. Now this is fine if the list to port checks the list to starboard, but structurally it might increase the tendency to completely fracture amidships. But there was nothing to do except continue the operation. The list increased, and so did the difference in trim at the forward and after sections. Our trusses at the main-deck level started to buckle, but they did not fracture.

We started pumping, I think about six o'clock in the morning. It was two the following morning when the ship floated. There was a difference of ten or twelve degrees between the lists of the forward and after sections. But the ship showed no great tendency to capsize. A very strong wind was blowing and there was a heavy swell in the bay. It was sweeping around the south end of the breakwater and causing us trouble, so I did not dare take the ship out with all the barges and cranes attached to it until the swell subsided. We just had to stand by and wait until after daybreak. Then we took the wreck outside without trouble and dropped it in our graveyard.

When this big freighter was removed, only the wholly submerged ship was left behind at pier 7. We had finally cleared away all the rubble, railcars, and miscellaneous vehicles along the side. We had also removed the Japanese tanker and the smaller ship on the north side.

Let me describe the removal of the Japanese tanker, because it is an interesting story. The deck was awash. It had been damaged and looked as if it could not be made tight to hold air pressure. I decided as a result to try and roll it upside down and take it out on an air bubble. It would save a lot of time. I thought that if we removed the mast, stack, and bridge structure we might be able to float it out on its side. The ship was small, perhaps a couple thousand tons. With the help of a crane we lifted off the topside erection, then the mast, and we started pumping air inside to see if we could possibly float the wreck. As we pumped, the air in the list of the ship increased and the bilge started to come up. Very soon the ship floated. It was riding on a pocket of air in its port bilge. It had listed about 120 degrees to starboard. Then we moved it outside, but instead of moving it to the graveyard we moved it to a buoy and had divers look it over. It had little damage, so I showed it to a representative of Admiral James Fife's submarine organization, for they were looking for a salvaged ship to run in some supplies. This was a tanker, but hatches could be cut in the deck. It had a diesel engine, and the submarine base was better able to fix up a diesel engine than a steam engine. So we got a couple of cranes for an afternoon, and by pulling with the cranes, using controlled blowing in the compressed-air compartments, and ballasting, we rolled it upright and pumped it dry. The ship was towed to Subic, where it was rebuilt. I believe it made a couple of trips to Australia.

This was the first time we tried moving ships out upside down or almost upside down. We found it eliminated a lot of work and speeded up clearance. We learned our technique with this ship and used it to remove eight more ships from Manila Harbor.

After that big ship was removed, only one remained on the south side of pier 7. The army now wanted me to try and remove it. I was afraid of making a failure of this job. Also I felt that the amount of tonnage to be trucked away from the pier could not be increased, because there was simply not enough room at the pier to take any more. But the army in Manila did not think so. They offered to give me the lumber to build a complete cofferdam. (One of the reasons the removal of this ship had not been given any priority was the estimate I had earlier submitted to the army of the lumber needed for a complete cofferdam.)

Now I realized that we could not build a complete cofferdam on this ship very easily because of the strong swell that swept in daily. I thought it would be foolish to start such a job. It would take months to cut up the ship, it would have to be done in a very hot season, and it would require a large force of divers. And there was real concern for the health of our divers. I suspected that much of the pressure to remove the ship was due to questions raised by visiting VIPs. Every day we had visitors, and the first thing they saw was the masts, bridge, and stack of this ship projecting above water. Why had we left this ship here? Why did we not take it out so we could have another Liberty berth? These eager beavers knew it all with their questions and suggestions. I finally cut the mast, stack, and bridge away from the wreck, thinking it might stop the pressure, but it only made things worse. Tugs and barges ran into the ship. Visitors noted the space and wondered why it was not being used.

No matter how much pressure was applied, I would not consider undertaking this work by cutting the ship up in place. Finally I decided to try to roll it upside down. I had only rolled tankers upside down before this. We got a lot of mobile cranes on the pier. We tried to wash the harbor bottom from under the offshore bilge of the wreck. I needed a hole for the ship to fall into as we rolled it over. We not only used mobile cranes on the pier, but I had beach gear laid to anchors in the harbor bottom. I used floating cranes and improvised pontoons. Finally we got the ship over ninety degrees, but in doing that we had skewed it. We couldn't roll it anymore unless we found some deeper water. I had divers go down and trim away more of the structure on the main deck. Then I arranged to borrow an army dredge, a suction dredge. Finally it looked as if we had a hole big enough for our purpose. In fact, the hulk was beginning to roll into it even before we took any strain with our hogging lines. But to be perfectly safe, I asked the operator to make two more sweeps. This proved disastrous. There was a big bang. The suction on the dredge had apparently picked up an unexploded air bomb, and the cutter head had detonated the bomb. There was no more cutter head, and the dredge was inoperative for some weeks until a new cutter head could be obtained from the States.

When we put air in the hull, we found a few holes in the bottom and the divers patched them. Then we continued pumping, but the results were not encouraging. It looked as if we were licked.

Now I thought I would try to bull the job through, so we got all the available cranes secured to the two ends and started pumping again. The ship came afloat, moved some distance, then got out of control. I let it sink to the bottom and then started all over again. Again we got it to float, but now we wasted no time getting it out of the harbor.

When Huie had arrived with his men I put the gang to work on North Harbor. There turned out to be over two hundred wrecks there. I paid little attention to North Harbor; Huie cleaned this up and then began work on the jobs on the Passig River, which I had bypassed. There were about two hundred wrecks in that area too. For some weeks we had reported forty to sixty wrecks cleaned up per week, but when we no longer had small craft our weekly average dropped to about four to six. This was around the end of May, and we had only big ships left to deal with.

In clearing North Harbor Huie removed a couple dozen Sugar Charlies with wood hulls.* He dumped them temporarily on the north side of pier 17. He had piled up about a dozen when we found them disappearing faster than we dumped them. The natives were cutting them up for firewood. There would be fifty to a hundred natives down there with hammers and saws, just taking the wood away. We had all kinds of trouble along the waterfront, but the looting there was not to be compared with what went on in town. We even saw wood paving blocks on the main streets downtown being dug up for kindling.

Our most important job in Manila was the opening of the main harbor entrance. The Japanese did a perfect job blocking it—far more efficient than any similar job the Germans had done in Europe. The man who directed the job knew what he was doing. There were five ships sunk in a staggered line across the entrance. There was no gap between the ships for a passage. Four of them were old interisland ships and one was the *Luzon*, the flagship of the Yangtze patrol.

The decks of these ships would not hold air, so we couldn't move them that way. The bulkheads inside were ruptured. The Japanese always put their explosives on a bulkhead line to impair transverse bulkheads. The decks were underwater, so cofferdams would be needed if we were to try and lift the ships by pumping. But the afternoon swell would have washed away any cofferdam unless it was very small.

The army had a number of Quonset cells which had been used to make up floating piers. I obtained a number of these and fitted them with lengths of chain. At the ends we fitted some hooks. We then cut a six-inch-diameter hole in one corner of each Quonset and filled it up with enough water to give a slight negative buoyancy. In this condition the Quonset was lowered by one of our floating cranes. A diver found the hole and inserted the hook. He then took an air hose and stuck it in the vent hole of the Quonset. This blew the water out of the Quonset and filled it with air, giving about eight tons of lift to

*Sugar Charlies are small boats used to haul sugarcane to refineries.

the hook. But problems developed, because the wrecks were so deteriorated that the hook at the end of the chain cut right through the plating like a knife. A few ingenious solutions were devised to circumvent this problem. Then we got every crane and LCT with sheerlegs to start lifting. I also had the ends of air hoses stuck in as many openings around the sides of the wreck as possible. When we got ready to pull, we started pumping air into the wreck in the hope that some of the air might give additional lift.

I was more surprised than anyone else to see the wreck start sliding away from the entrance. My figures had not led me to hope for any such success. With similar efforts we then moved the other three interisland ships.

The fifth ship was the *Luzon*. This was the last ship the Japanese had sunk at the entrance. It had effectively closed the gap. Ships sunk to plug a gap or close a channel have got to be sunk quickly, so the current cannot take them away before they hit bottom. There was no doubt that the *Luzon* had gone down quickly. The magazine had been blown up when a switch was thrown on the bridge. The crew went down with it.

I had the steering wheel of the *Luzon* taken off and sent to the Naval Academy Museum. I thought the ship would be more difficult to remove; therefore I took time to fit additional Quonset cells around the side. I also tried a new scheme of mine. I built a couple of wooden cofferdams, which were floated into place and with weights sunk until the bottom made contact with an area of the main deck that had no openings. These cofferdams were nothing but rectangular boxes without a bottom. One section of a cofferdam was about six by eight feet. The bottom of the sides had canvas padding. Once the cofferdams were in contact with the deck a three-inch pump started pumping water out. Each contributed about twelve tons more in lift. The *Luzon* started to slide away from the entrance as easily as the other ships did.

About this time Doc Schlesinger advised me to get the men out of the tents where they had been living and into buildings. Our concern was what was going to happen to our divers and other personnel when the rainy weather came. We could not have them in tents. We needed lumber. Requisitions put in to the Service Force for lumber were ignored. We were told we were working with the army and to get our supplies from them. The Service Force did have an enormous supply of lumber. It was being brought into Manila and, in sight of everyone, was being unloaded by SeaBees into lighters. The lumber was to be used to build a tremendous Seventh Fleet headquarters. I was disgusted with this project. At the rate the war was going it was quite evident to me that it would be over before the Seventh Fleet compound was ever completed. My speculation proved accurate. The war was over before construction was much more than started. The compound was never occupied by the navy.

Anyway, I watched the SeaBees unloading the Service Force lumber into lighters. At four o'clock every afternoon they knocked off and went back to their billets, and the lighters remained alongside the ship that was being unloaded. One night a lighter was not properly secured. It drifted loose. I sent our boat over and had the lighter towed to our slip in front of the Manila Hotel. I found good lumber on the lighter, just what we needed to build some houses. I had a spare lighter that we had borrowed from the army, and I had this taken out and secured alongside the Liberty ship. The next morning the SeaBees came back and started work as usual. The empty lighter we put alongside was loaded with lumber and taken away. I waited a day or so to see if there was any stink, but there was none. So I had the lumber from the towed lighter unloaded and stored behind the hotel. At the next opportunity I substituted this empty lighter for another full load. After we had three or four loads of lumber I decided we had enough to build a couple of two-story houses, each sixty by thirty feet, to take care of our men in the rainy season. I designed the buildings myself, adopting a shipyard type of fabrication and assembly to expedite the construction. Then I turned the work over to our firefighters. They supervised the work and did the layout. The construction was done by some Filipino carpenters and guerrillas.

No one in the navy ever asked me where the lumber came from. Neither SeaBees nor the Service Force ever mentioned any lumber missing. The only one who wanted to know where I got the lumber was General Casey, MacArthur's chief engineer. I told him I stole it. As the army was so short of lumber, he knew I could not have stolen any lumber from them, so he asked no more questions. I was tempted several times to tell Admiral Kinkaid, but he was such a gentleman and at the same time so serious and conscientious that I thought it best to keep quiet.

We had a job which received much publicity, the recovery of silver pesos from the waters around Corregidor. Within two weeks of my arrival in Manila I was asked what could be done about the pesos, deposited in Manila Bay just before the surrender to the Japanese. I refused to discuss this subject. I was out to clean up Manila Harbor and I had no time for any other work. The subject did not die. It was noted that I had some army divers working for me. This was after I had received many of our lost navy divers. The army divers had not been sent out to clean up Manila Bay—why could I not use them?

I mentioned the subject to General MacArthur. As the pressure was building, he said it was a job that would have to be done, but it was not to take precedence over harbor clearance work.

A week or two went by, and General MacArthur himself brought up the subject again. It had been reported that natives living near the bay were swimming out at night to pick up pesos. Military intelligence had found some pesos which appeared to have been in the water for a long time. General MacArthur said the money had been removed from the vaults of the Manila

Bank and taken to Corregidor before the surrender. Several huge bargeloads had been taken out and dumped in the bay. It was in boxes. The total value, as I remember, was something like thirteen million U.S. dollars. The United States had both a legal and a moral obligation to recover this money. MacArthur wanted to make an attempt to recover it before any trouble arose between the military police and the natives. I had made excellent progress on the harbor work. Could I arrange a few men now to work on the silver?

I told him I was ready to start. I would station an ARS in the area. I no longer needed the ARSs anyway. I wanted to avoid any scandalous rumors. I had read of many projects involving the recovery of money or valuables from the sea, and invariably there had been scandals of some sort; even where every effort had been made to keep treasure from disappearing, there had been stories and rumors of scandalous conduct by someone involved. I asked for an army finance officer and an army MP officer to be stationed on the ARS to take possession of the pesos as they were brought to the surface. I wanted the MP officer to see the divers as they removed their diving dress so that no silver was concealed. The pesos brought up would be counted on deck, and the army finance officer would give the CO of the ARS a receipt for the day's take. I told the general I would look over the divers and pick out those men who were due for early return to the United States. These would be employed at Corregidor until they were ready to go home. This arrangement was approved.

I made up a team of divers, I gave the CO of the ARS his orders, and he left with an army finance officer and an MP on board. The army gave us information on the location of the silver. A few days went by, and then I got a message from the CO of the ARS. He reported no trace of silver. I contacted the army again and an army sergeant was flown to Manila to talk with me. He had served on the barge that had taken the silver out at night. He had been in the Bataan death march and had only recently been released from a Japanese prison. He was quite foggy but recognized the chart I had and said the silver had been dumped at the spot marked on that chart with an X. He said the barge was taken out late at night. As soon as it had arrived at this marked spot, the silver was dumped over, box by box. I asked him how he knew the barge was at this particular spot when the silver was dumped. He said that he stood facing the bow of the barge and held his left arm out. When his left forefinger lined up with a certain point on Corregidor, the order was given to start dumping. I asked if anyone else had any points to take a line on, to be sure the barge was at this designated point. He did not know. He said the Japanese had found out about the silver and had forced some of the Americans to go back and point out the location. Perhaps the Japanese had removed all the silver. Intelligence had investigated this. They said the Japanese had removed a couple million pesos.

We were told the pesos had been dumped in water about sixty feet deep. The divers had gone down and found that after they hit the bottom they stirred up a fine mud that clouded the water. They had very little visibility and had to be guided largely by sense of touch.

I decided to go down and take a look myself. Nothing was found around the sixty-foot curve, so I made another trip down, looking at the map and trying to put myself in the position of the men who had sneaked out at night to dump the silver, expecting the Japanese to open fire at any moment. I decided there was a great chance of the money being dumped in water much deeper than sixty feet. The MPs had found some natives with pesos, which indicated that perhaps my reasoning was incorrect. Nevertheless, I instructed the ship to start a search in deeper water. This they did.

It was not until they started searching at a ninety-foot depth that any successful results were obtained. One diver noted a mound on the bottom. He found it was a pile of small wooden boxes about two feet in length, and they proved to be boxes of silver pesos.

The boxes were so deteriorated that they fell apart before they could be taken to the surface, so the ship had to improvise a net to take the boxes. Once the divers had retrieved all the boxes they could, they had to get down on their hands and knees and sift the fine silt to pick up stray pesos. It took them several days. Then it took a day or so of further searching to find another pile. This work kept up for weeks. Once four mounds were found close together. Most of the silver was in depths of between 90 and 130 feet, but once the divers went inshore and found a pile in water much less than sixty feet. That was where the Filipinos were getting their pesos.

Doc Schlesinger told me the divers were griping about doing all this work and not being able to sneak even a peso for a souvenir. I made arrangements with the army to put pesos up for sale as souvenirs for anyone who would buy one. Many of the men were buying the souvenirs, but the divers doing the work thought this was a cheap stunt and they were still trying to figure out how to get away with some.

Then I hit on a solution. The press wanted to go down and photograph the operation. There was no transportation to Corregidor and the army would provide none. The naval base would provide none. I passed the word that a way to buy pesos for the divers was urgently needed. A fund of $150 or so would do. Somehow or other transportation would be found if this fund was raised. It was.

The recovery of the silver continued during the remainder of my stay. When I left the Philippines I believe something like seven million dollars in pesos had been recovered. It was becoming harder and harder to locate mounds of boxes.

I was just about to ask for orders back to Washington when the war ended. The Japanese surrendered. All high-priority work on the harbor had been done. My replacements had arrived.

When I left, every pier in Manila could be used to tie up ships. There were more berths available there at the time I left in August than there had been before the Japs damaged the place.

The battle for Okinawa was a long and bloody one. The Japanese had anticipated the contest and placed about one hundred thousand defenders in strategic spots around the island. Sixty thousand were regulars of the Imperial Army. Against this formidable bastion came Admiral Spruance's Task Force 58, the largest and most powerful fleet ever assembled. Of its fifteen hundred ships, twelve hundred were assigned to the amphibious forces. During the battle they transported and supported one hundred eighty thousand assault troops of the Tenth Army (five infantry and three marine divisions). It took all that to subjugate an island only sixty miles long with a land mass of 465 square miles.

The cost was great. Thirteen thousand Americans were killed and thousands wounded. Fifteen naval vessels were sunk and more than two hundred others damaged, some beyond repair. But the gain was also great, for after the battle Allied air power had substantial bases within a reasonable distance of the industrial heart of Japan; the fleet had the means of setting up a complete blockade of the home islands; and it had a ready base for the coup de grace, the planned invasion of Japan (which dissipated with the advent of the atomic bomb).

The campaign for Okinawa found the Japanese military in a last desperate stand. They were now fighting for the survival of their nation. The time had come for them to use all they had—all their remaining air, naval, and human resources—against the Allied invaders. Suicide air attacks were launched in droves. The first of ten massive attacks employed 355 kamikaze pilots in old planes that were hurled against the fleet and the troops already landed.

An extremely valuable adjunct to the Allied fleet in this battle was the escort carrier, sometimes called the jeep carrier. It was developed by the Americans in World War II, although the British had experimented with a small carrier, HMS *Argus*, as far back as 1916. Henry J. Kaiser, the shipbuilder on the West Coast, was given a contract to build fifty or fifty-five carriers of ten thousand tons, which could make nineteen knots and carry twenty-four or more planes. When these first made their appearance early in 1943, almost all of them were consigned to the

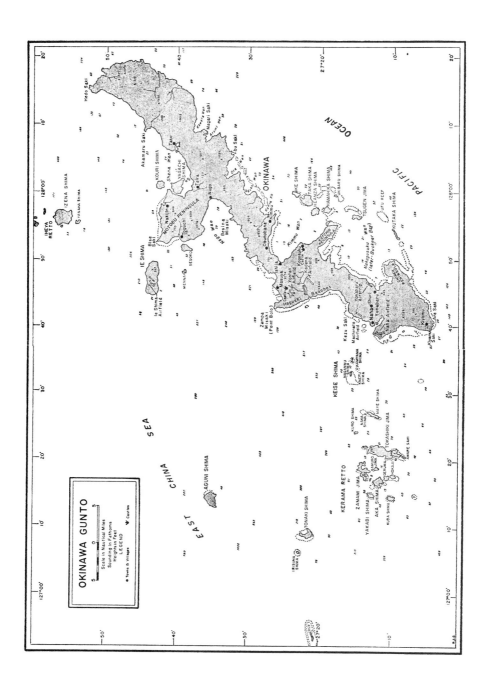

Pacific Fleet. Twenty-five or thirty participated in the battle for Okinawa, some in the amphibious support group, others in logistic support. Among them was the *Makassar Strait*, under the command of then-Commander Herbert Riley. She had been working as a trainer ship, but for the Okinawa campaign she assumed the role of combat air support. From D-day almost until the close of the contest she provided air cover for the ground forces.

Since the following excerpt, from the oral history interviews of Admiral Riley, deals almost exclusively with the pilots on the *Makassar Strait*, the circumstances under which they operated are of considerable interest. The men were young, some only nineteen or so. They were all without combat experience, and when they became involved in the Okinawa campaign the duty was tremendously rigorous. They were called upon to fly a number of missions every day and to be extremely versatile in their tasks. Fighter pilots in that battle often acted as bomber pilots and some were even engaged in strafing missions. Their jeep carrier, because of its small size, made landings difficult. It pitched and rolled in any kind of sea, requiring extreme vigilance from the pilots. Even off duty the men were obliged to respond to general quarters when an enemy attack on the ship was anticipated or under way, and at the height of the campaign a carrier might be subjected to twenty or thirty raids a day.

So there were many actions, duties, and demands—and the contest went on for a long time. D-day was 1 April (some of the pilots called it Love Day), but the island was not officially declared secure until 21 June. Eighty-odd days of unremitting demands and the constant din of battle inevitably resulted in pilot strain. An officer who was part of this experience in a carrier off Okinawa once said that the young pilots on his ship, when off duty, engaged in a ghoulish exercise to relieve their tensions: they mounted the forecastle above the flight deck on their ship to watch and criticize the tactics of attacking Japanese pilots. In retrospect it is easy to understand why the skipper of the *Makassar Strait* met with such great success when he employed an original technique to lessen the tension for his young pilots. It is equally easy to believe that there was never a single case of combat fatigue among his fliers during that long ordeal.

COCKTAIL PARTIES
IN THE *MAKASSAR STRAIT*

VICE ADMIRAL HERBERT RILEY

HERBERT DOUGLAS RILEY was born in Maryland on 24 December 1904. After attending Baltimore Polytechnic Institute, he entered the U.S. Naval Academy, from which he graduated in 1927. He was designated naval aviator in 1930 and thereafter had duty in all types of naval aviation squadrons. In one tour at the naval air station in Anacostia, he was a test pilot and a VIP transport pilot, with additional duty at the White House as naval aide to President Roosevelt.

With the advent of World War II he had duty as an operations officer with Commander, Fleet Air, West Coast. Riley participated in air operations at Guadalcanal and saw service as section head of the aviation plans division of the Navy Department. In 1944 he took command of the USS *Makassar Strait* and participated in the Iwo Jima and Okinawa operations. In the postwar period Riley had a number of interesting tours as deputy airborne commander for the atom bomb tests at Bikini; part of the Long-Range War Plans Office in the navy's strategic plans section; naval assistant to Secretary of Defense James Forrestal; aide to Secretary Louis Johnson; student at the National War College; assistant chief of staff for Plans, Commander in Chief, Atlantic Fleet; Deputy Chief of Staff, Supreme Allied Commander, Atlantic; commander of the USS *Coral Sea*; and chief of staff to Carrier Division 2. In January 1954 Riley became assistant director (later he was director) of politico-military policy in the Navy Department. He was Commander, Carrier Division 1, with duty in the Seventh Fleet, and Chief of Staff, Pacific

Command, from 1958 until 1961, when he became deputy chief of naval operations for fleet operations and readiness. His final position was director of the Joint Staff, Joint Chiefs of Staff (1962-64), in which capacity he served during the Cuban Missile Crisis.

Vice Admiral Riley retired from active duty on 1 April 1964 and died at his home on Kent Island, Maryland, on 17 January 1973.

I needn't go into what combat air support is. Everybody knows that. But I will tell you one thing that happened in the *Makassar Strait* which I think was quite distinctive.

When we first got into close air support work, my pilots, although they'd been on many combat air patrols, had never fired at live targets and they had never really been in combat. In the *Makassar Strait* the executive officer and I were the only two regulars, that is, the only two Naval Academy graduates. There were a couple of other regulars who'd been enlisted men formerly and had been promoted as high as lieutenant, but other than that there were no professional officers aboard that ship. Both the ship's company and the entire air group, including the air group commander, were made up of reserve officers. None of them had ever been in combat. None of them had any naval experience.

I'll concentrate on the air group. This was a bunch of eager kids. They really had rushed into aviation. They had been given their wings quickly and been pushed into the battle area. Until a man gets into combat, there is no good way to judge how he will stand up to it. People that you imagine would be perfectly calm and suave about it blow up; others you wouldn't ever bet on turn out the opposite. I decided I wanted to watch these boys closely to see how they responded. I had been in combat myself.

There was medicinal liquor aboard all of the carriers to be used under supervision of the flight surgeons. We had two flight surgeons on board. Their supply was generous, but they were supposed to issue it only when they thought it was needed as a tranquilizer, for morale purposes, etc. Liquor had its uses, believe me.

The trouble was that the flight surgeons were reserve officers, serving their first sea duty. It was left entirely to them just how the liquor was dispensed. It was dispensed, all right, but in various weird ways.

After the first combat mission in which my people were engaged I called the exec to the bridge and turned the conn over to him. Then I went down to the ready room and walked around to see how things were going with these kids. Of course they were very excited, as high as kites, all of them. I found sheer bedlam in the ready room. The flight surgeons were there. They had brought their liquor along and they were using water glasses. They would pour a slug of liquor, warm whiskey in a water glass, and hand it to each pilot as he came in, saying "Here's your medicinal liquor."

At the same time the ACI officers were buzzing around trying to debrief everybody at once. They would turn to one pilot and say, "What did you see? Did you hit your target? Did you take this out? Tell us exactly what you saw. Was it damaged before you hit it?" Half of the pilots didn't know whether they'd hit their targets or not. They were so excited they never even looked back. They dove down, dropped their bombs, did their strafing runs, and so forth, but they were just too excited. This was their first round. And it was a first for the medical officers and the ACI officers. It was sheer bedlam. How anybody could be debriefed properly or get any good from the liquor was beyond me.

I got to thinking about what I had witnessed. I thought, We've got to do something about this; this is awful. So first I called in the ACI officers. I said, "There will be no more debriefing in the ready room. The debriefing will be done individually, not collectively. You'll never get anywhere with three or four combat intelligence officers asking questions of a pilot while he is talking to somebody else. You were getting nonsense answers like, 'I don't know, ask Joe, he saw it.' Something like that. You'll never get any combat intelligence that way. You will have to set up your shop near the ready room and call pilots in before they leave the area, while all is fresh in their minds. And you will talk to them with no interruptions."

I had been thinking about the dispensing of the liquor. I knew that these kids needed to get calmed down, there was no doubt about that. And liquor had beneficial uses as a tranquilizer. But certainly this was not a good way to dispense it, by pouring a slug of raw liquor for pilots to gulp down, with nothing else in it, no ice or water or anything. Now half of these kids were nineteen-year-olds, and generally they didn't know much about drinking in those days at that age. They'd had a drink, sure, but they didn't know much about drinking. They all felt impelled to drink, since this was medicinal liquor furnished to them officially aboard ship—they *had* to drink it. It would be unheard of not to.

I recalled that every one of the Kaiser-class ships (they're alike as peas in a pod) had facilities, so-called facilities for a captain and a captain's cabin, an in-port cabin as well as a sea cabin. They also had similar facilities for a flag officer, should the ship happen to become a flagship. They had a cabin for the task group commander, a modest number of rooms for the staff. The flag cabin was identical to the captain's in-port cabin. In our ship this space was just going to waste. The rooms weren't used for anything since we had no admiral aboard and would not be used until and unless we did. I thought we might as well as get some use out of the flag space. I went down and took a good look at it. It had one of the standard old sideboards—you know, the kind that was bolted to the deck and the bulkhead, standard old navy stuff

338

that came out of BuShips blueprint umpty ump and was specified for that type of ship.

It was a drab place, so I got to thinking about improving it. I looked at the way the sideboards were secured and then I sent for the first lieutenant of the ship. The various shops came under his supervision. I told him what I wanted him to do. I wanted him to take the sideboards away from the bulkhead, to pull them out. They would be ideal bars. There were two of them, so I had them butted together and then brought out from the bulkhead far enough for a man to get behind them. I even had him fashion a rail at the bottom! Then I got enough chairs in there, comfortable chairs which were provided for the flag cabin. I had the carpenter's shop make up some low tables for cocktail tables, about three of them. I had somebody else search the ship to get some magazines. The *Playboy* equivalent in those days was *Esquire*. It had the centerfold with the beautiful babe, you may remember. I had people get all the *Esquire*s around the ship and take the centerfolds from them. We practically papered the bulkhead with them. The whole place was decorated with them—cocktail tables, the bar, everything.

Then I got the flight surgeons in there and said, "Gentlemen, you are responsible for the liquor, so you will provide the wherewithal to make this into a club. And this is going to be a club with a lot of rules. I have the rules all written out. Here they are. As far as you're concerned, one of you is going to be in charge. We're going to have a cocktail party every afternoon, and one of you is going to be the host at the party. You are going to see that the liquor is handled in accordance with these rules. Here are the rules for the liquor. The liquor will be kept in the bar. You'll bring it down and you'll take it back when the place closes. The bar will be open at certain specified times. All pilots who are on the dusk flight, the final flight of the day, are not invited to the party, nor those assigned to the standby flight that goes out in case of emergency. Remember, they are not invited. Every other pilot who, to the best of our knowledge, has finished flying for the day is invited to come to the party. But first, when they come back to the ready room from the last flight, they are to be debriefed by the ACI officer. They are then to go down to the living area and get a shower. They are to get into fresh khaki. Then they can come up to the flag cabin for the cocktail party. You two will see to it that no one, but *no* one, has more than two drinks. That is the maximum anybody can get and nobody can give his drink to somebody else so somebody can get three. This is a medicinal order; no more than two drinks, that's the max. Many will take one drink, to show that they're drinking, to prove they can; and you will find some of them will just toy with it. They won't really want a second, and they're never to be urged to have a second drink.

"Another item: there is often jealousy between the officers assigned to a ship and the officers assigned to its air group. That was true in prewar days. We want to be sure there isn't that feeling in this ship. The best way I can think to prevent jealousy is to develop a spirit of camaraderie between the air group and the ship's officers. Now this liquor is furnished for the pilots. That is the only reason it is aboard. Nobody really rates it but the pilots. But we'll make it so that every day the air group—they can work it out any way they want—is to invite three ship's officers as guests. I predict that it will be a popularity contest to see who gets invited. This ought to promote good spirit between the air group and the ship, because if the air group doesn't like some ship's officer he is not going to be invited. So ship's officers will try to make the air group officers like them so they will be invited. Just three officers can be invited by the air group each day, three people from the ship. I don't care if it is the same three people who are invited. If they're that popular, all right. The air group commander will determine the rules by which the air group invites the three ship's officers.

"Further, the skipper or the exec are always invited. They can come any time they want to. The chances are the number of times the skipper or exec will be there will be very remote, because they'll be too darned busy with other duties. I won't be able to leave the bridge for long, but I will make it a point to come sometimes. I will have the exec stand by for me while I run down, and I will stay there long enough to have a drink with the boys, then go back up. But that's the limit. The guests will be the flight surgeons, the three invitees, the skipper, the exec, and the pilots who are not out on the final flight or scheduled for emergency standby. Nobody else can come. We'll see how this works."

The flight surgeons were dubious about this. They saw what I'd done with the flag cabin; they approved of it, that was fine. But these rules were absolutely inflexible. Pilots had to be debriefed, they had to get their showers and get into fresh khaki, and only then could they come down and have their drinks.

I found a couple of Filipino boys aboard who had worked in a BOQ ashore and knew something about mixing drinks. Of course, we didn't have any bars in the BOQ in those days, but they had managed to learn enough about bartending and always loved it. They didn't drink very much themselves, but they loved to mix drinks. I checked them out. We made all sorts of mixes for the liquor so it would be a little more palatable. We trained the boys to make drinks that you would normally get at a bar. We had no vodka or gin so we couldn't make drinks with them, but we could make enough other drinks.

I went down there the first day. Of course everybody was a little awkward, didn't know what it was all about, but they thought it was a great idea and they warmed to it. I saw to it that the exec dropped in once in a while, and always one of the flight surgeons was there. I went down there probably three times in all, and the exec probably did the same.

Occasionally there'd be a mixup so that some pilot from another carrier had to land and spend the night aboard. Sometimes this would happen because of weather, if we were on the edge of a typhoon or something like that. I remember one time we had a lot of visitors aboard. Of course, any overnight visitor was always invited as a guest at the cocktail party.

The *Makassar Strait* had a cocktail party every day from early in the Okinawa operation until we came off combat air support and went to Guam. This thing was meticulously managed. You can make your own mind up as to what good it did, if any, but I never had one single case of combat fatigue in that air group. I never had a pilot who became so tensed up that we wondered whether to send him out or not. The pilots got into the spirit of the thing. This was the most relaxing diversion you could imagine.

The club was only open for forty-five minutes or an hour, and when it closed the pilots went to dinner. Things were set up so they had dinner later than the normal wardroom time.

This little daily party gave the pilots something to look forward to. The ship's officers had the opportunity to be invited. They understood that it was the air group's liquor and they didn't begrudge it. There never was any bad feeling between the air group and the ship's officers. A popularity contest is what it amounted to.

I never saw a gimmick that was so successful in accomplishing what it was designed to do. And we used the same amount of liquor as anybody else.

I remember, one time, there was a pilot from the *Hornet* who had to land aboard. He was invited to the party, under the standard operating procedure we had. The next day, when we were ready for the first launch, he was on the flight deck, waiting to return to his ship. Just before he got into his airplane, he came right below the wing of the bridge, cupped his hands, and yelled up, "Thank you very much for your hospitality, Captain. I sure did enjoy that cocktail party."

I told everybody, "We've got something good going, and we've got to handle it properly. The surest way for it to get out of hand is for the story to get exaggerated. I'm perfectly willing to say this is my project, and I'll take full responsibility for it if anybody wants to argue about it. But we're not going to talk about it because somebody, not knowing how it's done, may say, 'There'll be nothing like this.' And we want it." So we kept it throughout the combat period. Word did get around through the visiting pilots. I heard many, many comments about the *Makassar Strait* cocktail parties long after I was detached from the ship, but they always were favorable comments. The thing worked like a charm with those kids.

The denouement of the war with Japan was at hand when Allied leaders met in Potsdam, Germany, on 17 July 1945. On that very day, the start of the Potsdam Conference, Harry Truman, who had recently become president after the death of Roosevelt, was apprised of the success of the atomic explosion at Alamogordo, New Mexico. The way was open for the final blow at Japan.

The Potsdam Declaration, issued on 26 July, called for the unconditional surrender of all Japanese armed forces under threat of a stark and awesome alternative, "prompt and utter destruction." The declaration did not mention that such destruction would be wrought by an atomic bomb, but the clause brought matters to a head in the councils of Japan. The cabinet was deeply divided. The emperor's stalwarts were for surrender. They were fearfully conscious of the tragedy confronting the nation. But the war party was adamant and fanatical. They wanted to fight to the death, to invite a bloody invasion of the homeland with full knowledge of the dire consequences.

Meanwhile, the Japanese foreign minister, working through his ambassador in Moscow, was trying frantically to persuade the Russians to act as mediators in peace talks with the Allies. But the Russians themselves wanted to join the war against Japan, whose looming defeat promised beguiling fruits. So a reply to the Allied ultimatum was delayed. This was both costly and tragic. The Americans interpreted the Japanese silence as a rejection of surrender and proceeded with plans to drop the newly tested bomb. President Truman was on his way home from Potsdam when he gave his final order. B-29s of the Twentieth Army Air Force were to drop two bombs on two separate cities. Hiroshima was bombed on 6 August and Nagasaki on 9 August. That day the Russians declared war on the shattered remains of the Japanese empire. The following day, 10 August, Japan acquiesced to the Potsdam ultimatum.

Events moved fast after that. The emperor issued his rescript on 14 August and made a recording to be broadcast over national radio on 15 August. Behind the scenes, however, the war party was not giving up. A military coup was contemplated. The commanding general of the Imperial Guards Division was assassinated after he refused to obey the surrender orders of the emperor. Hara-kiri was committed by some war leaders. But saner heads prevailed. The emperor's message was broadcast. Japan had surrendered. The people heard their emperor's voice over radio and were stupefied by the revelation that the empire was defeated. They still appeared stunned when the first American occupation troops arrived at Atsugi airport two weeks later.

All this is but prelude to the surrender ceremony on board the U.S. battleship *Missouri* in Tokyo Bay on 2 September. An account of that ceremony and the preparations leading up to it is given by her former skipper, Admiral Stuart S. ("Sunshine") Murray. Then–Captain Murray was the man charged by Admiral Nimitz with arranging the details of the historic signing. The reader will find his recollections graphic, succinct, and humorous. What he reports on the elaborate security precautions taken for the event measures the American fear that dissident members of the war party would strike in some unexpected way. Certain kamikaze pilots were known to have boasted that they would crash on the *Missouri* when she entered Tokyo Bay.

On 2 September a total of 258 Allied warships of all types assembled in the bay for the surrender. Most of the aircraft carriers of the American and British fleets remained outside the bay in order to launch their planes for a flyover at the climax of the event.

Some of Admiral Murray's details differ from what was reported in the press of the day and in histories since. What is significant, however, is not whose version is correct—it hardly matters how many pens MacArthur used when signing the surrender documents—but rather that the following account has a resonance that could only come from the person who was closest to events on that September day.

A HARRIED HOST
IN THE *MISSOURI*

ADMIRAL STUART S. MURRAY

STUART SHADRICK MURRAY was born in Delia, Texas, on 22 March 1898. He had many connections in Oklahoma and was appointed from that state to the U.S. Naval Academy, where he graduated in 1918. Next he received instruction at the submarine base in New London, Connecticut. After early commands of R- and S-class submarines, Murray was put in charge of fitting out the *Porpoise* at the Portsmouth Navy Yard; he commanded her until 1937.

In November 1940 he assumed command of Submarine Division 15, based at Pearl Harbor. The division, subsequently designated Submarine Division 21 and moved to the Philippines, was in Manila when the Japanese struck in December 1941. In 1942 and 1943 Murray was chief of staff to Commander, Submarine Force, Southwest Pacific, and to Commander, Submarine Force, Pacific Fleet. Following a tour as commandant of midshipmen at the Naval Academy, he assumed command of the USS *Missouri* (May–November 1945). Under his command the *Missouri*, as flagship of Admiral William F. Halsey, participated in actions against Okinawa and the Japanese homeland. Later duty assignments included Commander, Amphibious Training Command, U.S. Atlantic Fleet; Commander, Sumarine Force, U.S. Atlantic Fleet; Commander, Hawaiian Sea Frontier; and Commander, Pearl Harbor Naval Base.

Admiral Murray retired in 1956 in the rank of admiral and died in Washington, D.C., in 1980.

The decision about where the Japanese surrender would take place was made in Washington by President Truman. There seemed to be considerable argument as to whether the surrender should be on a carrier, an amphibious ship, or ashore. President Truman settled all that by telling the secretaries of the navy and the army that it would be on the USS *Missouri*. When the *Missouri* had been christened he, a senator from Missouri at the time, was the principal speaker, and his daughter, Margaret, broke the bottle of champagne.

I might add that we on the *Missouri,* including Admiral Halsey, whose flagship she was, didn't know anything about this. We were milling around—that is the best word for it—well south of Japan after the fifteenth of August when we got some mail. It was brought out to us in the operating area. As soon as it had been distributed, my chief yeoman came dashing up with a letter and said, "Captain, the *Missouri* is going to be the surrender ship. Here's a clipping from the Santa Barbara paper." That was his home town. "My wife just sent it." There was a letter from my wife with a similar clipping.

I went down to Admiral Robert Carney, Halsey's chief of staff, and asked him what he knew. "Here's the dispatch," he said. "It just came in five minutes ago." That was our first word of the matter.

Well, we continued on till finally on the twenty-fifth or twenty-sixth of August we heard that the emperor had gotten orders out to all of his forces and that we were to go on in. The *Missouri* was to enter Tokyo Bay, just off Yokosuka, to stage the surrender on September 2.

As soon as this happened we knew we would have to clean up ship and paint some of the parts that were just red lead or had old paint. After all, we had been at sea for a month and a half or longer since we left Leyte at the end of July. So I asked Rear Admiral Arthur Radford if we could find out if anyone in the task group had paint. No one was supposed to have paint out in the war zone because of the fire hazard. But any bo'sun worth his salt would always have five or ten gallons or more of paint cached away just in case. I found our bo'sun had three five-gallon cans that he admitted to. How much more I never knew. But we also had quite a bit of paint sent over by various other ships. No one asked any questions.

We still didn't know what the plans were—how many people there were going to be. In talking with Admiral Carney we had fixed on our own idea of the ceremony, and among other things we decided to have the surrender on the starboard side of the galley deck. It was a verandah deck just outside of my cabin door.

We started holystoning the decks to get the paint off, because we had painted them war color to make them less visible—war color and black in lots of places on the topside. It was hard to get off, so the holystone was the only thing. Of course, navy regulations for years had said to us, "Thou shalt not holystone decks," but we did and everyone knew we were going to because it was the only way to get it off. It was interesting to see a bunch of sailors out there with sand and holystone. We were kept busy with that.

Finally on about the twenty-sixth of August, some Japanese naval officers came out on a destroyer. At that time we were only forty or fifty miles south of Sagami Won, which is just west of Tokyo. We received this Japanese destroyer. Arrangements had been made for it to come out when the Yokosuka naval shipyard and the naval district surrendered. When the officers came aboard they had their dress swords on. They were lined up as they came off the high line. Marines were stationed at the four corners of the verandah deck. The officers were disarmed by the flag secretary. They went down and formally surrendered to Admiral Carney, then went back after about half an hour's talking and questioning. Their purpose was to come and officially turn over the keys to the city of Yokosuka (the naval district area) because that was where we were going to be anchored and where the marines and navy landing party would go ashore first.

Later we were told that early on the morning of the twenty-seventh we would be met by pilots who would take us and our escort ships into Tokyo Bay about the twenty-ninth or thirtieth of August.

According to plan, we rendezvoused with the Japanese destroyers, which had been demilitarized. Their guns were depressed in the deck and plugged. They came alongside and Japanese pilots were transferred to our ship one at a time. Four marines, all armed with submachine guns, were on the verandah deck. A good number of the pilots were naval officers. The principal one was a civilian. As they came over, they would be landed in the middle of the verandah and immediately be told to take off their arms and put them down or hand them over to the flag lieutenant. Quite a little stash of arms was taken off these pilots. They wore their dress swords and daggers, but so far as I know none of them had pistols. Then they were each escorted by a marine up the ladder to Admiral Carney's messroom, where they were interviewed.

I could tell by the expressions on the faces of some of these men as they stood there and saw marines from all angles, from above, alongside, with a submachine gun turned on them, that they were not the least bit happy. I don't blame them. I wouldn't have been either.

When Admiral Carney had finished with them, he sent them to me. The chief pilot, the civilian, was assigned to us. He had been chief pilot for Tokyo Bay before the war and supposedly knew the bay perfectly. He and a half-dozen other pilots came up on the bridge of the *Missouri* to show us the minefields. They had given maps of the minefields to Admiral Carney. Then we proceeded alongside a Japanese destroyer assigned to us. We also had, of course, a screen of our own destroyers, about a dozen of them, going ahead of us and leading the ships into Sagami Won.

I told the Japanese destroyer to take position up ahead with our destroyers. He didn't want to understand. The chief pilot told him in Japanese to take position and pointed out to him exactly where it was. A stream of Japanese came back from the Jap ship. By this time he had cast off about one hundred feet away from us and was cruising along. He was just going to stay in that position. The chief pilot said, "He doesn't want to take position ahead," so I insisted on telling him again, but it didn't bring about a change in position. So I told the starboard broadside of five-inch guns and the forty-millimeter battery on turret two to train on him. When those guns swung around on him, he understood real fast. He took off at full speed. I told him, too, to ping with his sonar gear and to report to the screen commander. (We thought some kamikaze-type submarines might be loose and didn't want to take any chances.) But the screen commander reported back to me that the Japanese skipper didn't use his ASDIC and wouldn't try it. After another order, to which he paid no attention, we turned turrets one and two around in addition to the other ones. Before the turrets were actually in position, he started pinging. You could hear him through the hull of the *Missouri,* he was pinging so hard.

When the Japs brought their maps of the minefields up on the bridge and we broke out ours, we found that they matched perfectly, except that ours extended out about half a mile further to the west. And the Jap naval commander exclaimed, "Where you get, where you get? I have lots of trouble getting this and I was the one who laid most of those mines. Where you get this?"

And my answer, "Our submarines made it."

Then he said, "I only lay these in here. They not tell me they went out more than that."

He was quite uncomfortable, because I think he figured that we suspected him of trying to get us to run over the mines. That's one of the things we'll never know, but I kept plenty of room between the *Missouri* and the mines shown on the maps.

While the chief pilot was on the bridge with about half a dozen of the others, I engaged them in conversation, since they had little to do and no place to go. I asked about conditions in Japan, how come they surrendered. I thought his answer was very interesting. The others agreed with him. He said that the inside of Japan was nothing but a shell which would fall if anyone really came in and tried to invade it, but they would pretty much fight to the last man to defend it just the same. As far as the mainland of Japan was concerned, they were really relieved that the surrender was taking place. Then he said, "You know, if there ever is another big war we're going to be on your side. You licked the pants off of us, there is no question about it; we were thoroughly defeated and whipped. We may not agree with you, but whatever side you're on in the next war we're going to be in there with you. I don't speak for just myself but all the Japanese people that I have heard express any opinion."

After we anchored, we sent the other pilots to the ships they would pilot into Tokyo Bay. Only the chief pilot remained with us. They all spoke excellent English, for one of the requirements for their pilots was to speak good English.

The next day, August 28, orders were received for the landing forces to proceed into the Yokosuka area and land on the morning of the twenty-ninth. Admiral Oscar Badger, in the *San Diego,* was in command of the naval ships—the cruisers and destroyers—and had to be sure everything was squared away for the landing force of marines. The *Missouri,* the *Wisconsin,* and the *Iowa,* accompanied by other ships, were told to proceed into Tokyo Bay after daylight on the twenty-ninth, presumably after the marine party had landed on Japanese soil at daybreak. We were on hand in case heavier gunfire support should be needed. As we went in past Kamakura Peninsula, we saw the coast-defense guns that were marked on our charts. They were big guns—I would judge sixteen- or eighteen-inch—pointed toward the sky at about a forty-five-degree angle and very visible. They were supposed to be completely demilitarized at this point, and all the gun crews were absent. But I knew full well that those guns could be trained rapidly on some ship going by, so I kept the crew at general quarters all the way in. Not only that, we had our turrets trained to follow each one of the Japanese guns.

Nothing happened. It was all fine. There had always been the thought that some diehard Japanese might put a few rounds rapidly into the *Missouri,* because by that time the Japanese undoubtedly knew where the surrender was going to be signed. Some of our destroyers had been taken into the bay the day before. They had been searching all over. We had received a report that they had caught a small one- or two-man submarine sneaking down from the Yokohama area and had sunk it. Another one had been caught starting out of the harbor and heading towards Tokyo. So we had that concern, plus the fact we didn't know when some lone kamikaze plane might choose that time to come in and smash into our deck with a one- or two-thousand-ton bomb tied to it. Of course, we kept the carrier task force planes over us all the time. The carriers themselves were not allowed to come into Sagami or Tokyo Bay. They were left to patrol off the entrances and furnish cover for the ships in both places.

As we rounded the bend in the channel heading north to Tokyo Bay, we saw the battleship *Nagato* about four miles ahead of us. She was tied up at the dock in Yokosuka. Her guns were up in the air but they were also trained toward us. That was quite a shock at first. But as we passed around the line where her guns were trained we saw they didn't follow us, so we figured we were pretty safe.

Then we received a message from the landing forces. They were ashore and had taken the crew off the *Nagato.* They figured they had that situation under control.

349

We went in and anchored at the spot designated for us, which we found out later was chosen particularly because it was close to where Admiral Perry had anchored in 1853, when Americans first came to Japan and opened it up to the outside world.

General MacArthur arrived in Japan that same day by plane from his headquarters in the Philippines. He went to the outskirts of Tokyo, towards Yokohama, to set up headquarters. He drove through roads and streets lined with Japanese soldiers and his own American army guard. Admiral Nimitz came the next day on a destroyer. He went aboard the battleship *South Dakota,* which was anchored about half a mile from the *Missouri.*

The next day, on the thirtieth, Admiral Halsey and Admiral Carney and I went over to the *South Dakota* to see Admiral Nimitz and get further information on the surrender ceremony. He was to arrange the surrender ceremony under the overall direction of General MacArthur. Then I went back to the *Missouri* while Halsey and Carney stayed on for a while. My more detailed orders would come down to me through Admiral Halsey rather than directly through Nimitz.

The next day, on the thirty-first of August, we got the final word from Admiral Nimitz. We were to make up a complete list of available spaces for about 225 correspondents from all over the world and about 75 photographers, including two Japanese, who would be allowed to take pictures. All of these spaces were to have a view of the surrender deck and the signing. The photographers were to have the best places. We were told we could have the ceremony broadcast within the ship and for recording purposes. This was to be relayed back to the United States via the *Wisconsin,* the press ship. That pleased us because we didn't want a jam of reporters all trying to get into the radio room at the same time in order to get the story out first.

We made up the list of places, marked them in order of priority, and sent copies to both MacArthur and Nimitz. Correspondents and photographers were to draw lots for the numbers so that when they came aboard on September 2 they would be taken directly to their spots. There were only a limited number of spaces from which you could see the surrender deck so we had to go vertical and not very much horizontal.* Since we knew the only safe way was to escort them to their assigned places, we trained some of our sailors as escorts. They had to come from the main turret crew, because we were still manning our antiaircraft battery and figured we would have to continue doing so during the ceremony just in case there was a final dying gasp of resistance. There would have been a wonderful haul of senior leaders if a kamikaze plane had landed on that surrender deck.

On September 1 Admiral Sir Bruce Fraser (on the *King George V*), sent

---

*That is, they had to make use of the upper deck spaces.

over a beautiful polished mahogany deal table and two very nice upholstered chairs. He knew that we didn't have any particular table in view for the surrender ceremony and had asked Admiral Halsey if he could send one over for the ceremony. We thought it was a good idea and accepted with thanks. It gave the British a chance to say, "We contributed something to the surrender ceremony."

We had to drill for the Japanese delegation coming aboard. We had been told that the Japanese delegation, headed by Prime Minister Mamoru Shigemitsu, would consist of eleven Japanese. Shigemitsu was premier, and representing the emperor and the government of Japan. General Yoshijiro Umezo, chief of the Imperial General Staff, would sign as representative of all the armed forces of the empire. There would also be three representatives of the civilian government, three from the Imperial Army, and three from the Imperial Navy. There was a total of eleven men. We also found out that Premier Shigemitsu had a wooden leg, for his real one had been blown off in Shanghai several years before. That presented a problem.

The Japanese delegation was going to be delivered to the vicinity of the *Missouri* by destroyer on the morning of the second of September. The destroyer would be off our bow, very close aboard, by about eight o'clock in the morning, so that there would be no question of the delegation getting aboard in time. Then they would be sent over by a small boat at the proper time. General MacArthur had said that he didn't want them on the *Missouri*'s weather deck more than five seconds and he didn't want them to be even a fraction of a second late getting up to the galley deck and the place of signing. Nine o'clock was the official time. Well, it's kind of hard to try and run something within five seconds. The whole process involved walking up a gangway, across a deck, up another deck, and then about twenty feet more to get into position.

We took young sailors and swab handles and strapped them to their trousers so they couldn't bend their legs. They got in a small boat exactly like the one the Japanese delegation would come over in. They would play Shigemitsu, who was rapidly named Peg-Leg Pete by all the sailors and officers. We practiced this routine about twenty times in order to discover how long it took them to get out of the boat from a sitting position, up on the bottom platform of the forward gangway and on the ship, then across the quarterdeck to the ladder up to the verandah deck, in front of my cabin, where the surrender documents would be signed. These sailors were pretty good. In fact, the slowest time in twenty attempts was one and a half minutes, ninety seconds. I figured the sailors were more ambitious than the Japanese would be, so I doubled the time and figured that three minutes was the minimum we could allow. We couldn't allow more than that or they would arrive too soon. We thought then that we had it all set. The boat would come alongside about four minutes before nine. One or two minutes would be

351

controlled by the sailor standing at the bottom of the platform of the gangway; if necessary he could push the boat out a little bit and tell the coxswain not to let the Japanese get up yet. Well, that was one of the details we thought we had all set.

Another detail that we finally got word on the night before was that no ties and no side arms of any sort were to be worn by anyone at the ceremony. The officers would wear khaki with their shirt collars open and with overseas caps or regular caps.

It was decided that there would be eight side boys for a full admiral, six for a rear admiral, and four for a captain. The Japanese premier would rate eight, but no side honors except piping aboard would be given the other Japanese. The side boys would salute and there would be attention on deck and that was all. There was no marine guard of honor and no playing of martial marches, which are ordinarily accorded under full honors.

We marked with circles the standing positions for the various visitors on the deck and the several platforms erected to provide additional space. Of course, we had a list of all those who were definitely coming and we made allowance for several who might come. Then suddenly we received word that the secretary of the navy was sending some visitors and he wanted us to have a good place for them. So we decided to set them up on top of turret two, where they'd have a good bird's-eye view of everything and not interrupt the rest of our plans. They were to sit in chairs because it was safer if they sat. They wouldn't fall off.

There was one ticklish item. Fleet Admiral Nimitz and General of the Army MacArthur each rated five stars. General MacArthur had a red flag with five stars and Fleet Admiral Nimitz had a blue flag with five stars. I asked Admiral Nimitz if he wanted both of them at the same height and he said very emphatically yes; since this was a navy ship afloat, his flag would be on the starboard side and General MacArthur's on the port side. That sounds like a simple thing, but when you try to get two flags 120 feet in the air, to the top of a masthead, it's not so simple. We solved the problem by welding a bar on the top of the mainmast. Attached to this bar we had the two flags, one on the starboard side and one on the port side. They were each prepared so that with a yank on the halyards the correct flag would break and fly in the breeze as each gentleman came aboard. Of course, we were flying Admiral Halsey's flag all the time, since he was aboard, but at the time we broke Admiral Nimitz's flag, his would be hauled down. It was a nasty little problem at first, getting this horizontal bar up there. But we had to rig it because we didn't want either one of the men to see his flag lower than the other. I'm sure neither one would have noticed, but certainly some member of the staffs would have picked it up.

Then it was suggested that cards be given out certifying that Joe Doaks was aboard the *Missouri* at the time. The cards were to be signed by General

MacArthur and Admiral Nimitz, one on the left and the other on the right, with Admiral Halsey's signature in the middle and mine as captain of the ship down in the lower righthand corner. Our expert printers on the *Missouri* lifted General MacArthur's signature and Admiral Nimitz's from an article the two had signed in *The Saturday Evening Post*. Admiral Halsey gave us his signature. I said I would sign all of them so that we could keep track of them and prevent the distribution of a bunch of extras. Only one was to be given to each person physically aboard the *Missouri* during the ceremony. Several people did ask for additional cards, including Admiral Nimitz, who wanted to send one to the secretary of the navy and to Admiral King. I had to tell him no; it said right on the card that it was intended only for those who were physically aboard. There were a few extra left over because of our uncertainty about last-minute guests, but when it was all over I took those extras and also the plate from the print shop and burned them in the incinerator. This was witnessed by the executive officer and two members of the crew so there was no question as to what happened.

We were not exactly relaxed on the morning of September 2. We knew there were too many things hanging fire. Since we had a lot to do and since we were missing two-hundred plus men and about twenty officers, who were still ashore with the landing party, we had a very early reveille.

The newspaper correspondents and the photographers arrived about seven-thirty aboard two destroyers. When they landed they were told to show their assignments to the escorts. They were taken directly to their places and told to stay there. We had an average of one escort for every two correspondents. The escorts stayed with them during the ceremony so there wouldn't be any wandering around. We knew they would want to. We did the same thing with the photographers. Our preparations with numbers and circles on the deck were very important. We didn't have any trouble with them, at first anyway.

At eight we hoisted a clean set of colors at the mainmast and a clean Union Jack at the bow, as we were at anchor. These were just regular ship's flags, GI issue, that we'd pulled out of the spares, nothing special about them, and they had never been used anywhere so far as we knew. Some of the articles in the press said we flew the same flag that was on the White House or the U.S. Capitol on December 7, 1941, and that MacArthur took it up to Tokyo and flew it over his headquarters there. This was baloney; it was nothing like that. It was just a plain, ordinary GI flag and a Union Jack. We turned them both in to the Naval Academy Museum when we got back to the East Coast in October.

The only special flag there was a flag that Commodore Perry had flown on his ship in that same location eighty-two years before. It had been sent in its glass case from the Naval Academy Museum. An officer messenger brought it out. We hung it over the door of my cabin, facing the surrender deck so everyone there could see it. This was a thirty-one-star flag; that's all the states we had at that time, thirty-one. It was facing the Japanese as they came on deck.

Admiral Nimitz came aboard about two minutes after eight, and we hoisted his five-star flag and hauled down Admiral Halsey's four-star one.

General MacArthur and his staff arrived on the destroyer about eight-forty and came along the port side. Admiral Nimitz, Admiral Halsey, and I met him as he came aboard and escorted him to Halsey's cabin.

Along with General MacArthur and his staff was an army colonel from Washington. He had flown out with the surrender papers. They were to be signed first by the Japanese and then by the Allied powers. We had placed our beautiful mahogany table and its two fine chairs on deck in the central spot, and it looked very nice there.

It was the first time we had seen the surrender documents. We took one look at them and all hell broke loose. There were two of them, about forty inches by twenty inches wide, and they had to be placed next to each other, widths touching. Our beautiful mahogany table was forty by forty. We couldn't use it. So I called the four sailors nearest to me and we headed for the wardroom, which was on the deck below my cabin. We got there and were going to grab the wardroom table and take it up on the deck. But it was bolted down. So we dashed down to the next compartment, to the crew's mess. The messcooks had just finished cleaning up all the tables from breakfast and were hanging them from the overhead to get them out of the way. Well, we grabbed a table, bringing howls from the messcooks. They didn't know what we were about and they didn't want their table taken away from them. It was their table; they were supposed to clean and take care of it. We shouted, "You'll get it back," and took it on up. We had to have a cover for the table, so on the way I yanked a green cover off the first wardroom table I came to. I said to some guys on deck to set up the mess table and spread the green cloth on it. It really looked very nice.

No one knew about our difficulty at the time. I told MacArthur about it later and he laughed and said the table was a good touch anyway. Someone later echoed that, saying, "That's a beautiful common touch, to use the crew's general mess table and a green cloth from the wardroom." There were a few sarcastic remarks as well, because it appears that the tablecloth I'd yanked off the wardroom table had a lot of coffee spots on it. At the Naval Academy Museum they wanted to know why I didn't at least get a clean one. Nobody was thinking about that at the time, least of all I.

We got the surrender papers about fifteen minutes before the Japanese were supposed to start in the destroyer toward the side of the *Missouri*. All the VIPs were settling in their places, and Admiral Nimitz went to take his place as the official signer for the United States.

After we got the table covered and the documents on it, I noticed that

Admiral Nimitz was having a discussion with the Russian official delegate, a lieutenant general. I walked over to the admiral and asked if there was anything I could do. He said the delegate wanted the Russian newspaper correspondent to stand in line right behind him, where only the signer delegates and their deputies were allowed to stand. When Admiral Nimitz told me that, I figured the best way to take care of the trouble was to use some of the marines I had around as guards. So I motioned to them to grab the correspondent and take him back where he belonged. He apparently understood what was happening because he dashed through the line of signers and the line of VIPs and started up the ladder to get on top of number-two turret. Two husky marines, each with a Colt .45 at his side, were chasing him. He'd gotten about halfway up the ladder when they caught up with him. They grabbed his legs, pulled him down, and then escorted him with a little arm pressure, one on each side, to his assigned position, a couple of decks higher than where he had been. I told the marines to stay with him the whole time, and he gave us no more trouble. The people on deck, the signers and VIPs together, really thought it was a wonderful joke, and so did the Russian general. In fact, he slapped Admiral Nimitz on the back and said, "Wonderful, wonderful, wonderful." I judge that his neck was saved. He didn't have to order the man off and he didn't have to say he couldn't stay there. He was really relieved when we took care of the situation with a couple of marines.

The Japanese had a newsreel photographer assigned to a position on the forty-millimeter-gun platform on the starboard wing of the verandah deck. Two marines were assigned to him because I feared he might try to pull a fancy kamikaze trick with his camera and kill some of the central people. So these two marines each had a hand on this Jap; they put him in his place and told him to stay there. There was no question the Jap got the word. When he first got there, I looked at him and he was shivering. He was in his place but he was shaking, so I don't know how good his pictures could have been. There was no question he was kept under control.

By about eight-thirty the Japanese delegation had gotten into small boats from the destroyer. They were about two hundred yards from the *Missouri*. We called them alongside about eight-fifty. The boat had drifted in and was only about fifty yards off. It came alongside about eight-fifty-five. This was perhaps a minute before the time we had allowed in practice runs, but I didn't think Shigemitsu's heart was going to be in this, so that extra minute was all right. We signaled to the sailor on the bottom of the gangway, who was to help him aboard. They started up. I walked over and was standing on the top platform of the quarterdeck, the gangway, so I could see where they were. I thought that Shigemitsu would never get moving out of that boat. But finally he started up. Really and truly he just crept out. He went up the gangway and across the deck with the other men in the delegation following him, for he was, of course, the emperor's direct representative. They were led by an army colonel in charge of the arrangements to get the delegation there. He had to slow down all the time to keep from running away from Shigemitsu. Well, the Japanese finally got to the ladder going up from the foredeck to the verandah deck. Time was running out, and just as Shigemitsu's top hat appeared on the level with the verandah deck, on the stroke of nine, General MacArthur stepped out of Admiral Halsey's cabin, one deck above. He took one look, saw the Japanese still coming, turned around, and went back into the cabin. The Japanese proceeded and took their positions in line. Something like two and a half or three minutes after nine, General MacArthur came down and took his position on the after side of the surrender table.

He made a few remarks about hoping this would usher in permanent peace, a prayer was said, and the "Star-Spangled Banner" was played. MacArthur then turned to the Japanese and said, "The Japanese emissaries will now come forward and sign the surrender documents."

I had moved over about two feet toward the gangway going up to the surrender deck to get a better view, but that was all. I stayed on the quarterdeck during the ceremony. From there I could run things and besides, the commanding officer is supposed to be down there to greet arriving guests and say goodbye to departing guests.

Shigemitsu, who was accompanied by one of his civilian representatives (Kase was the anglicized version of his name), came forward and rather awkwardly sat in the big chair. As he did so his wooden leg hit the tie rod that held the legs of the table up. Our fingers were all crossed, all those who knew about the mess table. He hit it so that it rattled. You could hear it down on the quarterdeck. But it only moved, it didn't collapse.

Shigemitsu seemed to have quite a bit of trouble determining where to sign. He was fumbling around and Mr. Kase wasn't helping him any. Finally General MacArthur said, "Sutherland, show him where to sign." So Lieutenant General Richard Sutherland came over from where he had been standing with the VIPs and pointed out the place to sign. Then Shigemitsu signed both documents, since one copy was for the Allies and the other was the official Japanese copy. After that General Umezo, chief of staff of the Imperial Staff, signed for all the Japanese armed services. Then MacArthur signed for the Allied powers. He used several pens. I have a picture taken over the top of his head showing that five pens were used, not six as has been said. Following MacArthur, Admiral Nimitz signed as the official U.S. representative. He was followed by the representative for Nationalist China, the United Kingdom representative, the representative for the Union of Soviet Socialist Republics, the Commonwealth of Australia, the Dominion of Canada, the provisional government of France, the Netherlands, and New Zealand.

While the signing ceremony was going on, a Russian cameraman on the platform just forward of the surrender deck sneaked down from the platform, crept along with his camera, and started up the ladder to the surrender deck. He had been assigned an excellent place, though the legs of the Japanese delegation probably interfered with some of his view. I suppose he thought he would have a good chance of sneaking onto the deck without anyone seeing. The difficulty was, he walked right in front of me and the chief bo'sun's mate, who was about my size. I nodded my head toward the bo'sun's mate and we walked over and caught him as he started up the steps. We grabbed him by the trouser legs. His suspenders didn't hold very well and his trousers dropped down to his knees. We dragged him down, the chief got him by the back of his coat and I got him by his feet, and we carried him, face down, across the deck. We swung him up on his platform, about four or five feet higher up.

The other photographers there had been watching. Undoubtedly they had the idea they would do the same thing if he got away with it. They could hardly contain their amusement. He didn't try it again.

General MacArthur, when he signed, asked Lieutenant General Jonathan Wainwright of the U.S. Army and Lieutenant General Sir Arthur Percival of the British Army to come and stand alongside him. Wainwright, captured when Corregidor fell, had been a POW; Percival had been taken prisoner while in command at Singapore. They were both emaciated and had been flown in the day before from a prison in Manchuria. MacArthur gave the first pen he used to General Wainwright and the second one to General Percival. The other three he put in his own pocket.

When the ceremony was over General MacArthur said, "These proceedings are now closed." Mr. Kase, who came forward to pick up the Japanese part of the papers, questioned the position of a signature. The Canadian representative had not signed that copy in the proper place. After a moment General Sutherland and the colonel who had led them in corrected the matter with an arrow. Kase took his copy, folded it, and the Japanese delegation went down the gangway.

Just as the ceremony ended, there was a big flyover of U.S. planes. It was really quite a sight.

General MacArthur left in his destroyer, Admiral Nimitz departed in his. All the other visitors left gradually. By about eleven o'clock we were clear of everyone except General Sutherland, who was having lunch with Admiral Halsey and Admiral Carney. The general's daughter was married to Admiral Carney's son, so they were like kinsfolk visiting.

I was sitting in my cabin with the heads of the ship's departments, drinking coffee and relaxing, when someone said, "We had better save the table and the cloth. Somebody might want to give them to the museum." We jumped up, dashed out on the deck, and found the table was gone. In a crumpled pile alongside the bulkhead was the green cloth, so we threw that into my cabin, then dashed down to the mess hall. Sure enough, the mess-cook was happily setting up his table for lunch. I had to take it away from him again, but this time I explained why. I said that he should be proud of his mess table and should tell the crew who were to eat there to use another. He agreed because there was nothing else he could do. Then we took it up and put it in my cabin for safekeeping.

Admiral Nimitz had left the U.S. copy of the surrender documents for the *Missouri* to take back to the States. So I had those in the cabin also, and they had to be locked up.

APPENDIX

The following is a list of names that appear in the excerpts of this volume. For information on the oral historians, see the biographies that precede their respective pieces.

ADOUE, CHARLES
Leading designer for Standard Oil Company of New Jersey. Commander Triest used his services in drawing up the Operation Bobcat plans of December 1941.

ANDERSON, COMMANDER CHARLES E.
Beachmaster for the amphibious landings at Iwo Jima and Tinian and for other central Pacific operations.

ARNOLD, GENERAL HENRY H., USA
Became general of the air force in 1949. He figures in the story of the Tokyo Raid.

AULT, LIEUTENANT COMMANDER WILLIAM
Air group commander of the USS *Lexington* at the time of the Battle of the Coral Sea.

BADGER, REAR ADMIRAL OSCAR C.
In command of cruisers and destroyers for the landing of marines at Yokosuka, 29 August 1945.

BARBEY, VICE ADMIRAL DANIEL E.
Commander, Task Force 78, Seventh Fleet, during the invasion of the Philippines.

BERKEY, ADMIRAL RUSSELL S.
As captain of the USS *Santa Fe* he formed part of Task Force 53.4's fire support group for the Gilbert Islands operations of the Fifth Fleet in November–December 1943.

BIGGS, CAPTAIN BURTON B.
In the cruiser *Indianapolis* at the time of the invasion of Tarawa.

BLANDY, REAR ADMIRAL WILLIAM H. P.
Commander, Amphibious Support Force, Task Force 52, Fifth Fleet.

BREWSTER, SENATOR RALPH
A member of the Joint Congressional Committee to Investigate the Pearl Harbor Disaster, 1945–46.

BROWNING, REAR ADMIRAL MILES R.
In rank of captain, operations officer for Admiral Halsey at the time of the Tokyo Raid in 1942.

BUCKMASTER, VICE ADMIRAL ELLIOTT
Captain in command of the USS *Yorktown* at the time of the Battle of Midway in 1942.

BURKE, LIEUTENANT COMMANDER RICHARD
Commanding officer of UDT 7 at Saipan.

CARNEY, ADMIRAL ROBERT BOSTWICK
In the rank of rear admiral, chief of staff to Admiral William F. Halsey, commander of the Third Fleet.

CASEY, MAJOR GENERAL HUGH JOHN, USA
Chief engineer of U.S. Army Forces, Far East (1942–44) and the commanding general of the Army Service Command (1944–45).

CATES, MAJOR GENERAL CLIFTON B., USMC
Commanding general of the Fourth Marine Division at Tinian.

CHILLINGWORTH, VICE ADMIRAL CHARLES F., JR.
In rank of lieutenant commander, captain of the destroyer *Dewey* during the Battle of the Coral Sea.

COMSTOCK, COMMODORE MERRILL
Chief of staff to Vice Admiral Charles A. Lockwood.

CONOLLY, ADMIRAL RICHARD LANSING
As a rear admiral, in command of Task Force 53, Southern Attack Force, Fifth Fleet at Tinian.

CRACE, REAR ADMIRAL J. G., RN
In command of Task Group 17.3, Allied Support Group, Task Force 17, during the Battle of the Coral Sea.

CRUZEN, VICE ADMIRAL RICHARD HAROLD
In rank of captain, operational officer to Admiral Kinkaid at Leyte Gulf.

CUNNINGHAM, ADMIRAL SIR ANDREW, RN
In command of the British Fleet in the Mediterranean in 1943.

DAVISON, VICE ADMIRAL RALPH EUGENE
As a rear admiral, in command of Task Group 38.4, Third Fleet, at Leyte Gulf.

DE BOLD, LIEUTENANT JOHN
Executive officer to Lieutenant Commander Draper Kauffman of UDT 5 during the invasion of Saipan.

DIBB, ENSIGN RAM
Wingman with Lieutenant Commander John S. Thach at the Battle of Midway.

DIXON, REAR ADMIRAL ROBERT ELLINGTON
As a lieutenant commander, part of Air Group 1 of the USS *Lexington* at the Battle of the Coral Sea.

DOOLITTLE, LIEUTENANT GENERAL JAMES HAROLD, USA
As a lieutenant colonel, led the raid on Tokyo in April 1942.

DUDDLESTON, LIEUTENANT COMMANDER
Recruited from the Standard Oil Company of New Jersey to supervise the construction job on Christmas Island in 1942, the first project of the Seabees.

EARLY, REAR ADMIRAL ALEXANDER RIEMAN, JR.
In the rank of captain, served as commander of Service Squadron 10, with headquarters on Manus Island.

ERSKINE, MAJOR GENERAL GRAVES B., USMC
In command of the Third Marine Division for the invasion of Iwo Jima.

FARBER, VICE ADMIRAL WILLIAM SIMS
Served on the staff of Commander in Chief, U.S. Naval Forces, in World War II.

FIFE, ADMIRAL JAMES
As a vice admiral in 1944–45, Commander, Submarines, Southwest Pacific, and commander of Task Force 71.

FITCH, ADMIRAL AUBREY WRAY
As rear admiral, in command of the USS *Lexington* at the Battle of the Coral Sea.

FLATLEY, VICE ADMIRAL JAMES HENRY, JR.
As a lieutenant, practiced trial runs against the recovered Japanese Zero with Jimmy Thach. Named Thach's new theory the Thach Weave.

FLETCHER, ADMIRAL FRANK JACK
For the Midway operation, commanded the Carrier Striking Force, Task Force 17, Pacific Fleet.

FLUCKEY, REAR ADMIRAL EUGENE BENNETT
As a commander, an ace submariner in the central Pacific, being awarded the Medal of Honor for his successful exploits.

FORRESTAL, JAMES V.
Secretary of the navy in World War II, following the death of Secretary Frank Knox.

FORRESTEL, VICE ADMIRAL EMMET PETER
Captain on the staff of Admiral Spruance during the Battle of the Philippine Sea.

FRASER, ADMIRAL SIR BRUCE, RN
Commander in chief of the British Pacific Fleet in the latter days of World War II.

FUQUA, REAR ADMIRAL SAMUEL GLEN
A lieutenant commander in the battleship *Arizona* when the Japanese attacked Pearl Harbor.

GHORMLEY, VICE ADMIRAL ROBERT LEE
Commander of the South Pacific Force and South Pacific Area in April 1942.

GLASSFORD, VICE ADMIRAL WILLIAM A., JR.
As a rear admiral, in command of Task Force 5, Striking Force, U.S. Asiatic Fleet, in January 1942.

GRAHAM, TURKEY
Seaman in the USS *Arizona* at the time of the Japanese attack.

GRANT, MAJOR GENERAL WALTER, USA
In command of a small garrison of army regulars in the Philippines in 1940.

GREENE, GENERAL WALLACE MARTIN, JR., USMC
Operations officer to Major General Thomas E. Watson, USMC, when Watson was in command of the Second Marine Division at Saipan.

GRUNERT, MAJOR GENERAL GEORGE, USA
Commander under Admiral Thomas C. Hart, commander in chief of the Asiatic Fleet, in 1941.

HAAS, LIEUTENANT COLONEL, USMC
As commanding officer of the First Battalion, Twenty-third Marines at Tinian, ordered the jeep with a public address system to persuade the thousands of civilians to come forward at the end of hostilities.

HALL, ADMIRAL JOHN LESSLIE, JR.
In 1943, as rear admiral, in command of the Sea Frontier Forces, Western Task Force, Mediterranean.

HALSEY, FLEET ADMIRAL WILLIAM FREDERICK, JR.
Commander of the Third Fleet in the central Pacific.

HANLON, ADMIRAL BYRON HALL
While a captain, in command of the UDTs for the campaign in the Ryukyus.

HARA, REAR ADMIRAL CHUICHI, IMPERIAL JAPANESE NAVY
In command of Japanese carriers at the Battle of the Coral Sea.

HARRIS, BRIGADIER GENERAL FIELD, USMC
Chief of staff to Rear Admiral Mitscher, Commander, Aircraft, Solomon Islands.

HELFRICH, VICE ADMIRAL CONRAD EMILE, ROYAL DUTCH NAVY
Succeeded Admiral Hart as ABDA float commander in February 1942.

HENDERSON, COMMANDER GEORGE
Served as executive officer in the USS *Hornet* during the Tokyo Raid.

HILGER, MAJOR JOHN A.
Commanded a B-25 during the Tokyo Raid.

HOFFMAN, CAPTAIN MELVIN
Ascertained the maneuvering capabilities of the captured Japanese Zero in 1942.

HOLLOWAY, ADMIRAL JAMES LEMUEL, JR.
In the rank of captain, skipper of the battleship *Iowa* when she put in for repairs at Manus in 1944.

HOOVER, ADMIRAL JOHN HOWARD
While vice admiral, served as Commander, Aircraft, Central Pacific (1943–44).

HORN, REAR ADMIRAL PETER HARRY
While commander, served as communications officer for Admiral Richmond Kelly Turner at Saipan.

HUIE, CAPTAIN B. S., USNR
In command of Task Group 77.8, Service Force, Seventh Fleet.

JONES, CAPTAIN DAVID M., USA
In command of a B-25 for the Tokyo Raid.

JONES, CAPTAIN JAMES L., USMC
In command of seventy marines in the submarine *Nautilus* for the landing on Apamama.

KAISER, HENRY J.
A West Coast industrialist who built a number of merchant ship hulls in World War II for conversion to small escort carriers.

KETTERING, CHARLES F.
As vice president of General Motors, an interested spectator at the training of B-25 army pilots who would operate from a navy carrier.

KING, FLEET ADMIRAL ERNEST J.
Commander in Chief, U.S. Naval Forces, in World War II.

KOGA, ADMIRAL MINEICHI, IMPERIAL JAPANESE NAVY
Commander in chief of the Combined Japanese Fleet after the death of Admiral Yamamoto in 1943.

KRUEGER, LIEUTENANT GENERAL WALTER, USA
Commanded the Expeditionary Troops and the Sixth Army for the Philippines campaign.

KURIBAYASHI, LIEUTENANT GENERAL TADAMICHI, IMPERIAL JAPANESE ARMY
In command of the Japanese 109th Infantry Division at Iwo Jima.

KURITA, VICE ADMIRAL TAKEO, IMPERIAL JAPANESE NAVY
In command of the First Japanese Striking Force during the Battle of Leyte Gulf.

KUSAKA, ADMIRAL KINICHI, IMPERIAL JAPANESE NAVY
In command of both army and navy forces during the campaign for the Solomon Islands.

LEE, VICE ADMIRAL WILLIS AUGUSTUS, JR.
In command of the battle line of the Third Fleet during the invasion of the Philippines.

LOCKWOOD, VICE ADMIRAL CHARLES ANDREWS
Commander, Submarines, Pacific, in World War II.

LOVELACE, LIEUTENANT COMMANDER DONALD ALEXANDER
Lost his life on the USS *Yorktown* during the Battle of Midway.

LOW, ADMIRAL FRANCIS STUART
As a rear admiral, chief of staff for the Tenth Fleet from May 1943 to January 1945.

LYNCH, CAPTAIN OLIVER DEMOUY
As a lieutenant commander, executive officer of the *Nautilus* during the action at Tarawa.

MACARTHUR, GENERAL OF THE ARMIES DOUGLAS, USA
Supreme Commander, Allied Forces, Southwest Pacific Area, in World War II.

MANG, COMMANDER LEWIS WILBUR
Attached to an army air forces experimental unit at the time of Tinian and brought information on the new firebomb to the Amphibious Force.

MASON, VICE ADMIRAL CHARLES PERRY
Rear admiral in command of Aircraft, Solomon Islands. Relieved by Admiral Mitscher in April 1943.

MASSEY, LIEUTENANT COMMANDER LANCE EDWARD
Commanded a torpedo squadron on the *Yorktown* at the Battle of Midway.

MILLER, CAPTAIN RAYMOND V.
As part of the CEC, he was officer in charge of construction in the Bureau of Yards and Docks.

MITCHELL, MAJOR JOHN W., USA
His squadron of P-38s was involved in shooting down the plane carrying Japan's supreme naval commander, Admiral Yamamoto, in the South Pacific.

MITSCHER, ADMIRAL MARC
As a rear admiral, succeeded to command of Aircraft, Solomon Islands, on 1 April 1943.

MOREELL, REAR ADMIRAL BEN
Chief of the Navy's Bureau of Yards and Docks from 1937 to 1945.

MORISON, REAR ADMIRAL SAMUEL ELIOT
Historian of U.S. naval operations during World War II and author of a fifteen-volume work on the subject.

MYDANS, SHELLEY
A correspondent for *Time* magazine.

NIMITZ, FLEET ADMIRAL CHESTER WILLIAM
Commander in Chief, Pacific, and Commander in Chief, Pacific Ocean Area, during World War II.

NISHIMURA, REAR ADMIRAL SHOJI, IMPERIAL JAPANESE NAVY
Commander of the Japanese Southern Force at the Battle for Leyte Gulf.

OGATA, COLONEL KIYOUCHI, IMPERIAL JAPANESE ARMY
Commander of the Fiftieth Infantry Regiment, Twenty-ninth Division, at the Battle for Tinian Island.

O'HARE, LIEUTENANT COMMANDER EDWARD HENRY
Lost his life in an air battle off Tarawa on 24 November 1943.

O'KANE, REAR ADMIRAL RICHARD HETHERINGTON
A submarine commander in the Pacific who won the Medal of Honor for his exploits.

OLDENDORF, VICE ADMIRAL JESSE BARRETT
As a rear admiral, had command of a fire support unit during the Battle of Leyte Gulf.

OSMENA, SERGIO
> President of the Philippine Republic. Landed on Philippine soil on 20 October 1944 with General MacArthur in the celebrated return to the Philippines promised by MacArthur.

OZAWA, VICE ADMIRAL JISABURO, IMPERIAL JAPANESE NAVY
> In command of the Japanese Mobile Force of the Combined Fleet in the Battle of Leyte Gulf.

PARKS, REAR ADMIRAL LEWIS SMITH
> As a captain, served as wolf pack commander in 1944 in submarine operations in the central Pacific.

PARSONS, CHARLES
> Acted as liaison between the headquarters of General MacArthur and the coastwatchers in the Philippines.

PERCIVAL, LIEUTENANT GENERAL SIR ARTHUR, BRITISH ARMY
> A prisoner of war after the fall of Singapore. Honored at the surrender ceremony on the deck of the battleship *Missouri* in Tokyo Harbor.

PETERSON, REAR ADMIRAL GEORGE EDMUND
> In the central Pacific, commanded the submarine wolf pack that included the *Parche, Bang,* and *Tenosa.*

POWNALL, VICE ADMIRAL CHARLES ALAN
> As a rear admiral, figured in the fast carrier strikes in the Gilbert and Marshall islands in the central Pacific.

PULLER, LIEUTENANT COLONEL LEWIS B.
> Commanded the First Battalion, Seventh Marine Regiment, at the Battle of Matanikau River on Guadalcanal.

PURNELL, REAR ADMIRAL WILLIAM REYNOLDS
> Chief of staff to Admiral Hart, commander in chief of the Asiatic Fleet, in 1941.

QUEZON, MANUEL LUIS
> President of the Philippines from 1935 to 1944. With the Japanese conquest of the islands, became president of the Philippine government in exile.

RADFORD, ADMIRAL ARTHUR WILLIAM
> While a rear admiral, in command of Task Group 58.4 of the Fifth Fleet, and later of Task Group 38.4 of the Third Fleet.

RAMSEY, VICE ADMIRAL PAUL HUBERT
> While a lieutenant commander, had a fighter squadron on the *Lexington* at the Battle of the Coral Sea.

RICHARDSON, SETH W.
A Washington, D.C., attorney who served as chief counsel for the Joint Congressional Committee to investigate the Pearl Harbor Disaster.

RING, REAR ADMIRAL MORTON LOOMIS
A commander on the staff of Rear Admiral Marc Mitscher on Guadalcanal in 1943.

ROCHEFORT, CAPTAIN JOSEPH JOHN
In charge of the combat intelligence unit at Pearl Harbor until he was called to Washington in October 1942.

ROCKEY, MAJOR GENERAL KELLER E., USMC
In command of the Fifth Marine Division for the landing on Iwo Jima.

ROCKWELL, ADMIRAL FRANCIS WARREN
As a rear admiral, commandant of the Sixteenth Naval District in the Philippines at the time of the Japanese conquest.

ROSENMAN, JUDGE SAMUEL IRVING
Special counsel to Presidents Roosevelt and Truman.

SCHMIDT, MAJOR GENERAL HARRY, USMC
In command of the Fourth Marine Division at Tinian.

SHERMAN, ADMIRAL FREDERICK CARL
In the rank of captain, in command of the USS *Lexington* at the time of the Battle of the Coral Sea.

SHIGEMITSU, MAMORU
The foreign minister of Japan, a strong advocate of peace, and the personal representative of the emperor at the surrender ceremony.

SHIMA, VICE ADMIRAL KIYOHIDE, IMPERIAL JAPANESE NAVY
In command of the Second Japanese Striking Force at the Battle for Leyte Gulf.

SLESSINGER, DR. RICHARD
A medical doctor on the staff of Admiral Sullivan for most of the salvage operations in Europe and at Manila.

SMITH, GENERAL HOLLAND, USMC
As a lieutenant general, in command of the Second and Fourth Marine Divisions at Saipan and Tinian.

SOUCEK, VICE ADMIRAL APOLLO
Air officer in the *Hornet* during the Tokyo Raid.

SPRAGUE, ADMIRAL THOMAS LAMISON
As a rear admiral, in command of Task Group 77.4's Escort Carrier Group ("Taffy 1") at the Battle of Leyte Gulf.

SPRUANCE, ADMIRAL RAYMOND AMES
In command of the Fifth Fleet during World War II.

STARK, ADMIRAL HAROLD RAYNSFORD (BETTY)
Chief of naval operations at the outbreak of World War II.

SUTHERLAND, LIEUTENANT GENERAL RICHARD K., USA
Chief of staff to General MacArthur in World War II.

SVERDRUP, MAJOR GENERAL LEIF JOHN, USA
Chief of engineering troops under General MacArthur in the Philippines.

TOOTLE, ENSIGN MILTON, USNR
A pilot in the USS *Yorktown* at the Battle of Midway.

TRUE, REAR ADMIRAL ARNOLD ELLSWORTH
In the rank of commander, skipper of the destroyer *Hammann* at the Battle of Midway.

TURNER, ADMIRAL RICHMOND KELLY
As a vice admiral, in command of the Joint Expeditionary Force at Saipan and Tinian.

UMEZU, GENERAL YOSHIJIRO, IMPERIAL JAPANESE ARMY
Chief of the Imperial General Staff at the signing of the surrender on board the battleship *Missouri*.

VANDEGRIFT, GENERAL ALEXANDER, USMC
As a major general, in command of the First Marine Division at Guadalcanal.

VAN LEER, LIEUTENANT COMMANDER WAYNE
Attached to the Bureau of Yards and Docks at the inception of Operation Bobcat.

WAINWRIGHT, LIEUTENANT GENERAL JONATHAN M., USA
Surrendered the remnant of U.S. forces on Bataan in 1942 and became a prisoner of war.

WATANABE, CAPTAIN YASUJI, IMPERIAL JAPANESE NAVY
On the staff of Admiral Yamamoto at the time of the latter's death in the Solomons.

WATSON, MAJOR GENERAL THOMAS E., USMC
In command of the Second Marine Division at Saipan.

WILKINSON, VICE ADMIRAL THEODORE STARK
Deputy commander of the Seventh Fleet under Vice Admiral Thomas Kinkaid.

WILLOUGHBY, MAJOR GENERAL CHARLES A., USA
  Chief of intelligence for General MacArthur.

WITHERS, REAR ADMIRAL THOMAS, JR.
  In charge of supervising the submarine building program at the Portsmouth, New Hampshire, navy yard in 1944.

WROTEN, COMMANDER WILEY
  A salvage officer on the staff of Commodore William A. Sullivan.

YAMAMOTO, FLEET ADMIRAL ISOROKU, IMPERIAL JAPANESE NAVY
  Commander in chief of the Combined Japanese Fleet.

YONAI, ADMIRAL MITSUMASA, IMPERIAL JAPANESE NAVY
  Commander in chief of the Japanese Imperial Fleet in 1936. Served as prime minister in 1940 and as minister of the navy in 1945.

YORK, CAPTAIN EDWARD J., USA
  Commander of a B-25 for the Tokyo Raid.

BIBLIOGRAPHY

ORAL HISTORIES

Anderson, James. U.S. Naval Institute, 1981. Interviewed by the editor.

Burke, Admiral Arleigh. U.S. Naval Institute, 1979. Interviewed by the editor.

Dennison, Admiral Robert L. U.S. Naval Institute, 1973. Interviewed by the editor.

Duncan, Admiral Donald B. Oral History Research Office, Columbia University, 1964. Interviewed by the editor.

Forbis, James L. U.S. Naval Institute, 1981. Interviewed by the editor.

Hart, Admiral Thomas C. Oral History Research Office, Columbia University, 1962. Interviewed by the editor.

Hill, Admiral Harry W. Oral History Research Office, Columbia University, 1967. Interviewed by the editor.

Irvin, Rear Admiral William D. U.S. Naval Institute, 1978. Interviewed by the editor.

James, Rear Admiral Ralph K. U.S. Naval Institute, 1972. Interviewed by the editor.

Johnson, Vice Admiral Felix L. U.S. Naval Institute, 1972. Interviewed by the editor.

Kauffman, Rear Admiral Draper L. U.S. Naval Institute, 1979 (vol. 1). Interviewed by the editor.

Kinkaid, Admiral Thomas C. Oral History Research Office, Columbia University, 1961. Interviewed by the editor.

McCollum, Rear Admiral Arthur H. U.S. Naval Institute, 1971 (vol. 2). Interviewed by the editor.

Miller, Rear Admiral Henry. U.S. Naval Institute, 1971 (vol. 1). Interviewed by the editor.

Moore, Rear Admiral Charles J. Oral History Research Office, Columbia University, 1967. Interviewed by the editor.

Moore, Right Reverend Paul, Jr. Oral History Research Office, Columbia University, 1980. Interviewed by the editor.

Moorer, Admiral Thomas H. U.S. Naval Institute, 1975 (vol. 1). Interviewed by the editor.

Murray, Admiral Stuart S. U.S. Naval Institute, 1970 (vol. 1). Interviewed by Commander Etta Belle Kitchen, USN (Rct.).

Ramage, Vice Admiral Lawson P. U.S. Naval Institute, 1974. Interviewed by the editor.

Read, Rear Admiral William Augustus. Oral History Research Office, Columbia University, 1964. Interviewed by the editor.

Riley, Vice Admiral Herbert D. U.S. Naval Institute, 1971 (vol. 1). Interviewed by the editor.

Russell, Admiral James S. U.S. Naval Institute, 1974. Interviewed by the editor.

Strean, Vice Admiral Bernard M. U.S. Naval Institute, 1974. Interviewed by the editor.

Stroop, Vice Admiral Paul D. U.S. Naval Institute, 1970. Interviewed by Commander Etta Belle Kitchen.

Sullivan, Rear Admiral William A. Oral History Research Office, Columbia University, 1969. Interviewed by the editor.

Thach, Admiral John S. U.S. Naval Institute, 1971 (vol. 1). Interviewed by Commander Etta Belle Kitchen.

Tolley, Rear Admiral Kemp. U.S. Naval Institute, 1976. Interviewed by the editor.

Triest, Captain Willard G. U.S. Naval Institute, 1972. Interviewed by the editor.

Worthington, Rear Admiral Joseph M. U.S. Naval Institute, 1972. Interviewed by the editor.

BOOKS

Barbey, Daniel E. *MacArthur's Amphibious Navy*. Annapolis: Naval Institute Press, 1969.

Blair, Clay, Jr. *The U.S. Submarine War Against Japan*. Philadelphia: J. B. Lippincott, 1975.

Buell, Thomas B. *Master of Sea Power: A Biography of Fleet Admiral Ernest J. King*. Boston: Little, Brown, 1980.

————. *The Quiet Warrior: A Biography of Admiral Raymond A. Spruance*. Boston: Little, Brown, 1974.

Costello, John. *The Pacific War*. New York: Rawson, Wade, 1981.

Holmes, Wilfred J. *Double-Edged Secrets: U.S. Naval Intelligence in the Pacific During World War II*. Annapolis: Naval Institute Press, 1979.

Hough, Frank, Verle Ludwig, and Henry L. Shaw, Jr. *Pearl Harbor to Guadalcanal*. Vol. 1, *History of U.S. Marine Corps Operations in World War II*. Washington, D.C.: Historical Branch, U.S. Marine Corps, 1975.

Leutze, James. *A Different Kind of Victory: A Biography of Admiral Thomas C. Hart*. Annapolis: Naval Institute Press, 1981.

Lewin, Ronald. *The American Magic: Codes, Ciphers and the Defeat of Japan*. New York: Farrar Straus Giroux, 1982.

Lord, Walter. *Day of Infamy*. New York: Henry Holt, 1957.

Millis, Walter. *This is Pearl! The United States and Japan, 1941*. New York: William Morrow, 1947.

Morison, Samuel Eliot. *History of United States Naval Operations in World War II*. 15 vols. Boston: Little, Brown, 1962.

————. *The Two-Ocean War: A Short History of the U.S. Navy in the Second World War*. Boston: Little, Brown, 1963.

Potter, E. B. *Bull Halsey*. Annapolis: Naval Institute Press, 1985.

Potter, E. B., and Chester Nimitz. *The Great Sea War*. New York: Bramhall House, 1963.

Prange, Gordon W. *At Dawn We Slept: The Untold Story of Pearl Harbor*. New York: McGraw-Hill, 1981.

Toland, John. *Infamy: Pearl Harbor and Its Aftermath*. Garden City: Doubleday, 1982.

———. *The Rising Sun: The Decline and Fall of the Japanese Empire*. New York: Random House, 1970.